THE TRIANGULAR CONSTITUTION

This book offers a new account of modern European constitutionalism. It uses the Irish constitutional order to demonstrate that, right across the European Union, the national constitution can no longer be understood on its own, in isolation from the EU legal order or from the European Convention on Human Rights. The constitution is instead triangular, with these three legal orders forming the points of a triangle, and the relationship and interactions between them forming the triangle's sides. It takes as its starting point the theory of constitutional pluralism, which suggests that overlapping constitutional orders are not necessarily arranged 'on top of' each other, but that they may be arranged heterarchically or flatly, without a hierarchy of superior and subordinate constitutions. However, it departs from conventional accounts of this theory by emphasising that we must still pay close attention to jurisdictional specificity in order to understand the norms that regulate pluralist constitutions. It shows, through application of the theory to case studies, that any attempt to extract universal principles from the jurisdictionally contingent interactions between specific legal orders is fraught with difficulty. The book is an important contribution to constitutional theory in general, and constitutional pluralism in particular, and will be of great interest to scholars in the field.

The Triangular Constitution

Constitutional Pluralism in Ireland, the EU and the ECHR

Tom Flynn

·HART·

OXFORD · LONDON · NEW YORK · NEW DELHI · SYDNEY

HART PUBLISHING

Bloomsbury Publishing Plc

Kemp House, Chawley Park, Cumnor Hill, Oxford, OX2 9PH, UK

HART PUBLISHING, the Hart/Stag logo, BLOOMSBURY and the Diana logo are
trademarks of Bloomsbury Publishing Plc

First published in Great Britain 2019

Copyright © Tom Flynn, 2019

Tom Flynn has asserted his right under the Copyright, Designs and Patents Act 1988
to be identified as Author of this work.

All rights reserved. No part of this publication may be reproduced or transmitted in any form or by any
means, electronic or mechanical, including photocopying, recording, or any information storage
or retrieval system, without prior permission in writing from the publishers.

While every care has been taken to ensure the accuracy of this work, no responsibility for
loss or damage occasioned to any person acting or refraining from action as a result of any
statement in it can be accepted by the authors, editors or publishers.

All UK Government legislation and other public sector information used in the work is
Crown Copyright ©. All House of Lords and House of Commons information used in
the work is Parliamentary Copyright ©. This information is reused under the terms
of the Open Government Licence v3.0 (http://www.nationalarchives.gov.uk/doc/
open-government-licence/version/3) except where otherwise stated.

All Eur-lex material used in the work is © European Union, http://eur-lex.europa.eu/, 1998–2019.

A catalogue record for this book is available from the British Library.

Library of Congress Cataloging-in-Publication data

Names: Flynn, Tom (Thomas Joseph Sheridan), author.

Title: The triangular constitution : constitutional pluralism in Ireland, the EU and the ECHR / Tom Flynn.

Description: Oxford, UK ; Chicago, Illinois : Hart Publishing, 2019. | Based on author's thesis
(doctoral – University of Edinburgh, 2014) issued under title: Universality of interface norms under
constitutional pluralism : an analysis of Ireland, the EU and the ECHR. |
Includes bibliographical references and index.

Identifiers: LCCN 2019001265 (print) | LCCN 2019001819 (ebook) |
ISBN 9781509916184 (EPub) | ISBN 9781509916160 (hardback)

Subjects: LCSH: Constitutional law—Ireland. | Law—Ireland—European influences. |
International and municipal law—Ireland. | European Union. | Convention for the Protection
of Human Rights and Fundamental Freedoms (1950 November 5) | BISAC: LAW / International.

Classification: LCC KDK1227.5 (ebook) | LCC KDK1227.5 .F59 2019 (print) | DDC 342.4—dc23

LC record available at https://lccn.loc.gov/2019001265

ISBN: HB: 978-1-50991-616-0
ePDF: 978-1-50991-617-7
ePub: 978-1-50991-618-4

Typeset by Compuscript Ltd, Shannon
Printed and bound in Great Britain by CPI Group (UK) Ltd, Croydon CR0 4YY

To find out more about our authors and books visit www.hartpublishing.co.uk.
Here you will find extracts, author information, details of forthcoming events
and the option to sign up for our newsletters.

Acknowledgements

THERE MAY BE only one name on the front of this book, but it owes its existence, in ways great and small, to a large cast of remarkable people. I am deeply grateful to each of them.

In particular, thanks are due to my PhD supervisors at the University of Edinburgh, Professor Niamh Nic Shuibhne and Dr Cormac Mac Amhlaigh, for their expertise, advice and support. Their generosity and professionalism is boundless. I am also indebted to my internal and external examiners, Professor Neil Walker and Professor Donncha O'Connell, and to the entire research community at Edinburgh Law School.

My editors at Hart Publishing, Bill Asquith and Rosamund Jubber, have been enthusiastic and supportive of this project from the very beginning. Thanks also to Anne Bevan for her meticulous copy editing, and to the production editor, Linda Staniford.

During the development of this book, it has been my privilege first to work at the University of Warwick, and then at the University of Essex. I owe an enormous debt of gratitude to the current and former academic and administrative staff of the Schools of Law at both these institutions. In particular, I would like to thank my friends and colleagues Dr Stephen Connelly, Dr Emily Jones, Professor Theodore Konstadinides, Professor Dora Kostakopoulou, Professor John McEldowney, Dr Tara Mulqueen, Professor Rebecca Probert, Professor Maurice Sunkin, Dr Anastasia Tataryn, Dr Illan rua Wall and Dr Ania Zbyszewska.

Thanks also to Professor Gareth Davies and to Dr Matej Avbelj, and to the participants in the conference on 'Legal Pluralism in the European Union' held at Vrije Universiteit Amsterdam in November 2017.

Special thanks to Alan Bolster, Jodie Graves, Fiona Hegarty, Dr Wendy van der Neut, Dr Inês Sofia Oliveira, Ken Page, Caoimhe Rehill, Philippa-Lucy Reekie, Dr Nayha Sethi and Alison Treacy for their unstinting love, support and friendship.

My comrades Philip Karsgaard, Daniel P McCarthy, Dr Daniel Shand and Luke Smithson are a constant source of strength. May our pilgrimage ever gain momentum.

Finally – but most of all – I would like to thank my parents, Peter and Teresina, my sisters, Rachael and Olivia, my brothers-in-law, Kieran and Donnacha, and my nephew Oliver, for everything. Tolstoy was wrong: not all happy families are alike. This one is unique, and this book is dedicated to them.

Tom Flynn
Colchester
October 2018

Table of Contents

Acknowledgements	*v*
Table of Cases	*xiii*
Table of Legislation	*xxiii*
Introduction	*xxv*

I.	Context: Constitutional Pluralism	*xxvi*
II.	Problem: Interface Norms	*xxvii*
III.	Field: Justification of Choice of Jurisdictions	*xxix*
IV.	Chapter Outline	*xxxi*

1. European Constitutional Pluralism and the Triangular Constitution 1

Introduction 1

- I. Constitutional Pluralism's Origins in the EU 2
    - A. Constitutionalisation and Disorder 2
    - B. Beginnings: MacCormick's 'Radical Pluralism' and 'Pluralism Under International Law' 5
    - C. The Three Major Claims of Walker's Pluralism 7
- II. The Constitutional Pluralists and the Critics 11
    - A. Constitutionalism and Pluralism: A Contradiction in Terms?....12
        - i. Constitutional Pluralism Not Constitutionalist? 14
        - ii. Constitutional Pluralism Not Pluralist? 19
        - iii. Reconciling the Dichotomy: Constitutional Pluralism, Pluralist Constitutionalism 21
    - B. 'Going Their Own Ways': Different Conceptions of Constitutional Pluralism 23
- III. Metaconstitutional Pluralisms 28
    - A. Sabel and Gerstenberg: Polyarchic Coordinate Constitutionalism 30
        - i. Interface Norms Under Polyarchic Coordinate Constitutionalism 33
    - B. Maduro: Contrapunctual Law 34
        - i. Interface Norms Under Contrapunctual Law 35
    - C. Kumm: Cosmopolitan Constitutionalism 37
        - i. Interface Norms Under Cosmopolitan Constitutionalism 40
- IV. Two Problems of Metaconstitutional Pluralism 44
    - A. The Rule of Law, Integrity and Epistemology 44
    - B. The Universality of Interface Norms 51

viii *Table of Contents*

V. Triangular Constitutionalism 53
   A. The Triangular Constitution as a Composite Constitutional
      Polyarchy 53
   B. From the Triangular Constitution to Triangular
      Constitutional*ism* 56

2. The Vertical Frame 60
  Introduction 60
  I. The Terms of Engagement Between Irish Law and EU Law 61
    A. Incorporating EU Law in Ireland 61
      i. A Closed Legal Order 61
      ii. Opening the Legal Order: A Three-Pronged Approach 62
    B. The 'Licence to Join' and the ex ante Review of EU Norms 65
      i. Domestic Reservation of Ultimate Constitutionality
        by Conditional Recognition: The European Communities
        (Amendment) Act 1986 66
      ii. 'Penultimate Judicial Supremacy' and the Boundaries
        of Government Action: Title III of the SEA 69
      iii. Analysis: Conditional Recognition, 'Scope and Objectives'
        and the Attitude of the Court 71
    C. The 'Exclusion Clause' and the ex post Review of EU Norms 75
      i. Ripples and Torpedoes 75
      ii. *SPUC v Grogan*: An Aberration? 77
      iii. The 'Torpedo Effect' Torpedoed 79
      iv. Analysis: Democratic Legitimacy, 'Areas of Great
        Sensitivity' and a Hierarchy of Norms 82
    D. Conclusion: Hierarchy and Polyarchy, Specificity
      and Universality 86
  II. The Irish Legal Order and the European Convention
    on Human Rights 88
    A. The Relationship Defined, Pre- and Post-Incorporation 88
      i. 1950–2003: Pride and Prejudice 88
      ii. 2003 to the Present Day: The European Convention
        on Human Rights Act 2003 92
        a. Origins 92
        b. The Act's Provisions 93
    B. The ECHR Act 2003 and Polyarchy 95
      i. Otherness and Embeddedness 96
      ii. Unconstitutionality and Unconventionality:
        A Question of Priority 98
    C. Conclusion: *Legislative* Interface Norms 100
  III. Conclusion 101

Table of Contents   ix

3. The Horizontal Frame 103
   Introduction 103
   I.   The Pre-Accession Terms of Engagement Between the EU
        and the ECHR 104
        A.   The ECHR from the CJEU's Viewpoint 104
             i.   The Normative Status of the Convention
                  Within the EU 106
             ii. ECtHR Case Law Before the CJEU 109
        B.   The EU from the ECtHR's Viewpoint 112
             i.   Review of Primary EU Law 112
             ii. Review of Secondary EU Law 113
             iii. Review of Actions of the Union's Institutions 116
             iv. Institutional Matters: The CJEU's Advocates
                  General and Article 6 ECHR 118
        C.   Conclusions: Metaconstitutional Interface Norms 122
   II. The Draft Accession Agreement and Opinion 2/13 123
        A.   Specificity and Autonomy 124
             i.   Article 53 ECHR and Article 53 of the Charter 125
             ii. Article 344 TFEU 126
             iii. Mutual Trust 127
             iv. The Common Foreign and Security Policy (CFSP) 128
        B.   Institutional and Procedural Mechanisms 129
             i.   The Co-Respondent Mechanism 129
             ii. The 'Prior Involvement' of the CJEU 130
             iii. Protocol No 16 ECHR 131
        C.   Conclusions: Constitutional and Metaconstitutional
             Interface Norms 132
   III. Labour Rights and Constitutional Conflict 134
        A.   The CJEU, Labour Rights and Market Freedoms:
             An Indelicate Balance? 135
             i.   The Right to Take Collective Action as a Fundamental
                  Right 135
             ii. Conceptualising Collective Action 137
             iii. Justifying its Exercise 138
        B.   The ECtHR and Labour Rights: The Ground Shifts 141
             i.   The 'Integrated' Approach to Interpretation
                  and Article 11 143
        C.   Managing Impending Judicial Conflict in Europe 145
   IV. Conclusion 149

x *Table of Contents*

4. The Triangular Frame 151
   Introduction 151
      Aims and Structure of the Chapter.. 151
      Prologue: The Situation Prior to 1983.. 155
   I. Avoidance, Engagement and Conditional Recognition 158
       A. *AG (SPUC) v Open Door Counselling and Dublin*
          Well Woman 158
          i.   Avoidance of Triggering Engagement: The High Court
               Judgment... 159
          ii. Engagement Avoided Again, More Narrowly:
               The Supreme Court Judgment....................................... 161
       B. *SPUC v Grogan* 163
          i.   Engagement Begins: The High Court Judgment.............. 163
          ii. *Solange* in Ireland: The Supreme Court Judgment........... 164
   II. Polyarchic Deliberation.. 166
       A. The Right to Receive and Impart Information 167
          i.   The Right as a Corollary to the Freedom to Provide
               Services 167
               a. A Less Reticent Approach 169
          ii. The Right as Part of Freedom of Expression.................. 171
          iii. Political Resolution: The Fourteenth Amendment 177
       B. The Right to Travel.. 178
          i.   'A Spurious and Divisive Uniformity'? The High Court
               Judgment... 179
          ii. Conflict Avoided, for Now: The Supreme Court
               Judgment... 182
          iii. Potential Conflict Resolved Politically: The Thirteenth
               Amendment.. 184
       C. The Right to Private and Family Life 185
          i.   (Temporary?) Reverse Conditional Recognition:
               The Judgment of the Majority 188
          ii. Unconvincing Constitutionalism: The Dissent
               Regarding A & B 191
   III. The Nature of the Relationships and the Universality
        of Interface Norms.. 196
   IV. Conclusion.. 202

5. Towards Triangular Constitutionalism: Universalising
   the Triangular Constitution 204
   Introduction 204
   I. The Triangular Constitution Assessed.. 205
       A. Interface Norms Within the Triangular Constitution:
          Universal Categories, Particular Norms.................................. 208
       B. The Principle of Legality 208

		C. The Protection of National Specificity	212
		D. The Principle of Conditional Recognition	216
II.		From the Particular to the Universal	219
		A. The Rule of Law in Dangerous Times	222
		B. Jurisdictional Specificity	227
III.		Conclusion	230

Bibliography 232
Index 243

Table of Cases

Ireland

High Court

A and B v Eastern Health Board, Judge Mary Fahy and C
[1998] 1 IR 464 189
AG v X [1992] 1 IR 1.. 83, 85, 154, 175–76, 178,
180–82, 184, 194
AG (SPUC) v Open Door Counselling Ltd [1988] IR 593 .....78–79, 158–68, 172,
180, 195, 198, 202
Carmody v Minister for Justice [2005] 1 JIC 2103 97–99
Crotty v An Taoiseach [1987] IR 713 ....63, 65–71, 73–76, 81,
86–87, 101, 124, 214–15, 217
Dada v Minister for Justice [2006] IEHC 166 97
Doherty v South Dublin County Council (No 2) [2007] 2 IR 696 97
Dublin City Council v Liam Gallagher [2008] IEHC 354 100
Foy v an t-Árd Chláraitheoir (No 1) [2002] IEHC 116 ....97, 101
Foy v an t-Árd Chláraitheoir (No 2) [2007] IEHC 470 .... 97–98, 101, 213
G v An Bord Uchtála [1980] IR 32 ....157, 159
Heaney v Ireland [1994] 2 ILRM 420 90
Lawlor v Minister for Agriculture [1990] 1 IR 356.................................. 76–77
Law Society of Ireland v Competition Authority [2006] 2 IR 262 99
Leonard v Dublin City Council [2008] IEHC 79 97
Lelimo v Minister for Justice [2004] 2 IR 178 97
Meagher v Minister for Agriculture [1994] 1 IR 329 .... 75, 77
Norris v Attorney General [1984] IR 36 ....90, 159
Ó Laighléis, In re [1960] IR 93 .... 89, 91
O'Leary v Attorney General [1993] 1 IR 102 90
Roche v Ireland (unreported, High Court, 17 Jun 1983) 71
Ryan v DPP [1989] IR 399 180
SPUC v Grogan [1989] IR 753...................................... 77–82, 85–87, 101, 158,
163–67, 180, 182,
189, 198–99, 206, 210,
214–15, 217–18
The State (Keegan) v Stardust Compensation Tribunal [1986] IR 642.............83
The State (Quinn) v Ryan [1965] IR 70 ....71, 173

xiv *Table of Cases*

Court of Criminal Appeal

The People v Shaw [1982] IR 1 173
The People (Attorney General) v Cadden (1956) 91 ILTR 97 156

Supreme Court

AG v X [1992] 1 IR 1 .... 83, 85, 154, 175–76, 178,
180–82, 184, 194
AG (SPUC) v Open Door Counselling Ltd [1988] IR 593 .....78–79, 158–68, 172,
180, 195, 198, 202
Byrne v Ireland [1972] IR 241 159
Campus Oil v Minister for Industry [1983] IR 82 164
Carmody v Minister for Justice [2010] 1 IR 635 97–100
Crotty v An Taoiseach [1987] IR 713 .... 63, 65–71, 73–76, 81,
86–87, 101, 124, 214–15, 217
DPP v Delaney [1997] 3 IR 453 83
Educational Company of Ireland v Fitzpatrick (No 2) [1961] IR 345 159
G v An Bord Uchtála [1980] IR 32 .... 157, 159
Heaney v Ireland [1996] 1 IR 540 90
Lobe & Osayande v Minister for Justice [2003] IESC 1 91
McGee v Attorney General [1974] IR 284 .... 156–57, 159
Mead (unreported, Supreme Court, 26 Jul 1972) 159
Meagher v Minister for Agriculture [1994] 1 IR 329 .... 75, 77
Meskell v CIÉ [1973] IR 121 .... 159, 173
Murphy v Roche [1987] IR 106 100
Nathan v Bailey Gibson [1998] 2 IR 162 75–77
Norris v Attorney General [1984] IR 36 .... 90, 159
Ó Laighléis, In re [1960] IR 93 .... 89, 91
O'Leary v Attorney General [1995] 1 IR 254 90
Ryan v Attorney General [1965] IR 294 .... 91, 156
Ryan v DPP [1989] IR 399 180
Society for the Protection of Unborn Children v Grogan
[1989] IR 753 .... 77–82, 85–87, 101,
158, 163–67, 180, 182,
189, 198–99, 206,
210, 214–15, 217–18
The People v O'Callaghan [1966] IR 501 180
The People (DPP) v MS [2003] 1 IR 606 89
The People (DPP) v Shaw [1982] IR 1 83
The State (Keegan) v Stardust Compensation Tribunal [1986] IR 642 83
The State (Quinn) v Ryan [1965] IR 70 .... 71, 173
The State (Woods) v Attorney General [1969] IR 385 99
Wireless Dealers' Association v Fair Trade Commission (unreported,
Supreme Court, 14 Mar 1956) 71

Table of Cases xv

Other National Courts

Czech Constitutional Court

Judgment of 31 Jan 2012, Pl ÚS 5/12, *Slovak Pensions XVII* ('*Holubec*') 38, 77, 209, 230

German Federal Constitutional Court

Application of Wünsche Handelsgesellschaft, Re the
(Case 2 BvR 197/83), [1987] 3 *Common Market Law Review* 225
('*Solange II*') .... xvi, 4
Brunner v European Union Treaty (Case 2 BvR 2134/92
and 2959/92 JZ 1993, 1100), [1994] 1 *Common Market Law Review* 57 5
Gauweiler (Case 2 BvR 2728/13), order of 14 Jan 2014, available in English
at <www.bundesverfassungsgericht.de/SharedDocs/Entscheidungen/
EN/2014/01/rs20140114_2bvr272813en.html> xviii
Gauweiler (Case 2 BvR 2728/13), judgment of 21 Jun 2016, available
in English at <www.bundesverfassungsgericht.de/SharedDocs/
Entscheidungen/EN/2016/06/rs20160621_2bvr272813en.html> 6
*Internationale Handelsgesellschaft mbH v Einfuhr- und Vorratsstelle
für Getreide und Futtermittel* (Case 2 BvL 52/71), [1974] 2
Common Market Law Review 540 ('*Solange I*').............................. xvi, 3–4
Ratification of the Treaty of Lisbon, Re (Case 2 BvE 2/08) [2010] 3
Common Market Law Review 13..xviii, 6

United Kingdom House of Lords

R v Secretary of State for Transport, ex parte Factortame
[1991] 3 All ER 769 5

United States Supreme Court

Brown v Allen (1953) 344 US 443..48
Griswold v Connecticut (1965) 381 US 479 157
Marbury v Madison (1803) 5 US 137 32
Roe v Wade (1973) 410 US 113..157

Court of Justice of the European Union

General Court

AC-Treuhand v Commission (Case T–99/04) (ECLI:EU:T:2008:256,
[2008] ECR II–1501 107
Connolly v Commission (Case T–203/95) ECLI:EU:T:1999:101,
[1999] ECR II–443 117

xvi   *Table of Cases*

Connolly v Commission (Joined Cases T–34/96 and T–163/96)
    ECLI:EU:T:1999:102, [1999] ECR II–463 117
Connolly v Commission (Case T–214/96) ECLI:EU:T:1999:103,
    [1999] ECR II–517 117
Mannesmannröhren-Werke v Commission (Case T–112/98)
    ECLI:EU:T:2001:61, [2001] ECR II–729 107
Mayr-Melnhof Kartongesellschaft v Commission (Case T–347/94)
    ECLI:EU:T:1998:101, [1998] ECR II–1751 107

Court of Justice

*Accession by the Community to the European Convention for the Protection
    of Human Rights and Fundamental Freedoms*
    (Opinion 2/94) ECLI:EU:C:1996:140, [1996] ECR I–1759 105–06,
                                                                                109, 114, 132
*Accession of the European Union to the European Convention
    for the Protection of Human Rights and Fundamental Freedoms*
    (Opinion 2/13) ECLI:EU:C:2014:2454 .... 51–52, 104–06,
                                                                                108, 111, 116, 118,
                                                                                122–34, 145, 147–50,
                                                                                207, 213, 221
Åkerberg Fransson (Case C–617/10) EU:C:2013:105 .... 108, 125, 136, 172
Amministrazione delle Finanze dello Stato v Simmenthal
    (Case 106/77) ECLI:EU:C:1978:49, [1978] ECR 629 38
Arben Kaba v Secretary of State for the Home Department (Kaba II)
    (Case C–466/00) ECLI:EU:C:2003:127 (Opinion),
    ECLI:EU:C:2002:447 (Judgment), [2003] ECR I–2219 .... 120, 211
Bosman (Case C–415/93) ECLI:EU:C:1995:293,
    [1995] ECR I–4921 .... 137, 140
*Bosphorus Hava Yolları Turizm ve Ticaret Anonim Şirketi v Minister
    for Transport, Energy and Communications and others*
    (Case C–84/95) ECLI:EU:C:1996:179, [1996] ECR I–3953 108
Cinéthèque and Others v Fédération Nationale des Cinémas Français
    (Joined Cases 60 and 61/84) ECLI:EU:C:1985:329, [1985] ECR 2605 170
Comet BV v Produktschap voor Siergewassen (Case 45/76)
    ECLI:EU:C:1976:191, [1976] ECR 2043 38
Commission v European Investment Bank (Case C–15/00)
    ECLI:EU:C:2003:396, [2003] ECR I–7281 3
Commission v Germany (Case 205/84) ECLI:EU:C:1986:463,
    [1986] ECR 3755 170
Commission v Germany (Case C–271/08) ECLI:EU:C:2010:183
    (Opinion), ECLI:EU:C:2010:426 (Judgment) [2010] ECR I–7091 148
Commission v Ireland (Case C–459/03) ECLI:EU:C:2006:345,
    [2006] ECR I–4635 106

Table of Cases xvii

Commission v Luxembourg (Case C–319/06) ECLI:EU:C:2008:350,
[2008] ECR I–4323..135, 141
Connolly v Commission (Case C–273/99 P) ECLI:EU:C:2001:126,
[2001] ECR I–1575..117
Connolly v Commission (Case C–274/99 P) ECLI:EU:C:2001:127,
[2001] ECR I–1611..117
Cowan v Trésor Publique (Case 186/87) ECLI:EU:C:1990:102,
[1989] ECR 195 170
Dassonville (Case 8/74) ECLI:EU:C:1974:82, [1974] ECR 837....................161
Decker (Case C–120/95) ECLI:EU:C:1998:167, [1998] ECR I–1831..............136
*Draft Agreement Between the Community and the Countries
of EFTA Relating to the Creation of the EEA* (Opinion 1/91)
ECLI:EU:C:1991:490, [1991] ECR I–6079...106
Emesa Sugar (Free Zone) NV v Aruba (Case C–17/98)
ECLI:EU:C:2000:70, [2000] ECR I–675..119
ERT (Case C–260/89) ECLI:EU:C:1991:254, [1991] ECR I–2925...........105, 171
Eugen Schmidberger, International Transporte und Planzüge v Austria
(Case C–112/00) ECLI:EU:C:2003:333, [2003] ECR I–5659 .... 31, 136–40
Firma Foto-Frost v Hauptzollamt Lübeck-Ost (Case 314/85)
ECLI:EU:C:1987:452, [1987] ECR 4199 .... 38, 76
*Firma Molkerei-Zentrale Westfalen/Lippe GmbH v Hauptzollamt
Paderborn* (Case 28/67) ECLI:EU:C:1968:17, [1968] ECR 143 3
Flaminio Costa v ENEL (Case 6/64) ECLI:EU:C:1964:66,
[1964] ECR 585 .... 3, 69
Francovich v Italy (Case C–6/90) ECLI:EU:C:1991:428, ECR I–5357..............75
GB-INNO-BM v Confédération du Commerce Luxembourgeois
(Case C–362/88) ECLI:EU:C:1990:102, [1990] ECR I–667 169–70
Gebhard (Case C–55/94) ECLI:EU:C:1995:411, [1995] ECR I–4165 139–40
Geitling v High Authority (Joined Cases 36, 37, 38 & 40/59)
ECLI:EU:C:1960:36, [1960] ECR 423.. 4, 105
Georgios Orfanopoulos v Land Baden-Württemberg
(Joined Cases C–482/01 and C–493/01) ECLI:EU:C:2004:262,
[2004] ECR I–5257 108
*Gouvernement de la Communauté française and Gouvernement wallon v
Gouvernement flamand* (Case C–212/06) ECLI:EU:C:2007:398,
[2008] ECR I–1683 121
Hauer v Land Rheinland-Pfalz (Case 44/79) ECLI:EU:C:1979:290,
[1979] ECR 3727..4
Hoechst v Commission (Joined Cases 46/87 and 227/88)
ECLI:EU:C:1989:337, [1989] ECR 2859 ....110, 118, 145,
200, 210
Ilonka Sayn-Wittgenstein v Landeshauptmann von Wien
(Case C–208/09) ECLI:EU:C:2010:806, [2010] ECR I–13693.............. 31, 85,
182, 215

xviii Table of Cases

Internationale Handelsgesellschaft mbH v Einfuhr- und Vorratsstelle für Getreide und Futtermittel (Case 11/70) ECLI:EU:C:1970:114, [1970] ECR 1125 .... 3, 69, 200

ITWF & FSU v Viking Line (Case C–438/05) ECLI:EU:C:2007:292, [2007] ECR I–10779 .... 34, 86, 135–41, 143, 145–49, 195, 216

Kadi and Al Barakaat v Council and Commission (Joined Cases C–402/05 P and C–415/05 P) ECLI:EU:C:2008:461, [2008] ECR I–6351 .... 3, 31, 37, 108, 202, 209

Kamberaj (Case C–571/10) EU:C:2012:233 108

Kohll (Case C–158/96) ECLI:EU:C:1998:171, [1998] ECR I–1931 136

Laserdisken ApS v Kulturministeriet (Case C–479/04) ECLI:EU:C:2006:549, [2006] ECR I–8089 106

Laval un Partneri v Svenska Byggnadsarbetareförbundet (Case C–341/05) ECLI:EU:C:2007:809, [2007] ECR I–11767 .... 34, 85–86, 135–41, 143, 145–49, 195, 216

Limburgse Vinyl Maatschappij NV and Others v Commission (Joined Cases C–238/99 P, C–244/99 P, C–245/99 P, C–247/99 P, C–250/99 P to C–252/99 P and C–254/99 P) ECLI:EU:C:2002:582, [2002] ECR I–8375 .... 110, 150, 210

Luisi and Carbone v Ministero del Tesoro (Joined Cases 286/82 and 26/83) ECLI:EU:C:1984:35, [1984] ECR 377 .... 168, 170, 179

Malgožata Runevič-Vardyn and Łukasz Paweł Wardyn v Vilniaus Miesto Savivaldybės Administracija (Case C–391/09) ECLI:EU:C:2011:291, [2011] ECR I–3787 .... 31, 85, 182, 215

Mangold v Helm (Case C–144/04) ECLI:EU:C:2005:709, [2005] ECR I–9981 34

Marleasing SA v La Comercial Internacional de Alimentación SA (Case C–106/89) ECLI:EU:C:1990:395, [1990] ECR I–4135 75

Meki Elgafaji, Noor Elgafaji v Staatsecretaris van Justitie (Case C–465/07) ECLI:EU:C:2009:94, [2009] ECR I–921 108

Melloni (Case C–399/11) ECLI:EU:C:2013:107 .... 125–27, 146

Moser v Land Baden-Württemberg (Case 180/83) ECLI:EU:C:1984:233, [1984] ECR 2539 168

Nold v Commission (Case 4/73) ECLI:EU:C:1974:51, [1974] ECR 491 4

NV Algemene Transport- en Expeditie Onderneming van Gend en Loos v Nederlandse Administratie der Belastingen (Case 26/62) ECLI:EU:C:1963:1, [1963] ECR 1 2

Omega Spielhallen- und Automatenaufstellungs-GmbH v Oberbürgermeisterin der Bundesstadt Bonn (Case C–36/02) ECLI:EU:C:2004:614, [2004] ECR I–9609 .... xvi, 31, 84–85, 136–38, 147, 171, 182, 200, 215–16

Table of Cases xix

Ordre des barreaux francophones et germanophone and Others
(Case C–305/05) ECLI:EU:C:2007:383, [2007] ECR I–5305 108
Orkem v Commission (Case 374/87) ECLI:EU:C:1989:387,
[1989] ECR 3283 .... 110, 118,
145, 200, 210
P v S (Case C–13/94) ECLI:EU:C:1996:170, [1996] ECR I–2143 105
Parti Ecologiste 'Les Verts' v Parliament (Case 294/83)
ECLI:EU:C:1986:166, [1986] ECR 1339 3
R v Bouchereau (Case 30/77) ECLI:EU:C:1977:172,
[1977] ECR 1999 .... 170, 181
Roquette Frères SA v DGCCRF (Case C–94/00) ECLI:EU:C:2002:603,
[2002] ECR I–9011 .... 110, 150, 210
Rüffert v Land Niedersachsen (Case C–346/06) ECLI:EU:C:2008:189,
[2008] ECR I–1989 .... 135, 141
Ruiz Zambrano (Case C–34/09) ECLI:EU:C:2010:560 (Opinion),
[2011] ECR I–1177 161
Rutili (Case 36/75) ECLI:EU:C:1975:137, [1975] ECR 1219 105
Schindler (Case C–275/92) ECLI:EU:C:1993:944, [1994] ECR I–1039 84
Sgarlata and others v Commission (Case 40/64) ECLI:EU:C:1965:36,
[1965] ECR 215 .... 4, 105
SPUC (Ireland) v Grogan (Case C–159/90) ECLI:EU:C:1991:378,
[1991] ECR I–4685 ....78, 166–73, 178–79,
181–82, 198–200, 215–16
Stauder v City of Ulm (Case 29/69) ECLI:EU:C:1969:57,
[1969] ECR 419 .... 4, 105
Stork v High Authority (Case 1/58) ECLI:EU:C:1959:4,
[1959] ECR 17 .... 4, 105
Torfaen Borough Council v B&Q (Case C–145/88) ECLI:EU:C:1989:593,
[1989] ECR 3851 170
Van Duyn v Home Office (Case 41/74) ECLI:EU:C:1974:133,
[1974] ECR 1337 181
Van Wesemael (Joined Cases 110 and 111/78) ECLI:EU:C:1979:8,
[1979] ECR 35 170
Varec SA v Etat belge (Case C–450/06) ECLI:EU:C:2008:91,
[2008] ECR I–581 108
Walrave and Koch (Case 36/74) ECLI:EU:C:1974:140, [1974] ECR 1405 137
Webb (Case 279/80) ECLI:EU:C:1981:314, [1981] ECR 3305 170
Weber v Parliament (Case C–314/91) ECLI:EU:C:1993:109,
[1993] ECR I–1093 3
Wouters and Others (Case C–309/99) ECLI:EU:C:2002:98,
[2002] ECR I–1577 137

xx   *Table of Cases*

Council of Europe

European Commission of Human Rights

Brüggemann and Scheuten v Germany (1981) 3 EHRR 244 172
M & Co v Germany (1990) 64 *Decisions and Reports* 138 .... 112, 114–15
van Volsem v Belgium App No 14641/89 (decision, ECmHR,
    9 May 1990) 142
X v UK (1980) 19 *Decisions and Reports* 244 172
X & X v Germany App no 342/57 (decision, ECmHR, 4 Sep 1958) 112

European Court of Human Rights

A, B & C v Ireland (2010) 53 EHRR 13 .... 186–91, 193–94, 201,
                                            203, 214, 218, 221
Airey v Ireland (No 1) (1979–80) 2 EHRR 305 90
Avotiņš v Latvia App no 17502/07 (judgment, ECtHR, 23 May 2016) 149
Bosphorus Hava Yolları Turizm ve Ticaret Anonim Şirketi v Ireland
    (2005) ECHR 440 .... xvi, 18, 31, 114–19, 121–23,
                                      129, 131, 145–46, 149–50,
                                      207, 211, 213, 215, 218
Burden v UK (2008) 47 EHRR 38 187
Chiragov v Armenia App no 13216/05 (judgment, ECtHR, 16 Jun 2015) 56
Connolly v 15 Member States of the EU App no 73274/01
    (decision, ECtHR, 9 Dec 2008) 116, 207
Cooperatieve Producentenorganisatie van de Nederlandse
    Kokkelvisserij UA v the Netherlands App No 13645/05 (decision,
    ECtHR, 20 Jan 2009) 120, 211
Demir and Baykara v Turkey (2009) 48 EHRR 54 .... 142–45, 147–48, 200
Dudgeon v UK (1982) 4 EHRR 149 90
Enerji Yapı-Yol Sen v Turkey (2009) ECHR 2251 .... 142, 144–45, 200
Funke v France (1993) 16 EHRR 297 .... 110, 210
Goodwin v UK (2002) 35 EHRR 18 .... 34, 98, 112
Handyside v UK (1976) 1 EHRR 737 175
Hobbs v UK App no 63684/00 (decision, ECtHR, 18 Jun 2002) 187
Hrvatski Liječnički Sindikat v Croatia App no 36701/09 (Judgment,
    ECtHR, 27 Nov 2014) 148
Ireland v UK (1978) 2 EHRR 25 187
James and Others v United Kingdom App no 8793/79 (judgment,
    ECtHR, 21 Feb 1986) 92
JJ v the Netherlands (1999) 28 EHRR 168 119
KDB v the Netherlands (1998) ECHR 20; 119
Kress v France (2001) ECHR 382. 119–121
Lawless v Ireland (1961) 1 EHRR 1 89
Lobo Machado v Portugal (1996) 23 EHRR 79 119

Table of Cases xxi

Loizidou v Turkey (preliminary objections) App no 15318/89
   (1995) Series A no 310 .... 18, 31, 56
Lotarev v Ukraine App no 29447/04 (judgment, ECtHR, 8 Apr 2010) 187
Markt Intern and Beerman v Germany (1990) 12 EHRR 161 172
Matthews v UK (1999) 28 EHRR 361. .... 113–15, 117
Michaud v France (2012) ECHR 2030 .... 115, 131, 146
MSS v Belgium and Greece (2011) 53 EHRR 2 115
N v UK (2008) 47 EHRR 885 142
National Union of Belgian Police v Belgium (1979–80) 1 EHRR 578 142
Niemitz v Germany (1992) 16 EHRR 97 .... 110, 210
Norris v Ireland (1991) 13 EHRR 186 .... 90, 174
Open Door and Dublin Well Woman v Ireland (1992)
   15 EHRR 244 .... 163, 172–74, 176–77,
                                        187, 189, 200–01, 214
Reinhardt and Slimane-Kaïd v France (1998–II) 28 EHRR 59. 119
Schettini and Others v Italy App no 29529/95 (decision, ECtHR,
   9 Nov 2000) 142
Schmidt and Dahlström v Sweden (1976) 1 EHRR 632 .... 136, 141–42, 144
SH and Others v Austria (2011) ECHR 1879 189
Silver and Others v UK (1983) 5 EHRR 347 172
Société Colas Est v France (2004) 39 EHRR 373 .... 110, 210
Sunday Times v UK (1979–1980) 2 EHRR 245 172–73
Sunday Times v United Kingdom (No 2) (1991) ECHR 50 5
Swedish Engine Drivers Union v Sweden (1976) 1 EHRR 617 .... 142, 144
UNISON v UK App no 53574/99 (decision, ECtHR, 10 Jan 2002). 142
Vermeulen v Belgium (2001) 32 EHRR 15 (fix in text) 119–20
Vo v France (2005) 40 EHRR 259 187

Table of Legislation

Ireland

Department of Health, 'General Scheme of a Bill to Regulate
Termination of Pregnancy', 27 Mar 2018, <health.gov.ie/wp-content/
uploads/2018/03/General-Scheme-for-Publication.pdf> 191
European Communities Act 1972 ....62–64, 66, 86,
96–97, 159, 206,
209–10
European Convention on Human Rights Act 2003 ....58, 88, 90,
92–102, 107, 111,
187, 206–07, 209–10
Health (Family Planning) Act 1979 157
Protection of Life During Pregnancy Act 2013 ....78, 154–55, 190
Referendum (Amendment) (No 2) Act 1992 185
Thirty-sixth Amendment of the Constitution Act 2018 .... 152–53, 178

(Former) United Kingdom of Great Britain and Ireland

Offences Against the Person Act 1861.......................................90, 155–56, 190
Statute Law Revision Act 1892.. 156
Statute Law Revision (No 2) Act 1893.. 156

United Kingdom of Great Britain and Northern Ireland

Human Rights Act 1998 ....94–95, 128, 187

European Union

Act Concerning the Election of the Representatives of the Assembly
by Direct Universal Suffrage [1976] OJ L 278 113
Charter of Fundamental Rights of the European Union
[2016] OJ C 202/2 .... 103, 108–12,
125–26, 127, 133–36,
143, 144, 146–48,
207, 209–11

xxiv   *Table of Legislation*

Council Directive 73/148/EEC of 21 May 1973 on the abolition
of restrictions on movement and residence within the Community
for nationals of Member States with regard to establishment
and the provision of services [1973] OJ L 172. ....160, 181
Declaration on Article 6(2) of the Treaty on European Union
[2016] OJ C 202/1, 337...125
Explanations Relating to the Charter of Fundamental Rights
[2007] OJ C 303/17 ....110, 207
Parliament and Council Directive 96/71/EC Concerning the Posting
of Workers in the Framework of the Provision of Services
[1997] OJ L 18/1 136
Protocol (No 1) on the Role of National Parliaments in the European
Union [2010] OJ C 83/203 and Protocol (No 2) on the Application
of the Principles of Subsidiarity and Proportionality
[2010] OJ C 83/206 41
Protocol (No 8) relating to Article 6(2) of the Treaty on European
Union on the Accession of the Union to the European Convention
on the Protection of Human Rights and Fundamental Freedoms
[2016] OJ C 202/273 125
Rules of Procedure of the Court of Justice [2012] OJ L 265/1 179
Treaty of Lisbon amending the Treaty on European Union and the
Treaty establishing the European Community [2007] OJ C 306 108
Treaty on European Union (Treaty of Amsterdam) [1997] OJ C 340............107
Treaty on European Union (Treaty of Maastricht) [1992] OJ C 191.............107

Introduction

THIS IS A work of applied constitutional theory. It takes as its field of study three interacting legal orders – those of Ireland, the European Union and the European Convention on Human Rights – and posits them as a unified, yet non-unitary, whole: a triangular constitutional order. In doing so, it draws on the rich literature of the concept of constitutional pluralism in order to posit a new way of thinking about constitutionalism in Europe, one that refuses, as a matter of principle, to regard any part of the constitutional whole – national, Union or Convention – as the final arbiter of constitutionality, or the possessor of ultimate normative authority over the other parts.

These are inauspicious times for such a proposal. Though the proposed remedies differ, the diagnosis is widely shared: Europe is unwell. Ten years ago, as the Lisbon Treaty finally came into force, the hope was that the European Union's 'semi-permanent Treaty revision process'[1] was at an end, and the enlarged Union could settle into a period of stability and consolidation. It was not to be: the decade since has been one of multiple, overlapping crises – financial, economic, political and constitutional – which have strained the very sinews of the European project, and have resulted in an atmosphere of conflict and fragmentation. With the United Kingdom narrowly voting to leave the Union in 2016, and the electoral rise across the continent of political forces – reductively and unhelpfully grouped together as 'populists' – exhibiting various kinds of nativism, racism and authoritarianism, the question of how the Union and its Member States relate to one another has attained a new resonance. This book does not propose some all-encompassing solution, and, as we shall see, is suspicious of any universal constitutional master-theory by which all Europe's ills can be cured. Neither the Union nor its Member States have showered themselves in glory in the past decade, and in different ways each has been tried and found wanting. The proposal is therefore more modest: a constitutional worldview that acknowledges the advantages and disadvantages of constitutionalism at the national, supranational and international level, and attempts to institute a balance between these three levels, allowing the space for political and legal contestation required of any constitutional order worthy of the name, while still respecting the need for legal stability and certainty.

---

[1] B de Witte, 'The Closest Thing to a Constitutional Conversation in Europe: The Semi-Permanent Treaty Revision Process' in P Beaumont, C Lyons and N Walker (eds), *Convergence and Divergence in European Public Law* (Oxford, Hart Publishing, 2002) 39.

xxvi   *Introduction*

I. CONTEXT: CONSTITUTIONAL PLURALISM

'National law' and 'international law' were once quite easily distinguishable. The former operated within the territorial and conceptual borders of the Westphalian nation state; the latter dealt with the interstices between these states. However, the years since 1945 have seen the rise of one of the defining features of modern public law: the non-state legal system or normative order. This phenomenon entails, as its logical corollary, a shift or transfer of institutional normative power away from traditional actors, such as states and governments, and towards various international, transnational and supranational organisations – public,[2] private[3] and sometimes a hybrid of the two[4] – with concomitant difficulties for received notions of public accountability and democratic legitimacy. Though frequently possessed of the kind of jurisgenerative authority once thought the sole preserve of state legal orders, non-state legal systems lack many of the features commonly thought essential for the legitimation of the exercise of public power. Furthermore, given that this transfer of power has occurred without states *relinquishing* their claims to sovereignty and autonomy (the 'transfer' in this sense perhaps better characterised as a 'pooling'), the prospect arises of legal conflict between the state and non-state orders in cases where their jurisdictions overlap.

Accordingly, much effort has gone into the attempt to conceptualise and to legitimise these orders – and to explain their relationships with each other and with more traditional legal orders – by transplanting the idea of *constitutionalism* (defined by Neil Walker as 'the normative discourse through which constitutions are justified, defended, criticised, denounced or otherwise engaged with')[5] from its state-based incubator and developing a theory to fit the post-state configuration,[6] while keeping that which made constitutionalism desirable in the first place. In this way, the United Nations Charter is reconceived as a kind of 'constitution' for the international community,[7] while attempts have been made similarly to 'constitutionalise' the international trade regime of the World Trade Organization.[8]

---

[2] Such as the United Nations.

[3] Such as the International Standardization Organisation or the World Anti-Doping Agency (N Walker, 'Beyond Boundary Disputes and Basic Grids: Mapping the Global Disorder of Normative Orders' (2008) 6 *International Journal of Constitutional Law* 373, 382).

[4] Such as the Internet Corporation for Assigned Names and Numbers (ICANN) (ibid).

[5] N Walker, 'The Idea of Constitutional Pluralism' (2002) 65 *Modern Law Review* 317, 318.

[6] By 'post-state' here, I do not mean to imply that the State is no longer of any relevance – quite the contrary, as the book will demonstrate – but simply that the State can no longer be considered in isolation.

[7] B Fassbender, 'The United Nations Charter as Constitution of the International Community' (1998) 36 *Columbia Journal of Transnational Law* 529; and B Fassbender, '"We the Peoples of the United Nations": Constituent Power and Constitutional Form in International Law' in M Loughlin and N Walker (eds), *The Paradox of Constitutionalism: Constituent Power and Constitutional Form* (Oxford, Oxford University Press, 2007).

[8] See, inter alia, E-U Petersmann, 'The WTO Constitution and Human Rights' (2000) 3 *Journal of International Economic Law* 19; DZ Cass, *The Constitutionalization of the World Trade*

Introduction xxvii

The focus of this book is on one particularly promising, yet particularly controversial, manifestation of this discourse: constitutional pluralism. However, as Matej Avbelj and Jan Komárek point out, '[t]he concept has gained so many meanings that often the participants in the debate talk past each other, each endorsing a different understanding of what constitutional pluralism actually means'.[9] These different understandings of the idea will be outlined in chapter one, but, at its simplest, constitutional pluralism is the notion that interacting legal systems that are (or claim to be) constitutional in nature need not – and should not – necessarily be regarded as being *hierarchically* arranged, with one 'on top of' the others. Rather, the relationships between the orders can be conceived of *heterarchically*, so that conflict between them can be avoided, managed and ultimately resolved interactively and dialogically, without necessarily relegating one legal order to an inferior status or, conversely, privileging it over and above the others. This is a significant departure from the tradition of state-based constitutionalism, which presupposes and requires a hierarchical arrangement of the legal order. Of the many different conceptions of constitutional pluralism in the literature, this book focuses on a particular subset: the 'metaconstitutional'[10] theories, which seek to posit or discover an overarching normative framework for the management and resolution of conflict between constitutional orders while still preserving their autonomy, and not integrating them into a new whole. This metaconstitutional framework – a system of constitutional norms about constitutional norms – serves a bridging function between the orders, providing certain adjudicative principles, or 'interface norms' by which they can accommodate and manage the competing claims of each other order in the given constitutional heterarchy. However, analysis of these interface norms reveals an interesting – and significant – problem.

II. PROBLEM: INTERFACE NORMS

It is important to distinguish at the outset between two different kinds of interface norm. First, there are the *substantive* 'norms-at-the-interface' between legal orders. By this, I mean the norm or norms around which a concrete case of interaction or potential conflict between legal orders revolve, such as the conflict between the right to human dignity and the freedom to provide services in the

---

Organization (OUP 2005); JL Dunoff, 'Constitutional Conceits: The WTO's "Constitution" and the Discipline of International Law' (2006) 17 *European Journal of International Law* 647; J Lawrence, 'Contesting Constitutionalism: Constitutional Discourse at the WTO' (2013) 2 *Global Constitutionalism* 63.

[9] M Avbelj and J Komárek (eds), 'Four Visions of Constitutional Pluralism (symposium transcript)' EUI Working Papers LAW 2008/21, 1.

[10] See generally N Walker, 'Flexibility Within a Metaconstitutional Frame: Reflections on the Future of Legal Authority in Europe' in G de Búrca and J Scott (eds), *Constitutional Change in the EU: From Uniformity to Flexibility* (Oxford, Hart Publishing, 2000).

xxviii *Introduction*

Court of Justice of the European Union (CJEU) case of *Omega*,[11] or between the right to property and a state's international obligations in the European Court of Human Rights (ECtHR) case of *Bosphorus*.[12] Any norm can become a norm-at-the-interface if its application in a given case gives rise to questions of jurisdictional overlap between legal orders; this book will consider many of them, but they are not its focus.

Secondly, and more importantly, there are the *metaconstitutional* norms – interface norms proper – which, according to Nico Krisch, 'regulate to what extent norms and decisions in one sub-order have effect in another ... [and] are the main legal expression of openness and closure, friendliness or hostility among the different parts'.[13] Most notably, the principle of conditional recognition, epitomised in the *Solange*[14] jurisprudence of the German Bundesverfassungsgericht (BVerfG) recurs throughout different conceptions of metaconstitutional pluralism. It is this second-order type of interface norm that is the focus of the book, because while there is a certain amount of disagreement in the literature as to the *identity* of these norms, there is near unanimity as to their *nature* – a position that I argue to be problematic, and that a triangular conception of constitutionalism seeks to overcome.

Specifically, there is an always inherent – and sometimes explicit – claim in the literature that second-order interface norms are *universal* by nature: that however we classify them or frame them, their application need not be adjusted to any given institutional or jurisdictional circumstance. In their presentation and analysis of interface norms, scholars in the field draw on various sources – the jurisprudence of the CJEU, the ECtHR, and (especially) the BVerfG – but rarely consider whether and how the specific relations between the institutional actors in any given case may have influenced the choice and application of interface norms. In this regard, the 'founder' of constitutional pluralism, Neil MacCormick, wrote that '[t]he settled, positive character of law is jurisdiction-relative ... Moral judgments, however personal and controversial, are not in this way relativistic ... These judgments apply universally'.[15] But concerns relating to democracy and individual rights – the normative core of the principle of conditional recognition – are both legal and moral in nature. Are they (and should they be) universal or particular in their application?

---

[11] Case C-36/02 *Omega Spielhallen- und Automatenaufstellungs-GmbH v Oberbürgermeisterin der Bundesstadt Bonn* ECLI:EU:C:2004:614, [2004] ECR I-9609.

[12] *Bosphorus Hava Yolları Turizm ve Ticaret Anonim Şirketi v Ireland* [2005] ECHR 440.

[13] N Krisch, *Beyond Constitutionalism: The Pluralist Structure of Postnational Law* (Oxford, Oxford University Press, 2010) 285–86.

[14] Reported in English as *Internationale Handelsgesellschaft mbH v Einfuhr- und Vorratsstelle für Getreide und Futtermittel* (Case 2 BvL 52/71) [1974] 2 CMR 540 (*Solange I*); *Re the Application of Wünsche Handelsgesellschaft* (Case 2 BvR 197/83) [1987] 3 CMLR 225 (*Solange II*).

[15] N MacCormick, *Questioning Sovereignty: Law, State and Nation in the European Commonwealth* (Oxford, Oxford University Press, 1999) 14–15.

Introduction xxix

The major question that this book seeks to answer is therefore as follows: are the interface norms between legal orders under metaconstitutional pluralism universal, capable of application regardless of the relationship between the specific orders themselves and between the institutional actors involved?

The following chapters therefore seek to question a largely unchallenged presumption. They do so through the adoption of a version of constitutional pluralism which starts from the 'coordinate constitutionalism' of Charles Sabel and Oliver Gerstenberg as an analytical framework to test the hypothesis of interface norm universality across three categories of postnational legal relationship, isolated in the first instance and then drawn together holistically, and drawing on a wide array of norms-at-the-interface: first, the 'vertical'[16] relationships between the European Union (EU) and its Member States, and between the ECtHR and the states signatory to the European Convention on Human Rights (ECHR); secondly, the 'horizontal' relationship between the EU and the ECtHR; and, finally, the 'triangular' panoply of State, Union and Convention. Taken as a whole, this panoply is described throughout as the triangular constitution.

III. FIELD: JUSTIFICATION OF CHOICE OF JURISDICTIONS

Nowhere has the growth of non-state legal actors been more obvious than in Europe, where the legal orders of the EU and the Council of Europe have intermingled with, infiltrated, and – in places – supplanted state-centred law to an unprecedented degree. Just as the constitutional credentials of the two most significant European non-state actors are the most developed of their transnational peers, so too is the academic discourse on non-state constitutionalism most developed with reference to the European experience. It is for this reason that the law of the EU and of the ECHR are two parts of the main focus of this book.[17] The choice of the third, the law of Ireland, requires further explanation.

First, the choice of a single jurisdiction for analysis across the vertical and triangular relationships allows us to control for jurisdictional variables in a way that a more wide-ranging survey would not. There is a pronounced trend within the literature on constitutional pluralism to cherry-pick certain 'highlight' cases from different jurisdictions in order to demonstrate points or illustrate arguments. This approach lacks the continuity and focus of reliance on a single

---

[16] 'Vertical' is in quotes because a truly heterarchical arrangement of legal orders would admit to no x-axis. The terms 'vertical' and 'horizontal' will be used throughout, but only as a heuristic device: no concession to hierarchy is implied.

[17] Note, however, that the system of law overseen by the ECtHR is not a system based on direct effect and primacy, like that of the EU. The description of this system as being 'constitutional' therefore needs further justification: see ch 1, section II.A.i.

xxx *Introduction*

jurisdiction as an exemplar of the nation state in the postnational European legal sphere. Having said this, and though the book focuses heavily on Irish jurisprudence, it is not intended to be confined or unique to Ireland. Whereas the cases to be studied – and the interface norms they involve – may or may not be universal, the issues and themes involved are *universalisable*, to some extent at least, across EU Member States. As we shall see, the analysis of the particular triangular constitution presented here opens the door to a more wide-ranging normative theory of triangular constitutional*ism*, capable of application, with the necessary modifications, right across the Union.

Secondly, the nature of Ireland's constitutional order makes it a suitable candidate, combining the enclosed, self-referencing and self-authorising nature of the classical constitution of a sovereign state with a history of apparent openness to the postnational configuration, though the level of this openness varies as between the EU and the ECHR, a point returned to below.

Thirdly, there is a rich seam of constitutional jurisprudence to be mined with respect to the relatively long Irish experience of European integration. This jurisprudence has not generally been analysed in the round to date, taking the European constitutional constellation as a whole, but instead with the focus either on one particular legal order, or on discrete, substantive norms-at-the-interface rather than the metaconstitutional interface norms involved. As a result, the jurisprudence is under-theorised, despite the fact that, as we shall see, it very much lends itself to further analysis of the nature of the relationships between constitutional orders in the Europe of the early twenty-first century. Moreover, this large body of jurisprudence shows the constitutional frame not to be quite as open as its plain text – and the history of Irish 'loyalty' to European integration – might suggest. Again, this is not unique to Ireland – the BVerfG's decision in *Lisbon*[18] and particularly its request for a preliminary reference in *Gauweiler*[19] signalled a degree of relative closure in a jurisdiction generally regarded as constitutionally open. However, whereas the German jurisprudence has been analysed extensively in the literature, the Irish cases have yet to receive the same treatment.

Finally, and related to the foregoing, Alexander Somek notes that '[i]t is indeed a quite remarkable fact about European constitutional theory that in its most visible form it scarcely amounts to more than a series of glosses on lengthy opinions by the German Federal Constitutional Court'.[20] While I would not necessarily go quite so far, it is certainly true that there is a tendency in the literature to focus on the jurisprudence of large and powerful actors. In testing the universality of interface norms developed with reference to such actors, it is

---

[18] Reported in English as *Re Ratification of the Treaty of Lisbon* (2 BvE 2/08) [2010] 3 CMLR 13.
[19] *Gauweiler* 2 BvR 2728/13, decision of 14 January 2014, available in English at: www.bundesverfassungsgericht.de/SharedDocs/Entscheidungen/EN/2014/01/rs20140114_2bvr272813en.html.
[20] A Somek, 'Monism: A Tale of the Undead' in M Avbelj and J Komárek (eds) *Constitutional Pluralism in the European Union and Beyond* (Oxford, Hart Publishing, 2012) 346.

therefore a novel contribution to turn the lens to an economically, demographically and geographically peripheral state, such as Ireland.

IV. CHAPTER OUTLINE

As a work of applied constitutional theory, the approach taken to theory and practice throughout this book is both 'top-down' and 'bottom-up'. Under the top-down approach, the theory is our starting point, which we use to conceptualise the basic relations between the legal orders. Thus conceptualised, we feed the empirical evidence of the relations and interactions back into the theoretical analysis, refining and adjusting it cyclically.

Chapter one situates the argument, defines our terms and provides a literature review examining the concept of constitutional pluralism: its origins, its development and some of its specific applications to the EU and the ECHR, particularly as regards interface norms. It considers some of the many criticisms of the theory, and the attempts to navigate a way through them. It concludes by positing a particular form of constitutional pluralism, triangular constitutionalism, as an analytical framework to engage with the question of the universality or particularity of metaconstitutional interface norms.

Chapter two begins the empirical investigation, and parses the relationships between the legal orders in the 'vertical' frame: the nature of the relationships between Ireland and the EU, and Ireland and the ECHR; the means by which the norms of these non-state legal orders are received within the domestic order; and the question of priority in cases of conflict, along with the choice and application of interface norms in such cases.

Chapter three examines the 'horizontal' side of the triangle, that is, the relationship between the Union and the Convention. Importantly, though this relationship is characterised as being 'horizontal', there is an important 'triangular' element to it, given the as-yet indirect (but still concrete) nature of the linkages between the systems, and the role of states as intermediaries between the two European orders.

Chapter four is the broadest in scope, and concludes the empirical study, investigating a specifically 'triangular' instance of interaction between all three orders: the issue of the regulation of abortion in Ireland. Importantly, the substantive questions of whether and how abortion rights should be regulated is not the focus of this analysis. Instead, the analysis is specifically on the metaconstitutional aspects of how the issue has played out in the triangular constitution: how each legal order conceives of its role, its rights and its duties; and how these potentially competing conceptions find expression in interface norms.

Chapter five draws the three frames together, with a theoretical re-examination of what became clear when the inter-order relationships were looked at in isolation, and what becomes clear when all three are pulled together into one holistic frame: that the norms and the metaconstitution are not in fact universal.

xxxii *Introduction*

As a result, theories of metaconstitutional pluralism need to pay much greater attention to the specific nature of any given constitutional order and its relationship with other orders in the constitutional heterarchy. The chapter concludes by suggesting that triangular constitutionalism may provide just such an explanatory and normative framework, capable of application in any and every Member State, notwithstanding the non-universality of metaconstitutional interface norms.

1

European Constitutional Pluralism and the Triangular Constitution

INTRODUCTION

A MAJOR FEATURE of the European legal landscape in the early twenty-first century is the existence of multiple, overlapping, interlocking normative orders – national, supranational and international. The questions then arise as to how best to describe and conceptualise this plurality of legal orders, and the ways in which the orders relate to each other. This book proposes a theoretical and practical framework for answering these questions – the theory of triangular constitutionalism – and does so by providing an in-depth empirical investigation of the workings of one particular triangular constitution: the constitutional order of Ireland, the European Union (EU) and the European Convention on Human Rights (ECHR), taken together. Later chapters will set out in detail the 'horizontal' and 'vertical' workings of this triangular constitution, but first, there is some significant groundwork to be laid.

This chapter begins, in section I, by situating the argument in the broadest terms, first by setting out the initial development of the idea of *constitutional pluralism* in the context of the constitutionalisation of EU law, and then by outlining a particular refinement and condensation of the theory into a 'lowest-common-denominator' conception.

In section II I seek to define my terms, starting with the preliminary conceptual and definitional difficulty of attempting to reconcile and combine two ideas, 'constitutionalism' and 'pluralism', which by some accounts are irreconcilable opposites. Having suggested that constitutionalism and pluralism are not in fact opposites, but rather end points on a spectrum, I propose a distinction between 'constitutional pluralism' in the strict sense, and 'pluralist constitutionalism', a distinction which can clarify some disagreements in the literature.

In section III, I narrow the focus of the discussion to the normatively thicker 'metaconstitutional' theories of pluralist constitutionalism, as opposed to the looser conceptions of 'radical pluralism', or the more prescriptive accounts of constitutional pluralism in the strict sense, which advocate or require specific constitutional and institutional reforms in order to become operationalised. I analyse the approaches of three major contributions in the area of metaconstitutional pluralism with reference to both the EU and the ECHR, highlighting their similarities and differences.

2   *Constitutional Pluralism*

Section IV identifies two particular, related problems that arise from the overview of the various conceptions of pluralism in the literature, and especially the metaconstitutional conceptions: the potential (or at least alleged) threat to legal integrity and the rule of law caused by the absence of a single actor empowered to give the 'final say' in cases of constitutional conflict; and the alleged universality of the 'interface norms' which regulate the relationships between the legal orders. This latter issue, in particular, will be a major focus of this work.

Finally, section V outlines my conception of the legal orders of Ireland, the EU and the ECHR as a unified – but not unitary – composite whole: the triangular constitution. I suggest that this explanatory framework may be capable of being generalised into a normative theory – triangular constitutionalism – capable of application to each Member State of the Union, but that this can only be done by paying close attention to jurisdictional specificities. While triangular constitutionalism may be *universalisable*, it is not itself universal.

I. CONSTITUTIONAL PLURALISM'S ORIGINS IN THE EU

A. Constitutionalisation and Disorder

The story of the European Communities' (and later the Union's) growth from a classical, treaty-based creature of international law, nothing more than a set of binding obligations between states, to the autonomous, supranational legal order that exists today is well known, and will not be recounted at great length here.[1] Suffice it to say that the then European Court of Justice (ECJ),[2] through its formulation and elaboration of the twin doctrines of the direct effect of Community law and its primacy over national law, effected the steady 'constitutionalisation' of the Community. The famous statement from *van Gend en Loos* that '[t]he Community constitutes a new legal order of international law for the benefit of which the States have limited their sovereign rights'[3] lost its

---

[1] See generally, N MacCormick, *Questioning Sovereignty: Law, State and Nation in the European Commonwealth* (Oxford, Oxford University Press, 1999) ch 7 and references therein; P Craig and G de Búrca, *EU Law: Text, Cases, and Materials*, 6th edn (Oxford, Oxford University Press, 2015) chs 1 and 7–9. But let us bear in mind Arnull's warning against assuming too much: A Arnull, 'The Americanization of EU Law Scholarship' in A Arnull, P Eeckhout and T Tridimas (eds), *Continuity and Change in EU Law: Essays in Honour of Sir Francis Jacobs* (Oxford, Oxford University Press, 2008) 424–27.

[2] Aside from this historical context, the EU court at Luxembourg will generally be referred to as the Court of Justice of the European Union (CJEU) throughout this work for the sake of consistency, and at the risk of occasional anachronism. Where distinction between the Court of Justice proper and the General Court is necessary, the initialism ECJ will be used for the higher court (see Arts 13(1) and 19 of the Treaty on European Union (TEU)). Similarly, 'Union' will generally be preferred to 'Communit(y/ies)' throughout, again at the risk of anachronism.

[3] Case 26/62 NV *Algemene Transport- en Expeditie Onderneming van Gend en Loos v Nederlandse Administratie der Belastingen* ECLI:EU:C:1963:1, [1963] ECR 1, 12 (*van Gend en Loos*).

'of international law' qualifier five years later in *Molkerei-Zentrale*.[4] Not only was the EEC Treaty capable of 'producing direct effects and creating individual rights which national courts must protect',[5] but '[t]he law stemming from the Treaty, an independent source of law, could not, because of its special and original nature, be overridden by domestic legal provisions, however framed'.[6] By 1986, the ECJ felt confident enough in *Les Verts* to call the EEC Treaty the Community's 'basic constitutional charter'.[7]

This judicial constitutionalisation of the Union did not occur in a vacuum, but was aided by the agreement – or at least the acquiescence – of the Member States. There is the obvious fact that 22 of the 28 Member States acceded to the Community or Union long after 1964, aware of the implications of *van Gend* and *Costa*. But more importantly, Joseph Weiler notes that this constitutionalisation was 'brought about with the full collaboration of national governments [and] national parliaments, who again and again ... ratified the new order'.[8] He invokes Albert Hirschman's theory of exit and voice to show that as Community law developed, political intergovernmentalism provided a counterweight to legal supranationalism, 'allowing the Member States to digest and accept the process of constitutionalization', which they could do 'because they took real control of the decision-making process, thus minimizing its threatening features'.[9]

However, having had less of a Hirschmanian voice in the matter, the supreme and constitutional courts of some Member States were rather less enthusiastic, particularly the German Federal Constitutional Court, the Bundesverfassungsgericht (BVerfG). In its *Solange I* judgment,[10] the BVerfG claimed for itself the jurisdiction to review Community norms for conformance with fundamental rights as set out in the German Basic Law (Grundgesetz). This was in clear defiance of the ECJ's ruling in *Internationale Handelsgesellschaft*[11] (itself a stage in the proceedings that led to the *Solange I* judgment), which had

---

[4] Case 28/67 *Firma Molkerei-Zentrale Westfalen/Lippe GmbH v Hauptzollamt Paderborn* ECLI:EU:C:1968:17, [1968] ECR 143, 152.

[5] *van Gend en Loos* (n 3) 13.

[6] Case 6/64 *Flaminio Costa v ENEL* ECLI:EU:C:1964:66, [1964] ECR 585, 594 (*Costa*).

[7] Case 294/83 *Parti Ecologiste 'Les Verts' v Parliament* ECLI:EU:C:1986:166, [1986] ECR 1339, para 23, affirmed in Case C-314/91 *Weber v Parliament* ECLI:EU:C:1993:109, [1993] ECR I-1093, para 8; Case C-15/00 *Commission v European Investment Bank* ECLI:EU:C:2003:396, [2003] ECR I-7281, para 75; Joined Cases C-402/05 P and C-415/05 P *Kadi and Al Barakaat v Council and Commission* ECLI:EU:C:2008:461, [2008] ECR I-6351, paras 81 and 281 (*Kadi*).

[8] JHH Weiler, *The Constitution of Europe* (Cambridge, Cambridge University Press, 1999) 4, drawing on A Hirschman, *Exit, Voice, and Loyalty* (Cambridge, MA, Harvard University Press, 1970).

[9] Weiler, *The Constitution of Europe* (n 8) 36.

[10] Reported in English as *Internationale Handelsgesellschaft mbH v Einfuhr- und Vorratsstelle für Getreide und Futtermittel* (Case 2 BvL 52/71) [1974] 2 CMLR 540 (*Solange I*).

[11] Case 11/70 *Internationale Handelsgesellschaft mbH v Einfuhr- und Vorratsstelle für Getreide und Futtermittel* ECLI:EU:C:1970:114, [1970] ECR 1125 (*Solange II*).

4 *Constitutional Pluralism*

reserved such jurisdiction to itself. Faced with the threat of open rebellion by one of the most powerful and influential constitutional courts in Europe – and an apex constitutional actor in what has long been the continent's economic power-house – the ECJ staged a remarkable about-turn in its jurisprudence. Whereas once it had held that fundamental rights as they appear in national constitutions were entirely outwith the scheme of the Treaties,[12] or, later, were to be protected only insofar as they formed part of the constitutional traditions common to the Member States,[13] the ECJ held in *Nold*[14] that:

> [F]undamental rights form an integral part of the general principles of law, the observance of which [the Court] ensures. In safeguarding these rights, the Court is bound to draw inspiration from constitutional traditions common to the Member States, and it cannot therefore uphold measures which are incompatible with fundamental rights recognized and protected by the Constitutions of those States. Similarly, international treaties for the protection of human rights on which the Member States have collaborated or of which they are signatories, can supply guidelines which should be followed within the framework of Community law.[15]

The ECJ went on to develop its case law[16] to the satisfaction of the BVerfG, which held in *Solange II*[17] that as the EU's (and in particular the ECJ's) rights protection was now at a level comparable to its own, it would no longer exercise (but did not renounce) the jurisdiction it had claimed for itself.

It is in response to this 'disorder of normative orders'[18] – wherein the legal orders of both the EU and its Member States make claims to autonomy and to primacy in their own domain, with all the potential for jurisdictional overlap and conflict that this entails – that the various different strands and species of constitutional pluralism have been developed.

---

[12] Case 1/58 *Stork v High Authority* ECLU:EU:C1959:4, [1959] ECR 17; Joined Cases 36, 37, 38 & 40/59 *Geitling v High Authority* ECLI:EU:C:1960:36, [1960] ECR 423; Case 40/64 *Sgarlata and others v Commission* ECLI:EU:C:1965:36, [1965] ECR 215. See, in particular, *Geitling* 438: 'Community law, as it arises under the ECSC Treaty, does not contain any general principle, express or otherwise, guaranteeing the maintenance of vested rights'.

[13] Case 29/69 *Stauder v City of Ulm* ECLI:EU:C:1969:57, [1969] ECR 419; *Internationale Handelsgesellschaft* (n 10) para 3.

[14] Case 4/73 *Nold v Commission* ECLI:EU:C:1974:51, [1974] ECR 491.

[15] ibid para 13.

[16] See, in particular, Case 44/79 *Hauer v Land Rheinland-Pfalz* ECLI:EU:C:1979:290, [1979] ECR 3727. For a summary of developments, see N Fennelly, 'Pillar Talk: Fundamental Rights Protection in the European Union' (2008) 1 *Judicial Studies Institute Journal* 95, 97–106. See further, N Nic Shuibhne, 'Margins of Appreciation: National Values, Fundamental Rights and EC Free Movement Law' (2009) 32 *European Law Review* 230.

[17] Reported in English as *Re the Application of Wünsche Handelsgesellschaft* (Case 2 BvR 197/83) [1987] 3 CMLR 225.

[18] N Walker, 'Beyond Boundary Disputes and Basic Grids: Mapping the Global Disorder of Normative Orders' (2008) 6 *International Journal of Constitutional Law* 373.

B. Beginnings: MacCormick's 'Radical Pluralism' and 'Pluralism Under International Law'

The title of 'inventor' of constitutional pluralism – at least insofar as it relates to European law of both kinds – belongs to Neil MacCormick, who set out to show that:

> [S]overeignty and sovereign states, and the inexorable linkage of law with sovereignty and the state, have been but the passing phenomena of a few centuries, that their passing is by no means regrettable, and that current developments in Europe exhibit the possibility of going beyond all that.[19]

MacCormick illustrated this claim by reference to the UK's position within the legal orders of the European Communities and of the ECHR: to regard the UK as still being sovereign in the classical, all-encompassing sense is to blind ourselves to objective reality, but to regard the Communities as being sovereign, with Member States merely their subordinates, is to overstate the case.[20] Problematically, the traditional concept of sovereignty by its very nature – indivisible, exclusive, etc[21] – lends itself only to one of these either/or approaches. Alternatively, '[t]o escape from the idea that all law must originate in a single power source, like a sovereign, is thus to discover the possibility of taking a broader, more diffuse, view of law'.[22]

It is exactly this broader, more diffuse approach that MacCormick took in response to the *Maastricht* judgment[23] of the BVerfG two years later.[24] Here, the BVerfG held the Maastricht Treaty to be compatible with the Grundgesetz, but also drew a line in the sand: sovereignty in Germany continues to be vested in the German people, and Germany is still (for the BVerfG) a sovereign state. Accordingly, the competences of the EU are specified and limited, and its authority derived from and dependent on that of the Member States: neither the EU corporately, nor any of its individual actors – such as the Court of Justice – has interpretive *Kompetenz-Kompetenz*, the power to decide the limits of its own jurisdiction and powers. As a result, if the BVerfG detected an intrusion by a future EU legislative instrument into the still-sovereign sphere of German law,

---

[19] N MacCormick, 'Beyond the Sovereign State' (1993) 56 *Modern Law Review* 1, 1.

[20] ibid 5, citing the House of Lords judgment in *R v Secretary of State for Transport, ex parte Factortame* [1991] 3 All ER 769 and the ECtHR judgment in *Sunday Times v United Kingdom (No 2)* (1991) ECHR 50.

[21] See D Grimm, *Sovereignty: The Origin and Future of a Political and Legal Concept* (New York, Columbia University Press, 2015).

[22] MacCormick, 'Beyond the Sovereign State' (n 19) 8.

[23] Reported in English as *Brunner v European Union Treaty* (Case 2 BvR 2134/92 and 2959/92 JZ 1993, 1100) [1994] 1 CMLR 57.

[24] N MacCormick, 'The Maastricht-Urteil: Sovereignty Now' (1995) 1 *European Law Journal* 259.

6 Constitutional Pluralism

such instrument would have no binding power within Germany.[25] How can this be squared with the CJEU's long-standing jurisprudence on the autonomy and primacy of Community – and now Union – law? Clearly, the BVerfG and the CJEU cannot both be right. Or can they?

MacCormick observed that from the point of view of an institutional (rather than pure) theory of law, institutions and actors within municipal European legal systems derive their authority and competence from the national legal order, independently of whatever international or supranational organisations to which the state may belong. Equally, EU legal actors derive their authority and competence from the Treaties, without reference (for doctrinal purposes) to the ins and outs of the national law of any one Member State. The conclusion MacCormick drew from this observation is a clear statement of the fundamentals of constitutional pluralism, and merits quoting at length:

> [T]he doctrine of supremacy of Community law is not to be confused with any kind of all-purpose subordination of Member State law to Community law. Rather, the case is that these are interacting systems, one of which constitutes in its own context and over the relevant range of topics a source of valid law superior to other sources recognised in each of the Member State systems ... On the whole, therefore, the most appropriate analysis of the relations of legal systems is pluralistic rather than monistic, and interactive rather than hierarchical. The legal systems of Member States and their common legal system of EC law are distinct but interacting systems of law, and hierarchical relationships of validity within criteria of validity proper to distinct systems do not add up to any sort of all-purpose superiority of one system over another.[26]

This refusal to accept (from anything other than an internal epistemic perspective, on which more below in section IV.A) the claims of apex actors within both national and European law to total supremacy, one over the other, is one of the

---

[25] Much of this argument has been echoed more recently in somewhat different constitutional frames: see the BVerfG's judgment on the compatibility of the Lisbon Treaty with the *Grundgesetz*, reported in English as *Re Ratification of the Treaty of Lisbon* (2 BvE 2/08) [2010] 3 CMLR 13; and its preliminary reference to the CJEU regarding the Outright Monetary Transactions (OMT) programme of the European Central Bank, *OMT* (2 BvR 2728/13, available in English at: www.bundesverfassungsgericht.de/SharedDocs/Entscheidungen/EN/2016/06/rs20160621_2bvr272813en.html). See further JEK Murkens, '*Bundesverfassungsgericht* (2 BvE 2/08): "We Want Our Identity Back" – The Revival of National Sovereignty in the German Federal Constitutional Court's Decision on the Lisbon Treaty' [2010] *Public Law* 530; J Ziller, 'The German Constitutional Court's Friendliness towards European Law: On the Judgment of the *Bundesverfassungsgericht* over the Ratification of the Treaty of Lisbon' (2010) 16 *European Public Law* 53; M Niedobitek, 'The *Lisbon Case* of 30 June 2009 – A Comment from the European Law Perspective' (2009) 10 *German Law Journal* 1267; M Wendel, 'Exceeding Judicial Competence in the Name of Democracy: The German Federal Constitutional Court's *OMT* Reference' (2014) 10 *European Constitutional Law Review* 263; M Kumm, 'Rebel Without a Good Cause: Karlsruhe's Misguided Attempt to Draw the CJEU into a Game of "Chicken" and What the CJEU Might Do About It' (2014) 15 *German Law Journal* 203; M Claes and J-H Reestman, 'The Protection of National Constitutional Identity and the Limits of European Integration at the Occasion of the *Gauweiler* Case' (2015) 16 *German Law Journal* 917; A Pliakos and G Anagnostaras, 'Saving Face? The German Federal Constitutional Court Decides *Gauweiler*' (2017) 18 *German Law Journal* 213.

[26] MacCormick, 'The Maastricht-Urteil: Sovereignty Now' (n 24) 264.

hallmarks of constitutional pluralism. However, acceptance of the incommensurability of the sovereignty claims of the heterarchically arranged orders does not offer us any assistance in seeking to determine how conflicts between these orders might be resolved. Quite the opposite, for a clear hierarchical arrangement of the orders would enable us to look to our chosen actor (whether the CJEU or a national court) for the final say on the matter, but conceptualising them as being ordered heterarchically leaves us at a loss. This is why MacCormick later termed this initial formulation of constitutional pluralism as one of 'radical pluralism', which 'entails acknowledging that not every legal problem can be resolved legally'.[27]

MacCormick later moved away from this radical pluralism towards 'pluralism under international law', which, he admitted, is 'a kind of "monism" in Kelsen's sense',[28] whereby conflicts between legal orders are dealt with under the overarching normative authority of international law.[29] His main reason for doing so was in response to a problem of radical pluralism, which we shall, in section IV, see extended to the idea of constitutional pluralism *tout court*, that:

> Simply to remit to state courts an unreviewable power to determine the range of domestic constitutional absolutes that set limits upon the domestic applicability of Community law would seem likely to invite a slow fragmentation of Community law.[30]

However, the fact that pluralism under international law does admit to the existence of an authoritative frame for the resolution of disputes does not necessarily rob it of all its pluralist qualities. Accepting the hierarchically superior placement of public international law does not require the subsequent hierarchical arrangement of EU and Member State law one above the other – the two orders remain interactive and heterarchical in their ('horizontal') relationships with one another, subject only to the ultimate authority of the public international order. It is from these two conceptions of the idea of constitutional pluralism, one radical, one rather less so, that the literature has evolved.

C. The Three Major Claims of Walker's Pluralism

MacCormick's underlying scepticism towards claims to sovereignty in the classical sense by any modern legal or political actors[31] was taken up and

---

[27] MacCormick, *Questioning Sovereignty* (n 1) 119.

[28] ibid 121. Jaklič clarifies that this is Kelsen's *initial* conception of monism, which he later adjusted into a conception that allows for the supremacy either of international law or of national law: K Jaklič, *Constitutional Pluralism in the EU* (Oxford, Oxford University Press, 2014) 191, fn 13 and references therein.

[29] See further, N MacCormick, 'Risking Constitutional Collision in Europe?' (1998) 18 *Oxford Journal of Legal Studies* 517.

[30] MacCormick, *Questioning Sovereignty* (n 1) 120.

[31] Upon which he elaborated in MacCormick, *Questioning Sovereignty* (n 1): see, in particular, chs 7 and 8.

8 *Constitutional Pluralism*

developed by Neil Walker, who, in his exposition of the ontological basis of constitutional pluralism,[32] combines scepticism as to sovereignty-claims with a recognition of the fact that constitutionalism itself – which he defines as 'the normative discourse through which constitutions are justified, defended, criticised, denounced or otherwise engaged with'[33] – has 'been subject to a perhaps unprecedented range and intensity of attack'.[34] If claims to sovereignty are to be treated sceptically, and if the very concept of constitutionalism is a debased and antiquated one, then any attempt to frame and explain the European legal landscape and its multiple, competing, overlapping jurisdictions by means of a constitutionalist discourse, pluralist or otherwise, would be doubly quixotic.

Having set out what he believes to be the major criticisms of constitutionalism, and possible methods for them to be overcome,[35] Walker outlines a particular conception of constitutional pluralism as the best way of meeting the challenges, a conception which, echoing MacCormick:

> [R]ecognises that the European order inaugurated by the Treaty of Rome has developed beyond the traditional confines of inter-*national* law and now makes its own independent constitutional claims, and that these claims exist alongside the continuing claims of states. The relationship between the orders, that is to say, is now horizontal rather than vertical – heterarchical rather than hierarchical.[36]

However, let us be quick to note, as Walker himself does,[37] that this brief outline of the contours of pluralism does not even come close to answering all the objections of the critics (and, most likely, it raises a whole crop of new ones). This is why Walker calls it a 'lowest common denominator'[38] position, serving only as a common basis shared by the various species of pluralism, 'a series of preliminary steps beyond which the various pluralists ... and many others have gone their own ways'.[39]

Walker's baseline conception makes three fundamental claims: the explanatory, the normative and the epistemic. The first, explanatory, claim is that to persist with a monist conception of constitutionalism in Europe is to ignore reality. The only adequate way of accounting for the radical changes to the allocation and distribution of jurisgenerative power in the past half-century is conceptually to posit the different legal orders alongside each other horizontally, rather than in some vertical relationship (the precise arrangement of which will differ depending on one's own personal political preferences and/or institutional epistemic viewpoint). This explanatory claim is deeply persuasive.

---

[32] N Walker, 'The Idea of Constitutional Pluralism' (2002) 65 *Modern Law Review* 317.
[33] ibid 318.
[34] ibid.
[35] Which criticisms include constitutionalism's statist legacy, fetishism, normative bias, ideological exploitation and debased conceptual currency: see generally, ibid 319–39.
[36] ibid 337, emphasis in original.
[37] ibid.
[38] ibid 339.
[39] ibid 337.

The current configuration of the exercise of public power in Europe bears little relation to that of the nineteenth and early twentieth centuries. A monist view, whereby the exercise of all public power must draw on the same font of legitimacy, a common constitutional *Grundnorm* – whether national, international, or supranational – has little to offer given the competing claims to autonomy that characterise the legal landscape. The different accounts of constitutional pluralism in the literature all take this explanatory claim as their starting point.

But the kind of pluralism that Walker outlines is much more than an attempt simply to describe what actually happens in European constitutional practice. There is the second claim, where pluralism is presented as being *normatively desirable*, because of its claimed ability to transcend the flaws and shortcomings for which constitutionalism is (perhaps justly) criticised, while still retaining that which made constitutionalism a worthy discourse in the first place: the possibility of meaningfully bringing public power under public control. Not only is constitutional heterarchy posited as an observable, existing fact, but this fact is to be welcomed. For Walker, pluralism 'contend[s] that the only acceptable ethic of political responsibility for the new Europe is one that is premised upon mutual recognition and respect between national and supranational authorities'.[40] This normative claim is less clear-cut than the explanatory, but, as we shall see in sections II and III, the various strands of pluralism on offer do tend to commit themselves to the normative desirability of a political, judicial and legal (indeed constitutional) ethic of mutual recognition, mutual accommodation and mutual deference, even if this deference is conditional and contingent. Comity, the recognition of the other, and the acceptance of difference are all normative values inherent in, and expressed through, the different articulations of constitutional pluralism in the literature. However, this normative dimension of the discourse has been the subject of repeated criticism, both on its own terms, and for the way in which the discourse is claimed to have difficulty distinguishing between its descriptive and normative dimensions.[41] To the extent that this is true (which shall form part of the investigation in section III), a major reason for this is because the two dimensions are not entirely separate from one another in the first place, and partially overlap. The normative dimension arises, at least in the first instance, from the descriptive dimension: there is an inherent normative value in having a descriptively accurate account of how the legal universe actually works in practice, and being able to explain this description in coherent terms.[42]

---

[40] ibid.

[41] N Krisch, *Beyond Constitutionalism: The Pluralist Structure of Postnational Law* (Oxford, Oxford University Press, 2010) 69–70; D Sarmiento, 'Making Sense of Constitutional Pluralism: A Review of Klemen Jaklič's *Constitutional Pluralism in the EU*' (2015) 40 *European Law Review* 110; C Timmermans, 'The Magic World of Constitutional Pluralism' (2014) 10 *European Constitutional Law Review* 349, 350, 355.

[42] See M Avbelj and J Komárek, 'Four Visions of Constitutional Pluralism' (2004) 4 *European Constitutional Law Review* 524, 525–26; M Avbelj and J Komárek (eds), 'Four Visions of Constitutional Pluralism (symposium transcript)' EUI Working Papers LAW 2008/21, 19–20.

10   *Constitutional Pluralism*

This is the baseline or starting normativity of constitutional pluralism: its continuation, in the context of European integration, of the normative imperatives of constitutionalism as a modernist project that seeks to subject mere power to reason, and to temper public authority with public contestation and control. While sharing this baseline normativity, the various species of pluralism then go on to provide their own accounts of the *ought*, of why a specifically pluralist species of constitutionalism is preferable to either national or European constitutional monism. The approach taken in this book follows in this tradition, in that it seeks to provide an accurate description and explanation of lived experience (which in itself is a normative value), and to demonstrate that this explanation is in fact normatively preferable to the alternatives.

There is then the third, epistemic, claim: that there is no neutral position; no bird's-eye view; no 'Archimedean point' 'from which we can evaluate the strength and validity of the different, and in some respects contending, authority claims made from national and supranational constitutional sites'.[43] Instead, we can either accept the plausibility (and, crucially, the incommensurability) of each claim, and the heterarchical vision of their interrelationships that follows, or we can reject the plausibility of any given claim, which collapses us back into monism, with one system hierarchically inferior to the other. This claim of perpetual epistemic indeterminacy is at the root of much of the confusion and disagreement in the discourse surrounding constitutional pluralism, and can be described as the 'tightrope problem'. The problem operates in two dimensions. First, is this epistemic indeterminacy in fact sustainable, or must it inevitably collapse into monism, whether national or supranational? The danger is that by leaning too far either to one side or the other, constitutional pluralism falls off the tightrope, and returns us to one of the opposing monisms beyond which it tries to move. An undercurrent of this difficulty is the possibly inherent tension between constitutionalism and pluralism, whereby the two are regarded as being diametrically opposed and utterly irreconcilable. Even if the two are not regarded as being opposites, Klemen Jaklič takes issue with Walker's account of the epistemic claim being an *essential* component of a theory of constitutional pluralism, and argues that this epistemic indeterminacy can be remedied and foreclosed without rendering a given theory as a species of monism.[44]

The second dimension follows from the first: even if we *do* manage to stay on the tightrope, and not revert to one or other of the opposing monisms, does the existence and maintenance of this epistemic indeterminacy mean that constitutional pluralism lacks or threatens legal integrity, and is therefore incompatible with, or poses a threat to, legal certainty and the rule of law? If either dimension of this criticism is valid, then constitutional pluralism is a lose–lose discourse: if it falls off the tightrope, it collapses into monism and ceases to exist; if it stays on the tightrope, the uncertainty engendered undermines the rule of law.

---

[43] Walker, 'The Idea of Constitutional Pluralism' (n 32) 338.
[44] Jaklič, *Constitutional Pluralism in the EU* (n 28) 170–73.

The Constitutional Pluralists and the Critics   11

This epistemic tightrope issue, in both dimensions, is crucial for what follows, and before detailing the further development of the theories of constitutional pluralism – and of triangular constitutionalism – the undercurrent of the first dimension of the problem, the alleged dichotomy between constitutionalism and pluralism, must be addressed.

II. THE CONSTITUTIONAL PLURALISTS AND THE CRITICS

From the foundations laid by MacCormick, and their elaboration by Walker, the literature on constitutional pluralism has grown enormously, to the extent that Julio Baquero Cruz has labelled it a 'movement'[45] – though Baquero Cruz, a noted critic of the 'movement', was using the term exonymously and pejoratively. For Weiler, constitutional pluralism is a 'remarkably underspecified concept[] which allow[s] a multiplicity of meanings without offending any received understanding',[46] and has become 'the only party membership card which will guarantee a seat at the high tables of the public law professoriate'.[47] This underspecification is a particular target of Jaklič, who writes that despite constitutional pluralism becoming 'the dominant branch of constitutional thought'[48] in Europe,

> the various contributions hiding under the umbrella of 'constitutional pluralism' are strikingly different projects, much more so than has been commonly assumed and represented. In important respects they actually appear within wholly different discourses and deal with different sets of questions. When they are making contributions within the same topic, their positions often contradict one another, so much so that each author would clearly consider the other proposals as monist when judged by his own standards.[49]

Jaklič ultimately rejects the charge that 'the field, rapidly expanding with many more very different authors who currently claim to be pluralists, [is] just too messy and thus in a sense too vacuous to be able to provide any meaningful conception of pluralism'.[50] He does so in two steps: first by excising from the discourse entirely all the contributions he argues have been 'wrongly assumed and treated as if they were part of the pluralist branch when they could not possibly be',[51] and then by boiling the remainder down to what he takes to be

---

[45] J Baquero Cruz, 'The Legacy of the Maastricht-Urteil and the Pluralist Movement' (2008) 14 *European Law Journal* 389.

[46] JHH Weiler, 'Prologue: Global and Pluralist Constitutionalism – Some Doubts' in G de Búrca and JHH Weiler (eds), *The Worlds of European Constitutionalism* (Cambridge, Cambridge University Press, 2012) 9.

[47] ibid 8.

[48] Jaklič, *Constitutional Pluralism in the EU* (n 28) 6.

[49] ibid 7.

[50] ibid 190.

[51] ibid 218.

12 *Constitutional Pluralism*

their shared core – a shared core which differs from Walker's lowest common denominator – and from this developing his own particular conception of the theory. Before detailing this conception, those of other authors, or indeed the conception which this book proposes, the purpose of this section is preliminary and definitional: what we mean by constitutionalism, by pluralism, and therefore by constitutional pluralism.

A. Constitutionalism and Pluralism: A Contradiction in Terms?

At its core, *pluralism* is synonymous with *heterarchy*. It describes any situation where power-relations between two or more actors or systems are (at least partially or in some respects) heterarchical or horizontal, as opposed to hierarchical or vertical. Baquero Cruz objects to the use of the term 'heterarchy' in the literature, and laments the unfairness of '"[h]eterarchical" and "horizontal" [being] instinctively appealing notions, while "hierarchy" and "vertical" sound old-fashioned, "anti-modern", almost reactionary'.[52] He points out that that the *Oxford English Dictionary* declares the term obsolete, and in any event, it meant 'the rule of an alien', not 'rule by the many', which he takes to be the meaning implied by constitutional pluralists.[53] While this older meaning may well be obsolete, Ana Bobić imports a definition from anthropological literature which captures heterarchy's meaning in the context of constitutional pluralism nicely: 'the relation of elements to one another when they are unranked or when they possess the potential for being ranked in a number of different ways'.[54] In the specifically constitutional context, this heterarchical pluralism stands in contrast to hierarchical *monism*, whereby the relation of each element to one another is definitively ranked: power springs from one ultimate source and is distributed hierarchically.[55]

---

[52] Baquero Cruz, 'The Legacy of the Maastricht-Urteil and the Pluralist Movement' (n 45) 414.

[53] J Baquero Cruz, 'Another Look at Constitutional Pluralism in the European Union' (2016) 22 *European Law Journal* 356, 369.

[54] A Bobić, 'Constitutional Pluralism is not Dead: An Analysis of Interactions Between Constitutional Courts of Member States and the European Court of Justice' (2017) 18 *German Law Journal* 1395, 1399, fn 18, quoting C Crumley, 'Heterarchy and the Analysis of Complex Societies' (1995) 6 *Archaeological Papers of the American Anthropological Association* 1, 3.

[55] Note that monism is more usually set in opposition to dualism, not pluralism, and describes a system where national and international law are indivisible. Dualism, by contrast, separates the two systems, and requires a positive act of incorporation at the national level for international law to be valid within the national system. However, Walker distinguishes between monism in its philosophical and legal senses: the legal concepts of monism and dualism are both monist in the philosophical sense, in that the choice of how to deal with the interplay between national and international law is a decision internal to the national system. For this reason, Walker uses the term 'particularism' to describe the kind of philosophical, hierarchical monism we are dealing with here, in opposition to heterarchy: see N Walker, 'Constitutional Pluralism Revisited' (2016) 22 *European Law Journal* 333, 337, fn 12.

The Constitutional Pluralists and the Critics   13

From his survey of the literature, Jaklič extracts a minimal shared conception of heterarchy (and therefore of pluralism), which he calls 'heterarchy minimized'.[56] This imposes, as a requirement for the relationship between any two legal orders to be considered pluralist, that each order '*concede[s]* that neither is any longer ultimately superior over the other'.[57] This heterarchy is 'minimised' by the fact that the nature of such concession – procedural or substantive (or both), thin or thick – is left open.[58] In this way, Jaklič can accommodate within his shared core of constitutional pluralism various conceptions with very different approaches to the question of the 'final say'. As we shall see in section II.A.iii, this *requirement* of openness to the possibility of thick, substantive concessions, of a legal order openly recognising that it is no longer possessed of the final say, poses difficulties for the epistemic claim of Walker's pluralism, but is not insuperable.

There is a long intellectual tradition of *legal* pluralism, offering various conceptualisations of how different legal systems and orders can operate side by side.[59] But what makes our specific kind of pluralism *constitutional*? There is a tendency among some writers to identify constitutionalism with monism, and, therefore, to posit constitutionalism and pluralism in oppositional, binary, antagonistic terms. This is put forward most forcefully by Nico Krisch, who writes that constitutionalism in the postnational[60] sphere

> attempts to provide continuity with the domestic constitutionalist tradition by construing an overarching legal framework that determines the relationships of the different levels of law and the distribution of powers among their institutions. It seeks to redeem the modern, revolutionary promise of a human-made constitution as an antidote to the forces of history, power and chance.[61]

Pluralism, on the other hand

> is a less orderly affair. It sees such an overarching framework as neither practically possible nor normatively desirable and seeks to discern a model of order that relies less on unity and more on the heterarchical interaction of the various layers of law. Legally, the relationship of the parts of the overall order in pluralism remains open – governed by the potentially competing rules of the various sub-orders, each with its

---

[56] Jaklič, *Constitutional Pluralism in the EU* (n 28) 170.

[57] ibid 196, emphasis in original.

[58] ibid 170.

[59] On which see W Twining, 'Normative and Legal Pluralism: A Global Perspective' (2010) 20 *Duke Journal of Comparative and International Law* 473, 486–504; W Twining, 'Institutions of Law from a Global Perspective: Standpoint, Pluralism and Non-State Law' in M del Mar and Z Bańkowski (eds), *Law as Institutional Normative Order* (Farnham, Ashgate, 2009) 17.

[60] By which Krisch means the legal landscape where '[t]he classical distinction between the domestic and international spheres ... is increasingly blurred ... [and] law has become "postnational" – the national sphere retains importance, but it is no longer the paradigmatic anchor of the whole order' (Krisch, *Beyond Constitutionalism* (n 41) 5).

[61] ibid 23.

14   Constitutional Pluralism

own ultimate point of reference and supremacy claim, the relationships between them are left to be determined ultimately through political, not rule-based processes.[62]

Taken in isolation and in the abstract, these definitions have certain merits (and demerits), but they are fundamentally incompatible. The unity of constitutionalism – which Krisch takes to *require* monism and hierarchy, rather than pluralism and heterarchy – cannot be reconciled with the multiplicity of pluralism. If this is so, then talk of 'constitutional pluralism' is simply idle, a theoretically impossible cul-de-sac into which has been invested far too much time and intellectual effort. On this analysis, MacCormick's retreat from his radical pluralism to pluralism under international law is emblematic of the tension, and Krisch's dichotomous characterisation of the two concepts fits well with MacCormick's two positions, with radical pluralism as an example of Krisch's pluralism *simpliciter*, and pluralism under international law being recast instead as a species of what Krisch would call constitutionalism, notwithstanding the heterarchical relationship of the legal orders below the overarching level of international law. On this analysis, we are left with a dyad: constitutionalism-as-monism-as-hierarchy, set in opposition to pluralism-as-heterarchy. However, the idea that constitutionalism *requires* monism, and therefore that constitutional pluralism is a contradiction in terms, is open to serious challenge.

i. Constitutional Pluralism Not Constitutionalist?

The claim that a given theory that calls itself a species of constitutional pluralism is not, in fact, constitutionalist, comes in two varieties. We have just seen the criticism in its broadest form, advanced by Krisch, where constitutionalism is inherently monist, and therefore can *never* be pluralist, and therefore any genuinely pluralist theory cannot be constitutionalist. Jaklič advances a second, narrower, stipulative claim. Objecting strongly to Krisch's use of both terms, Jaklič writes that we can only speak of *constitutionalism* specifically and exclusively in the context of *self-standing* legal orders: that is, orders which are not in any way dependent on any other order for their authority, and which enjoy a direct link with the people to whom that authority is addressed.[63] The EU and its Member States, on this analysis, are both constitutional orders,[64] whereas international law is not, its link with the people being mediated through the State.[65] As we have seen, *pluralism* for Jaklič exists only in a situation where two confronting orders mutually recognise each other as being coequal 'and yet simultaneously coexistent over [a] shared piece of territory'.[66] *Constitutional pluralism*, therefore, can only exist where both of these requirements are met.

---

[62] ibid.
[63] Jaklič, *Constitutional Pluralism in the EU* (n 28) 212.
[64] ibid 220.
[65] ibid 211–12.
[66] ibid 195.

It is for this reason that Jaklič characterises the work of Krisch[67] and Daniel Halberstam[68] as being categorically separate from constitutional pluralism: though they refer to the foundational work of MacCormick and use similar terminology, the focus of their work on non-self-standing, international legal orders renders it non-constitutional, and the lack of recognition of co-equality between the orders renders it non-pluralist.[69] However, though Jaklič is right to reject Krisch's identification of constitutionalism with monism, and his resultant dichotomy between constitutionalism and pluralism, he does so only by stipulating a restrictive conception of constitutionalism that is itself open to question. It would seem that only on a statist conception of constitutionalism can we describe constitutionalism as being inherently monist (Krisch); and only on a still-too-statist conception can we describe talk of constitutionalism as being appropriate only in the context of self-standing legal orders (Jaklič). Constitutionalism is capable of being extended further beyond the State than either author is willing to accept.

It is precisely a statist conception of constitutionalism that Krisch employs in positing pluralism and constitutionalism as opposites.[70] We can in fact go further, for Krisch makes it clear that he has a particular *kind* of state constitutionalism in mind:

> [T]he line of tradition that traces itself back to the American and French revolutions, [which] stresses more the formal elements: the actual constitution (not only limitation) of government through an act of the people, as expressed in a constitutional document.[71]

This he contrasts to the older conception of constitutionalism, 'closer to British history and common law ideas, [which] emphasizes the importance of substantive constitutional values (rights, democracy, etc) as limitations to

---

[67] Krisch, *Beyond Constitutionalism* (n 41); N Krisch, 'The Case for Pluralism in Postnational Law' in G de Búrca and JHH Weiler (eds), *The Worlds of European Constitutionalism* (Cambridge, Cambridge University Press, 2012).

[68] D Halberstam, 'Local, Global, and Plural Constitutionalism: Europe Meets the World' in G de Búrca and JHH Weiler (eds), *The Worlds of European Constitutionalism* (Cambridge, Cambridge University Press, 2012); D Halberstam, 'Systems Pluralism and Institutional Pluralism in Constitutional Law: National, Supranational, and Global Governance' (2001) University of Michigan Law School Public Law and Legal Theory Working Paper Series, Working Paper No 229; D Halberstam, 'Constitutional Heterarchy: The Centrality of Conflict in the European Union and the United States' (2008) University of Michigan Law School Public Law and Legal Theory Working Paper Series, Working Paper No 111.

[69] Jaklič, *Constitutional Pluralism in the EU* (n 28) 219–25.

[70] See, generally, Krisch, *Beyond Constitutionalism* (n 41), especially chs 2–3. For detailed – and differing – responses to Krisch's dichotomy between constitutionalism and pluralism, see S Besson 'The Truth About Legal Pluralism' (2012) 8 *European Constitutional Law Review* 354, 357–59; G Shaffer, 'A Transnational Take on Krisch's Pluralist Postnational Law' (2012) 23 *European Journal of International Law* 565, 572–75; A Stone Sweet, 'The Structure of Constitutional Pluralism' (2013) 11 *International Journal of Constitutional Law* 491, 491–93.

[71] N Krisch, 'Europe's Constitutional Monstrosity' (2005) 25 *Oxford Journal of Legal Studies* 321, 330.

16   *Constitutional Pluralism*

government power'.[72] The problem here is that 'modern' revolutionary constitutionalism obviously bears little relation to the foundation and evolution of the European *ordre publique*. This was obvious even prior to the failed EU Constitutional Treaty, but that very failure highlighted that if we are to imagine and describe the European legal order – by which I mean here and throughout this book the whole panoply of State, Union and Convention – as being 'constitutional', it is the older, evolutionary conception of constitutionalism that we must adopt.[73] Nor is evolutionary constitutionalism necessarily synonymous with the 'weak' variety, without the judicial review of legislation and constitutional enforcement. One can share Weiler's scepticism of the 'Dicey bluff'[74] in a general sense, while still recognising that, say, the UK and German legal orders are both 'constitutional': they are just different kinds of constitutionalism, varying in their origins, development and consequences.

The argument that constitutionalism is inherently monist, and therefore that pluralism and constitutionalism are irreconcilable, is therefore perfectly true – even trivially so – if we are to take the revolutionary, documentary form of constitutionalism as our sole definition and point of reference. This sort of constitution is (or perhaps was) by its very nature authoritative, self-referential and self-contained. Quite aside from the fact that these adjectives do not necessarily apply to non-state European constitutionalism, they may not even accurately describe the constitutions of EU Member States any longer, given the EU's claim to primacy and hierarchical superiority within its areas of competence, and the openness of their legal orders to the influence of the ECHR.

This being the case, the claim that constitutionalism requires monism begins to take on water if we broaden our conception of constitutionalism to include the evolutionary, as I would argue we must. But this still leaves us with Jaklič's stipulative conception, whereby only self-standing legal orders can be described as constitutional, and can be discussed and analysed using the language of constitutionalism. The approach of this book, treating the legal order of the ECHR as a useful – and necessary – part of the constitutional analysis, therefore requires justification. Walker's account of constitutionalism as 'the normative discourse through which constitutions are justified, defended, criticised, denounced or otherwise engaged with'[75] is an altogether broader conception of the notion than the more prescriptive account given by Krisch and the more

---

[72] ibid 329–30.

[73] See further, M Avbelj, 'Questioning EU Constitutionalisms' (2008) 9 *German Law Journal* 1, 25: 'Constitutionalism is a social concept, which means that it does not have any essence of its own which is immutable and independent from the social constructionist forces in the society ... Consequently, there can be simply no justification for a claim that constitutionalism can not be severed from its statist pedigree', citing J Tully, *Strange Multiplicity: Constitutionalism in an Age of Diversity* (Cambridge, Cambridge University Press 1995) 9.)

[74] Weiler, *The Constitution of Europe* (n 8) 9, fn 2.

[75] Walker, 'The Idea of Constitutional Pluralism' (n 32) 318.

exclusionary account of Jaklič, but it leaves open the question of what is meant by 'constitutions'. As we have seen, for Krisch, 'constitutions' must be the founding documents that not only limit but also constitute and empower a polity and its institutions. The broader, evolutionary conception, adopted enthusiastically by Jaklič with respect to the EU, is that 'the constitution' is more than the mere document, and includes the accumulation of norms, practices, precedents and customs from which the order may derive its legitimacy and by which the actions of the order may be restrained. This conception builds on the statist origins of constitutionalism but opens the discourse to the state-*like* (but still non-state) self-standing constitutional order of the EU, with its direct link to the citizen. But there is then a yet broader conception, doing away with the requirement that the order be self-standing, whereby 'the constitution' is a reified thought-object. It comprises not only the actual document and the surrounding norms and practices, but also, crucially, the legal and sociological hinterland surrounding this agglomeration, and the discourse within it. This discourse includes the world-view and self-image of all of those working within and subject to the order, from high institutional actors to the individual citizen, along with the ways in which the 'constitution' interacts and overlaps with any other orders with which it comes into contact and enters into relations.

Matej Avbelj takes just this broader approach, of constitution-as-reified-thought-object, starting with the observation that

> [c]onstitutionalism is ... a social concept. This entails that it is non-essentialist. It does not have a DNA or any inherent meaning *an sich* ... The meaning and hence the very way of being of constitutionalism is thus a result of the process of a social construction.[76]

Avbelj looks at the concept across three dimensions, and argues that a genuine constitutionalism is a holistic one, drawing all three dimensions together.[77] The legal-institutional dimension looks at the actual constitutional document(s) and the institutions it or they establish; the socio-political puts flesh on the bare bones of the legal-institutional, focusing on the symbolic language of popular ownership of a constitution, popular consent to its enactment, and popular self-government under it; and the philosophical dimension consists of the constitution's *telos*: its values and objectives.[78] These three dimensions can be boiled down further, and simplified into a calculus of *empowerment*; *restraint*; and what Paul Craig calls the *metaconstitutional inquiry*: that discourse which asks questions such as 'why a constitution is legitimate, why it is authoritative

---

[76] M Avbelj, 'Can European Integration be Constitutional and Pluralist – Both at the Same Time?' in M Avbelj and J Komárek (eds), *Constitutional Pluralism in the European Union and Beyond* (Oxford, Hart Publishing, 2012) 386, citing R Dworkin, 'Hart's Postscript and the Character of Political Philosophy' (2004) 24 *Oxford Journal of Legal Studies* 1, 11 (footnote omitted).

[77] ibid 387.

[78] ibid 387–92.

18   Constitutional Pluralism

and how it should be interpreted' and includes 'the deeper justificatory rationale for the particular constitutional rules that a legal system has adopted'.[79]

Whether or not a given legal order is 'constitutional' – and thus, whether there is any point in speaking of 'constitutionalism' – is not an either/or question on this analysis, but one of degree. This broader, holistic approach enables us to conclude that Jaklič's limitation of constitutionalism to encompass only self-standing legal orders is too narrow. If a legal order makes claims for itself as an 'institutional normative order'[80] (empowerment) and limits those claims with, to take Craig's examples, '[i]ssues such as the accountability of government, broadly conceived, principles of good administration and mainstreaming of human rights'[81] (restraint), that legal order can lay claim, at the very least, to a 'thin'[82] or 'low-intensity'[83] constitutionalism. Just how thin or thick, low- or high-intensity the constitutionalism in question actually is – and how valid or invalid the claims – can then be analysed in the third stage, the metaconstitutional enquiry. Taking this approach, we can see that to imagine and engage with the ECHR legal order using the language of constitutionalism, rather than being a category error, is both appropriate and necessary. Certainly, the ECHR is not, like the EU, a legal order based on the principles of direct effect and primacy. It makes no claim to a self-standing autochthony and bears much more resemblance to a standard creature of international law. However, the Convention is interpreted authoritatively by an independent and autonomous court (empowerment), and the limitation of public power for the purpose of protecting human rights is its very raison d'être (restraint). The European Court of Human Rights (ECtHR) explicitly uses the language of constitutionalism to describe its activities and the Convention itself,[84] and, importantly, the right of individual petition establishes a direct link with the citizenry. This direct link is certainly more attenuated than that which exists between the citizen and the State, or the citizen and the EU, given the more limited remit of the Convention, the more limited jurisdiction and powers of enforcement of its Court, and the requirement of exhausting domestic remedies. However, to simply write off the

---

[79] P Craig, 'Constitutions, Constitutionalism and the European Union' (2001) 7 *European Law Journal* 125, 127 citing L Alexander, 'Introduction' in L Alexander (ed), *Constitutionalism: Philosophical Foundations* (Cambridge, Cambridge University Press, 1998). Note that 'metaconstitutional' in this sense is not the same thing as the metaconstitutional pluralisms outlined in section IV.

[80] MacCormick, *Questioning Sovereignty* (n 1) 131. See generally MacCormick, *Questioning Sovereignty* (n 1) ch 1; M del Mar and Z Bańkowski (eds), *Law as Institutional Normative Order* (Farnham, Ashgate, 2009).

[81] Craig (n 79) 128. While Craig was using these examples in the specific context of the EU, the points hold more generally.

[82] N Walker, 'European Constitutionalism and European Integration' [1996] *Public Law* 266 269.

[83] MP Maduro, 'The Importance of Being Called a Constitution: Constitutional Authority and the Authority of Constitutionalism' (2005) 3 *International Journal of Constitutional Law* 332, 334.

[84] *Loizidou v Turkey (preliminary objections)* App no 15318/89 (1995) Series A no 310, para 75 (*Loizidou*); *Bosphorus Hava Yolları Turizm ve Ticaret Anonim Şirketi v Ireland* [2005] ECHR 440, para 156 (*Bosphorus*).

The Constitutional Pluralists and the Critics   19

ECHR legal order as being 'non-constitutional', as Jaklič does, is to sacrifice an accurate description and full understanding of the interactions of legal orders in twenty-first century Europe at the altar of theoretical purity.[85] It ignores the very real authority that the ECHR itself possesses, and the very real effects it has on and interactions it has with the other constitutional orders – both State and EU – with which it comes into contact and of which it forms a part. Furthermore, this holistic, more finely graded, and less stipulative conception of whether a given legal order qualifies as constitutional can be extended to the question of whether the relationships between legal orders are constitutional (hierarchical, but *not* necessarily monist), pluralist (heterarchical), or somewhere in between, as we shall soon see.

ii. Constitutional Pluralism Not Pluralist?

The inverse criticism, that constitutional pluralism is not pluralist, has been made most consistently and most forcefully by Baquero Cruz, who writes that '[i]n practice, the various pluralist strategies to clean up the mess of "heterarchy" look very much like variations of the national constitutional position'.[86] On this analysis, constitutional pluralism is far too (national) constitutionalist and nowhere near pluralist enough, if it is pluralist at all, and is little more than a misguided effort to lend intellectual respectability to a bald rejection of European integration, and a concomitant retreat to a kind of constitutional chauvinism, with the State as the be-all and end-all of the constitutional order. In the current political and constitutional climate in Europe, Baquero Cruz argues that this is actively dangerous, and has written trenchantly – indeed movingly – about the dangers posed by the fading memory of pan-European war.[87]

We can share his fears in this regard without sharing his diagnosis. In the continuing absence of a European demos, a European politics, and an incontrovertible we-the-People 'moment' of popular legitimation, a universally shared, rigid, hierarchically constitutionalist conception of EU law and its relationship with national law is arguably *more* likely to lead to fragmentation and its resulting dangers, not less: rigidity can be brittle, and can snap. If the various conceptions of constitutional pluralism in the literature owe more to the jurisprudence of national constitutional courts – and in particular the BVerfG – than they do to the case law of the CJEU, this is only because the centralising tendencies of the latter leave far less room for a pluralist analysis than do the more contingent and relational attempts of national courts to reconcile their own interpretive supremacy over the national constitution, and that constitution's authority and

---

[85] Note also MacCormick, *Questioning Sovereignty* (n 1) 116: 'the institutional theory of law insists on a degree of sociological realism, hence is not in the Kelsenian sense a pure theory'.

[86] Baquero Cruz, 'Another Look at Constitutional Pluralism in the European Union' (n 53) 372.

[87] ibid 357–64.

20   *Constitutional Pluralism*

legitimacy, with the exigencies of EU law. It is only since the coming into force of Article 4(2) TEU, with its obligation of respect for the constitutional identities of the Member States, that the Union has been required as a matter of primary law to pay anything like the same kind of attention to national constitutionalism that the very fact of EU membership has always obliged national constitutional law to pay to the Union.[88] This is not to say that national court resistance to, say, EU legislative *Kompetenz-Kompetenz* is 'pluralist'. For the epistemological reasons to be outlined below in section IV.A, it cannot be. But to cast constitutional pluralism as some sort of witting or, worse, unwitting rearguard action against European integration is to ignore the significant lengths to which writers in the area have gone to try to broaden the horizons of national constitutionalism. If 'the various pluralist strategies' really do 'look very much like variations of the national constitutional position', what drastic variations they are! While in certain, rare, limited, justifiable circumstances they agree with the national constitutionalist claims that the authority of EU law *is* not and *ought* not to be unlimited, and that the limits of this authority cannot only be policed by the Union institutions themselves, they also go far beyond this, and call on – in fact require – national constitutional thought to undergo a significant process of introspection and readjustment in order properly to account for the fundamental changes brought about by European integration.

A rather different objection is made by Gareth Davies, who, echoing the 'tightrope problem' outlined above, writes that

> where there are multiple sources of apparently constitutional law one always takes precedence and the other is then no longer constitutional. Dialogue may help the legal sources reconcile, but it does not change the normative hierarchy between them.[89]

On this account, the disapplication of a norm from one order in a heterarchy collapses the pluralist heterarchy into monist hierarchy, and we are left with constitutionalism, not pluralism. But is this really the case? In order to engage with Davies' criticism, let us compare it with another situation by rephrasing it: what about a case where there are not 'multiple *sources* of *apparently* constitutional law', but rather 'multiple *provisions* of *definitely* constitutional law'?

What I have in mind is a classic situation of two constitutional rights being in conflict in a given case, such as the right to freedom of expression and the right to privacy, both of which we can well imagine being given some sort of specific recognition in a hypothetical (state) constitutional order. While the particular calculus a judge will employ in determining any given dispute will differ from case to case, and from place to place, it is unrealistic to imagine that a victory for the person expressing themselves means that the right to privacy 'is no longer

---

[88] See Timmermans (n 41) 355–57 and references therein; Bobić (n 54) 1407–09.

[89] G Davies, 'Constitutional Disagreement in Europe and the Search for Pluralism' in M Avbelj and J Komárek (eds), *Constitutional Pluralism in the European Union and Beyond* (Oxford, Hart Publishing, 2012) 269.

constitutional', or that some definitive normative hierarchy between the two has been established. Similarly, a victory for the person seeking to protect his or her privacy does not mean that the right to freedom of expression has been destroyed for all time coming. Rather, it is just that two rights were in conflict in a particular way and a resolution was necessary. If we assume that the constitutional order does not regard either of these rights as being inherently more important than the other, then the specific means of resolution will not establish a hierarchy between them where there was none previously. Instead, the particular facts and context of the case will be the decisive factors, along with the deeper justificatory rationales for why these two rights are worthy of protection in the first place, such as human dignity in the case of privacy, or the public interest in knowing the truth in the case of expression.

How, and to what extent, does this then differ from the case discounted by Davies, where there is conflict not between the norms of *a* legal *order* but between the norms of legal *orders*? I suggest that the two situations can be seen as being at the very least partially analogous. It is an overstatement to imagine that the disapplication in a given case of a norm from one 'constitutional' order in favour of a norm from another 'constitutional' order necessarily makes one order 'more constitutional' than the other. Our choice of the norm of one order over that of the other may well be capable of justification for reasons that have nothing to do with preferring one order over the other as a matter of principle. Moreover, this justification does not necessarily have to be viable or acceptable only from the perspective of the 'victorious' order. The order from which the disapplied norm originates can, in theory, recognise that there were good reasons for the disapplication, without doing violence to its own authority, integrity or self-image as a constitutional order. At least, this is the case if we accept the possibility of a temporally unlimited conception of dialogue between legal orders, with no 'end point', a possibility to which we will return in section IV.

Though we may reject the assertion that constitutional pluralism cannot be genuinely pluralist, there is still the question of how pluralist it *can* be, and how pluralist it *should* be. It is to this that we now turn.

iii. Reconciling the Dichotomy: Constitutional Pluralism, Pluralist Constitutionalism

Just as the first order question of the constitutionality of a legal order admits of answers altogether more complex than a simple denial or recognition of constitutionality, so too does the second order question of the relationships between legal orders (constitutional/hierarchical, pluralist/heterarchical or otherwise) allow us to give much more nuanced answers. There is still value in the criticisms, however, in that they force us to be clearer in our meanings: to what extent are the different constitutional pluralisms in the literature constitutional, and to what extent are they pluralist?

22 *Constitutional Pluralism*

There is a qualitative difference between what we could call theories of 'constitutional pluralism' in the *strict* sense and 'pluralist constitutionalism'.[90] This is more than a semantic quibble, because the two ideas approach the problem – the resolution and reconciliation of seemingly opposing realities – from different angles and different starting points. Constitutional pluralism in the strict sense can be seen as trying to collar, tame and stabilise the inherent unpredictability of a radical conception of pluralism (that is, to make pluralism more constitutional). MacCormick's pluralism under international law, to which he retreated from what he called radical pluralism, is an example of constitutional pluralism, properly so-called in this sense.[91] It takes pluralism as its starting point and attempts to constitutionalise it by the imposition of an authoritative framework for the resolution of conflict. Conversely, a theory of pluralist constitutionalism can be seen as trying, in the first instance, to make constitutionalism more pluralist, taking as its starting point the stability and predictability of state constitutionalism, while rescuing it, in Walker's sense,[92] from the fact that a globalising world has robbed it of much of its previous descriptive force and accuracy; and, secondly, to open it to the polycentricity inherent in European integration. Put simply, constitutional pluralism seeks to narrow the overly broad, and pluralist constitutionalism seeks to broaden the overly narrow. As will be seen below and throughout, this book takes the latter approach: triangular constitutionalism is a species of pluralist constitutionalism.

If we accept that constitutionalism and pluralism are not irreconcilable, we can recast MacCormick's two conceptions in ways that do not fit Krisch's either/or schema. In this light, MacCormick's radical pluralism is indeed a species of constitutional pluralism – rather than pluralism *simpliciter* in Krisch's sense – but is only 'constitutional' in the thin, descriptive sense that it deals with the arrangement, hierarchical or otherwise, of legal orders which themselves make valid (constitutional) claims to normative authority, whether in the normatively thick sense of national constitutionalism, the 'small-c' constitutionalism of the EU, or the 'smaller-c' constitutionalism of the ECHR.[93] Its reliance on politics, rather than law, for the ultimate resolution of disputes between orders places it more towards the pluralist end of the spectrum, but does not altogether rob it of its constitutional pedigree. Conversely, the recognition of public international law as an overarching frame makes pluralism under international law the more constitutional of MacCormick's two legal pluralisms, though it owes rather more to the constitutionalised internationalism of Bardo Fassbender[94] than to

---

[90] Timmermans hints at, but does not pursue, such a distinction when he says that if he had to 'express a preference, it would be in favour of a variant of pluralism that is constitutionalised as much as possible' (Timmermans (n 41) 358).

[91] See further, MacCormick, 'Risking Constitutional Collision in Europe?' (n 29).

[92] Walker, 'The Idea of Constitutional Pluralism' (n 32) passim.

[93] N Walker, 'Big "C" or Small "c"?' (2006) 12 *European Law Journal* 12.

[94] See B Fassbender, 'The United Nations Charter as Constitution of the International Community' (1998) 36 *Columbia Journal of Transnational Law* 529; and B Fassbender, '"We the Peoples of the United Nations": Constituent Power and Constitutional Form in International Law' in

The Constitutional Pluralists and the Critics   23

more traditional, state-based theories, or, indeed, to the various conceptions of constitutional pluralism which will be introduced in the next section. Similarly, distinguishing between constitutional pluralism in the strict sense and pluralist constitutionalism allows us to reconcile the epistemic discrepancy between Walker's and Jaklič's core or lowest-common denominator conceptions. For Walker, it is impossible for a legal order to make thick, substantive concessions regarding the question of the final say under constitutional pluralism. There being no Archimedean point from which we can gauge the relative strength of competing claims to finality, the question must be left open. For Jaklič, such concessions are in fact possible, provided the theory closes the question of the final say only in order to ensure the continued existence of some deeper, systemic pluralism at the most foundational level. However, the two authors are speaking at cross purposes, and the distinction between constitutional pluralism proper and pluralist constitutionalism provides the key: Walker's starting point is constitutionalism, which he seeks to pluralise with his requirement of ongoing, heterarchical epistemic contestation. Jaklič starts with pluralism, which he allows to be constitutionalised in the interests of preserving this core, foundational heterarchy.

B. 'Going Their Own Ways': Different Conceptions of Constitutional Pluralism

Having clarified our meanings of constitutionalism and pluralism, and posited the distinction between constitutional pluralism in the strict sense and pluralist constitutionalism, we can now further situate ourselves within the wider literature. In the specific context of the EU, rather than in the broader postnational context of Halberstam and Krisch, Avbelj outlines six conceptions of constitutionalism, all of which have pluralist aspects, though to greatly varying degrees: 'socio-teleological constitutionalism', represented by the work of Weiler;[95] 'epistemic meta-constitutionalism', represented by Walker;[96] the 'best

---

M Loughlin and N Walker (eds), *The Paradox of Constitutionalism: Constituent Power and Constitutional Form* (Oxford, Oxford University Press, 2007) 269.

[95] Avbelj, 'Questioning EU Constitutionalisms' (n 73) 11–12, citing, inter alia, JHH Weiler, 'Fin-de-Siècle Europe' in R Dehousse (ed), *Europe After Maastricht: An Ever Closer Union?* (Munich, Beck 1994); JHH Weiler, 'The Reformation of European Constitutionalism' (1997) 35 *Journal of Common Market Studies* 97; JHH Weiler, 'In Defence of the Status Quo: Europe's Constitutional *Sonderweg*' in JHH Weiler and M Wind (eds), *European Constitutionalism Beyond the State* (Cambridge, Cambridge University Press, 2003); JHH Weiler, 'On the Power of the Word: Europe's Constitutional Iconography' (2005) 3 *International Journal of Constitutional Law* 173.

[96] Avbelj, 'Questioning EU Constitutionalisms' (n 73) 13–15, citing, inter alia, Walker, 'The Idea of Constitutional Pluralism' (n 32); N Walker, 'Late Sovereignty in the European Union' in N Walker (ed), *Sovereignty in Transition* (Oxford, Hart Publishing, 2003); N Walker, 'Flexibility Within a Metaconstitutional Frame: Reflections on the Future of Legal Authority in Europe' in G de Búrca and J Scott (eds), *Constitutional Change in the EU: From Uniformity to Flexibility* (Oxford, Hart Publishing, 2000).

24 Constitutional Pluralism

fit universal constitutionalism' of Mattias Kumm;[97] the 'harmonious discursive constitutionalism' of Miguel Poiares Maduro;[98] Ingolf Pernice's 'multilevel classical constitutionalism';[99] and the 'reductionist constitutionalism' of Charles Sabel and Oliver Gerstenberg.[100] Jaklič employs a different schema for four of these authors: on his account, Walker's pluralism is 'epistemic', Weiler's is 'substantive', Maduro's is 'interpretive and participative', and Kumm's is 'institutional'. To these we can add Jaklič's own conception, which he variously dubs the 'distinctive', 'fully sound', 'more universalist', or 'superior' approach,[101] but can rightly and most usefully be described as 'utopian'.[102] The work of Walker, Kumm, Maduro and Sabel and Gerstenberg is of particular relevance for what follows, whereas that of Pernice, Weiler and Jaklič is not. The purpose of this section is to explain why.

Though neither Avbelj nor Jaklič group the work of Kumm, Maduro, and Sabel and Gerstenberg together, there is a significant amount of common ground between them. Most importantly, they all share Walker's third, epistemic, claim, where each legal order recognises the claim to final authority of each other order as being correct *only* from within the perspective of that other order. The final say *across* orders is, and must be, and ought to be, left open. Building on this epistemic claim, these authors propose a conception (though in different ways and to varying degrees) of inter-systemic 'metaconstitutional'[103] principles whereby conflict between legal orders can – in the first place – be avoided, and – if necessary – be resolved. These metaconstitutional pluralisms therefore seek either (in their explanatory dimension) to *identify*, or (as part of their normative dimension) to *posit* a series of norms that serve a bridging function between legal orders, while (in their epistemic dimension) still seeking to maintain the essentially heterarchical nature of the relationships between them and without falling off the oxymoronic tightrope and collapsing the orders into a monist

---

[97] Avbelj, 'Questioning EU Constitutionalisms' (n 73) 15–18, citing M Kumm, 'The Jurisprudence of Constitutional Conflict: Constitutional Supremacy in Europe Before and After the Constitutional Treaty' (2005) 11 *European Law Journal* 262.

[98] Avbelj, 'Questioning EU Constitutionalisms' (n 73) 18–19, citing, inter alia, MP Maduro, 'The Heteronyms of European Law' (1999) 5 *European Law Journal* 160; MP Maduro, 'Contrapunctual Law: Europe's Constitutional Pluralism in Action' in N Walker (ed), *Sovereignty in Transition* (Oxford, Hart Publishing, 2003).

[99] Avbelj, 'Questioning EU Constitutionalisms' (n 73) 19–20, citing, inter alia, I Pernice, 'Multilevel Constitutionalism in the European Union' (2002) 27 *European Law Review* 511.

[100] Avbelj, 'Questioning EU Constitutionalisms' (n 73) 20–22, citing, inter alia, J Cohen and C Sabel, 'Directly-Deliberative Polyarchy' (1997) 3 *European Law Journal* 313; O Gerstenberg and C Sabel, 'Directly-Deliberative Polyarchy: An Institutional Ideal for Europe?' in C Joerges and R Dehousse (eds), *Good Governance in Europe's Integrated Market* (Oxford, Oxford University Press, 2002). Avbelj later (and less pejoratively) describes this sort of theory as 'pragmatic constitutionalism': M Avbelj and J Komárek, 'Introduction' in M Avbelj and J Komárek (eds), *Constitutional Pluralism in the European Union and Beyond* (Oxford, Hart Publishing, 2012) 6.

[101] Jaklič, *Constitutional Pluralism in the EU* (n 28) passim.

[102] Sarmiento (n 41) 110.

[103] Walker, 'Flexibility Within a Metaconstitutional Frame' (n 96).

whole. It is in this respect that these versions of pluralism are *meta*constitutional: they identify or posit *constitutional rules about constitutional rules*. In terms of the distinction introduced above, these metaconstitutional pluralisms are species of pluralist constitutionalism. Their starting point is the coherence and order and predictability of constitutionalism, which they then pluralise specifically by leaving the question of the final say open. The approach in this book, of triangular constitutionalism, is situated firmly within this metaconstitutional branch of the discourse.

Pernice's 'multilevel constitutionalism', however, is virtually indistinguishable from standard federal constitutionalism at the state level, and in cases of conflict between legal orders always weighs on the side of the application of EU law.[104] It will therefore play no part in what follows.

The normative core of Weiler's theory is the notion of 'constitutional tolerance', which celebrates as a virtue distinct to the *sui generis*,[105] evolutionary constitutionalism of the EU that the institutional actors of the Member States

> accept [the legal doctrines of EU constitutionalism] as a continuously renewed, autonomous and voluntary act of subordination, in the discrete areas governed by Europe, to a norm that is the aggregate expression of *other* wills, *other* political identities, *other* political communities.[106]

To deal with cases of constitutional conflict, Weiler proposes the creation of a 'constitutional council', consisting of members of national constitutional or supreme courts, and chaired by the President of the CJEU, to decide questions of Union competence after the adoption of Union law but before it has come into force.[107] In one formulation of the proposal, Weiler asks, but does not answer, whether 'this proposal betray[s] my own craving for the mono-centrism of the old constitutional order'.[108] On one analysis, the answer to this question must

---

[104] Avbelj, 'Questioning EU Constitutionalisms' (n 73) 20. Franz Mayer and Mattias Wendel have mounted a defence of multilevel constitutionalism as a species of constitutional pluralism, arguing that it is neither 'a [specifically] German quarrel' nor 'a quarrel about nothing'. However, René Barents' reply argues that it is, in fact, both: see FC Mayer and M Wendel, 'Multilevel Constitutionalism and Constitutional Pluralism' in M Avbelj and J Komárek (eds), *Constitutional Pluralism in the European Union and Beyond* (Oxford, Hart Publishing, 2012); and R Barents, 'The Fallacy of European Multilevel Constitutionalism' in M Avbelj and J Komárek (eds), *Constitutional Pluralism in the European Union and Beyond* (Oxford, Hart Publishing, 2012). In his mapping analysis, Jaklič pays little attention to the theory, aside from noting Walker's description of it as a species of monism: Jaklič, *Constitutional Pluralism in the EU* (n 28) 41, fn 52, citing Walker, 'Late Sovereignty in the European Union' (n 96) 13–14, fn 31.

[105] It is in this sense that Weiler used the word *Sonderweg* (see Weiler, 'In Defence of the Status Quo: Europe's Constitutional *Sonderweg*' (n 95)).

[106] Weiler, 'On the Power of the Word' (n 95) 188, emphasis added.

[107] Weiler, 'The Reformation of European Constitutionalism' (n 95) 127; JHH Weiler, 'The European Union Belongs to its Citizens: Three Immodest Proposals' (1997) 22 *European Law Review* 150, 155–56; JHH Weiler, 'A Constitution for Europe? Some Hard Choices' (2002) 40 *Journal of Common Market Studies* 563, 573–74.

[108] Weiler, 'The Reformation of European Constitutionalism' (n 95) 127.

26   *Constitutional Pluralism*

be *yes*: though Weiler's constitutional tolerance does recognise constitutional *plurality*, and evinces a strong commitment to the normative imperatives of pluralism as outlined in the second claim of Walker's lowest-common-denominator conception, its pluralism operates ultimately at the deepest level of the self-image of legal orders, their institutions and their citizens, rather than at the hard edge of legal conflict between the orders. Its prior acceptance of the hierarchical constitutional claims of the EU order ('subordination', above) would seem to undermine any truly heterarchical aspects of the theory in terms of the avoidance and resolution of constitutional conflict. As Avbelj notes:

> [I]t fails to explain how its constitutional vision of the integration can be then genuinely tolerant and thus truly legitimate if a normative ideal of constitutional tolerance is introduced only when the constitutional framework of a clearly hierarchical nature is already in place.[109]

However, Jaklič's answer to Weiler's question regarding his craving for monocentrism is *no*: he specifically classifies Weiler as a constitutional pluralist[110] due to Weiler's refusal to accept either of the opposing monisms of state or EU constitutional supremacy on their own, already existing terms.[111] For Jaklič, the 'ethical building blocks'[112] of constitutional tolerance are the means by which 'both of the monist sources mutually tame one another',[113] providing a way beyond the two monisms towards what Jaklič takes to be an ethically sound, substantive conception of constitutional pluralism. Which analysis is correct, Avbelj's or Jaklič's? Again, the distinction between constitutional pluralism in the strict sense and pluralist constitutionalism provides the key. Just as with MacCormick's 'pluralism under international law', Weiler's constitutional tolerance is a species of constitutional pluralism in the strict sense. It takes pluralism as its starting point, but fears leaving the question of the final say open for its potential to undermine the mutual, voluntary infra-systemic readjustments required by constitutional tolerance. It attempts to remedy this potential for indeterminacy by superimposing a specifically constitutional method of dispute resolution: a hierarchical solution designed to allow for heterarchy to exist below it. The prescriptivism of the proposal for a specific, institutional reform of the Union, requiring Treaty amendment – and its closure of the question of the final say – distinguishes the theory from the metaconstitutional conceptions, which seek to explain the actual practice of European constitutionalism, and limit their proposals to interpretive and jurisprudential principles which can be applied within the already existing legal and institutional framework, rather

---

[109] Avbelj, 'Questioning EU Constitutionalisms' (n 73) 24, fn 112.

[110] Somewhat to Weiler's surprise: see JHH Weiler, 'Christmas Reading? Christmas Gifts? Some Suggestions from the Editor-in-Chief' (*EJIL: Talk!*, 29 December 2014), available at: www.ejiltalk.org/christmas-reading-christmas-gifts-some-suggestions-from-the-editor-in-chief/.

[111] Jaklič, *Constitutional Pluralism in the EU* (n 28) 74–75.

[112] ibid 77–89.

[113] ibid 80.

The Constitutional Pluralists and the Critics   27

than wholesale adjustment to the institutional makeup of the constitutional order(s). Seen in this way, as a theory of constitutional pluralism in the strict sense, the categorisation of Weiler's constitutional tolerance as being non-heterarchical which is inherent in Avbelj's analysis, and Jaklič takes to be inherent in Walker's approach,[114] does not hold. It is not that Weiler's conception is not pluralist, it is just a different *kind* of pluralism to the epistemic pluralism of Walker, with its claim of perpetual indeterminacy, and the metaconstitutional pluralisms that Walker's approach has inspired.

Similarly outside the scope of metaconstitutional pluralism is Jaklič's own theory. The first parts of his work aim to map and assess the theories of MacCormick, Walker, Weiler, Maduro and Kumm in great detail, through four different discursive frames: the *who*, which deals with the question of the final say in cases of conflict; the *how*, which refers to the manner or method through which constitutional interpretation and discourse should be engaged with; the *what*, concerning the substantive content of this discourse; and a final, more abstract, 'foundational' discourse which seeks to 'elaborate[] a distinctive plural-ist conception – actually explain[ing] the notion of *heterarchy* – at the deepest systemic level'.[115] On this analysis, Jaklič categorises MacCormick as dealing largely with the foundational discourse, Walker and Maduro mostly with the *how*, Kumm mostly with the *who*, and Weiler with the *what*.

It is the discourse of the *what*, defined more specifically as the question of 'what exactly should be the content of the substantive identities that Europe (the Europeans) and its nation-states (the national citizens) ought to adopt at their respective constitutional sites',[116] that most captures Jaklič's imagination. Having found each of the sub-branches of constitutional pluralism to be 'bare',[117] Jaklič sets out to develop a 'distinctive', 'fully sound', 'more universalist', 'substantive', 'superior' conception, which can 'unleash a new democratic potential implicit in Europe's new post-sovereign context', containing 'the seed of a new historic advancement of democracy for the Europeans and non-Europeans alike', where 'the sound pluralist model of democracy would gradually, but inevitably, arise out of the particular sound foundation of consti-tutional pluralism'.[118] This is heady stuff. In its utopianism and its use of the language of inevitability, it offers a kind of liberal foil to the withering away of the State under socialism. Jaklič envisages a refined nation state that

> make[s] it clear that, in the sphere that affects 'external others'[119] equally, its previ-ously sovereign territory is now open to inclusion of those 'others' ... They are offered such inclusion through some coexisting common supranational project

[114] ibid 95.
[115] ibid 11–12.
[116] ibid 30.
[117] ibid 8.
[118] ibid 8–9.
[119] By which Jaklič means those who are not 'members' of 'the nation-state people as the single ultimate source of authority over the nation-state territory' (ibid 301).

28   *Constitutional Pluralism*

that is not limited to the regional Europe, but to which the nation-state now opens itself through such a refinement at the level of its foundational principle. Such more inclusive foundational principle is more able to capture the unconditional universal respect and its ideal of essential humanity than does some monist monopolization of territory under the superstate strategy still underpinned by its monist foundational principle. It also better fulfils those ideals than some monopolization that aspires to be internally pluralist, but is externally still monist, limited to some regional Europe, such as was the case with most of our pluralists examined earlier.[120]

However, this idea is so abstract in its formulation, so unmoored from the actual practice of national and European constitutionalism as it actually stands, and so far beyond the territory on which the discourse surrounding constitutional pluralism has taken place to date, that it stands quite apart from that discourse. For a theory that purports to elaborate a foundation for 'democracy's third coming',[121] Jaklič's utopian pluralism has remarkably little to say about the actual workings of constitutional democracy, politics and law in contemporary Europe. Its concern for advancing a conception of constitutionalism based on 'a particular quality of equal respect between human beings as the bearers of the kind of dignity that nothing else in this world possesses',[122] may be morally praiseworthy, but it is a very different project from that of the constitutional pluralists. It operates almost entirely at the level of pure theory, and makes little reference to actual practice, lived experience, or the parlous current state of constitutional democracy in Europe and the wider world.[123]

We saw, above, that Weiler's proposal of specific Treaty reform for solving the question of the 'final say' distinguished his conception from the metaconstitutional species of pluralism. Jaklič's altogether more fundamental proposal of utopian pluralism takes (or claims to take) constitutional pluralism as its starting point, but (d)evolves so far beyond this starting point, and in such a different direction, that it constitutes a very different theory indeed.

III. METACONSTITUTIONAL PLURALISMS

This leaves us with the theories of Sabel and Gerstenberg, Maduro, and Kumm. At the heart of these metaconstitutional pluralisms are the specific norms constituting the overarching metaconstitutional framework, which offer guidance in the avoidance and resolution of conflicts between orders. These have been termed 'interface norms' by Krisch, which 'are the main legal expression of openness and closure, friendliness or hostility among the different parts'.[124] This is the description that will be adopted throughout this book, and a major

---

[120] ibid 301.
[121] ibid 259, and ch 10 passim.
[122] ibid 264. See further K Jaklič, 'Liberal Legitimacy and Intact Respect' (2014) 27 *Ratio Juris* 409.
[123] See also Sarmiento (n 41).
[124] Krisch, *Beyond Constitutionalism* (n 41) 285–86.

Metaconstitutional Pluralisms   29

part of the discussion in section IV below is focused on the nature of the interface norms supplied, inferred or suggested by each of the metaconstitutional conceptions of pluralism. However, two preliminary matters must be dealt with here.

First, we have already seen that Krisch rejects the concept of (meta)constitutional pluralism as an impossibility and posits his own theory as being specifically pluralist rather than constitutional. This he makes clear when he writes that:

> Unlike in a constitutionalist structure, the strength of the respective claims in a pluralist order is not assessed by a single decision-maker or from a central vantage point. The pluralist setting distinguishes itself precisely by the fact that the conflict rules do *not* have an overarching legal character; they are normative, moral demands that find (potentially diverging) legal expressions only within the various sub-orders.[125]

But as we have seen, we need not accept this characterisation of affairs. The fact that 'the rules are set by each sub-order for itself'[126] does not necessarily render them non-constitutional, especially in light of the above discussion of the finely graded, rather than either/or, nature of constitutionalism, and in particular when we consider the rules as being *meta*constitutional. In fact, Krisch tacitly concedes as much when he goes on to write that:

> This can lead to incoherences in the overall order ... [y]et the rule of law also poses demands on decision-makers in a pluralist setting: its asks legislators and judges to pursue the values of legal certainty and predictability by striving for consistency in the overall order. At times this goal may be trumped by other values – autonomy, democracy, and rights among them. If another order does not deserve respect on the basis of its autonomy pedigree, overall consistency need not be ensured.[127]

It is precisely this sort of contingent, relational analysis that supplies metaconstitutional pluralism with its constitutional credentials, and distinguishes it from radical pluralism, contrary to Krisch's a priori distinction between the two.

The lines quoted above also hint at the second preliminary issue: the use of the phrase interface *norms* to describe the means by which the relations between legal orders can be regulated. As we have seen, Krisch also characterises these 'norms' as 'rules', 'demands' and even 'values'. Elsewhere, he writes of the need for 'a more finely tuned legal and doctrinal instrumentarium'[128] and 'doctrinal tools'.[129] Bobić speaks similarly of 'expressions', 'concepts' and 'keywords' used by national constitutional courts and the CJEU when navigating the boundaries of national and EU law.[130] The issue is compounded by the varying ways

---

[125] ibid 296, footnote omitted.
[126] ibid 286.
[127] ibid 296.
[128] ibid 286.
[129] ibid.
[130] Bobić (n 54) 1414.

30 Constitutional Pluralism

in which the different metaconstitutional theories classify their conceptions of interface norms. As we shall see, they are most frequently described as 'principles'. Kumm is explicit in his outline of what has come to be called 'cosmopolitan constitutionalism'[131] that he adopts and relies on Robert Alexy's conception of norms as consisting of both rules and principles,[132] under which:

> [P]rinciples are norms which require that something be realized to the greatest extent possible given their legal and factual possibilities. Principles are optimization requirements, characterized by the fact that they can be satisfied to varying degrees and that the appropriate degree of satisfaction depends not only on what is factually possible but also on what is legally possible. The scope of the legally possible is determined by opposing principles and rules.
>
> By contrast rules are norms that are always either fulfilled or not. If a rule validly applies, then the requirement is to do exactly what it says, neither more nor less. In this way rules contain fixed points in the field of the factually and legally possible. This means that the distinction between rules and principles is a qualitative one and not one of degree. Every norm is either a rule or a principle.[133]

Therefore, though the phrase 'interface norms' which will be used throughout the analysis is Krisch's, this does not require us to accept his constitutionalism/pluralism dichotomy, nor does it limit the discussion to hard and fast legal rules. The various understandings of interface norms encompass not just rules and principles, but, in certain conceptions, 'doctrinal instrumentaria' in Krisch's sense and Bobić's 'concepts': whole toolkits encompassing a variety of considerations as to how legal orders relate to one another.

Let us now examine the various metaconstitutional pluralisms in more detail, and in particular their conceptions of interface norms.

A. Sabel and Gerstenberg: Polyarchic Coordinate Constitutionalism

Sabel and Gerstenberg take as their starting point the CJEU's development of a fundamental rights jurisprudence at the behest of Member State courts, most notably the BVerfG, as set out in section I above. They note, however, that later

---

[131] See section III.C.3, below.

[132] Kumm, 'The Jurisprudence of Constitutional Conflict' (n 97) 290, fn 70, citing R Alexy, *A Theory of Constitutional Rights* (Oxford, Oxford University Press, 2002) 44–110; J-R Sieckmann, *Regelmodelle und Prinzipienmodelle des Rechtssystems* (Baden-Baden, Nomos, 1990); R Dworkin, *Taking Rights Seriously* (Cambridge, MA, Harvard University Press, 1977). See also M Kumm, 'Who is the Final Arbiter of Constitutionality in Europe?: Three Conceptions of the Relationship Between the German Federal Constitutional Court and the European Court of Justice' (1999) 36 *Common Market Law Review* 351, 375, fn 47, citing R Dworkin, *Law's Empire* (London, Fontana, 1986); R Alexy, *A Theory of Legal Argumentation* (Oxford, Clarendon Press, 1989); N MacCormick, *Legal Reasoning and Legal Theory* (Oxford, Clarendon Press, 1978).

[133] Alexy, *A Theory of Constitutional Rights* (n 132) 47–48.

Metaconstitutional Pluralisms 31

judgments such as *Schmidberger*[134] and *Omega*[135] – where attempts are made at reconciling the market freedoms of the EU with national commitments to freedom of expression and the right to human dignity respectively – had the effect of solving an old problem only to recreate the same problem at a level further abstracted from national constitutionalism. In rising to the challenge of developing its own fundamental rights jurisprudence, the CJEU has extended its jurisdiction 'in ways that overlap and potentially compete with that of Member States in matters of visceral concern'.[136] This is not just an issue within the confines of the EU and its relations with its parts, but is compounded by the EU's place in the broader international order. *Kadi*[137] is given as an example: instead of national courts making demands of the supranational CJEU, the supranational CJEU makes demands of the Security Council of the United Nations, a jurisgenerative body unused to having its decisions reviewed in courts of law.[138] In the European sphere, the problem is complicated by the overlap between the CJEU's jurisprudence on fundamental rights and the position of the ECtHR as the overseer and guardian of the Convention, which the ECtHR has gone so far as to describe as a 'constitutional instrument of a European public order'.[139]

There is therefore in Europe a potential tripartite clash of jurisdiction concerning the meaning and scope of human and fundamental rights. Though the jurisdictions of the EU, the ECtHR and states are separate, they are not neatly compartmentalised or hermetically sealed. Sabel and Gerstenberg suggest that this problem is in the process of being resolved by

> the formation of a novel order of *coordinate constitutionalism* in which Member States, the ECJ [and] the ECtHR ... agree to defer to one another's decisions, provided those decisions respect mutually agreed essentials. This coordinate order extends constitutionalism ... beyond its home territory in the nation state through a jurisprudence of mutual monitoring and peer review that carefully builds on national constitutional traditions, but does not create a new, encompassing sovereign entity.[140]

---

[134] Case C-112/00 *Eugen Schmidberger, International Transporte und Planzüge v Austria* ECLI:EU:C:2003:333, [2003] ECR I-5659.

[135] Case C-36/02 *Omega Spielhallen- und Automatenaufstellungs-GmbH v Oberbürgermeisterin der Bundesstadt Bonn* ECLI:EU:C:2004:614, [2004] ECR I-9609. To this we can add Case C-208/09 *Ilonka Sayn-Wittgenstein v Landeshauptmann von Wien* ECLI:EU:C:2010:806, [2010] ECR I-13693; and Case C-391/09 *Malgožata Runevič-Vardyn and Łukasz Paweł Wardyn v Vilniaus Miesto Savivaldybės Administracija* ECLI:EU:C:2011:291, [2011] ECR I–3787: see Bobić (n 54) 1408.

[136] CF Sabel and O Gerstenberg, 'Constitutionalising an Overlapping Consensus: The ECJ and the Emergence of a Coordinate Constitutional Order' (2010) 16 *European Law Journal* 511, 512.

[137] *Kadi* (n 7).

[138] Sabel and Gerstenberg (n 136) 512. See further M Avbelj, F Fontanelli and G Martinico (eds), *Kadi on Trial: A Multifaceted Analysis of the Kadi Trial* (Abingdon, Routledge, 2014).

[139] *Loizidou* (n 84) para 75; *Bosphorus* (n 84) para 156.

[140] Sabel and Gerstenberg (n 136) 512, emphasis added. Jaklič makes no mention at all of the work of Sabel and Gerstenberg in his mapping analysis, but given that their work on the subject deals specifically with the relationship between the EU and the (for Jaklič) 'non-constitutional' ECHR, we can safely assume that he would regard their work as being beyond the pale of his conception of constitutional pluralism.

32 Constitutional Pluralism

This coordinate constitutional order is described in terms of John Rawls' idea of overlapping consensus,[141] whereby general agreement on fundamental matters of principle does not rest on a single set of shared (in this case, constitutional) values, but rather:

> On the contrary, the parties to an overlapping consensus know that they have reached agreement on essentials, such as the attractiveness of democracy as a system of government or of respect for the individual as a condition of freedom and fairness, through differing, only partially concordant interpretations of such comprehensive ideas.[142]

The acknowledgement of these differences, rather than being a cause of friction, is precisely what drives each actor to reserve to themselves the right to their own interpretation of overlapping principles, while simultaneously affording that right to competing actors, within broader or narrower limits. For Sabel and Gerstenberg, it is the *Solange* principle – the principle of deference leavened by watchfulness – that provides the necessary doctrinal instrument for articulating each actor's viewpoint while providing the opportunity for this viewpoint to be adjusted in light of those of competing actors.

Coordinate constitutionalism is not a new idea, but it is one with a chequered history in the statist constitutional frame. As Christine Bateup notes:

> Coordinate construction is the oldest conception of constitutional interpretation as a shared enterprise between the courts and the political branches of government, having been first espoused by James Madison. While acknowledging that issues of constitutional interpretation would normally fall to the judiciary in the ordinary course of government, Madison rejected the view that judicial decisions had any unique status, as the [US] Constitution did not provide for any specific authority to determine the limits of the division of powers between the different branches. Similarly, Thomas Jefferson considered that each branch of government must be 'co-ordinate and independent of each other', and that each branch has primary responsibility for interpreting the Constitution as it concerns its own functions.[143]

Though this idea was eventually torpedoed in the American context by the US Supreme Court's assumption of the ultimate right to determine the meaning of the Constitution and the legitimate sphere of action of each actor established thereunder[144] (as well as the eventual acquiescence of competing actors in this analysis), it is not difficult to transplant the idea to the modern, postnational configuration. The 'deliberative polyarchy'[145] of the ECHR system takes the place of the constitutional state, and each normative order within the

---

[141] J Rawls, 'The Idea of an Overlapping Consensus' (1987) 7 *Oxford Journal of Legal Studies* 1.

[142] Sabel and Gerstenberg (n 136) 513.

[143] C Bateup, 'The Dialogic Promise: Assessing the Normative Potential of Theories of Constitutional Dialogue' (2005–06) 71 *Brooklyn Law Review* 1109 1137 (footnotes omitted).

[144] *Marbury v Madison* 5 US 137 (1803). See further RH Jackson, *The Struggle for Judicial Supremacy* (New York, Knopf, 1941).

[145] Sabel and Gerstenberg (n 136) 513.

polyarchy takes the place of the constitutional actors empowered under coordinate constitutionalism to make their own interpretations of what the consensus requires, subject to an ongoing dialogic reframing and re-evaluation of these interpretations.

i. Interface Norms Under Polyarchic Coordinate Constitutionalism

The explanatory claim of constitutional pluralism is evident in polyarchic coordinate constitutionalism's acknowledgment of the messy reality of coexisting, competing, cooperating normative orders, and – although the authors are nowhere explicit on the point – *seems* to agree with the normative claim, in that this incipient dialogic polyarchy is presented as being preferable to the full-scale, hierarchical constitutionalisation of the EU or ECHR orders. Moreover, the statement, quoted above, that coordinate constitutionalism 'carefully builds on national constitutional traditions, but does not create a new, encompassing sovereign entity'[146] clearly casts the theory as a species of metaconstitutional pluralism, accepting of Walker's third claim, with the final say left open. However, the theory is unique among metaconstitutional pluralisms in its conception of interface norms. Rather than positing specific, universally applicable interface norms in the abstract and in advance, it is the principles of overlapping consensus themselves that do the substantive work of regulating relations between the legal orders in the polyarchy, and this only at the point of application. Sabel and Gerstenberg note two essential features of an overlapping consensus. First, it is 'a freestanding political view, which draws on shared democratic ideals of the parties to the consensus and which can be affirmed by them on the basis of their opposing, but reasonable, comprehensive outlooks.[147] Secondly, and crucially, it 'arises in practice not from a simultaneous deduction from overlapping first principles to convergent conclusions, but rather from an ongoing historical interaction between the emergent, common political view and the diverse comprehensive views underlying it.[148] The centrality of this *temporal* element, with its focus on the ongoing (and potentially permanent) dialogue between sites in the polyarchy, is what most distinguishes coordinate constitutionalism from the metaconstitutional pluralisms to be discussed in sections III.B and III.C below, and what marks the theory as the least prescriptive of the three. It also serves as a riposte to Davies' temporally foreclosed conception of dialogue, whereby dialogue may help different sources of law reconcile, but the disapplication of a norm from one constitutional order permanently relegates that order to non-constitutional status. For Sabel and Gerstenberg, the emergence of an overlapping consensus is an iterative, three-stage process whereby certain (unspecified, varying) liberal principles first come to be accepted as

---

[146] ibid 512.
[147] ibid.
[148] ibid.

34   Constitutional Pluralism

'boundary conditions on political contest'.[149] There then emerges 'agreement on the kind of public reason – the kinds of reasons acceptable in arguments – that applying liberal principles of justice involves',[150] followed by the third stage, in which there is the secular dialogic reinforcement of these liberal principles by the use of public reason by actors within the polyarchy.[151] Sabel and Gerstenberg write that this three-stage process is exactly what has happened in the sphere of European integration: first, 'certain areas of decision making ... were taken off the agenda of exclusively domestic decision making and established as European supranational norms with primacy over domestic law'[152] both as a response to the European experience of war and in order to solve political and economic problems that states could not deal with alone. Secondly, the *Solange* dialogue was the means by which the CJEU began to take seriously fundamental rights protection. Thirdly, continuing dialogue regarding fundamental rights in the EU legal order – and in the legal order overseen by the ECtHR – constitutes the secular reinforcement of this overlapping consensus.[153]

It is therefore through the principles of overlapping consensus and its operationalisation by means of the *Solange* principle that specific interface norms emerge under coordinate constitutionalism over time, rather than being posited beforehand.[154] *Solange* is on this view 'a master framework for creating other frameworks and with them the necessity and methods for establishing mutual regard of constitutional traditions'.[155] Though Sabel and Gerstenberg do not posit specific interface norms in advance, the claim to universality is inherent in their theory: this master framework creates a 'de-nationalised precedent for de-nationalising precedents, which, loosened from their moorings in national constitutional tradition, can become part of the overlapping consensus'.[156]

B. Maduro: Contrapunctual Law

The aim of Maduro's theory is twofold: the avoidance of constitutional conflict in the first place, followed by its effective management when it does arise.[157]

---

[149] ibid, citing Rawls (n 141) 159ff and 161.

[150] ibid, citing Rawls (n 141) 162.

[151] ibid.

[152] ibid.

[153] Sabel and Gerstenberg give as examples Case C-341/05 *Laval un Partneri v Svenska Byggnadsarbetareförbundet* ECLI:EU:C:2007:809, [2007] ECR I-11767 (*Laval*); Case C-438/05 *ITWF & FSU v Viking Line* ECLI:EU:C:2007:292, [2007] ECR I-10779 (*Viking*); and Case C-144/04 *Mangold v Helm* ECLI:EU:C:2005:709, [2005] ECR I-9981 in the EU context, and the case of *Goodwin v UK* (2002) 35 EHRR 18 with respect to the ECHR: Sabel and Gerstenberg (n 136) 545. *Viking* and *Laval* will be discussed in depth in ch 3, below.

[154] In fact, Sabel and Gerstenberg explicitly disclaim the possibility of such norms being posited beforehand: 'If this view captures the jurisgenerative logic of the *Solange* jurisprudence, there can be no meta-criteria such as the best fit of all constitutional cases ... by which to harmonise all decision making' (Sabel and Gerstenberg (n 136) 550).

[155] Sabel and Gerstenberg (n 136) 545.

[156] ibid.

[157] Maduro, 'Contrapunctual Law' (n 98).

This he attempts by analogy to the musical theory of counterpoint, whereby different voices exhibit both independence and interdependence simultaneously, resulting not in cacophony but in harmony.

Maduro describes his principles of contrapunctual law as

> the principles to which all actors of the European legal community must commit themselves and according to which the EU legal order must be structured as a system of law. This commitment is voluntary but it may still be presented as a limit to pluralism. It can nevertheless be argued that this is the limit to pluralism necessary to allow the largest extent of pluralism possible.[158]

Something similar was said above about MacCormick's and Weiler's proposals for solving the problem of the final say. However, for Maduro, this limit to pluralism arises from principles internal to each system, and not the imposition of an external factor, whether public international law in the case of MacCormick or a Constitutional Council in the case of Weiler.

Maduro explicitly does not set out to provide a completely theorised third way between national and European monism. Borrowing a phrase from Sunstein, he writes that the aim of the contrapunctual principles is to achieve 'incompletely theorised agreements',[159] whereby different actors may proceed from different bases and by different routes, but nevertheless come up with the same (or at least different but compatible) results. We can further see the absence of an attempt to construct a *via media* in the following statement:

> Borrowing the language of systems theory, we may say that the problem of compatibility between different legal systems or sub-systems is presented as a problem of coordination whose only answer can be found in each system adapting its own set of perspectives to the possible contacts and collisions with other systems.[160]

Maduro's approach is therefore aimed at modification of the existing, internal perspectives of both national and EU apex actors, instead of leaving them intact and bridging them with an entirely new discourse or philosophy, or the imposition of an overarching framework or authoritative decision-maker. In this sense it more clearly embraces Walker's third, epistemic claim than does the more concrete theory of Kumm, to be discussed below. However, the theory is still metaconstitutional in nature in that Maduro posits specific principles of contrapunctual law – constitutional rules about constitutional rules – by which this internal modification of perspectives is to be achieved.

i. Interface Norms Under Contrapunctual Law

The principles of counterpoint are how Maduro conceives of interface norms under contrapunctual law. First, there is the principle of *pluralism itself*, which

---

[158] ibid 524, emphasis added.
[159] ibid 525.
[160] ibid.

36 Constitutional Pluralism

has two elements: (1) different legal orders must expressly acknowledge the existence and autonomy of their counterparts, which 'entails the recognition and adjustment of each legal order to the plurality of equally legitimate claims ... made by other legal orders';[161] and (2) 'pluralism requires such a discourse to take place in such a way as to promote the broadest participation possible'.[162] Here we see quite some overlap with Walker's requirement of inclusive coherence for constitutionalism,[163] that it must be attentive to its own democratic deficit, and we can clearly discern Maduro's acceptance and endorsement of the explanatory claim of constitutional pluralism. As was the case with Sabel and Gerstenberg, the normative claim is less clearly articulated, but rests on the importance Maduro attaches to the importance of participation and representation to the democratic legitimacy of the Union.[164]

The second contrapunctual principle is constituted by the requirements of *consistency* and *vertical and horizontal coherence*, whereby the decisions of courts across Europe must fit not only with the jurisprudence of the CJEU, but also with that of other national courts.[165] The reasons for this are practical as well as theoretical: Maduro notes that the sheer weight of the Court of Justice's caseload means that 'an increased amount of the burden of interpreting and applying EU law will fall *de facto* even if not *de iure* upon national courts'.[166] However, this increased (and necessary) role for national courts must not undermine the coherence and uniformity of the EU legal order and, for this reason, requires the development of a strong tradition of dialogue and mutual interest between national legal systems.

The third principle, *universalisability*, is related to but separate from the second. National judgments on EU law should be structured so as to permit their application, in principle at least, not just in the deciding Member State but also in any other. Maduro suggests that the taking seriously of this requirement would lead national courts to internalise the consequences of their judgments not just for their own legal system, or for the EU legal order itself, but for the whole pluralist array of legal orders existing in Europe. This, Maduro claims, 'will prevent national courts from using the autonomy of their legal system as a form of evasion and freeriding',[167] and so create a virtuous cycle whereby courts across Europe cooperate in the development and application of EU law, without insult to the autonomy of either their own legal systems or that of the EU, thereby seeking to avoid the dangers of fragmentation and breakdown.

---

[161] ibid 526.

[162] ibid 527.

[163] Walker, 'The Idea of Constitutional Pluralism' (n 32) 336.

[164] Maduro, 'Contrapunctual Law' (n 98) 518.

[165] Note, however, the touch of hierarchy in Maduro's phraseology here – a pluralist may wish to include the CJEU along the horizontal axis, rather than admit to the existence of a vertical axis. This is why I characterise my own use of the terms below in section V.B as merely heuristic.

[166] Maduro, 'Contrapunctual Law' (n 98) 528.

[167] ibid 530.

Finally, there is the principle of *institutional choice*. This recognises that an exclusive focus on the judgments and actions of courts is necessarily distorting, particularly when we adopt a pluralist conception of legal orders. Just as epistemic pluralism means that there is no one court of wise judges to whom we can turn when we need a final answer, nor is there one parliament, one government, or one administration that can decide legal, political and social issues. Pluralism necessarily multiplies and complicates the range of legal actors in and across polities, as well as the internal self-images of these actors; their relationships among themselves within polities; and their attitudes to other polities (and the actors these polities contain). Here Maduro refers to the dangers of what Neil Komesar has called 'single institutional analysis',[168] and suggests that multiple institutional analysis is a *requirement* of contrapunctual law. He does not, however, elaborate on the precise contours and meaning of this requirement.[169]

C. Kumm: Cosmopolitan Constitutionalism

In his 1999 analysis of the relationship between the BVerfG and the CJEU, Kumm defined the two Courts' opposing theses as 'European monism' in the case of the CJEU and 'democratic statism' on the part of the BVerfG, and proposed a *via media* in the form of 'European constitutionalism'.[170] He subsequently broadened his argument by not focusing exclusively on the jurisprudence of one national court and relabelled the positions as 'European constitutional supremacy', 'national constitutional supremacy' and 'constitutionalism beyond the state'.[171] More recently, Kumm expanded the analysis further in order to encompass the question of the relationship between the EU and the UN,[172] and has re-labelled the positions as 'legalist monism',[173] 'democratic statism'[174] and 'cosmopolitan constitutionalism'.[175] These more recent labels will be used below.

Under legalist monism, EU law, of any kind, is supreme over national law in cases of conflict; only the CJEU may review EU norms, and national

---

[168] ibid 530–31, citing N Komesar, *Imperfect Alternatives – Choosing Institutions in Law, Economics and Public Policy* (Chicago, IL, Chicago University Press, 1994).

[169] The challenge is taken up, however, in J Komárek, 'Institutional Dimension of Constitutional Pluralism' in M Avbelj and J Komárek (eds), *Constitutional Pluralism in the European Union and Beyond* (Oxford, Hart Publishing, 2012).

[170] Kumm, 'Who is the Final Arbiter of Constitutionality in Europe?' (n 132).

[171] Kumm, 'The Jurisprudence of Constitutional Conflict' (n 97) passim.

[172] A move prompted by the CJEU's decision in *Kadi* (n 7): see M Kumm, 'Rethinking Constitutional Authority: On the Structure and Limits of Constitutional Pluralism' in M Avbelj and J Komárek (eds), *Constitutional Pluralism in the European Union and Beyond* (Oxford, Hart Publishing, 2012) 39.

[173] Kumm, 'Rethinking Constitutional Authority' (n 172) 43–49.

[174] ibid 49–54.

[175] ibid 54–63.

38   *Constitutional Pluralism*

constitutional provisions may not be relied upon by national courts to justify any decision to disapply or suspend the application of EU law in any given state – a decision that national courts have no jurisdiction to make in the first place.[176] Of course, this is merely a succinct restatement of a long line of CJEU case law,[177] which is mostly – but by no means always[178] – followed by national supreme and constitutional courts.

Conversely, democratic statism holds that national apex courts, as creatures of their domestic constitution, are bound to regard that constitution as the font of all legal authority. This statism is *democratic*[179] because it is justified by reference to democratic constitutional theory:

> State law ultimately derives its authority from 'We the People' imagined as having acted as a *pouvoir constituant* to establish a national Constitution as a supreme legal framework for democratic self-government. International law, on the other hand, derives its authority from the consent of states.[180]

The consequences of democratic statism are twofold: first, the national constitution, being the supreme law of the land, is the sole point of reference for determining whether and under what circumstances international law (which on this analysis must include EU law)[181] is to be applied within the State. The legal universe is therefore dualist[182] in its structure, and '[t]he only relevant question is how to interpret the constitution with regard to the status it ascribes to EU law'.[183] Secondly, the lack of authority derived from 'We the People' in the international sphere means that international law remains afflicted with an 'aura of illegitimacy'.[184]

Kumm's third approach, cosmopolitan constitutionalism, derives from that of what he calls the '*sui generists*'. Here, the important question is not whether the final say rests with Luxembourg or with national courts. Instead, the emphasis is on the procedural and jurisprudential factors (that is – though he

---

[176] Kumm, 'Who is the Final Arbiter of Constitutionality in Europe?' (n 132) 354, citations omitted; Kumm, 'Rethinking Constitutional Authority' (n 172) 43.

[177] See, inter alia, *Costa* (n 6); Case 45/76 *Comet BV v Produktschap voor Siergewassen* ECLI:EU:C:1976:191, [1976] ECR 2043; Case 106/77 *Amministrazione delle Finanze dello Stato v Simmenthal* ECLI:EU:C:1978:49, [1978] ECR 629; Case 314/85 *Firma Foto-Frost v Hauptzollamt Lübeck-Ost* ECLI:EU:C:1987:452, [1987] ECR 4199.

[178] See the judgment of the Czech Constitutional Court in the 'Slovak pensions' case: Judgment of 31 January 2012, Pl ÚS 5/12, *Slovak Pensions XVII*, analysed in J Komárek, 'Playing with Matches: The Czech Constitutional Court Declares a Judgment of the Court of Justice of the EU *Ultra Vires*' (2012) 8 *European Constitutional Law Review* 323. See also M Bobek, '*Landtová, Holubec*, and the Problem of an Uncooperative Court: Implications for the Preliminary Rulings Procedure' (2014) 10 *European Constitutional Law Review* 54.

[179] Rather than 'conceptual' or 'realist': see Kumm, 'Rethinking Constitutional Authority' (n 172) 47–48.

[180] Kumm, 'Rethinking Constitutional Authority' (n 172) 48.

[181] ibid 49–50.

[182] Though recall Walker's distinction (n 55), between philosophical monism (particularism) and legal monism, whereby both legal monism and dualism are species of philosophical monism.

[183] Kumm, 'The Jurisprudence of Constitutional Conflict' (n 97) 266.

[184] Kumm, 'Rethinking Constitutional Authority' (n 172) 49.

did not initially use the phrase – the metaconstitution) that may serve to prevent constitutional conflict in the first place: by this approach, the problem of the final say is left unresolved because it is a problem that should never arise.[185] The problem with the *sui generist* approach for Kumm is that it is undertheorised and, as a result, cannot adequately answer the question of what kind of legal order the EU actually *is*. Here, the present author agrees, and recalls the further problem, noted by Tom Eijsbouts and others, that the language of '*sui generis*-ness' serves only to 'veil, or even wall off, the Union as a paradise for single-issue experts and officials, inaccessible to the common man and sometimes impervious to common sense',[186] a critique that ties in directly with Walker's account of the alleged limits of constitutionalist discourse.[187]

Kumm is essentially sympathetic to the *sui generist* approach,[188] and it is in response to its theoretical shortcomings that he develops his theory of cosmopolitan constitutionalism, under which 'a set of *universal principles* central to liberal democratic constitutionalism undergird the authority of public law and determine which norms take precedence over others in particular circumstances'.[189] As will be immediately clear, Kumm's conception of cosmopolitan constitutionalism is a species of metaconstitutional pluralism, but it goes further than either Sabel and Gerstenberg or Maduro in seeking, through his various principles, to *create* or *supply* precisely the Archimedean point that does not (yet) exist, from and through which constitutional conflict can be resolved or avoided in the postnational legal landscape. In this regard it departs from the epistemic claim of Walker's pluralism, and in positing specific, explicitly shared and trans-systemic principles for the avoidance and ultimate resolution of conflict, it is perhaps the most prescriptive account of metaconstitutional pluralism in the literature. Though it might seem that cosmopolitan constitutionalism owes rather more to democratic statism than to legalist monism – indeed, Kumm tacitly admits as much when he states that '[f]or so long as structural deficits remain on the level of the [EU], [EU] law will [not be], *and should not be*, recognised by national courts as the supreme law of the land without qualification'[190] – it should not be supposed that cosmopolitan constitutionalism is a kind of reactionary constitutional nationalism, insufficiently cognisant and respectful of the authority of EU law. Indeed, Kumm explicitly does *not* regard heterarchy as being always and in every case the best way of conceptualising the relationships between legal orders: '[C]onstitutional pluralism is no panacea and is not always attractive ...

[185] Kumm, 'The Jurisprudence of Constitutional Conflict' (n 97) 266–67. Kumm places Maduro's 'contrapunctual' conception of pluralism, discussed above in section III.B, under the '*sui generist*' rubric.

[186] WT Eijsbouts, L Besselink, J-H Reestman and JW Sap, 'Preface' (2005) 1 *European Constitutional Law Review* 1, 2.

[187] Walker, 'The Idea of Constitutional Pluralism' (n 32) 319–39.

[188] Kumm, 'The Jurisprudence of Constitutional Conflict' (n 97) 291.

[189] Kumm, 'Rethinking Constitutional Authority' (n 172) 54, emphasis added.

[190] Kumm, 'The Jurisprudence of Constitutional Conflict' (n 97) 301, emphasis added.

40   Constitutional Pluralism

[It] is not inherently superior to hierarchical constitutionalism. Whether it is or not itself depends on how potentially competing constitutional principles play out in particular contexts'.[191] Cosmopolitan constitutionalism therefore serves a dual purpose: it provides principles that allow us to determine, first, when heterarchy is preferable to hierarchy in the relations between legal orders; and, second, how the heterarchical relations should be structured in those cases where heterarchy is in fact preferable. Kumm summarises this dual function as follows:

> The refusal of a legal order to recognize itself as hierarchically integrated into a more comprehensive legal order is justified, if that more comprehensive order suffers from structural legitimacy deficits that the less comprehensive legal order does not suffer from. The concrete norms governing the management of the interface between legal orders are justified if they are designed to ensure that the legitimacy conditions for liberal-democratic governance are secured. In practice that means that there are functional considerations that generally establish a presumption in favour of applying the law of the more extensive legal order over the law of the more parochial one, unless there are countervailing concerns of sufficient weight that suggest otherwise.[192]

i. Interface Norms Under Cosmopolitan Constitutionalism

The interface norms of cosmopolitan constitutionalism are fourfold: 'the formal principle of *legality*, [the] jurisdictional principle[] of *subsidiarity*, the procedural principle of *democracy*, and the substantive principle of the *protection of basic rights or reasonableness*'.[193]

The keystone of these principles is legality, by which Kumm means that 'national courts should start with a strong presumption that they are required to enforce EU law, national constitutional provisions notwithstanding',[194] a presumption informed by the CJEU's (not at all unfounded) claim that any national review of EU norms would threaten the effective and uniform nature of those norms, and would undermine the entire scheme of the Treaties. Here we see the operationalisation of what we could call Kumm's ambivalence between hierarchy and heterarchy. As we saw in section I, the doctrines of primacy and direct effect were neither fashioned out of whole cloth nor sprung on unsuspecting Member States, and any deviation from their requirements must be justified.

The first principle that may justify such a deviation is subsidiarity, which provides a basis for national review in cases of unjustified EU usurpation of national competences. Writing in 2005, Kumm noted that:

> Much will depend on how the procedural and technical safeguards of the Constitutional Treaty will work in practice once the Treaty has been ratified. If the structural

---

[191] Kumm, 'Rethinking Constitutional Authority' (n 172) 65.
[192] ibid, emphasis removed.
[193] Kumm, 'The Jurisprudence of Constitutional Conflict' (n 97) 299, emphasis added.
[194] ibid.

safeguards will succeed in establishing a culture of subsidiarity carefully watched over by the Court of Justice, then there are no more grounds for national courts to review whether or not the EU has remained within the boundaries established by the EU's constitutional charter.[195]

Of course, the Constitutional Treaty never came into force, but the safeguards of which Kumm wrote are now to be found in the revised Subsidiarity Protocol and the new Protocol on the Role of National Parliaments.[196] There is a broad and deep literature on the subsidiarity principle,[197] which is beyond the scope of this book, but we can say with a degree of confidence that the 'culture of subsidiarity carefully watched over by the Court of Justice' spoken of by Kumm does not yet exist.

Kumm's second interface norm is the principle of democracy, or democratic legitimacy.[198] Of course, stated baldly like this, such a principle is far too broad to give us any guidance. Kumm therefore narrows down its implications:

> Given the persistence of the democratic deficit on the European level … national courts continue to have good reasons to set aside EU Law *when it violates clear and specific constitutional norms that reflect essential commitments of the national community.*[199]

The preference for the principle of legality, and thus the application of EU norms notwithstanding national specificities, is illustrated by the conditions Kumm attaches to the disapplication of EU norms under the principle of democracy: by 'clear and specific' he means that that the national norm in question 'has in fact been legislated by the constitutional legislator',[200] and not merely derived through interpretation by a constitutional court from an unclear or vague constitutional provision. Moreover, even if clear and specific, such a norm may not be a constitutional essential: a close analysis of the legislative history and public function of the norm would be necessary to establish whether it is in fact.[201]

---

[195] ibid 300.

[196] Protocol (No 1) on the Role of National Parliaments in the European Union [2010] OJ C 83/203 and Protocol (No 2) on the Application of the Principles of Subsidiarity and Proportionality [2010] OJ C 83/206.

[197] See A Estella, *The EU Principle of Subsidiarity and its Critique* (Oxford, Oxford University Press, 2002) and references therein. See further, G Davies, 'Subsidiarity: The Wrong Idea, in the Wrong Place, at the Wrong Time' (2006) 43 *Common Market Law Review* 63; M Kumm, 'Constitutionalising Subsidiarity in Integrated Markets: The Case of Tobacco Regulation in the European Union' (2006) 12 *European Law Review* 503; R Schütze, 'Subsidiarity after Lisbon: Reinforcing the Safeguards of Federalism?' (2009) 46 *Cambridge Law Journal* 525; X Groussot and S Bogojević, 'Subsidiarity as a Procedural Safeguard of Federalism' in L Azoulai (ed), *The Question of Competence in the European Union* (Oxford, Oxford University Press, 2014); GA Moens and J Trone, 'Subsidiarity as Judicial and Legislative Review Principles in the European Union' in M Evans and A Zimmermann (eds), *Global Perspectives on Subsidiarity* (Dordrecht, Springer, 2014).

[198] Kumm, 'The Jurisprudence of Constitutional Conflict' (n 97) 300.

[199] ibid, footnote omitted, emphasis in original.

[200] ibid 298, emphasis removed.

[201] ibid.

42   Constitutional Pluralism

The third and final interface norm is that of the protection of fundamental rights. As Kumm makes clear, this is essentially a recitation and condensation of the *Solange* doctrine of conditional recognition: 'If ... the guarantees afforded by the EU amount to structurally equivalent protections, then there is no more space for national courts to substitute the EU's judgment on the rights issue with their own'.[202]

As will by now be clear, all these justificatory interface norms are weighted towards the threshold principle of legality: taken in reverse, Kumm concedes that the EU's fundamental rights protection is (in general) structurally equivalent to that of the Member States; the requirements of clarity, specificity and essentiality heavily circumscribe the potential ambit of the principle of democracy; and the principle of subsidiarity is seen as being potentially self-extinguishing in the event that the EU develops a subsidiarity 'culture' overseen by the CJEU. Moreover, the principles of cosmopolitan constitutionalism are altogether more prescriptive as interface norms than those of contrapunctual law, which in turn were more prescriptive than the jurisgenerative mechanisms of Sabel and Gerstenberg. Maduro's requirements of pluralism, consistency and vertical and horizontal coherence, universalisability, and institutional choice – though they may guide a constitutional actor in shaping his or her institutional viewpoint, or in structuring his or her judgments – provide altogether less concrete guidance in cases of constitutional conflict. Though Kumm's principles of subsidiarity, the protection of clear, specific and essential national norms, and the protection of fundamental rights are not themselves step-by-step guides for resolving constitutional conflict, they do provide much firmer bases from which a judge faced with such a conflict could proceed. Whereas Maduro offers his principles as adjustments internal to each system, Kumm specifically posits his as the very same external, free-standing principles that Sabel and Gerstenberg (and Walker) believe not to be possible. However, what unites Kumm's and Maduro's theories is greater than that which divides them. They take as given Walker's explanatory claim of pluralism and are equally enthusiastic as to the normative desirability of such a configuration. Crucially, they both seek to extract or create, whether from historical legal practice or from first principles – or some combination of the two – a metaconstitutional frame for the management and resolution of conflict. For Kumm, this can be achieved by a set of jurisprudential principles separate from the competing legal orders, whereas Maduro focuses more on the internal rules that must be developed within the epistemic confines of each system, and Sabel and Gerstenberg emphasise the emergence of such rules through a cyclical dialogue.

But all these principles have another aspect, crucial for the present analysis: Kumm writes that his principles 'can be applied to the interpretation of

---

[202] ibid 299.

constitutions *in all Member States and the European legal order [itself]*.[203] Unlike Kumm, Maduro is not explicit on this point, but the universality of the principles of counterpoint is inherent in their very nature, particularly in the case of the principles of vertical and horizontal coherence, and universalisability. Contrapunctual law is a theory of EU law, and these are principles that, for Maduro, can be – and ought to be – put into effect throughout the Union. Sabel and Gerstenberg are less clear on the issue of universality. While on the one hand they regard the *Solange* principle as the shared (universal) means by which an overlapping consensus can be constitutionalised, they also expressly disclaim the possibility of there being any 'meta-criteria ... by which to harmonise all decision making',[204] preferring instead to rely on the jurisgenerative possibilities of inter-institutional dialogue. But the problem is that both '[a]greement on fundamentals'[205] and the *Solange* principle of conditional recognition are *themselves* 'meta-criteria', at the level of principle and procedure, if not at the level of specific application and substance.

For Kumm, this 'universal applicability'[206] of cosmopolitan constitutionalism and the interface norms thereunder is both a strength of the theory and a weakness. The weakness 'lies in the fact that it does not guarantee that the results such an interpretation leads to will be the same in every legal order'.[207] But this admission of non-universality as to result would seem at least partially to undermine the prior claim of universality as to application.[208] Moreover, in his development of the principles, Kumm does not cast his analytical net particularly widely, and the jurisprudence of the BVerfG and the text of the Grundgesetz are the primary resources from which he draws. In discussing clear, specific and essential national commitments, Kumm does mention the Greek Constitution's exclusive recognition of higher education from public, rather than private, institutions[209] and the Irish Constitution's (then) protection of the right to life of the 'unborn',[210] but does not go into detail. Sabel and Gerstenberg and Maduro develop their theories from a similarly restricted set of empirical bases. But can we draw such wide-ranging and far-reaching conclusions from analysing a relatively small number of possibly exceptional cases from a narrow range of jurisdictions? The question thus remains as to how universal these interface norms, and the metaconstitution they embody, really are.

---

[203] ibid 300.

[204] Sabel and Gerstenberg (n 136) 550.

[205] ibid.

[206] ibid, see also Kumm, 'Rethinking Constitutional Authority' (n 172) 54.

[207] Kumm, 'The Jurisprudence of Constitutional Conflict' (n 97) 300.

[208] Maduro writes of precisely the opposite happening, noting that the principles of contrapunctual law allow for incompletely theorised agreements, whereby actors may proceed from different bases but still come up with similar results (see section III.B.i above).

[209] Art 16, Greek Constitution (Kumm, 'The Jurisprudence of Constitutional Conflict' (n 97) 297).

[210] Art 40.3.3°, Irish Constitution; (Kumm, 'The Jurisprudence of Constitutional Conflict' (n 97) 297).

44 *Constitutional Pluralism*

IV. TWO PROBLEMS OF METACONSTITUTIONAL PLURALISM

Having set out these three conceptions of metaconstitutional pluralism, there are two important problems that must be addressed. The first is the claim first noted above in section II, that pluralism – and more specifically the epistemically open, metaconstitutional variants of pluralist constitutionalism – poses a threat to the concepts of legal certainty and legal integrity, and therefore to the rule of law. This is a serious charge and, as we are about to see, it is one I partially accept, but only because Walker's third claim (the inherent epistemic indeterminacy of constitutional pluralism) renders its off-the-shelf application *within* any given legal order problematic, if not impossible. However, the criticism is ultimately better regarded as *part of the analysis*, a factor that may lead us *in certain circumstances* to prefer a hierarchical conception of legal orders, rather than as a trump that leads us away from heterarchy in every instance: it tends to lead us towards pluralist constitutionalism. The second is the issue of the universality of interface norms, and, by extension, of the metaconstitution generally, which was adverted to throughout section III. While both these problems would be important in themselves in any circumstances, they have gained a new resonance and urgency in the febrile current state of constitutional politics within the Union, as we shall see.

A. The Rule of Law, Integrity and Epistemology

The most serious criticism of constitutional pluralism, and the most difficult to rebut, is the argument that by its inability or refusal to empower any one constitutional actor or order with the 'final say' in cases of irreconcilable conflict, constitutional pluralism undermines legal integrity, the rule of law and, by extension, democracy itself. This is a repeated criticism of the whole discourse on constitutional pluralism,[211] to the extent that rather than it being 'the dominant branch of constitutional thought',[212] as Jaklič would have it, Bobić's view, that criticism of constitutional pluralism 'is becoming as fashionable as the theory itself was at one time', seems closer to the mark.[213]

The most longstanding critic in this regard is again Baquero Cruz, who writes that:

> In law, pluralism enters into conflict with one of the main structural traits of legal systems as a tool of civilisation, which is order, security, predictability and certainty

---

[211] See P Eleftheriadis, 'Pluralism and Integrity' (2010) 23 *Ratio Juris* 365; Weiler, 'Prologue: Global and Pluralist Constitutionalism – Some Doubts' (n 46); Timmermans (n 41); Baquero Cruz, 'Another Look at Constitutional Pluralism in the European Union' (n 53); RD Keleman, 'On the Unsustainability of Constitutional Pluralism: European Supremacy and the Survival of the Eurozone' (2016) 23 *Maastricht Journal of European and Comparative Law* 136.

[212] Jaklič, *Constitutional Pluralism in the EU* (n 28) 6.

[213] Bobić (n 54) 1400.

in social and institutional relationships, in one's position, rights and obligations vis-à-vis the others ... If ... the law is excessively uncertain, then the legal system is not functioning correctly, and a structural precondition for a democratic constitutional order based on the rule of law would be lacking. In such circumstances even the best democracy would be unsustainable.[214]

This criticism must be taken seriously, for constitutional pluralism would be an unorthodox sort of constitutional theory if it leads, inexorably, to the destruction of the rule of law. Whereas Baquero Cruz's objection is a general one, operating at the level of basic principle, Daniel Keleman has more recently denounced the dangers of constitutional pluralism in the more specific and concrete context of the autocratic Hungarian government of Viktor Orbán, and its 'capture' of Hungary's Constitutional Court.[215] With the rise of governments similarly disrespectful of norms of constitutionalism in Poland, Italy and elsewhere, Keleman's belief that constitutional pluralism 'threatens to destroy the EU legal order'[216] sharpens the more general critique of Baquero Cruz, and must be taken just as seriously. There is no one, all-purpose rebuttal to the objections, but a number of points can be made.

First, the idea that pluralism – and more specifically, legal heterarchy – leads to the destruction of the rule of law, or of the Union legal order itself, because of the possibility of constitutional clashes ignores a large part of what we have seen pluralism, and in particular metaconstitutional pluralism, to be actually concerned with: the *avoidance* of such clashes. Baquero Cruz writes that pluralists

> do not seem to be concerned with the real everyday life of law, but only with the extraordinary and rather rare cases of disagreement. Their analysis takes for granted that the normative claims of Union law are generally effective, and that both systems routinely enter into radical contradictions – while the opposite is true: contradictions are rare, practice less than virtuous.[217]

But pluralism does not seek to justify national defiance of EU law resulting from the mere recalcitrance, backsliding or free-riding of the type described by Keleman. This sort of behaviour, all too common, is pathological, not constitutional. When the 'real everyday life of law' proceeds smoothly, it does not need to be theorised by constitutional pluralism: the CJEU's account of European constitutional supremacy suffices. When it does not, it usually ought to, and still does not necessarily need to be theorised by constitutional pluralism. But it is the cases of *principled* disagreement that interest the pluralist precisely *because*

---

[214] Baquero Cruz, 'Another Look at Constitutional Pluralism in the European Union' (n 53) 369–70. See also Baquero Cruz, 'The Legacy of the Maastricht-Urteil and the Pluralist Movement' (n 45) 417.

[215] RD Keleman, 'The Dangers of Constitutional Pluralism' in G Davies and M Avbelj (eds), *Research Handbook on Legal Pluralism in EU Law* (Cheltenham, Edward Elgar, 2018).

[216] ibid 392.

[217] Baquero Cruz, 'Another Look at Constitutional Pluralism in the European Union' (n 53) 369.

46 Constitutional Pluralism

they are extraordinary and rather rare, and the pluralist is interested not merely (and frequently not even) in *justifying* the disagreement, but in explaining it, resolving it and avoiding it in the first place. Moreover, this avoidance is not attempted through some rough-and-ready *modus vivendi* 'based on appeasement and institutional diplomacy',[218] but by a genuine attempt to determine – and give a sound theoretical basis to – the jurisprudential rules and the adjudicative principles whereby rupture is postponed indefinitely, in favour of a dialogic mutual articulation and resolution of difference. Keleman writes that pluralism 'may have been designed as a peaceful legal technology, but it is one that can be easily weaponized',[219] but this is equally true of constitutionalism itself: recall Walker's description of constitutionalism's susceptibility to ideological exploitation, whereby a whole array of widely divergent and conflicting political projects can 'clothe their interests, ideas or aspirations in constitutional garb',[220] not because of any shared principles or normative ideals, but purely as an instrumental effort to draw on the symbolic authority of constitutionalist discourse. The whole point of the metaconstitutional pluralisms outlined above is to try to provide or uncover the framework through which we can distinguish between principled disagreement (worthy of respect and careful attention), and unprincipled abuse of the very idea of constitutionalism.

Secondly, there is the possibility that, by regarding a hierarchical conception of the EU legal order as the only conceivable guarantor of predictability and stability, Baquero Cruz simply overstates his case. Kumm put this objection nicely:

> [T]he law is being disobeyed a lot of the time, in lots of systems, in lots of situations, by a lot of people. And it tends not to immediately lead into a civil war or anarchy. So, just as a sociological point, the practice of law tends to be pretty robust ... [I]t is difficult not be amused by the rhetoric of disaster, mutually assured destruction, complete disintegration etc. ... I never understood why only a monist construction of the legal world and an unqualified submission to the authority of law could conceivably save humanity from disaster.[221]

Less snappy, but somewhat more convincing, is Kumm's earlier analysis of what he calls the Cassandra and Pangloss scenarios.[222] If Baquero Cruz and Cassandra are correct, the review of EU norms by national courts leads to the Union devolving into a talking shop, abandoning any pretence at something more. Why engage in law-making if you know that your law will not be followed? Alternatively, if Dr Pangloss has his way, three substantial benefits would accrue to the Union as a result of acknowledging national court jurisdiction to review EU

---

[218] ibid.

[219] Keleman, 'The Dangers of Constitutional Pluralism' (n 215) 393.

[220] Walker, 'The Idea of Constitutional Pluralism' (n 32) 319 and 331–33.

[221] Kumm, quoted in Avbelj and Komárek, 'Four Visions (transcript)' (n 42) 29.

[222] Kumm, 'Who is the Final Arbiter of Constitutionality in Europe?' (n 170) 359–62.

norms. First, oversight by national courts might enhance the democratic quality of EU legislation and encourage more rigour in the CJEU's exercise of its own jurisdiction regarding Union competence and fundamental rights. Secondly, the horizontal discourse between state courts of the kind alluded to above by both Kumm and Maduro would become a reality. Thirdly, national courts could act as catalysts for a more informed public and enhanced popular debate on Union political issues. However, these possibilities are not conclusive: they are just that, possibilities. Moreover, they may be more applicable to the structurally 'looser', 'smaller-c'[223] setting of the relationship between the ECtHR and nation states: they do not address the core issue in the EU context that the EU is a legal system based on primacy and direct effect.

Baquero Cruz describes pluralism as a 'deforming lens that bars any future legal development in a non-pluralist direction'.[224] However, the same criticism could well be made in reverse: an insistence on a strictly hierarchical conception of the relationship between EU and national law might tend to act as a 'deforming lens', with its focus not on constitutional pluralism's quotidian aspect – that of conflict avoidance – but on the possible disaster scenario of total breakdown in communication and comity.[225] Nor, as Kumm has noted, is it necessarily the case that this is more likely under constitutional pluralism than under rigid hierarchical constitutionalism. The most significant fracture in the whole history of European integration – the UK's decision to leave the Union – did not arise from a legal dispute over *Kompetenz-Kompetenz*, rules of recognition, or some breakdown in the judicial management of overlapping claims to constitutional authority which could not be resolved or even papered over by politicians. Rather, it arose from the entirely false choice offered by its proponents between the recovery of a lost, insular, autonomous 'independence' on the one hand, and total submission to an overmighty, all-encompassing, 'sovereign' European Union on the other: precisely the two opposing, monist, national- or European-constitutional supremacist conceptions beyond which constitutional pluralism tries to move. To put it mildly, the Brexiteers are not constitutional pluralists.

The indeterminacy argument as a defence of the rule of law may well be an excellent reason not to become *too attached* to the heterarchical vision of constitutional relationships in Europe. Heterarchy is not always superior to hierarchy as a matter of principle, and may be less stable, but that does not necessarily make it inherently unstable, or too unstable to qualify as a legitimate conception of twenty-first century European constitutionalism. Stability, in this

---

[223] Walker, 'Big "C" or Small "c"?' (n 93).

[224] Baquero Cruz, 'The Legacy of the Maastricht-Urteil and the Pluralist Movement' (n 45) 417. Baquero Cruz directs his criticism here at what he calls radical pluralism, but it is clear from the context that his understanding of 'radical' pluralism is broader than the sense in which the term was used by MacCormick, and includes the metaconstitutional theories.

[225] See Keleman, 'The Dangers of Constitutional Pluralism' (n 215) 396–97 on 'exit [from the Union] as the proper remedy for irresolvable conflicts'.

48   *Constitutional Pluralism*

context, is a relative matter. Let us return momentarily to our earlier example of the rights to freedom of expression and to privacy coming into conflict within a single legal order. Prior to the judgment in that particular case being handed down, the heterarchical relationship between the two principles is inherently unpredictable. Neither party knows in advance who will win. Given their knowledge of the circumstances of the case, the general structure and tendencies of the legal system, and looking at the outcomes of previous cases, they may have some idea of how the issue will be decided and their relative chances of success, but all they know for certain is that the matter is arguable – and is being argued – both ways. But this unpredictability is not the same thing as instability, and neither does it threaten the integrity of the legal system as a whole, or its claim to protect both these important rights simultaneously and without contradiction. Again, something quite similar can be said regarding a conflict within a particular legal order between rules and principles each originating in different legal orders. The difference is that within our hypothetical state order, there is always an end point in sight: some actor or institution (a parliament, a supreme or constitutional court, the electorate etc) is endowed with the final say on the matter, and its answer, even when 'wrong', is always 'right' within the epistemic confines of the national order.[226] But within the metaconstitutional approaches outlined above, 'there is no final arbiter, and there should not be one'.[227] This explanatory and normative dismissal of the final say impels us to look again at the issue at the national level. To what extent is any final say really ever final? National apex courts can, and do, reverse earlier decisions. Constitutions can be amended to reverse earlier 'finalities', whether as the amendment's explicit purpose or by necessary implication. A more nuanced conception of the final say recognises the always and only ever *relative* nature of even the most authoritative decision. This element of temporal contingency is always present in the law but is usually unspoken. If I ask, 'what is the law in this area?', inherent in my question is the unspoken addendum: '*right now?*' I am not asking what the law was, nor what it may yet be, but by asking what the law currently is, I am not foreclosing the possibility of future change. My question is temporally closed, with its focus on the present, but this closure is relativised by my implicit acknowledgement that permanence in law is impossible. In recognising this only-ever relative nature of the final say, we can, at least in theory, open the way for a conception of constitutionalism less concerned with the achievement of *absolute* finality, and more concerned with keeping open the space for continued contestation, provided that the *relative* finality of agreement on certain principles is achieved. The question then becomes whether such a conception is in fact practical, a question which can only be answered in the light of lived experience.

---

[226] See Jackson J's aphorism in *Brown v Allen* 344 US 443, 540 (1953): 'We are not final because we are infallible, but we are infallible only because we are final'.
[227] Bobić (n 54) 1402.

The empirical studies in chapters two, three and four will therefore pay close attention to the lived experience of 'final' says in Europe, and better equip us to consider the matter further in chapter five.

Finally, the various metaconstitutional species of pluralism outlined here go far beyond simple reliance on (judicial) politics: they are not just jurisprudential frameworks for the management and avoidance of conflict but ask us (or, less explicitly but more commonly, lead us) to reconsider our fundamental notions of constitutionalism, identity, ownership and belonging: precisely the sort of discourse which Jaklič finds lacking in all but Weiler's writing, and precisely the sort of discourse which is emphatically *not* engaged in by the politically captured Hungarian Constitutional Court of which Keleman writes. It is too broad, then, to apply to all the various theories of constitutional pluralism – both the constitutionally pluralist and the plurally constitutionalist, the radical and the metaconstitutional – the charge that the rule of law will inexorably be damaged.[228] Such concern *may well* cause us to move towards and settle upon a conception of the relationships which is *more constitutionalised* – or, in the metaconstitutional frame, it may cause us to attach significant weight to the importance of the EU doctrines of primacy and direct effect – but this does not necessarily collapse us back to the former world of rigidity and hierarchy. It merely reminds us that we are dealing with serious matters and should not be too keen to throw off decades or even centuries of experience in seeking to make better sense of the modern world. The criticism can then be reconceived in its most useful form: not as a trump, which forces us back into old ways of thinking, but as a necessary and important part of the analysis in seeking to explain, theorise and justify the present constitutional configuration in Europe.

These problems of predictability, stability and integrity arise because they are inherent in the fact that constitutional pluralism began as a specifically and inescapably *external* discourse. By this I mean that it was epistemologically situated *outside* any given legal system. In order to view the inter-systemic legal order as a whole, constitutional pluralism must of necessity be unmoored from and unconstrained by the requirements of any one system.

By way of analogy, we can liken any given constitutional order to a camp fire in a night-time forest clearing. When we are 'doing' constitutional law in any capacity, whether as judge, politician, practitioner, plaintiff, scholar, or citizen, we are sitting around the constitutional camp fire, engaged in conversation. The fire itself is the focus of our attention, and its brightness blinds us to our surroundings. We know that there are other camp fires in nearby clearings; we know how to get to those clearings if we need to; but the conversations around those camp fires are different, and we cannot hear them from here. Similarly, when we are epistemically situated *within* a legal order, the logic and integrity

---

[228] For a defence of an explicitly radical conception of pluralism from the criticism from the rule of law, see Krisch, *Beyond Constitutionalism* (n 41) 276–85.

50   *Constitutional Pluralism*

of that legal order blinds us, not to the existence, but at least to the requirements and specificities of other legal orders.

When we engage in pluralist discourse, we do *not* sit around the camp fire – the light is too bright. Instead, we take a step back; we let our eyes adjust to the gloom; and we peer out from the undergrowth. Now, we can keep an eye on the surrounding forest. We can see all the camp fires, we can see people leaving one camp fire to go and join the conversation in the next clearing, and then returning with what they have learned. We are epistemically situated *outwith* any legal order, and are thus not bound by the logic, rules or doctrine of any order. This is neither a strength nor a weakness, but a structural necessity. As a result, no infra-systemically situated constitutional actor – whether judge, politician, administrator or citizen – can *be* constitutionally pluralist. A given judgment, policy, decision, belief or statement may be more or less 'pluralist' in a thin sense, in the extent to which it recognises, accommodates or welcomes the plurality (or multiplicity) of legal systems at work within the European legal panoply, but this is already determined by or contingent upon the particular structure and orientation of the legal system within which the actor is situated, along with the actor's own legal and political conception of the proper relationship between the systems.

This epistemic indeterminacy is not even a problem in this freestanding context, because our vantage point is itself indeterminate in the first place. We simply recognise the incommensurable authority claims and try to manage them. It is when we zoom in to any one order, when we enter the clearing and sit around the camp fire and attempt to put constitutional pluralism to work *within* that order, that indeterminacy becomes a problem, and a serious one.

To give a concrete example, a national supreme court judge may render a judgment which is more or less 'open' or 'closed' with respect to the relationship between the national constitution, the EU and the ECHR. We may step outside the legal system and subject the judgment to a constitutionally pluralist analysis. But regardless of how integrationist or insular the judgment, it will be (because it must be) a judgment generated from *within* the national constitutional system, and therefore bounded by the logic internal to that system. To speak of constitutional pluralism in this context is to make a category error: regardless of openness or closure, a national supreme court judgment cannot be constitutionally pluralist – it can only be constitutional.

If this is the case, then in order to become operationalised within any given legal order, and to do so in a workable way, respectful of legal integrity, constitutional pluralism must be able epistemically to both anchor itself and unmoor itself at will. It must become both an external *and* an internal discourse. It must 'zoom in', emerge from the undergrowth, enter the clearing and sit at the camp fire, while reserving the right and the ability to 'zoom back out', and return to the forest with what it has learned. As we shall soon see in section V, triangular constitutionalism attempts to do just this.

B. The Universality of Interface Norms

We saw, in section III, the different conceptions of interface norms under the various models of metaconstitutional pluralism. Fittingly, though the conceptions differed – from Sabel and Gerstenberg's evolutive, dialogic account of the emergence of interface norms through the jurisgenerative mechanism of the *Solange* principle, through Maduro's modification of the attitude and self-images of judicial actors, to Kumm's more prescriptive account of specific adjudicative principles – there is something of an 'overlapping consensus' present in the literature, for example, regarding the importance of the mutual recognition of each system's autonomy or of the *Solange* principle of conditional recognition.

In particular, however, we saw the claim that these interface norms, whatever form they may take, are universal in their applicability. This claim was an explicit feature of the work of Kumm,[229] but was also an inherent part of the theories of Maduro and Sabel and Gerstenberg. Problematically, all these writers draw on similar sources in developing their notions of metaconstitutional pluralism – the jurisprudence of the CJEU, the ECtHR and (especially) the BVerfG – but without focusing much attention on how the specific, contingent relationships between the judicial actors in question may have influenced the choice and application of interface norms in a given case. In this regard, Alexander Somek writes that '[i]t is indeed a quite remarkable fact about European constitutional theory that in its most visible form it scarcely amounts to more than a series of glosses on lengthy opinions by the German Federal Constitutional Court'.[230] While this probably goes too far, the fact remains that the entire discourse of constitutional pluralism draws far-reaching conclusions, ostensibly applicable across the entire European constitutional configuration, from a rather restricted set of premises. This problem is relevant in two dimensions. First, 'horizontally', (and as we shall see in chapter three) it is arguable that the relationship between the CJEU and the ECtHR is perhaps more hierarchical in nature than is sometimes thought, even without the EU's (stalled, but still legally required) accession to the Convention.[231] Moreover, pending and even after this accession,[232] states

---

[229] Kumm, 'The Jurisprudence of Constitutional Conflict' (n 97) 300; see also Kumm, 'Rethinking Constitutional Authority' (n 172) 54.

[230] A Somek, 'Monism: A Tale of the Undead' in M Avbelj and J Komárek (eds), *Constitutional Pluralism in the European Union and Beyond* (Oxford, Hart Publishing, 2012) 346.

[231] See B de Witte, 'The Use of the ECHR and Convention Case Law by the European Court of Justice' in P Popelier, C Van de Heyning and P Van Nuffel (eds), *Human Rights Protection in the European Legal Order: The Interaction Between the European and National Courts* (Cambridge, Intersentia, 2011) 22; HCH Hofmann and BC Mihaescu, 'The Relation Between the Charter's Fundamental Rights and the Unwritten General Principles of EU Law: Good Administration as the Test Case' (2013) 9 *European Constitutional Law Review* 73 (and references therein). See also K Lenaerts, 'Exploring the Limits of the EU Charter of Fundamental Rights' (2012) 8 *European Constitutional Law Review* 375, especially 384–86.

[232] On the issue of EU accession to the Convention, see Opinion 2/13 *Accession of the European Union to the European Convention for the Protection of Human Rights and Fundamental Freedoms* ECLI:EU:C:2014:2454; L Besselink, M Claes and J-H Reestman, 'Editorial: A Constitutional

52   *Constitutional Pluralism*

are interim actors in this relationship: important sites of constitutional power through which the relationship between the two European courts is mediated. Does this extra element change the choice and application of interface norms in a given case of conflict between legal orders? Secondly, 'vertically', there is the question of the relative strength and importance of each national polity within the broader legal orders, EU or ECHR, notwithstanding the formal principle of equality between states. The BVerfG, the jurisprudence of which is of foundational importance to metaconstitutional pluralism, is a particularly powerful constitutional actor in a particularly powerful European state. Can doctrines, toolkits, keywords, rules and principles developed largely with reference to its jurisprudence be transplanted, unchanged, right across the European polyarchy? The approach of this book is to bring more empirical grist to the theoretical mill. Its focus on the triangular relationship between Ireland, the EU and the ECHR allows for a more sustained analysis of the interaction between these orders in a specific jurisdictional context and configuration, and brings to the forefront the questions of universalism and jurisdictional contingency which the literature on constitutional pluralism to date has tended to downplay or ignore altogether. MacCormick wrote that '[t]he settled, positive, character of law is jurisdiction-relative ... Moral judgments, however personal and controversial, are not in this way relativistic ... These judgments apply universally'.[233] But the kinds of issues at play in the various conceptions of interface norms – Kumm's concern for democratic legitimacy, Maduro's principle of universalisability as a safeguard against free-riding, Sabel's and Gerstenberg's secular, self-reinforcing dialogue on fundamental rights – are frequently both legal and moral in nature. Are they, and should they, therefore be universal or particular in their formulation, in their application, in both, or in neither? Walker notes that in the development of his ideas of constitutional pluralism, 'MacCormick was searching for some notion of a unity of law standing beyond particular legal systems, but a unity which was not conceivable in terms of a new system to which the original legal systems would inevitably become subordinate'[.][234] Precisely the

---

Moment: Acceding to the ECHR (or Not)' (2015) 11 *European Constitutional Law Review* 2; T Lock, 'The Future of the European Union's Accession to the European Convention on Human Rights after Opinion 2/13: Is it Still Possible and is it Still Desirable?' (2015) 11 *European Constitutional Law Review* 239; S Peers, 'The EU's Accession to the ECHR: The Dream Becomes a Nightmare' (2015) 16 *German Law Journal* 213; D Halberstam, '"It's the Autonomy, Stupid!" A Modest Defense of Opinion 2/13 on EU Accession to the European Convention on Human Rights' (2015) 16 *German Law Journal* 105; P Gragl, 'The Reasonableness of Jealousy: Opinion 2/13 and EU Accession to the ECHR' in W Benedek, F Benoît-Rohmer, W Karl and M Nowak (eds), *European Yearbook on Human Rights 2015* (Vienna, Neuer Wissenschaftlicher Verlag, 2015); M Scheinin, 'CJEU Opinion 2/13 – Three Mitigating Circumstances' (*Verfassungsblog*, 26 December 2014), available at: www.verfassungsblog.de/cjeu-opinion-213-three-mitigating-circumstances/.

[233] MacCormick, *Questioning Sovereignty* (n 1) 14–15, citing N MacCormick, 'Comment [on G Postema's "The Normativity of Law"]' in R Gavison (ed), *Issues in Contemporary Legal Philosophy* (Oxford, Clarendon Press, 1987).

[234] N Walker, 'Reconciling MacCormick: Constitutional Pluralism and the Unity of Practical Reason' (2011) 24 *Ratio Juris* 369, 379.

same thing could be said of the metaconstitutional pluralists under discussion here. Walker notes – and discounts – one method by which this unity could be achieved: the 'covering-law universalism' of Michael Walzer,[235] which entails 'a version of legal unity so strong, so insistent on subordinating the local and particular to the epistemic and moral authority of the global and universal, that it does not countenance internal differentiation and division at all'.[236] A more justifiable possibility is Walzer's 'reiterative universalism'[237] where:

> [T]here is a general or universal quality to the norms that integrate the pluralist configuration. Yet the articulation of these common norms is not seen as a matter of simply 'reading off' the local version from some inert universal covering-law. Rather, it is a continuous and progressive process of recontextualization in which the universal is not just realized but also reshaped by the particular.[238]

My hypothesis is that interface norms under metaconstitutional pluralism are not universal, but rather context dependent. The intention in the chapters that follow is similar to Walzer's reiterative universalism: to apply a model of metaconstitutional pluralism to specific examples of constitutional conflict in Europe and to see whether, and how, these ostensibly universal interface norms can be 'not just realized but also reshaped by the particular'.

V. TRIANGULAR CONSTITUTIONALISM

A. The Triangular Constitution as a Composite Constitutional Polyarchy

This book takes, as its field of study, the legal orders of Ireland, the EU and the ECHR. Each of these legal orders makes valid – though differing – claims as to its own specifically *constitutional* nature. These constitutional orders also overlap significantly, both territorially and jurisdictionally. The explanatory hypothesis of this book is that if we are to speak meaningfully, the reified thought-object known in Ireland as 'the Constitution' is not just the national constitution, but rather the *Gestalt* of the national constitution, the Convention and the legal order of the EU taken together: a simultaneously fragmentary yet indivisible composite whole. The point holds when we shift our viewpoint from the Irish legal order to that of the EU or the ECHR: the European legal orders cannot be analysed in isolation, but only with simultaneous reference to each other and the national orders by which they are constituted. I will seek to demonstrate that the relationship between these three orders is interactive and dialogic, and

---

[235] M Walzer, 'Nations and Universe' in D Miller (ed), *Thinking Politically: Essays in Political Theory* (New Haven, CT, Yale University Press, 2007) 187.
[236] Walker, 'Reconciling MacCormick' (n 234) 379.
[237] Walzer (n 235) 184.
[238] Walker, 'Reconciling MacCormick' (n 234) 380.

54   Constitutional Pluralism

may manifest itself in given cases hierarchically or heterarchically, depending on the specific circumstances, and without such a specific manifestation necessarily being externally generalisable to the relationship between the orders as a whole, for all time. This holistic, composite constitutional construct is presented in this book as the *triangular constitution*, where the legal orders themselves form the vertices of the triangle, and the relationships and interactions between them constitute the triangle's sides. This constitution is *triangular* because the composite panoply of State, Union and Convention is a deliberative polyarchy in Sabel and Gerstenberg's sense, based on incompletely theorised agreements and overlapping consensus, each of the legal orders having normative authority within their own domains, each of them recognising the authority of the others (but not necessarily on the terms set by those others), and without any of them having entirely subsumed themselves under the authority and logic of any of the others, or depending on the others for their validity. And the triangle is *constitutional* because the orders each make claims – thinner or thicker, weaker or stronger, 'big C' or 'small c' – as to their own specifically constitutional nature. Where the model breaks with that of Sabel and Gerstenberg is in its conception of interface norms. Whereas Sabel and Gerstenberg expressly disclaim the possibility of there being any 'meta-criteria ... by which to harmonise all decision making',[239] preferring instead to rely on the jurisgenerative possibilities of inter-institutional dialogue (a distinction I have argued above to be problematic), I instead leave that question open while undertaking the analysis that follows. This agnosticism allows the model to comprehend and probe the conceptions of interface norms under cosmopolitan constitutionalism and contrapunctual law as well as the principle of overlapping consensus. Being the most prescriptive account in the literature, and the one in which the claim to universality is at its most explicit and its most central, the work of Kumm will be at the heart of the enquiry. Moreover, though Kumm and Maduro's theories were specifically developed within the context of the EU–Member State relationship, imagining the triangular constitution as a deliberative polyarchy allows us to broaden the analysis to include the Convention system while still encompassing and comprehending the interface norms formulated within that bilateral relationship, and enables us to investigate the extent to which these norms – and, conceivably, others as yet unidentified – may also play a part in the State–Convention and Convention–Union relationships.

A fundamental and distinctive feature of this composite polyarchy is its asymmetry. First, all of the three constitutional sites in the polyarchy partially differ from each other and also partially overlap, in their nature, structure, origins, tendencies, functions, and purpose. Secondly, and as a result of this, each order within the polyarchy relates to the others in different ways, *in a*

---

[239] Sabel and Gerstenberg (n 136) 550.

manner determined by each order for itself. Crucially, when we situate ourselves *at* one of the points of the triangle – when we 'zoom in', sit around the camp fire, and assume an epistemic viewpoint embedded within *one* of the legal orders (which I shall call the reference order), the logic of that order, and the integrity of law, *obliges* us to accept its ultimate authority. The fact that this ultimate authority may not be recognised (or at least may not be recognised in the same way or on the same terms) by the other orders may be, but is not necessarily, an embarrassment: the possibility of incompletely theorised agreements, of achieving coherent outcomes by divergent means, is entirely consistent with the logic of European integration, and as we shall see, does not necessarily have to lead to a breakdown in the integrity of the legal order(s). Leaving the question of the final say open may in fact make such a breakdown *less* likely, by providing exactly the space for contestation necessary for disputes to be resolved, and the animating tension necessary to drive competing actors towards resolution.

When the Irish constitutional order is the reference order, the national constitution is the foundation on which all else is built. If the EU and the ECHR were to vanish overnight, the Irish Constitution and legal system would still stand (albeit with gaping holes which would need to be patched, as the United Kingdom is now in the process of learning). The same is true in every Member State. But the converse is not true: within each Member State, the EU and the ECHR depend on the national legal order for their authority, enforceability and legitimation. If there were no national constitutions, then there would be no European legal orders. But the national constitutional orders are not self-contained. Rather, they are intricately linked with the European orders. A vast swathe of what we can properly call *Irish* law (that is, law having effect within Ireland, enforced by the Irish State, and which bestows rights and obligations on Irish citizens) has its origin outwith the domestic legal order. Moreover, though the national courts retain their interpretive authority over the national constitution, interpretive authority over the other two sources of what we can properly call Irish *constitutional* law rests with the CJEU and the ECtHR. In short, viewed in this holistic way, the Irish constitutional system does not operate, and cannot be analysed, in isolation.

When the EU is the reference order, the Treaties are the foundation. The fact that the Treaties are international agreements between sovereign states is neither here nor there: the Union has long since lost its international law milk teeth, and makes consistent and justifiable claims to autonomy and autochthony. While it is true that if there were no Member States there would be no Union, the specific means by and manner in which the state constitutions recognise, empower and (occasionally) police the competences of the Union are, from the central Union perspective, irrelevant. The legislative and/or constitutional provisions by which the Member States give effect to EU law within their legal orders vary widely in their form, effect and the extent of their conditionality, and none of this concerns the EU, so long as the efficacy, consistency and uniformity of EU law are ensured.

56 *Constitutional Pluralism*

With the Convention as the reference order, things differ again, and, being the least state-like of the three points of the triangle, they differ more significantly than when the EU or Ireland is the reference order. Though the ECtHR refers to the Convention as 'a constitutional instrument of European public order',[240] it has never made (because it could never make) the same kind of thick claims to constitutionalism as the EU. It does not claim to be an order based on direct effect and primacy, and the ECtHR frequently stresses the subsidiary and supervisory nature of its jurisdiction.[241] But this merely alters, rather than lessens, the constitutional credentials of the Convention system, and highlights how deeply it is intertwined with the constitutional systems of the signatories.

B. From the Triangular Constitution to Triangular Constitutional*ism*

Such is the asymmetric, composite, polyarchical structure of the triangular constitution. In the coming chapters, I will seek to demonstrate that this explanatory framework, built on the epistemic pluralism of Walker and the metaconstitutional pluralisms that share its epistemic claim, is a descriptively accurate way of explaining and conceptualising the constitutional landscape in one particular corner of Europe. But in the tradition of the second of Walker's three claims, this book also seeks to demonstrate that this triangular conception is in fact normatively preferable to any competing explanation. Then, beyond the specific triangular constitution of Ireland, the EU and the ECHR, this book seeks to go further still, and to develop, from the triangular constitution as an explanatory framework, a normative theory of triangular constitutional*ism*, capable, with the necessary modifications, of application as a general framework right across the Member States.

Triangular constitutionalism is a species of metaconstitutional pluralism. As with the theories of Sabel and Gerstenberg, Maduro, and Kumm outlined above, it takes constitutionalism, rather than pluralism, as its starting point. It acknowledges the need for the empowerment of certain public institutions in order to achieve certain public goals; the need for these institutions to be restrained in the exercise of these powers in order to protect certain public goods; and the need for both this empowerment and this restraint to be subject

---

[240] *Loizidou* (n 84) para 75.
[241] For a recent example, see *Chiragov v Armenia* App no 13216/05 (judgment, ECtHR, 16 June 2015) para 115: '[I]t is primordial that the machinery of protection established by the Convention is subsidiary to the national systems safeguarding human rights. The Court is concerned with the supervision of the implementation by Contracting States of their obligations under the Convention. It cannot, and must not, usurp the role of Contracting States whose responsibility it is to ensure that the fundamental rights and freedoms enshrined therein are respected and protected on a domestic level'.

to a continual public discourse of justification. It aims for reason over arbitrariness, and certainty over chance: it is a theory of constitutionalism, both within and beyond the (non-)state. But where it becomes pluralised is in its refusal, outlined above, to insist on a unitary model of 'the constitution'; or on the spatial differentiation of spheres of jurisdiction along Westphalian lines; or on the empowerment of a single actor with the final say over questions of constitutional conflict. Quite the contrary, it specifically recognises and embraces the observable fact that in each Member State of the EU, there are three interlocking, overlapping legal orders at work, each of which can be described as being constitutional, to greater or lesser degrees, and each of which, within its own domain, reserves – and ought to reserve – the final say to itself. Starting with the baseline normativity of the desirability of having a descriptively accurate understanding of the constitutional universe, triangular constitutionalism goes further, and proposes that, at least in certain circumstances, a heterarchical relationship between the constitutional orders is itself normatively desirable, most notably for its tendency to remedy the ill of constitutional *solipsism*, whether national or European. Its simultaneous embrace of *different* approaches, by *other* people, serves as a constant reminder to actors within each constitutional order that they owe responsibilities to the other orders, which, in turn, owe responsibilities to them. In this regard, triangular constitutionalism is not only a way of conceptualising the relationships between constitutional orders externally, but also of conceptualising – and refining – each order itself, internally. In discouraging constitutional solipsism, triangular constitutionalism seeks to broaden and pluralise the discourse, opening up and keeping open avenues of contestation beyond the particularist, and constantly reminding each order and the actors within each order that theirs is not the only way of seeing the world, and nor should it be.

Triangular constitutionalism accepts the reference order's ultimate authority within its own domain: the final say rests with the reference order, whichever that order that may be. This may solve the problem of integrity *within* each order, but not *between* them. It therefore does not solve the question of workability: if, say, a national order disapplies a norm of EU law, this may be acceptable from the national perspective but almost certainly not from the EU perspective. It is through the *deliberative* nature of the polyarchy, and the *temporally unlimited* nature of the discourse, that conflict between the orders is to be avoided, managed and resolved. No actor, externally, has the final say, precisely because no say is ever final. It is in the interactions between the legal orders that we see how each 'final' say is made, rebutted, refined, withdrawn, or – possibly – accepted by competing actors, in a mutual, cyclical attempt to do constitutional justice. Let us therefore turn from the points of the triangular constitution to its sides.

The relationships between Ireland, the EU and the ECHR have changed over time, due to Treaty and constitutional amendment, judicial (re)interpretation

58 *Constitutional Pluralism*

of the constitution(s), and legislative changes. We can parse these relationships into two 'vertical' frames and one 'horizontal' frame.[242] The 'vertical' frames are the relationships between Ireland and the EU on the one hand, and Ireland and the ECHR on the other. The 'horizontal' frame is the relationship between the EU and the ECHR. As we have seen, the metaconstitutional pluralisms of Kumm and Maduro seek to posit in advance certain rules-about-rules for the management of these relationships and of any conflicts that may arise. We also saw that Sabel's and Gerstenberg's approach differs, and focuses on the temporal element, the ongoing (and potentially permanent) dialogue between sites in the polyarchy. It uses the *Solange* device of conditional recognition as 'a master framework for creating other frameworks and with them the necessity and methods for establishing mutual regard of constitutional traditions';[243] a 'de-nationalised precedent for de-nationalising precedents, which, loosened from their moorings in national constitutional tradition, can become part of the overlapping consensus'.[244] These are the interface norms, metaconstitutional rules-about-rules – whether posited in advance or generated through a deliberative process – which are the heart of metaconstitutional pluralism.

This is where triangular constitutionalism departs from its metaconstitutional siblings. It is highly sceptical the claim of interface norm universality. The particular, substantive interface norms employed by the judicial actors at each site in the polyarchy in regulating the relationships between the different systems vary in their nature, from the legislative (for example, national acts incorporating the Convention, such as the European Convention on Human Rights Act 2003 in Ireland), through to the constitutional (for example, the means by which most Member States, including Ireland, authorise EU membership) to the metaconstitutional (most notably variations on the interface norm of conditional recognition). While we might well expect sub-constitutional and constitutional interface norms – being creatures of their own legal systems – to lean away from the universal, and towards the historically contingent and jurisdictionally specific, this tendency also applies with respect to the metaconstitutional interface norms employed: they will differ depending on jurisdiction, subject matter and much else. It is perfectly permissible and possible to posit broad, freestanding categories into which the various norms applied in regulating the relationships between legal orders in a polyarchy, and avoiding and resolving conflict between them, may fall. Such taxonomies are important and useful in helping us to analyse these inter-order relationships. However, the fundamental problem is that these categories are just that – categories, rather than substantive action-guiding rules or principles. For the actual rules or principles that regulate the relationships between legal orders – the substantive interface norms

---

[242] 'Horizontal' and 'vertical' are in quotes here to indicate that they are being used as heuristic devices only and imply no concession to hierarchy.
[243] Sabel and Gerstenberg (n 136) 545.
[244] ibid.

at work – we must assume a viewpoint internal to the reference order, and take into account its own constitutional text and its own particular *telos*. But when we do this, the norms cease to be metaconstitutional, and are so far evolved from their abstract, external description that they are incapable of universal, internal application. When we then zoom back out of a particular legal order, and attempt to metaconstitutionalise the particular constitutional interface norms at work, we lose precisely what it was that made those norms useful in the first place, and are left back with mere categories, not norms.

What triangular constitutionalism requires, therefore, is for close and systematic attention to be paid to jurisdictional specificity, at all three points of the triangle. By focusing on all three orders simultaneously, triangular constitutionalism can provide a more coherent account of their interactions than an account that focuses only on the 'vertical' (Maduro, Kumm) or mostly on the 'horizontal' (Sabel and Gerstenberg). In the 'horizontal' frame, the relationship between the EU and the ECHR is totally unlike that between the European orders and the various state orders. It is also a relationship that has changed over time and, regardless of whether and how the current impasse in the process of EU accession to the Convention is resolved, will continue to change. In the 'vertical' frames, there is not one triangular constitution, but rather 28 (soon to be 27) of them. There are therefore not two but 56 different 'vertical' relationships, given that each European state relates to the EU and ECHR legal orders in different ways. This being the case, triangular constitutionalism as an explanatory and normative theory is a general conceptual framework, but is not an overarching, one-size-fits-all, unified theory of European constitutionalism. Concretised at the level of application, there are 30 different triangular constitutions. This book attempts to map only one of them. But it is only with a full, holistic understanding of how each legal order relates to the others *in fact* that we can begin to answer the question of whether such a mixture of legal hierarchy and heterarchy is descriptively accurate, legally workable and normatively desirable.

2

The Vertical Frame

INTRODUCTION

THIS CHAPTER PARSES the relationships between the legal orders of the triangular constitution in the 'vertical' frame: the two sides of the triangle that deal with the relationship between state and non-state legal orders. As explained in chapter one, a central concern of this analysis is the universality or otherwise of metaconstitutional interface norms, but this question – and the broader question of the normative desirability of constitutional heterarchy – cannot be engaged with (let alone answered) without first demonstrating that the explanatory claim of the triangular constitution, the conception of the three legal orders as being part of a deliberative polyarchy, is in fact accurate. Accordingly, along with a discussion of interface norms, this chapter also aims to demonstrate the validity of such a conception, and will proceed in two major parts, one for each side of the vertical frame.

Section II seeks to set out the precise means by which the Irish constitutional order was 'opened' to that of the EU. In arguing for a non-hierarchical conception of the relationship between these two orders, it examines two instances of the national constitutional review of EU norms – ex post and ex ante – and engages in a preliminary analysis of the nature of the interface norms employed.

Section III performs the same function with respect to the interplay between the Irish legal order and that of the European Convention on Human Rights (ECHR), setting out its evolution from being a standard dualist relationship between national and international legal orders to something potentially more integrated and interactive.

The chapter concludes by suggesting that the relationship between the national system and both European systems is best regarded as being heterarchical; that the three systems form part of a tripartite, composite, constitutional whole; and that rather than being simple applications of the universal metaconstitutional interface norms posited by Mattias Kumm and Miguel Poiares Maduro, or developing interactively over time as posited by Charles Sabel and Oliver Gerstenberg, the norms that regulate the relationships between the orders are frequently *constitutional* or *legislative* in nature. That is, they are conflict-of-laws rules internal to the national legal system, and particular to that system. Whether (and how) they can be *metaconstitutionalised* – transplanted from their

The Terms of Engagement Between Irish Law and EU Law   61

national site of origin, departicularised, and made relevant to different national sites in the polyarchy – remains, at this stage of the analysis, an open question.

I. THE TERMS OF ENGAGEMENT BETWEEN IRISH LAW AND EU LAW

A. Incorporating EU Law in Ireland

i. A Closed Legal Order

The classical story of the constitutional evolution of the EU was recounted in chapter one. Quite aside from that narrative of judicial constitutionalisation, the Communities consisted from the very beginning of various institutions – an Assembly (later a Parliament), a Council, a Commission and a Court – which were to exercise very real normative power of a legislative, executive, administrative, or judicial character, necessarily implying the delegation or transfer of some aspects of these powers from national institutions to those of the Communities. As originally enacted in 1937, the Irish Constitution contained a number of provisions which would complicate – if not definitely exclude – membership of an international organisation of the scale, depth and breadth of the Communities and their later incarnations.[1]

First is the general issue of the source of constitutional authority, and the identity of those entitled to exercise it. Article 6 of the Constitution states that:

> All powers of government, legislative, executive and judicial derive, under God, from the people, whose right it is to designate the rulers of the State and, in final appeal, to decide all questions of national policy, according to the requirements of the common good.[2]

Having identified 'the people' as the source of all constitutional power[3] and having invoked tripartite separation of powers theory to divide the powers of government into the legislative, executive and judicial, Article 6.2 goes on to state that '[t]hese powers of government are exercisable only by or on the authority of the organs established by this constitution'. The particular institutions invested with governmental power are specified in later Articles, following the tripartite scheme. As regards the legislative power, Article 15.2.1° vests the 'sole and exclusive power of making laws' in the Oireachtas; Article 28.2 vests the executive power in the government, subject to the other provisions of the Constitution; and Article 29.4.1° vests the executive power insofar as it relates to external

---

[1] DR Phelan, *Revolt or Revolution: The Constitutional Boundaries of the European Community* (Dublin, Round Hall Sweet & Maxwell, 1997) 330–31. Note that the numbering of some provisions of both the Constitution and the Treaties has changed since the enactment of the Constitution and since Ireland's accession to the Union in 1972/73. For the sake of clarity, the current numbering will be used throughout.

[2] Art 6.1.

[3] Let us leave the role of God to one side as essentially unknowable.

62   *The Vertical Frame*

relations in the government in accordance with Article 28. Articles 34–37 – grouped under the heading 'The Courts'– deal with the judicial function, providing that '[j]ustice shall be administered in courts established by law by judges appointed in the manner provided by this Constitution'.[4] They establish a High Court with 'full original jurisdiction in and power to determine all matters and questions whether of law or fact, civil or criminal';[5] a Court of Appeal with a general appellate jurisdiction from the High Court;[6] and a Supreme Court as the court of final appeal, whose decisions 'shall in all cases be final and conclusive'.[7] Finally, there is the Constitution's dualist attitude to international law, Article 29.6 providing that '[n]o international agreement shall be part of the domestic law of the State save as may be determined by the Oireachtas'.

As will be clear, a dualist national constitutional scheme of this sort is essentially 'closed' in nature. It identifies 'the people' as the source of all governmental authority; vests the exercise of that authority in named institutions set up by the Constitution itself; and makes the domestic applicability of international law conditional on the specific incorporation of that law into the national legal system by the national legislature. A self-contained and self-referential normative order such as this is essentially incompatible with the autonomous and autochthonous jurisgenerative power of the Communities, as they then were. It was therefore clear that some form of amendment to the Irish Constitution would be necessary to 'open' the constitutional order in order to allow for Community membership.

ii. Opening the Legal Order: A Three-Pronged Approach

Accession to the Communities was achieved, and EC law made domestically effective, by three legal mechanisms: a constitutional 'licence to join', a constitutional 'exclusion clause', and a legislative measure giving effect to EC law within the jurisdiction.[8] Each of these will be set out in turn.

The first two were contained within the Third Amendment of the Constitution Bill 1972, which proposed the insertion into the Constitution of the following provision, originally as Article 29.4.3°:

> The State may become a member of the European Coal and Steel Community ..., the European Economic Community ... and the European Atomic Energy Community ... *No provision of this Constitution invalidates laws enacted, acts done or*

---

[4] Art 34.1.
[5] Art 34.3.1°.
[6] Art 34.4.
[7] Art 34.5.6°.
[8] Contemporary accounts of the instruments of accession are given in J Temple Lang, 'Legal and Constitutional Problems for Ireland of Adhesion to the EEC Treaty' (1972) 9 *Common Market Law Review* 16; and M Robinson, 'The Irish European Communities Act 1972' (1973) 10 *Common Market Law Review* 352.

The Terms of Engagement Between Irish Law and EU Law   63

measures adopted by the State necessitated by the obligations of membership of the Communities or prevents laws enacted, acts done or measures adopted by the Communities, or institutions thereof, from having the force of law in the State.

The first sentence of the Third Amendment has been termed the 'licence to join',[9] and has repeatedly been updated by referendum in order to enable the ratification of subsequent EU treaties.[10] The second sentence – italicised above – has been termed the 'constitutional exclusion clause',[11] and is now to be found on its own in Article 29.4.6°.[12] The Third Amendment Bill was passed by both Houses of the Oireachtas, triggering a referendum in accordance with the terms of Article 46.[13] This was held on 10 May 1972, and was approved by 83 per cent of the electorate, on a turnout of 71 per cent.[14]

The third provision enabling membership was the European Communities Act 1972 (ECA 1972), a short piece of ordinary legislation. Section 2 provided, in full, that:

From the 1st day of January, 1973, the treaties governing the European Communities and the existing and future acts adopted by the institutions of those Communities shall be binding on the State and shall be part of the domestic law thereof under the conditions laid down in those treaties.[15]

---

[9] *Crotty v An Taoiseach* [1987] IR 713, 756 (Barrington J).

[10] As the Constitution now stands, Art 29.4.3° authorises membership of Euratom; Art 29.4.4° states that 'Ireland affirms its commitment to the European Union within which the member states of that Union work together to promote peace, shared values and the well-being of their peoples'; Art 29.4.5° authorises ratification of the Lisbon Treaty and membership of the EU established thereunder; and Art 29.4.10° authorises ratification of the Treaty on Stability, Coordination and Governance in the Economic and Monetary Union (the Fiscal Stability Treaty (FST)).

[11] M Cahill, 'Constitutional Exclusion Clauses, Article 29.4.6°, and the Constitutional Reception of European Law' (2011) 18 *Dublin University Law Journal* 74, 78.

[12] The text of the exclusion clause has been updated to take into account the expiry of the European Coal and Steel Community (ECSC) and the depillarisation of the EU, but its meaning and effect have not been materially affected. Another exclusion clause, materially identical, is contained in Art 29.4.10° in relation to the FST. Accordingly, the analysis of Art 29.4.6° in this chapter applies with equal force to Art 29.4.10°.

[13] Art 46 sets out the only procedure by which the Constitution may be amended, 'whether by way of variation, addition or repeal' (Art 46.1), and requires a popular referendum, with a simple majority of votes cast for the amendment to be approved.

[14] *Referendum Results 1937–2015* (Department of Housing, Planning, Community and Local Government, Dublin 2016), available at: www.housing.gov.ie/sites/default/files/migrated-files/en/Publications/LocalGovernment/Voting/referendum_results_1937-2015.pdf. It is worthwhile to note, in relation to the issue of democratic legitimacy that informs much of Kumm's conception of cosmopolitan constitutionalism – and, more generally, the normative resistance of metaconstitutional pluralism to the wholesale primacy of EU law – that this was the second highest turnout in a referendum in Ireland's history, beaten only by the 76% turnout in the referendum on adopting the Constitution itself in 1937. Moreover, in 1937, the Constitution was approved by only 57% of those voting. Accordingly, in 1937, only 39% of the total electorate endorsed the Constitution, whereas, in 1972, fully 58% of the total electorate voted in favour of accession to the Communities – a fact rarely remembered in debates surrounding the Union's democratic legitimacy in Ireland. (Percentages have been rounded to the nearest whole figure.)

[15] The ECA 1972 has been repeatedly amended as the Communities and Union have developed, but the meaning and effect of s 2, mutatis mutandis, remains the same.

64   *The Vertical Frame*

Taken together, these three provisions enabled the direct and full-throated incorporation of Community law into the domestic legal order. The ECA 1972 performed the substantive legwork of making EC law domestically effective within a dualist system, backed up by a constitutional authorisation for membership of the Community, and a clause which ostensibly sought to immunise EC law from constitutional scrutiny. It might therefore appear that constitutional pluralism of any sort, and any heterarchical conception of the power relations between domestic and EU constitutional orders, is simply inapt for describing the Irish constitutional configuration. On this analysis, the three-pronged method of accession simply subsumed Irish constitutional law within the mantle and the logic of the Treaties, and that is all there is to it. Indeed, as we shall soon see, this has been the long-standing orthodoxy in Ireland, particularly as regards the 'exclusion clause' of Article 29.4.6°.

But the reality is altogether more complex. A close reading of the 'licence to join' and the 'exclusion clause' – and the case law surrounding them – suggests that a monist reading of the relationship is inaccurate; provides an opening for a pluralist analysis of the terms of engagement between the legal orders; and, more than this, demonstrates that a polyarchic arrangement is in fact a more convincing way of conceptualising these relations, and is normatively preferable. In developing his theory of contrapunctual law, outlined in chapter one, Maduro identified two different types of national constitutional challenge to the claim to ultimate authority made by European constitutionalism: first, there is the ex ante constitutional review of EU norms, especially including Treaty amendments.[16] Though the particular way in which such a review is conducted varies widely throughout the Union, '[t]his is effectively required by all national legal orders with regard to Treaty changes'.[17] Secondly, there is the altogether more controversial ex post national constitutional review of EU norms,[18] epitomised by the *Solange* jurisprudence of the German Federal Constitutional Court, the Bundesverfassungsgericht (BVerfG). This occurs in different ways and to greatly varying degrees across the Union, depending on the existence of mechanisms of constitutional judicial review, the status ascribed to the EU by the national constitution, and the attitudes of national constitutional courts.[19] This typology fits well with the case law on the 'authorisation' inherent in Article 29.4.3° and the 'exemption' suggested by Article 29.4.6°, and will therefore be used to examine the nature of the relationship between the Irish Constitution and EU law, and the nature of the interface norms – constitutional and metaconstitutional – regulating the relationship.

---

[16] MP Maduro, 'Contrapunctual Law: Europe's Constitutional Pluralism in Action' in N Walker (ed), *Sovereignty in Transition* (Oxford, Hart Publishing, 2003) 506–08.

[17] ibid 506.

[18] ibid 508–11.

[19] ibid.

B. The 'Licence to Join' and the ex ante Review of EU Norms

We have seen that Ireland's initial accession to the EU was backed up by an impressive expression of popular constitutional authorisation. However, if we are to take seriously the argument that 1 January 1973 was a watershed, after which provisions of the Irish Constitution could never outweigh the exigencies of European integration, it would follow that subsequent Treaty amendments would be entirely within the initial popular authorisation for EU membership. However, *Crotty v An Taoiseach*,[20] 'the only case solely dedicated to an analysis of the constitutional problems posed by membership',[21] provides convincing evidence for the proposition that *at least prior to the coming into force* of EU norms, the question of the compatibility of these norms with the Irish Constitution cannot be ignored or papered over. Accordingly, there remains at the very least a residual or gatekeeping role for national constitutionalism, and the argument of all-purpose subordination to EU law is weakened. From the internal perspective of a (dualist) national constitutional order, a non-state legal order that relies on national constitutional law for its validity cannot in any meaningful sense be considered hierarchically superior in normative terms.[22]

Crotty, an Irish citizen, sought an injunction restraining the Irish Government from finalising the ratification of the Single European Act (SEA); a declaration that the European Communities (Amendment) Act 1986 (which purported to make the SEA domestically effective) was repugnant to the Constitution; and a declaration that ratification of the SEA without a constitutional amendment would be in breach of the Constitution. The injunction was initially granted by the High Court, but upon full hearing of the issues, the Court discharged the injunction and the plaintiff's relief was denied. The plaintiff immediately appealed, and had his injunction re-granted pending the hearing. It was finally held by the Supreme Court that the 1986 Act was not repugnant to the Constitution.[23] However, while the Supreme Court held unanimously that the courts have no jurisdiction to interfere with the government's conduct of foreign policy, it went on to hold – by a 3:2 split[24] – that in any case where the government, in conducting foreign policy, purported to alienate any powers of

---

[20] *Crotty v An Taoiseach* [1987] IR 713 (*Crotty*).

[21] Phelan (n 1) 335.

[22] Maduro (n 16) 507–08.

[23] This part of the judgment was unanimous, and without dissenting opinions, as was required under the circumstances by then Art 34.4.5°: 'The decision of the Supreme Court on a question as to the validity of a law having regard to the provisions of this Constitution shall be pronounced by such one of the judges of that Court as that Court shall direct, and no other opinion on such question, whether assenting or dissenting, shall be pronounced, nor shall the existence of any such other opinion be disclosed.' This 'one-judgment rule' has since been removed from the Constitution by the Thirty-third Amendment of the Constitution Act 2013 (which established the Court of Appeal). A separate one-judgment rule still exists at Art 26.2.2°, in relation only to the constitutionality of Bills referred to the Supreme Court by the President under that Article.

[24] Then Art 34.4.5°'s unanimity requirement not applying, as this issue did not concern the constitutionality of a statute.

66   *The Vertical Frame*

government or fetter the sovereignty of the State, such purported action would be beyond the power conferred upon the government by the Constitution. On this basis, the majority held that the State's purported ratification of Title III of the SEA[25] was outwith the executive powers of the government in the sphere of external relations, and thus was void without specific constitutional licence to ratify, which could be achieved only by referendum. The issues of the constitutionality of the 1986 Act and Title III SEA will be dealt with in turn.[26]

i. Domestic Reservation of Ultimate Constitutionality by Conditional Recognition: The European Communities (Amendment) Act 1986

The 1986 Act purported to amend the ECA 1972 to make domestically effective certain provisions of the SEA, all of which consisted of amendments to the Treaties of Paris and Rome. Because the State was explicitly authorised to ratify these Treaties by the electorate in 1972, the question was therefore whether the licence to join of Article 29.4.3° entitled the State to ratify the Treaties as they stood in 1972, but not to ratify any subsequent treaties without a further constitutional amendment (as the plaintiff alleged); or, as the government claimed, whether it entitled the State:

> [T]o join Communities which were established by Treaties as dynamic and developing entities and that it should be interpreted as authorising the State to participate in and agree to amendments of the Treaties which are within the original scope and objectives of the Treaties.[27]

The Court agreed in essence with the State's argument, and in a passage much subsequently quoted, held that:

> [Article 29.4.3°] must be construed as an authorisation given to the State not only to join the Communities as they stood in 1973, but also to join in amendments of the Treaties *so long as* such amendments *do not alter the essential scope or objectives of the Communities*. To hold that [Article 29.4.3°] does not authorise any form of amendment to the Treaties after 1973 without a further amendment of the Constitution would be too narrow a construction; to construe it as an open-ended authority to agree, without further amendment of the Constitution, to any amendment of the Treaties would be too broad.[28]

Straightaway, we can see from the words italicised an – unreferenced – application of the *Solange* principle of conditional recognition. The Supreme

---

[25] Entitled 'Treaty Provisions on European Co-operation in the Sphere of Foreign Policy', the forerunner of the Common Foreign and Security Policy.

[26] It was not contended, and the Court held it to be clear, that ratification of the SEA – which, despite its name, was an international treaty between states referred to using the public international law terminology of 'High Contracting Parties', and not an infra-Community measure agreed upon between fellow Member States (*Crotty* (n 20) 784 (Henchy J)) – was not an act 'necessitated by the obligations of membership of the Communities': therefore we need not consider the 'exclusion clause' of Art 29.4.6° for present purposes (ibid 767 (Finlay CJ per curiam)).

[27] *Crotty* (n 20) 767 (Finlay CJ).

[28] ibid, emphasis added.

The Court chose a middle path between the outright denial or wholesale embrace of the evolutionary nature of the EC legal order. The acceptability of EC constitutional evolution to the national constitutional order was made conditional, and the Court reserved to itself the power to determine the breach or fulfilment of the substantive condition that the 'essential scope or objectives of the Communities' not be altered. The Court therefore conducted its own analysis of the SEA, the Treaties and the 1986 Act, without (direct) reference to the jurisprudence of any other court, including the Court of Justice of the European Union (CJEU).

The plaintiff alleged four areas where the 1986 Act went beyond what was permissible under Article 29.4.3°. First, a shift in the Council's voting procedures in six areas from unanimity to a qualified majority was alleged to be an unauthorised surrender of sovereignty.[29] Second, the establishment of the then Court of First Instance was said to be an unauthorised surrender of judicial power.[30] Third, the SEA added five new objectives to the EEC Treaty, allegedly taking it outside the terms of the initial authorisation of 1972.[31] Finally, the SEA gave the Council new powers relating to the provision of services, the working environment and the health and safety of workers 'which could encroach on existing guarantees of fundamental rights under the Constitution'.[32]

In its decision, the Court noted that:

> The capacity of the Council to make decisions with legislative effect is a diminution of the sovereignty of Member States, including Ireland, and this is one of the reasons why the Third Amendment to the Constitution was necessary. Sovereignty in this context is the unfettered right to decide: to say yes or no.[33]

However, the Court went on to note that whereas unanimity was a 'valuable shield'[34] against proposals the State might oppose, qualified or simple majority voting was of significant assistance with respect to proposals the State might support. Moreover, the EC Treaty itself already contemplated that decision-making in various areas would initially be unanimous, but would, over time, require only a qualified majority.[35] Accordingly:

> The Community was thus a developing organism with diverse and changing methods for making decisions and an inbuilt and clearly expressed objective of expansion and progress, both in terms of the number of Member States and in terms of the mechanics to be used in the achievement of its agreed objectives.[36]

---

[29] *Crotty* (n 20) 768.

[30] ibid.

[31] ibid. The new objectives added by Arts 20–21 and 23–25 SEA concerned economic and monetary policy; the health and safety of workers; economic and social cohesion; research and technological development; and environmental protection.

[32] *Crotty* (n 20) 768.

[33] ibid 769.

[34] ibid.

[35] ibid.

[36] ibid 770.

68　*The Vertical Frame*

The changes envisaged by the SEA as regards the Council's voting procedures were therefore neither unforeseeable nor unjustifiable and did not go beyond what had initially been authorised in 1972. The plaintiff's other objections fell on similar grounds, the Court noting that some of the judicial power of the State had been ceded to the CJEU by virtue of Ireland's accession to the Communities, and that the establishment of what is now the General Court was an internal reorganisation of power already ceded, and did not involve any further cession of power.[37] Though the SEA's separate and specific statement of various objectives was indeed an innovation, they were within the original objectives of the Communities, as set out in Articles 2 and 3 EEC.[38] Moreover, the Council's new powers did not 'alter the essential character'[39] of the Communities, and the plaintiff had not shown that they could threaten fundamental constitutional rights.[40] Within the hermetically sealed boundaries of Irish constitutional law, the changes to the Treaties effected by the SEA were held not to alter substantially the scope or objectives of the Communities, and accordingly, the 1986 Act, which incorporated those changes into domestic law, was constitutional.

This first part of the judgment in *Crotty* shows that it is for the Irish courts, and none other, to determine what does and does not constitute the essential scope and objectives of the Communities, and later the Union, as a matter of Irish law. Two consequences flow from this as regards the powers of the domestic judiciary vis-a-vis EC/EU law. As Diarmuid Rossa Phelan notes, if the Community law interpretation of the scope and objectives of the Community were to go beyond that of Irish law, 'then the European Communities Act (as amended) would be open to constitutional challenge so far as it purports to import into domestic law a rule which goes beyond the Irish constitutional law version'.[41] Second, acts or measures of Community law or implementing Community law which go beyond the Irish interpretation of the scope and objectives would not be 'necessitated' within the meaning of Article 29.4.6°, and would therefore prima facie be vulnerable to Irish constitutional attack, regardless of how one interprets Article 29.4.6°. It is submitted that despite the changes that have taken place since Phelan first proposed this analysis, his logic stands.[42]

Before moving on from the 1986 Act, there is another aspect of the decision which is important for present purposes, because it relates to the acceptance or otherwise of the CJEU's doctrine of primacy, and therefore to the question of hierarchy and heterarchy. The headnote to the case report of *Crotty* states that 'the proposed new Court of First Instance did not in any way extend the

---

[37] ibid.
[38] ibid.
[39] ibid.
[40] ibid.
[41] Phelan (n 1) 337.
[42] See further M Cahill, 'A Critical Assessment of Irish Scholarship on the Constitutional Reception of European Law' in T Mohr and J Schweppe (eds), *Thirty Years of Legal Scholarship* (Dublin, Roundhall, 2011) 244–46.

The Terms of Engagement Between Irish Law and EU Law   69

primacy of the [CJEU] over the Irish Courts beyond that already authorised in [Article 29.4.3°]'.[43] But nowhere in the relevant part of the judgment did the Supreme Court advert to the EU legal concept of primacy.[44] Instead, according to the Court, the CJEU was established 'to ensure that in the interpretation and the application of the Treaty the law is observed'[45] – a simple recitation of what is now Article 19 TEU. Furthermore, the Court only recognised the finality of the CJEU's jurisprudence insofar as it relates to the interpretation of the Treaty and on questions of its application as a matter of EU law. Recognising the CJEU's authority to interpret the Treaty is hardly a recognition of the absolute primacy of its judgments over those of national courts. Just as the only bodies competent to interpret the Irish Constitution authoritatively are the High, Appellate and Supreme Courts established thereunder – and specifically empowered to do so and for that interpretation to be final as a matter of Irish law – the CJEU is the only body competent to interpret the Treaties authoritatively, and to have its interpretation taken as final. This in no way amounts to the all-purpose subordination of one legal system to another – rather, it is a good example of exactly the sort of arrangement described by heterarchy. It stretches the Court's judgment – which at this point did not even refer to any cases of the CJEU, let alone *Costa v ENEL*[46] or *Internationale Handelsgesellschaft*[47] – past breaking point to regard the above as a wholesale endorsement of the CJEU's conception of primacy, regardless of what the headnote to *Crotty* may say. For judicial endorsement of the *Costa* jurisprudence, as we shall see in section I.C, one must look elsewhere.

ii. 'Penultimate Judicial Supremacy' and the Boundaries of Government Action: Title III of the SEA

Though the plaintiff was unsuccessful in challenging the constitutionality of the 1986 Act, the claim that Title III of the SEA could not be ratified without a referendum was upheld. The Court was in total agreement that Article 29.4.1° vests in the government the executive power of the State in connection with its external relations, and that the conduct of this power is outwith the purview of the courts (in that the courts have no foreign policy role or voice whatsoever). However, Article 29.4.1° specifically states that this foreign policy power is to be exercised *in accordance with Article 28*, which provides, at Article 28.2, that '[t]he executive power of the State shall, *subject to the provisions of this Constitution*,

---

[43] *Crotty* (n 20) 714–15.

[44] Curiously, the only mention of 'primacy' in the relevant part of the case is with regard to the Council, 'whose decisions have primacy over domestic law' – a statement made in passing, and without reference to authority (ibid 769).

[45] ibid 769 (Finlay CJ per curiam).

[46] Case 6/64 *Flaminio Costa v ENEL* ECLI:EU:C:1964:66, [1964] ECR 585.

[47] Case 11/70 *International Handelsgesellschaft mbH v Einfuhr- und Vorratsstelle für Getreide und Futtermittel* ECLI:EU:C:1970:114, [1970] ECR 1125.

70   *The Vertical Frame*

be exercised by or on the authority of the Government'.[48] For the majority of the Court, the portion of Article 28.2 emphasised above was sufficient to impart to the government, along with the *right* to conduct the State's foreign policy without judicial interference, the *obligation* not to go beyond what is permissible with respect to the totality of the Constitution. The threshold question of what is and is not permissible with respect to the Constitution is then a matter for the courts exclusively.[49] This idea was put most succinctly by Hederman J, whose brief judgment contains a neat *précis* of the majority's reasoning:

> The State's organs cannot contract to exercise in a particular procedure their policy-making roles or in any way to fetter powers bestowed unfettered by the Constitution. They are the guardians of these powers – not the disposers of them.[50]

According to the reasoning of the majority, Title III of the SEA obliged the State, and each ratifying State, 'to surrender part of its sovereignty in the conduct of foreign relations',[51] which, in Ireland's case, directly went against the claims to the sovereignty of the nation and of the State in Articles 1 and 5 of the Constitution. Furthermore, according to Henchy J's reading of Article 6.1, 'the common good of the Irish people is the ultimate standard by which the constitutional validity of the conduct of foreign affairs by the Government is to be judged'.[52] For the State to be bound to 'take full account' of the common positions of the Member States, as provided for by Title III of the SEA, was therefore enough of a derogation from the 'ultimate standard' of the common good of the Irish people to render the State's purported ratification of Title III of the SEA null and void, in the absence of a new 'licence to join' along the lines of that in the Third Amendment, which could only be provided by the people by way of referendum. Thus, the coming into force of the SEA was delayed pending such referendum, which was held in May 1987 and was carried by a large majority, albeit on a turnout of only 44 per cent.[53]

This part of the judgment in *Crotty* demonstrates that the system of authority under the Irish Constitution can be regarded as one of 'penultimate judicial supremacy'. The reason that this judicial supremacy is 'penultimate', rather than final, is that the final say on each matter is reserved to the citizens themselves, acting in concert, by way of referendum. However, let us recall the suggestion in chapter one of the only-ever *relative* nature of this 'final' say. Just as later court judgments can reverse earlier ones, so too can particular popular 'constitutional moments' be reversed by later such 'moments', as we shall see in chapter three. With this in mind, even the use of the word 'penultimate' here must be qualified.

---

[48] Emphasis added.
[49] *Crotty* (n 20) 778 (Walsh J); 786 (Henchy J).
[50] ibid 794 (Hederman J).
[51] ibid 787 (Henchy J).
[52] ibid.
[53] *Referendum Results* (n 14) 43.

The Terms of Engagement Between Irish Law and EU Law   71

This system of penultimate judicial supremacy is only penultimate within any given iterative cycle of constitutional deliberation, and the 'finality' of a decision of the Supreme Court must be qualified by its susceptibility to later judicial or popular reversal, which later reversal is itself qualified by the ongoing and always incomplete nature of the processes of constitutionalism.

Though the Constitution provides for a wide degree of autonomy for and separation between the legislative, executive and judicial powers, it is the judicial power that is charged with the penultimate defence of the Constitution. The judiciary may not interfere with the legislative process while it is ongoing,[54] but may rule on the constitutional validity of legislative norms once enacted.[55] Equally, the judiciary has no role or voice in the government's exercise of its foreign policy powers, except for a residual, threshold power to prevent the government 'fetter[ing] powers bestowed unfettered by the Constitution'. Whatever its merits and demerits – and no doubt there are many – this strong judicial power is the long-established orthodoxy in Ireland, as evidenced by the foundational statement of Ó Dálaigh CJ in *The State (Quinn) v Ryan*:

> It was not the intention of the Constitution in guaranteeing the fundamental rights of the citizen that these rights should be set at nought or circumvented. The intention was that rights of substance were being assured to the individual and that the Courts were the custodians of these rights. As a necessary corollary it follows that no-one can with impunity set these rights at nought or circumvent them, and that the Court's powers in this regard are as ample as the defence of the Constitution requires.[56]

A necessary corollary of this, taken in conjunction with the Constitution's amendability by way of referendum, is that if the citizenry believes the judiciary to have been *wrong* in its defence of the Constitution, that decision can be reversed and corrected by popular vote. Of the 38 constitutional referendums held in Ireland under the 1937 Constitution, 10 have been in direct or indirect response to judicial decisions,[57] with some endorsed and others reversed.

iii. Analysis: Conditional Recognition, 'Scope and Objectives' and the Attitude of the Court

The overview above has demonstrated that *Crotty* provides an exemplar of Maduro's first leg of the national legitimation of EU law: ex ante constitutional review. The question of the compatibility of the European Communities (Amendment) Act 1986 with the Constitution was a matter solely of Irish law

---

[54] *Wireless Dealers' Association v Fair Trade Commission* (unreported, Supreme Court, 14 March 1956); *Roche v Ireland* (unreported, High Court, 17 June 1983).

[55] The one exception to this is the procedure under Art 26, where the legislative process is still technically 'ongoing', the impugned Bill not yet having been signed into law by the President. However, the parliamentary leg of the process is, by this stage, complete.

[56] *The State (Quinn) v Ryan* [1965] IR 70, 122.

[57] Updated from *Referendum Results* (n 14).

72 *The Vertical Frame*

and was therefore apt for review by an Irish court without reference to other authorities ('higher' or otherwise). The government's attempt to ratify Title III of the SEA without consent was, under the accepted Irish theory of the separation of powers, subject to the control of the judiciary, and ultimately the electorate. These facts go some of the way towards demonstrating that the Irish and EU legal orders can be regarded as part of a heterarchical polyarchy – each order having ultimate authority on its own terms in its own domain – rather than being hierarchically integrated.

The substantive interface norm adopted by the Supreme Court with respect to the 1986 Act was the principle of conditional recognition subject to the 'scope and objectives' test, a standard noted by Phelan to be 'extremely vague ... the essential scope of the Community is far from clear, and what can come under its objectives is potentially limitless'.[58] Vague or otherwise, what is important is that this is a norm *internal to the Irish legal order*. This manifests in two senses. First, rather than being an overarching (metaconstitutional) rule, straddling legal orders and managing the relationships between them, it is a conflict-of-laws rule generated purely from within the national system. It is in this sense *constitutional*, not *meta*constitutional. Secondly, and relatedly, because this is a norm particularly and logically within the domain of Irish law, it is subject to the 'final' say of domestic constitutional actors.[59] The question of the legitimacy of the government's purported ratification of Title III of the SEA was similarly internal in nature.

Let us recall that Kumm posits the principle of conditional recognition as a universal, metaconstitutional interface norm justifying the disapplication of EU norms in the face of deficient protection for fundamental rights, whereas Sabel and Gerstenberg regard the principle as a more general doctrinal tool by which an overlapping consensus can be constitutionalised. Neither of these descriptions quite captures the Court's decision here, however, though the notion of conditional recognition as a doctrinal tool comes closest. The question of fundamental constitutional rights had been raised by the plaintiff, but the Court merely pointed out that no threat had been identified, and therefore engaged in no enquiry as to whether the EC legal order was equipped to guard against such a threat. Rather, the Court's concern – though expressed in both parts of the judgment in the language of sovereignty, defined as the unfettered right to decide – was *democratic legitimacy*. Accession to the Communities, and the diminution of sovereignty that this entailed, had been democratically authorised. With respect to the 1986 Act, the principle of conditional recognition was therefore employed as a means by which the Community legal order could, if necessary, be prevented from going beyond this authorisation without further recourse to the electorate. With respect to Title III of the SEA, the focus was

---

[58] Phelan (n 1) 336.
[59] ibid 336–67.

The Terms of Engagement Between Irish Law and EU Law   73

similarly on democratic legitimacy, but here conditional recognition played no role – rather, the government, in purporting to ratify Title III of the SEA without a referendum, had strayed beyond the bounds of the authority in foreign affairs granted to it by the Constitution.

Being a rule internal to a national system, the 'scope and objectives' test, though having democratic legitimacy as its central concern, does not fit with Kumm's conception of democratic legitimacy as a metaconstitutional interface norm capable of universal application – the protection of a 'clear and specific constitutional norm that reflect[s] essential commitments of the national community'.[60] It is clear from the examples Kumm gives – the former protection of the right to the life of the 'unborn' in Ireland and the non-recognition of private higher education in Greece[61] – that, by this, he meant an instance of national constitutional specificity, something particularly important in one state, which does not necessarily have echoes in other European constitutional orders. While it may well be possible to construct a retrospective argument that the Supreme Court was protecting the 'clear and specific' constitutional norm of Article 6 of the Constitution – its reservation to the people of the ultimate right to decide all questions of national policy – the Court framed its arguments in altogether more general terms. Moreover, there is nothing nationally specific about the Irish Constitution's claim of popular sovereignty. Rather, the 'scope and objectives' test derives from the particular, historically contingent means by which the Irish legal order had been opened to that of the Communities, and the legitimacy of the ratification of Title III of the SEA depended solely on how the Irish Constitution confers authority on the executive.

The Irish Supreme Court is a national court, and as such is obliged to operate within the terms of the national constitution. As was noted in chapter one, constitutional pluralism, by contrast, is a specifically external discourse. This being the case, the question then arises whether the internal, nationally specific approach of the Supreme Court in *Crotty* can be 'metaconstitutionalised' – that is, explained in more general, universal terms, from a perspective outwith the national legal system. In his discussion of the ex ante review of EU norms, Maduro notes the variety of ways that Member States deal with the issue: an express requirement in the constitutional text for national ratification of any 'constitutional amendment' of the EU;[62] the imposition of substantive conditions regarding the content and manner of the transfer of sovereignty;[63] and the imposition of conditions relating to other constitutional values and rules.[64] In terms of the decision in *Crotty*, the second of these categories describes the

---

[60] M Kumm, 'The Jurisprudence of Constitutional Conflict: Constitutional Supremacy in Europe Before and After the Constitutional Treaty' (2005) 11 *European Law Journal* 262, 300.

[61] ibid 297.

[62] Maduro (n 16) 506–07, citing the constitutions of Italy (Art 11); Spain (Art 93 ff); Belgium (Art 34); Germany (Art 23); Denmark (Art 20); Portugal (Art 7); and the Netherlands (Art 92).

[63] ibid 507, citing Denmark (Art 20); Sweden (Art 5); Austria (Art 92); and Belgium (Art 25).

[64] ibid, citing the *Maastricht* decisions of the French, German and Spanish courts.

74 The Vertical Frame

scope and objectives test, and the third describes the judicial oversight of the government's exercise of its foreign policy. However, these various methods of national oversight of EU constitutional development are so generally phrased, and subject to such diversity in their application, that they bear little resemblance to the clearly specified, narrowly delimited universal metaconstitutional interface norms posited by Kumm, or the open-ended, discursive development of trans-systemic interface norms described by Sabel and Gerstenberg. It may well be the case that any attempt to zoom out from a national constitutional order in order to formulate universal principles by which the ex ante review of EU norms could be conducted results in 'principles' so wide in their statement and general in their application that they cease to be in any way action-guiding and instead become broad categories, encompassing different, potentially conflicting approaches. Let us bear this thought in mind for now, before returning to it in considering the question of ex post constitutional review in section II.C.

While the specific principles that the Supreme Court applied in *Crotty* are deeply embedded in the text and nature of the Irish Constitution, the Court's general attitude to the autonomy of EC law does fit very well with one of Maduro's principles of contrapunctual law: the principle of pluralism itself, whereby different legal orders must expressly acknowledge the existence and autonomy of their counterparts, which 'entails the recognition and adjustment of each legal order to the plurality of equally legitimate claims ... made by other legal orders'.[65] The Court described the Community as 'a developing organism with diverse and changing methods for making decisions and an inbuilt and clearly expressed objective of expansion and progress'.[66] The metaphor nicely illustrates the great extent to which the Court was prepared to recognise the ('organic') growth of the Community, and, by holding that this growth was still within the initial 'licence to join' of 1972, to adjust the domestic constitutional order to accommodate it. But whereas the Court's decision fits well with one of the principles of contrapunctual law, it is much less in line with another: the principle of universalisability. In the High Court, counsel for the defendants in *Crotty* had specifically invited the Court to 'have regard to the fact that its decision will affect not only Ireland, but the other Member States of the European Communities as well, of which the total population affected comprises 300 million'.[67] Nowhere in their judgments did the High Court or Supreme Court Justices take counsel up on his suggestion, preferring, as I have shown, to regard themselves as purely domestic actors, and to treat the issues as being those of exclusively domestic law. There is a curious tension between this solipsism and the earlier recognition of the 'organic' nature of the Community, particularly as regards its expansion, which the judgment leaves unresolved.

---

[65] ibid 526.
[66] *Crotty* (n 20) 770.
[67] ibid 723 (Eoghan Fitzsimons SC for the defendants).

In *Crotty*, the impugned legislation and Treaty provisions had not yet come into force, and were thus not yet 'immunised' from review by the exclusion clause of Article 29.4.6°. If one believes that the exclusion clause of Article 29.4.6° is in fact *completely* exclusionary, ex ante constitutional review can be seen as a kind of once-off, 'last-chance-saloon' jurisdiction. Difficult questions of normative effectiveness and democratic legitimacy can be answered once, but only once, and consent once granted can never be withdrawn without complete withdrawal from the Union.[68] This can cause great difficulty in cases of subsequent, unforeseen constitutional conflict, and raises questions about just how exclusionary the exclusion clause can – or should – be. The resounding popular endorsement of 1972, and the less impressive but no less effective endorsements of 1986 and later, certainly provide a democratic basis for the effectiveness of EU law in Ireland, but they raise deep questions about the very nature of constitutions and constitutional law, and the temporal difficulty of regarding any given 'say' as 'final': once power has been democratically delegated, how and under what circumstances can it be reclaimed if necessary, and who decides when it *is* necessary? With these questions in mind, let us turn to Article 29.4.6°, and the second, much more controversial leg of Maduro's two conceptions of national constitutional challenge: the ex post national constitutional review of EU law.

C. The 'Exclusion Clause' and the ex post Review of EU Norms

i. Ripples and Torpedoes

Article 29.4.6° is a remarkable constitutional provision. At first blush, it seems to subordinate the entirety of the Irish Constitution to Union law without exception. Indeed, it would seem to do this at the second and subsequent blushes as well: Maria Cahill notes that this criticism was levelled at the amendment by a Labour Deputy during the Third Amendment Bill's passage through the Dáil,[69] and cites some statements from the bench that are supportive of this idea: in *Meagher v Minister for Agriculture*,[70] for example, Blayney J stated that '[i]t is well established that Community law takes precedence over our domestic law. Where they are in conflict, it is the Community law that prevails.'[71]

---

[68] On which see RD Keleman, 'The Dangers of Constitutional Pluralism' in G Davies and M Avbelj (eds), *Research Handbook on Legal Pluralism in EU Law* (Cheltenham, Edward Elgar, 2018), and the discussion thereon in ch 5 of this book.

[69] Justin Keating TD, 2 December 1971, available at: www.oireachtas.ie/en/debates/debate/dail/1971-12-02/3/, cited in Cahill, 'Constitutional Exclusion Clauses' (n 11) 81.

[70] *Meagher v Minister for Agriculture* [1994] 1 IR 329.

[71] ibid 360, citing (without comment) Case C-106/89 *Marleasing SA v La Comercial Internacional de Alimentación SA* ECLI:EU:C:1990:395, [1990] ECR I-4135 and Case C-6/90 *Francovich v Italy* ECLI:EU:C:1991:428, ECR I-5357. Cahill notes that this statement was quoted and endorsed in the Supreme Court by Hamilton CJ in the later case of *Nathan v Bailey Gibson* [1998] 2 IR 162, 173–74 (Cahill, 'Constitutional Exclusion Clauses' (n 11) 92, fn 52).

76 *The Vertical Frame*

Four years later, the Chief Justice of the Supreme Court stated that '[t]he democratic system in Ireland functions through three branches of government. However, in addition, the State is *subject* to the European institutions and provisions made therein'.[72] To see the practical effect of this, we can usefully add the earlier statement of Murphy J in *Lawlor v Minister for Agriculture* that 'it is no part of the function of this Court to determine whether or not any part of the EEC regulations were invalid'.[73] Though it was suggested in section I.B.i that the headnote to *Crotty* jumped the gun in alleging unqualified acceptance of the CJEU's doctrine of primacy, there is plenty of judicial support for the idea to be found elsewhere. Ana Bobić lists Ireland as one of the six Member States which have 'expressly accepted the primacy of EU law ... be it by way of a constitutional provision, or based upon the binding nature of the ECJ's case law'.[74] She does this on the strength of a publication of the Supreme Court itself, which states that the Court 'is constitutionally obliged to consider *and follow* EU law',[75] and that it '*must follow* EU law jurisprudence due to the requirements of EU membership, and the changes made to Ireland's Constitution to facilitate this membership'.[76] Indeed, the received interpretation of Article 29.4.6° is that it has what Cahill calls a 'torpedo effect' on the whole of the Constitution, 'whereby [it] destroy[s] the effect of every other provision',[77] rather than a 'ripple effect', 'whereby [it] temporarily displace[s], without destroying the effect, of the other provisions'.[78]

Nor are Irish judges and politicians alone in adopting the 'torpedo' explanation, that the function of Article 29.4.6° is automatically and irreversibly to neuter the Constitution when it comes to Union law. On the occasion of a visit to the European Court of Justice (ECJ) in Luxembourg by the President of Ireland in 1995, then President of the Court, Judge Gil Carlos Rodríguez Iglesias, stated in his welcoming address that:

> The Irish judiciary have been active in ensuring that the Community is based on the rule of law. The principle of primacy, which is *specifically recognised* in the Constitution of Ireland, and that of direct effect, are regularly applied in the Irish Courts. The procedure by way of preliminary ruling, which transforms every national judge into a Community judge and thus constitutes one of the dynamic forces of European integration, is one to which Irish judges have untrammelled access and of which they

---

[72] *Nathan v Bailey Gibson*, ibid, 222 (Hamilton CJ) emphasis added.

[73] *Lawlor v Minister for Agriculture* [1990] 1 IR 356, 378, following the CJEU judgment in Case 314/85 *Firma Foto-Frost v Hauptzollamt Lübeck-Ost* ECLI:EU:C:1987:452, [1987] ECR 4199.

[74] A Bobić, 'Constitutional Pluralism is not Dead: An Analysis of Interactions Between Constitutional Courts of Member States and the European Court of Justice' (2017) 18 *German Law Journal* 1395, 1413–14. The others are given as Austria, Belgium, Croatia, Luxembourg and Malta.

[75] Supreme Court of Ireland 'National Report', 26th Congress of the Conference of European Constitutional Courts (2014), available at: www.confeuconstco.org/reports/rep-xvi/LB-Irlande-EN. pdf, 1, emphasis added.

[76] ibid 3, emphasis added.

[77] Cahill, 'Constitutional Exclusion Clauses' (n 11) 90.

[78] ibid.

make regular use. By their vigilance, the Irish courts ensure that the rights of the citizens of the Union receive adequate protection and are properly safeguarded.[79]

With respect to Judge Rodríguez Iglesias, it is submitted that the emphasised part of the above statement is based on a superficial reading of Article 29.4.6°. In order for the principle of primacy to be 'specifically recognised', the Constitution would first have to specify – that is, mention – primacy, which it does not, and then endorse it, which it cannot, because it never mentions it. Be this as it may, if the Chief Justice of the Irish Supreme Court[80] and the President of the Court of Justice take as their reading of Article 29.4.6° that it renders all Union law, without exception, permanently immune from constitutional challenge in Ireland, one could be forgiven for expecting this to be the end of the matter. However, there is a unanimous judgment of the Supreme Court, *Society for the Protection of Unborn Children (SPUC) v Grogan*,[81] which predates the above-quoted judgments in *Lawlor*, *Meagher*, and *Nathan*, which has never been expressly overturned, and which provides a quite different – more convincing and more principled – account of the effect of Article 29.4.6° and of the terms of engagement between Irish law and European law.

ii. SPUC v Grogan: An Aberration?

SPUC v Grogan is the only case where the Irish judiciary dealt head-on with a case of potential conflict and collision between a right protected under the Irish Constitution and a right protected under EU law. This unanimous decision of the Supreme Court is directly along the lines of the German *Solange* jurisprudence,[82] but has come to be regarded as an outlier, and has been generally ignored – though never explicitly reversed – despite its obvious precedential value. In this regard, Gerard Hogan and Gerry Whyte state that the arguments in *Grogan* are 'isolated ones and entirely confined to an area of great sensitivity and it is unlikely that they would nowadays be followed'.[83] This is an unprincipled approach. Why should the mere fact that abortion is (or, now, perhaps *was*) an area of great sensitivity lessen the precedential value of a unanimous judgment of the Supreme Court? Moreover, recognition of this precedential value need not imply approval of the constitutional, medical and social background

---

[79] GC Rodríguez Iglesias, 'Memorandum: Visite de Mme le Présidente d'Irlande, le 16 mai 1995' (No 212/95) (internal CJEU memorandum, copy with author), emphasis added.

[80] *Nathan* (n 72) 222 (Hamilton CJ).

[81] *Society for the Protection of Unborn Children v Grogan* [1989] IR 753 (*Grogan*).

[82] Cahill, 'Constitutional Exclusion Clauses' (n 11) 75. Cahill, like Maduro (see nn 62–65), notes other courts which have taken similar approaches – defensive of national constitutional provisions but still open and receptive to the power of EU law – including the constitutional courts of the Czech Republic, Denmark, Italy and Spain. On the Czech court, see M Bobek, '*Landtová, Holubec*, and the Problem of an Uncooperative Court: Implications for the Preliminary Rulings Procedure' (2014) 10 *European Constitutional Law Review* 54.

[83] G Hogan and G Whyte, *JM Kelly: The Irish Constitution*, 4th edn (Dublin, Tottel, 2003) 535.

78   *The Vertical Frame*

of the case (the protection of the right to life of the 'unborn' and its effect on the availability of abortion in Ireland), nor of the arguments advanced and the relief sought by the plaintiffs. It simply requires taking the case seriously precisely *because* it concerned a controversial issue: exactly the kind of issue that is most likely to cause constitutional conflict between constitutional orders. Let us therefore take *Grogan* seriously, and investigate the implications it may have for our understanding of Article 29.4.6°, rather than turning a blind eye in the hope and on the assumption that a similar constitutional collision, concerning different issues, will never happen.

The facts of the case may be familiar to the European lawyer, on account of the preliminary reference sought by the High Court.[84] Briefly, the plaintiff society, an anti-abortion campaign group, sought an injunction restraining various student groups from publishing information on the identity, location and method of communication with abortion clinics outside the state. The argument of the defendants was that pregnant women had a right under EU law to travel to another Member State to receive services, including therefore a right to travel in order to procure an abortion in a Member State where it is legal to do so. As a corollary, they also had a right under EU law to receive information about abortion clinics outside Ireland but within the Union; and by further extension, the defendants had a right to publish and distribute such information. This argument was made despite the fact that none of this series of mutually dependent and mutually reinforcing rights had actually been recognised in EU law at that time, whether by Treaty provision, legislation, or judgment of the CJEU.

Article 40.3.3° of the Constitution, inserted by referendum in 1983, provided (later in part, but at the time in full) that:

> The State acknowledges the right to life of the unborn and, with due regard to the equal right to life of the mother, guarantees in its laws to respect, and, as far as practicable, by its laws to defend and vindicate that right.[85]

The defendants' argument in *Grogan* was thus predicated on the widespread belief – indeed, the judicial, political and social orthodoxy – that Article 29.4.6° has Cahill's 'torpedo effect' on the rest of the Constitution.

In the High Court, Carroll J considered the year-old Supreme Court judgment in *Attorney General (SPUC) v Open Door Counselling Ltd*,[86] but distinguished it on the ground that that case had turned on the question of whether there

---

[84] Which was handed down by the CJEU in Case C-159/90 *SPUC (Ireland) v Grogan* ECLI:EU:C:1991:378, [1991] ECR I-4685 (referred to in this book as *Grogan* (CJEU) to distinguish it from the domestic proceedings).

[85] The meaning of 'unborn' was left undefined in law for 30 years, until the enactment of the Protection of Life During Pregnancy Act 2013, s 2(1): '"unborn", in relation to a human life, is a reference to such a life during the period of time commencing after implantation in the womb of a woman and ending on the complete emergence of the life from the body of the woman'.

[86] *Attorney General (Society for the Protection of Unborn Children) v Open Door Counselling and Dublin Well Woman* [1988] IR 593.

The Terms of Engagement Between Irish Law and EU Law   79

was a right to receive information about abortion services abroad in the context of one-to-one counselling (the Supreme Court had held that there was not). Because the present case was concerned with the question of whether there was a stand-alone right, outside the counselling context, to receive information relating to abortion services outside the jurisdiction, Carroll J held that a preliminary reference to the CJEU was necessary to determine the matter. Pending word from Luxembourg, Carroll J made no decision as to the injunction sought by the plaintiff.

iii. The 'Torpedo Effect' Torpedoed

On appeal to the Supreme Court, Carroll J's judgment was overturned in unusually strong terms, and SPUC's injunction granted and made permanent. Though the Court was unanimous as to the result of the case, the reasons contained in the three written judgments are quite diverse. However, two major threads can be drawn out for the present analysis. First, the paramount importance of the fundamental rights provisions of the Constitution was emphasised, offering little support for the 'torpedo effect' orthodoxy surrounding the 'exclusion clause' and preserving for the domestic judiciary a role in their vindication, even in the face of EU norms. Secondly, the Court hinted darkly as to possible repercussions if the CJEU were ever to hold that the defendants were in possession of the rights they had claimed. Though these two threads are conceptually distinguishable, they are inextricably linked and will be discussed together.

Finlay CJ 'rejected as unsound'[87] the idea that the facts of the case could be meaningfully distinguished from those in *Open Door* as Carroll J had held – the application for the injunction was in reality:

> An application to restrain an activity which has been clearly declared by this Court [in *Open Door*] to be unconstitutional and therefore unlawful and which could assist and is intended to assist in the destruction of the right to life of an unborn child, a right acknowledged and protected under the Constitution. That constitutionally guaranteed right must be fully and effectively protected by the courts.[88]

Here we see the first of SPUC's major threads: it would seem that when it comes to *at least one right* guaranteed by the Constitution, the Supreme Court saw itself as being obliged to protect that right, regardless of any other provision of the Constitution, emphatically including Article 29.4.6°. Indeed, Finlay CJ went on to suggest as much in his very next sentence:

> If and when a decision of the [CJEU] rules that some aspect of European [Union] law affects the activities of the defendants impugned in this case, the consequence of that decision on these constitutionally guaranteed rights and their protection by the courts will *then* fall to be considered *by these courts.*[89]

[87] *Grogan* (n 81) 764.
[88] ibid 764–65, emphasis added.
[89] ibid 765, emphasis added.

80 *The Vertical Frame*

The conclusion that Cahill draws from this is, I argue, entirely correct and essential to any analysis of the relationship between Irish and EU law: specifically, she asserts that the Chief Justice 'expressly acknowledged and established for the Irish courts the power to review a decision of the European Court of Justice on the grounds that it was contrary to a fundamental right protected by the Irish Constitution'.[90] The words italicised in the above quote encapsulate this second major thread of *SPUC*. They were a shot across the bow: a warning, in no uncertain terms, that if the CJEU were ever to hold that, as a matter of EU law (recognised, polyarchically, as the exclusive interpretive domain of the CJEU), pregnant women had any of the rights claimed by the defendants, then the response of the Irish courts could not be predicted and obedience could not be guaranteed. As we can see, this part of the judgment in *Grogan* very much lessens the force of the argument that Article 29.4.6° subordinates the entire Constitution, without exception, to EU law for all time coming.

The judgment of Walsh J, with whom Hederman J concurred, was particularly scathing of Carroll J's judgment at first instance, and lends further weight to the 'ripple' interpretation of Article 29.4.6°:

> When the present matter came before the High Court it was clear beyond all doubt that the activities complained of were contrary to the Constitution. The decision of the High Court judge to adopt the course which she did, namely, to leave the matter undecided, was in effect to suspend the provisions of [Article 40.3.3°] for an indefinite period. *It is not open to any judge to do anything which in effect suspends any provisions of the Constitution for any period whatsoever.*[91]

Walsh J continued in equally strong terms, holding that '[i]t is the undoubted duty of this Court to ensure that the protection guaranteed by [Article 40.3.3°] is not put in abeyance'.[92] He then discussed, without deciding, an argument of counsel for the plaintiff that had been raised during the hearing, and which merits quoting at length:

> It has been sought to be argued in the present case that the effect of [Article 29.4.6°], which was necessary to permit our adhesion to the treaties of the European Communities, is to qualify all rights including fundamental rights guaranteed by the Constitution. [The insertion of Article 40.3.3° was] subsequent in time, by several years, to the [insertion of Article 29.4.6°]. That fact may give rise to the consideration of the question of whether or not [Article 40.3.3°] itself qualifies [Article 29.4.6°]. Be that as it may, *any answer to the reference received from [the CJEU] will have to be considered in the light of our own constitutional provisions.* In the last analysis only this Court can decide finally what are the effects of the interaction of [Article 40.3.3°] and [Article 29.4.6°].[93]

---

[90] Cahill, 'Constitutional Exclusion Clauses' (n 11) 95.
[91] *Grogan* (n 81) 767–68, emphasis added.
[92] ibid 768.
[93] ibid 768–69, emphasis added.

The Terms of Engagement Between Irish Law and EU Law   81

This paragraph triggers a number of observations. First, Walsh J noted, but did not explicitly accept or reject, the argument that Article 29.4.6° has a 'torpedo effect' on the rest of the Constitution. Secondly, he raised the possibility that a subsequent amendment to the Constitution could qualify the effect of the alleged 'exclusion clause'. On one view, this would render the clause not very exclusionary after all. Alternatively, if the exclusion clause was capable of being qualified, then it must have had at least some exclusionary effect prior to such popular qualification, but presumably more of the 'ripple' than 'torpedo' variety. Thirdly, Walsh J followed Finlay CJ in implying that any future CJEU jurisprudence on point would be 'considered' in the light of Irish constitutional provisions and not automatically followed, as the CJEU would argue it should be. Fourthly, Walsh J reserved to the Irish courts all interpretive power over the Irish Constitution – hardly a revolutionary proposition, but again one that lends itself to the ideas of polyarchy and heterarchy, rather than to agreement with either of the monist or particularist conceptions of the relationship between the EU constitutional order and that of the Member States.

Before we leave Walsh J, one final line of his judgment is worthy of inspection:

> [I]t cannot be one of the objectives of the European Communities that a member state should be obliged to permit activities which are clearly designed to set at nought the constitutional guarantees for the protection within the State of a fundamental human right.[94]

Let us remember that only a few years previously, in *Crotty*, the Supreme Court had held unanimously that, as a matter of Irish law, just what constitutes the scope and objectives of the Community in the context of Treaty amendment falls to be determined by the Irish courts, and no other. Because *Grogan* concerned certain substantive (claimed, but not explicitly granted) rights under EU law and not Treaty amendments, this part of Walsh J's judgment echoes the scope and objectives test but transplants it to a different frame. His reference to the objectives of the Communities would thus seem to have at least the potential to qualify the exclusionary effect of Article 29.4.6°. This can be analogised to the 'penultimate judicial supremacy' leg of *Crotty*, that is, that though the Constitution provides for no judicial role in the government's exercise of its foreign policy powers, such powers are ultimately subject to the provisions of the Constitution as a whole, the interpretation of which is a matter for the judiciary (subject, in the (relatively) 'final' instance, to override and reversal by the electorate). Extending the analogy, Article 29.4.6°, on its face and in its ordinary everyday effect, immunises EU law from constitutional challenge, but does not go so far as to oblige the judiciary 'to permit activities which are clearly designed to set at nought the constitutional guarantees for the protection within the State

---

[94] ibid 769.

82   *The Vertical Frame*

of a fundamental human right'. The fact that this sentence was expressed in general terms, and was not confined to the protection of the right to life of the 'unborn', makes even less convincing the idea that *SPUC v Grogan* is 'confined to an area of great sensitivity' and lends weight to the argument that the 'ripple effect' is the preferable interpretation of Article 29.4.6°.

iv. Analysis: Democratic Legitimacy, 'Areas of Great Sensitivity' and a Hierarchy of Norms

The parallels between the decision in *Grogan* and Kumm's conception of the principle of democratic legitimacy as an interface norm are immediately apparent. This is hardly surprising, given that the Irish constitutional provision on the right to life of the 'unborn' was specifically given by Kumm as an example of where the application of the principle might justify the rebuttal of the presumption of legality of EU norms.[95] But the specific circumstances under which the case arose, the way in which the principle was applied, and how all of this differs from Kumm's conception, are especially interesting. Rather than being a case of straightforward conflict between a norm of EU law and a 'clear and specific constitutional norm that reflect[s] essential commitments of the national community',[96] *Grogan* was more contingent and conditional in nature. The rights under EU law claimed by the defendants were derived from the Treaties but not specified therein, and their existence had never been confirmed by the CJEU. As a result, the overall effect of the decision in *Grogan* was one step removed from how Kumm conceives of the principle of democratic legitimacy. Rather than relating directly to the relationship between EU and Irish constitutional norms, the principle was adopted in interpreting the Irish constitutional provision that itself regulates the relationship. This extra layer of abstraction shifts the principle from the realm of the metaconstitutional to that of the constitutional – the Supreme Court used Kumm's principle of democratic legitimacy not to disapply a norm of EU law, but to interpret one norm of Irish constitutional law – the exclusion clause – in such a way that it assumed a position (potentially) subordinate to another norm (protecting a fundamental right).

The fact that the fundamental right in question in the case was the right to life, and specifically the right to life of the 'unborn', raises two related questions. First, was the Court's approach focused specifically on the protection of the right to life of the 'unborn' and therefore limited to the contingent (and pathological) context of the Irish abortion controversy, or might other constitutional rights warrant similar vigilance? Despite the widespread view that the judgments in *Grogan* were 'isolated ones' 'unlikely to be followed', the judgments

---

[95] Kumm (n 60) 297.
[96] ibid 300.

The Terms of Engagement Between Irish Law and EU Law   83

were clearly phrased in general and abstract terms, capable of application to *any* of the fundamental rights guaranteed by the Constitution. At no point did the Supreme Court give any indication that the right to life of the 'unborn' was being afforded protection above and beyond any other constitutional right. This leads to the second question, whether the Supreme Court was relying – though not explicitly – on a hierarchical conception of constitutional rights and norms. The Supreme Court has repeatedly recognised a hierarchy of norms under the Constitution when two provisions are in seemingly irresolvable conflict, with a particularly heavy weight attached to the right to life.[97] However, the difficulty inherent in trying to formulate a definitive and all-encompassing hierarchy has also been recognised,[98] most relevantly for present purposes in the statement of Henchy J in *The State (Keegan) v Stardust Compensation Tribunal* that:

> The concept of 'accepted moral standards' [by which the ranking in a hierarchy of norms may be judged] represents a vague, elusive and changing body of standards which in a pluralist society is sometimes difficult to ascertain.[99]

By 'pluralist', Henchy J was referring here to social pluralism, that is, a society consisting of individual citizens with varying political, religious, social and moral beliefs – but the point holds when one extends it from the realm of diversity among citizens to that of diversity among legal systems. In the modern European state, where the individual must daily navigate a plurality of legal orders – both in the sense of 'hard' law (state law, EU law) and 'soft' law (religious codes of orthodoxy and orthopraxy, rules of social interaction) – the difficulty of determining a universal standard, whether moral or legal, against which conduct can be judged becomes even more pronounced. We can further extend this difficulty to the attempt to posit overarching metaconstitutional rules by which conflicts between heterarchically arranged legal orders may be regulated. It was noted in section I.B.iii that Kumm's conception of the principle of democratic legitimacy seems especially concerned with instances of national constitutional specificity. There is therefore a twofold problem with the principle. First, it means that the number of cases to which it could apply is essentially limited: it is therefore a rather narrow means of dealing with cases at the boundaries, rather than a general principle of (meta)constitutionalism. Examples of Greek and Irish constitutional specificity have already been mentioned, to which we could add the *laïque* nature of the French State;[100] the particular way in which the right to human dignity is expressed in the German Grundgesetz;[101]

---

[97] On the importance of the right to life see, inter alia, *The People (DPP) v Shaw* [1982] IR 1 (right to life superior to right to personal liberty); *AG v X* [1992] 1 IR 1 (superior to right to travel, see ch 4 of this book); *DPP v Delaney* [1997] 3 IR 453 (superior to inviolability of the dwelling).

[98] See Egan J's example in *AG v X* [1992] 1 IR 1, 92 of a woman's right to bodily integrity outweighing a rapist's right to life in the case of an attempted rape resulting in the death of the attacker.

[99] *The State (Keegan) v Stardust Compensation Tribunal* [1986] IR 642, 658.

[100] French Constitution, Art 1.

[101] German Basic Law, Art 1.

84   *The Vertical Frame*

and quite possibly as many others as there are Member States. This is the mirror image of the problem discussed above in section I.B.iii: whereas the attempt to take decisions predicated on specific national circumstances and to universalise them may leave us with principles so broad as to offer little guidance, similarly, to posit general principles capable of being put into effect universally may leave us, at the level of application, with nothing more than an exceptional method of dealing with a few dozen exceptional instances of national specificity, or, less charitably, recalcitrance.

Related to this is the second issue, that national specificity is not necessarily something to which the CJEU is blind in its jurisprudence, and therefore may not necessarily be best protected (if indeed it ought to be protected at all) primarily or in the first instance at the national level. An example is the case of *Omega*,[102] where the issue was whether it was permissible for the German authorities to ban the importation from elsewhere in the EU of equipment for the game of 'laser-tag', whereby participants could 'play at killing' other human beings. For the national authorities, such activity contravened Article 1(1) of the Grundgesetz, which provides specific protection for the concept of human dignity – the importance and sensitivity of which for the German constitutional order is evidenced by its prominent placement within the Basic Law and its unamendability (or, given the impossibility of permanence in law, its unamendability *within the logic of the Basic Law*). While the protection of human dignity is inherent in, if not the basis of, the protection of all human rights, nowhere else in national European constitutions does it receive the specific formulation to be found in the Grundgesetz. Accordingly, the question was whether the national ability to restrict such activity was dependent on 'the condition that that restriction be based on a legal conception that is common to all Member States'.[103]

The CJEU emphasised the centrality of proportionality to its framing of the relevant test: while the question of whether the formulation given to the national protection of a right is common to all Member States is a legitimate part of the analysis, it is not the only concern. At the level of determining whether there had been a breach of free movement rules, it was the notion of human dignity specific to EU law that was relevant, whereas the specific nature of the German Constitution's version of human dignity was relevant to the subsequent proportionality test. Critically, the fact that the Grundgesetz formulates the right to human dignity rather differently from other constitutions was not enough for

---

[102] Case C–36/02 *Omega Spielhallen- und Automatenaufstellungs-GmbH v Oberbürgermeisterin der Bundesstadt Bonn* ECLI:EU:C:2004:614, [2004] ECR I–9609 (*Omega*). For analysis see MK Bulterman and HR Kranenborg, 'Case Comment: What if Rules on Free Movement and Human Rights Collide? About Laser Games and Human Dignity: The Omega Case' (2006) 31 *European Law Review* 93; N Nic Shuibhne, 'Margins of Appreciation: National Values, Fundamental Rights and EC Free Movement Law' (2009) 32 *European Law Review* 230.

[103] *Omega* (n 102) para 23, emphasis added. This requirement of commonality was the seeming result of the CJEU's earlier judgment in Case C-275/92 *Schindler* ECLI:EU:C:1993:944, [1994] ECR I-1039.

The Terms of Engagement Between Irish Law and EU Law   85

the measure to be disproportionate.[104] In other cases, the abolition of titles of nobility[105] and the spelling of names using the orthography of the national language[106] have been held to be similarly nationally specific rules that are not necessarily disproportionate interferences with free movement.[107] The relevance to *Grogan* is clear: the right to life obviously receives some form of protection in all Member State constitutions, but nowhere else was it afforded directly to the 'unborn' in the manner of the Irish Constitution until 2018. In the light of the subsequent *Omega* judgment, Walsh J's statement in *Grogan* that the State should not be 'obliged to permit activities which are clearly designed to set at nought the constitutional guarantees for the protection within the State of a fundamental human right' can be seen as entirely justifiable – indeed as positively *communautaire* – and not a mere piece of national supremacist grandstanding.

An in-depth look at Irish abortion litigation, across all three points and sides of the triangular constitution, will form the basis of chapter four, but for now it is worth continuing this line of thought, regarding constitutional traditions which are *not* common to the Member States, with reference to the case of *Attorney General v X*,[108] where Costello J said in the High Court that:

> I think the attainment of the fundamental objectives of the Treaty is *enhanced* by laws which assist in the development of a Community in which legitimate differences on moral issues are recognised and which does not seek to impose a spurious and divisive uniformity on its members on such issues.[109]

As we shall see, the Supreme Court did not address this reasoning, finding itself able to resolve the case as a matter of domestic law. But Costello J's statement is at least conceptually compatible with Walsh J's judgment in *Grogan* and the CJEU's approach in *Omega*, *Sayn-Wittgenstein*, and *Runevič-Vardyn*. 'Unity in diversity' is obviously not the same thing as 'spurious and divisive uniformity', and it is for precisely this reason that the CJEU has recognised, to an extent, the legitimacy of difference in national approaches to questions of fundamental rights,[110] The effective and uniform application of Union law is doubtless

---

[104] *Omega* (n 102) paras 36–40.

[105] Case C-208/09 *Ilonka Sayn-Wittgenstein v Landeshauptmann von Wien* ECLI:EU:C:2010:806, [2010] ECR I-13693.

[106] Case C-391/09 *Malgožata Runevič-Vardyn and Łukasz Paweł Wardyn v Vilniaus Miesto Savivaldybės Administracija* ECLI:EU:C:2011:291, [2011] ECR I-3787.

[107] As well as relying on *Omega*, which was a pre-Lisbon decision, both of these (post-Lisbon) cases also noted the importance of Art 4(2) TEU's requirement that the EU respect the constitutional and national identities of Member States: *Sayn-Wittgenstein* (n 105) para 92; *Runevič-Vardyn* (n 106) para 86.

[108] *AG v X* [1992] 1 IR 1.

[109] ibid 16, emphasis added.

[110] A recognition lent weight by the coming into force of Art 4(2) TEU. Cases where the CJEU adopts an altogether less accommodating approach to national specificity, in the context of labour rights, will be discussed in ch 4, below: see Case C-341/05 *Laval un Partneri v Svenska*

86 *The Vertical Frame*

important, perhaps foundationally so, but it is a stretch to say that it is *the* most important norm in the European constitutional constellation. Again, it is important to emphasise that none of this should be taken as signifying agreement with the former constitutional restriction of abortion in Ireland: the point is an abstract and general one, concerning constitutional principle and constitutional authority. Different national conceptions of fundamental rights and their requirements *are* possible within the Union, and it is not *necessarily* the case that this is either undesirable in itself or poses a threat to the integrity of the Union legal order. This question of differing conceptions of rights and their requirements across jurisdictions is a key element for further study in chapter three and chapter four.

D. Conclusion: Hierarchy and Polyarchy, Specificity and Universality

This section has demonstrated the means by which the Irish constitutional order, initially self-contained and 'closed' in nature, was 'opened' to enable membership of what is now the EU. Between them, the ECA 1972, the 'licence to join', and the 'exclusion clause' incorporated EU law into the Irish system, democratically authorised membership of the Union and ostensibly immunised its law from constitutional challenge. However, analysis of *Crotty* and *Grogan*, still the leading cases on the issues, demonstrates that to regard the Irish and EU legal orders as being hierarchically integrated in all circumstances – despite being the widespread and consistent orthodoxy – is mistaken. While in the ordinary, quotidian run of things, norms of EU law enjoy hierarchical superiority in the Irish legal order (as they generally should), the judicial imposition of the 'scope and objectives' test in *Crotty* – which has in practice resulted in the requirement of a referendum for Treaty amendments – demonstrates that EU law is received into the Irish legal order on terms *set by the Irish order itself*, undermining, from the domestic perspective, the CJEU's autonomy claim, while still being respectful of the 'organic' nature of the EU legal order, and this without contradiction. Moreover, *Grogan* demonstrates that Cahill's interpretation of Article 29.4.6° as having a 'ripple' rather than 'torpedo' effect on the rest of the Constitution is correct: when faced with potential conflict between the two orders, the Irish

---

Byggnadsarbetareförbundet ECLI:EU:C:2007:809, [2007] ECR I-11767; and Case C-438/05 *ITWF & FSU v Viking Line* ECLI:EU:C:2007:292, [2007] ECR I-10779. For discussion, see R Eklund, 'A Swedish Perspective on *Laval* (2007–2008) 29 *Comparative Labor Law & Policy Journal* 551; ACL Davies, 'One Step Forward, Two Steps Back? The *Viking* and *Laval* Cases in the ECJ' (2008) 37 *Industrial Law Journal* 126; C Joerges and F Rödl, 'Informal Politics, Formalised Law and the "Social Deficit" of European Integration: Reflections after the Judgments of the ECJ in *Viking* and *Laval*' (2009) 15 *European Law Journal* 1; A Veldman, 'The Protection of the Fundamental Right to Strike within the Context of the European Internal Market: Implications of the Forthcoming Accession of the EU to the ECHR' (2013) 9 *Utrecht Law Review* 104.

The Terms of Engagement Between Irish Law and EU Law   87

Supreme Court indicated a willingness to enforce a constitutional norm protecting a fundamental right in preference to a (claimed, potential) norm which would nullify that right's effectiveness. The vision of the two legal orders that results from this is polyarchic in nature: both legal orders make justifiable claims to legislative and interpretive autonomy in their own domains. Though this may in result in the appearance of hierarchy in the ordinary course of affairs, the two legal orders remain distinct and analytically severable – part of a polyarchy within which heterarchy can exist. But the analysis above only focused on the decisions and attitudes of one part of this polyarchy, and so it has not yet shown to be *deliberative*. This will be done in chapter four, with reference to the interactions and dialogue that have occurred regarding the question of abortion.

In demonstrating the polyarchic nature of the relationships between the legal orders, close attention was paid to the specific principles applied by the Irish Supreme Court in its decisions. The principle of conditional recognition – Sabel and Gerstenberg's doctrinal tool for the constitutionalisation of an overlapping consensus – was of fundamental importance in both *Crotty* and *Grogan*, but in a manner significantly different from that envisaged by those authors. The Irish legal order permits the evolution of the EU legal order *so long as* it does not go beyond the 'scope and objectives' of the Treaties. If this condition is breached, a further popular authorisation is necessary. Similarly, the Supreme Court loyally and dutifully applies norms of EU law, including judgments of the CJEU, *so long as* these norms do not – to borrow Walsh J's phrase – 'set at nought the constitutional guarantees for the protection within the State of a fundamental human right'.[111] However, being a national court bound by a national constitution, the Supreme Court formulated and applied its interface norms based on the specific text of the Constitution and on the historically contingent means by which EU law had been made effective in the State. They are therefore internal interface norms, constitutional in nature, and not metaconstitutional. They deal with matters that are both nationally specific, for example, the right to life of the 'unborn', and much more general, for example, the Constitution's conception of popular sovereignty. The question then arises as to whether they can be universalised into metaconstitutional interface norms, independent of any one legal system; and, relatedly, whether they bear any resemblance to the metaconstitutional interface norms posited by Kumm and Maduro. It was suggested above that any such attempt is beset by difficulty, and that the specific principles posited by Kumm, in particular, do not reflect Irish constitutional experience.

These questions will be analysed further in the chapters to follow, but for now let us turn our attention to the other 'vertical' side of the triangle: the relationship between Irish law and the ECHR.

---

[111] *Crotty* (n 20) 769.

88 *The Vertical Frame*

II. THE IRISH LEGAL ORDER AND THE EUROPEAN CONVENTION ON HUMAN RIGHTS

The nature of the Convention legal order and the method of its reception in Ireland make the task of positing the two as part of a deliberative polyarchy more straightforward than is the case with reference to Ireland and the EU. Though the European Court of Human Rights (ECtHR) reserves supreme interpretive authority over the Convention to itself, it has never claimed for its judgments the same kind of primacy over national law as does the CJEU. Moreover, as we shall see, the method by which the Convention has been incorporated into the Irish legal system has no parallel with the 'exclusion clause' of Article 29.4.6°, simplifying the task of presenting the two systems as being non-hierarchically arranged.

While Ireland was a founding member of the Council of Europe, an original signatory to the Convention in 1950, and one of the first States to accept the right of individual petition to Strasbourg in 1953, it was not until 2003 that the Convention was made domestically effective, making Ireland the last Contracting Party to incorporate the Convention into its own legal system. The method chosen for incorporation was legislative, under the European Convention on Human Rights Act 2003 (ECHR Act 2003), rather than constitutional. In this section, the nature of the relationship between the two legal orders will first be set out, both prior to and after incorporation in 2003. This will then be followed by an outline of how this incorporation justifies a polyarchic conception of the relationship between the legal orders.

A. The Relationship Defined, Pre- and Post-Incorporation

i. 1950–2003: Pride and Prejudice

In a comprehensive comparative study of the effect of the Convention on the legal systems of Ireland and the UK (or, rather, England and Wales), Samantha Besson states that '[b]ecause Irish courts always had to enforce the Irish Bill of Rights, there was no domestic pressure for the development of a European human rights catalogue and court'.[112] While it is true that there was little domestic pressure for something along the lines of the Convention, it is not quite true that the Irish courts 'always' had to enforce constitutional rights. The 1937 Constitution, like the 1922 Constitution before it, contains a catalogue of

---

[112] S Besson, 'The Reception Process in Ireland and the United Kingdom' in A Stone Sweet and H Keller (eds), *A Europe of Rights: The Impact of the ECHR on National Legal Systems* (Oxford, Oxford University Press, 2008) 43.

The Irish Legal Order and the European Convention on Human Rights   89

justiciable rights, but these rights had little real impact until the 1960s. In the (extra-curial) words of a former Chief Justice of the Irish Supreme Court:

> [W]hile the Constitution was successfully invoked in scattered instances [in the first two decades of its existence], it was the appointment of Cearbhall Ó Dálaigh as Chief Justice in 1961 which signalled the beginning of the new era. He was joined on the court on the same day by Brian Walsh and it soon became clear that litigants and advocates who looked to the text of the Constitution itself, rather than to constitutional theory as expounded in the British tradition by Dicey and others, would receive a sympathetic audience.[113]

For all its superficial and substantive resemblance to the written, republican constitutions of the Franco-American tradition, and notwithstanding the changed understanding and reality of rights adjudication from the 1960s, the Diceyan seam runs deeply in both the text of the Constitution and the body of law constructed around it. To take just two examples, its model of parliamentary democracy is in many regards a carbon copy of the United Kingdom's;[114] and the law relating to the judicial review of administrative action borrows heavily from the judgments of English courts, both before and after Irish independence. The legacy of British constitutionalism can also be detected in the Constitution's embodiment of the concept of dualism, and the courts' enthusiastic defence thereof.

As was mentioned above in section I, Article 15.2.1° vests the legislative function in the Oireachtas, and Article 29.6 provides that '[n]o international agreement shall be part of the domestic law of the State save as may be determined by the Oireachtas'. As early as 1960, the Supreme Court held in Ó Laighléis[115] that, taken together, these provisions created an 'insuperable obstacle to importing the provisions of the [Convention] into the domestic law of Ireland'.[116] The courts over the next 40 years held fast to this strict approach to the direct application of the Convention, approving the rule in Ó Laighléis as late as 2003, just prior to the enactment of the ECHR Act.[117] One important side effect of this judicial resistance to reliance on the Convention is described by Donncha O'Connell:

> [T]his view of dualism, as a legal fact, has permeated the discourse on human rights in the political domain. Thus, dualism has become 'internalised' as a political value with the result that international human rights obligations have been 'externalised',

---

[113] R Keane, 'Judges as Lawmakers: The Irish Experience' (2004) 4 *Judicial Studies Institute Journal* 1, 9–10.

[114] Note, for instance, that the provisions of Arts 20–25, under the heading of 'Legislation', bear more than a passing resemblance to the UK Parliament Act 1911 and to the general British theory (up to 1937) of the power-relations between the upper and lower Houses of Parliament.

[115] *In re Ó Laighléis* [1960] IR 93.

[116] ibid 124 (Maguire CJ). Notably, this case was the domestic precursor to the very first case decided by the ECtHR (with the plaintiff using the English language form of his name): *Lawless v Ireland* [1961] 1 EHRR 1.

[117] *The People (DPP) v MS* [2003] 1 IR 606, 611 (Keane CJ).

90   *The Vertical Frame*

as it were, as matters to be resolved exclusively through arguably flawed international enforcement mechanisms and, ultimately, international diplomacy. In other words, the separation of international and domestic law under the concept of dualism can be seen as an effectively immutable norm.[118]

This is the leitmotif of the Convention's reception in Ireland prior to incorporation. Before we explore the reasons for this 'externalisation' of human rights discourse, and its consequences for a pluralist analysis of the Irish and Convention legal orders, it is worth noting that the courts' strict refusal to apply the Convention domestically did not result in the Convention having *no* effect upon the Irish legal order. The relatively few cases decided by the European Commission and Court of Human Rights against Ireland did lead to reform, though this was often piecemeal, belated and somewhat grudging. For example, the decision in *Airey*[119] that the absence of a legal aid scheme in civil matters amounted to a breach of Article 6(1) ECHR led to such a scheme being set up, but on a merely administrative rather than legislative basis. In *Norris*,[120] the ECtHR held that the provisions of the Offences Against the Person Act 1861 and the Criminal Law (Amendment) Act 1885 (both Acts of the former Parliament of Great Britain and Ireland which had the effect of criminalising male homosexual conduct) were a violation of Article 8 ECHR. This led to the enactment of the Criminal Law (Sexual Offences) Act 1993 and the repeal of the impugned provisions five years after the ECtHR had handed down judgment in the case.

However, these are cases where the State had been held to be in breach of its obligations under the Convention as a matter of international law by the bodies established thereunder, and so executive and legislative remedy of the breaches, however tardy, in no way offended the principle of dualism. Judicial opposition to the notion of giving effect either to the Convention or to judgments of the ECtHR prior to the State having been found in violation is clearly illustrated by the Supreme Court's refusal, in *Norris v Attorney General*[121] (the precursor to the ECtHR case mentioned above) to follow *Dudgeon v UK*,[122] in which the ECtHR had already held the very same nineteenth-century statutes, in the context of Northern Ireland, to be in violation of Article 8 ECHR. As Besson notes, despite the increasing frequency of judicial references to the Convention in the High Court from the 1980s as an aid to legislative interpretation, the Supreme Court was careful not to lend its weight to this slight shift in attitudes.[123]

---

[118] D O'Connell, 'Watched Kettles Boil (Slowly): The Impact of the ECHR Act 2003' in U Kilkelly, (ed) *ECHR in Irish Law*, 2nd edn (Bristol, Jordan 2009) 5–6.

[119] *Airey v Ireland (No 1)* [1979–80] 2 EHRR 305.

[120] *Norris v Ireland* [1991] 13 EHRR 186.

[121] *Norris v Attorney General* [1984] IR 36.

[122] *Dudgeon v UK* [1982] 4 EHRR 149.

[123] Besson (n 112) 52, citing, inter alia, *O'Leary v Attorney General* [1993] 1 IR 102 (HC), [1995] 1 IR 254 (SC); *Heaney v Ireland* [1994] 2 ILRM 420 (HC), [1996] 1 IR 540 (SC).

The Irish Legal Order and the European Convention on Human Rights 91

Why this insistence on keeping the Convention at (more than) arm's length from the domestic system? The legalistic explanation is that given by the Supreme Court in *Ó Laighléis*: the Constitution's requirement of dualism. This is certainly justifiable, though it must be said that the Supreme Court adhered to this strict construction long after such an approach to interpretation gave way to an altogether more flexible (or, if you prefer, 'activist') approach to the protection of fundamental rights from the 1960s. For example, Article 15.2.1°'s reservation of all law-making power to the Oireachtas never posed any difficulty for the Supreme Court's development, from 1965, of a doctrine of 'unenumerated rights' – supposedly inherent, but nowhere specified, in the Constitution.[124] Whatever other criticisms may be levelled at the Irish judiciary, and despite a relatively less 'activist' approach since the turn of the century,[125] it has rarely been seen since the 1960s as being in hock to textual formalism. The dualist approach to international law inherent in Article 29.6 and 15.2.1°, taken alone, does not suffice to explain this wary judicial attitude to the Convention and the judgments of the ECtHR.

The explanation presented here is twofold. First, there was a widespread conviction that the constitutional provisions for the protection of individual rights were sufficient, to the extent that placing any reliance on the Convention would be otiose (or even lead to a *reduction* in rights-protection),[126] and, secondly, a concomitant suspicion of the interpretive methodology of the ECtHR.[127] These two ideas, one of pride and one of prejudice, had both legal and political consequences: legally, they were instrumental in the judiciary's largely sceptical treatment of the Convention; and, politically, they shed light on why it took 50 years for the State to make the Convention domestically effective.

As regards the first reason – that of the Irish Constitution's sufficiency on its own, or even of its superiority to the Convention – it is worth noting that there are areas where the rights afforded by the Convention go above and beyond those provided for by the Constitution, and vice versa.[128] This notwithstanding, there is no doubting that the Irish record before the ECtHR is quite good.

---

[124] Beginning with *Ryan v Attorney General* [1965] IR 294. See generally Hogan and Whyte (n 83) ch 7.3.

[125] I Bacik, 'A Human Rights Culture for Ireland?' in I Bacik and S Livingstone, *Towards a Culture of Human Rights in Ireland* (Cork, Cork University Press, 2001) 37–42.

[126] K Lesch Bodnick, 'Bringing Ireland Up to Par: Incorporating the European Convention for the Protection of Human Rights and Fundamental Freedoms' (2002) 26 *Fordham International Law Journal* 418; AZ Drzemczewski, *European Human Rights Convention in Domestic Law: A Comparative Study* (Oxford, Oxford University Press, 1983) 170–74; Besson (n 112) 43–44. See also *Lobe & Osayande v Minister for Justice* [2003] IESC 1, Fennelly J, dissenting: 'It may … be possible to argue persuasively that an act which does not satisfy the minimum standards of the Convention should not lightly be considered compatible with the more rigorous demands of the Constitution' (no page or paragraph numbers in transcript).

[127] O'Connell (n 118) 8, citing conference papers delivered by the then Minister for Justice in October 2003, and Hardiman J of the Supreme Court in February 2001.

[128] Bacik (n 125) passim, especially at 17–23, noting the wider scope of the 'family' under Art 8 ECHR and the more extensive protection of freedom of expression under Art 10 ECHR.

92   The Vertical Frame

Analysis of the ECtHR's database shows that only 25 of the more than 100 cases taken against Ireland have proceeded to judgment on the merits, though 18 of these have resulted in findings of a violation of the Convention. However, to suggest that this low number of cases and violations can be ascribed in the main to 'the lively and strong human rights tradition in Ireland'[129] is to risk letting self-satisfaction obscure the many deficiencies in the protection of rights under the Constitution.[130] The length and expense of taking a case to Strasbourg (particularly given that seeking domestic redress may be just as long and expensive, depleting both funds and patience in the exhaustion of domestic remedies) and Ireland's small population should be taken into account. One must also not forget the litany of human rights abuses at the hands of (or with the connivance of) the State with regard to the treatment of, in particular, women and children, against which both the Constitution and the Convention were singularly useless – an important reminder of the limits of an excessively juridified, legalistic approach to the protection of fundamental rights.[131]

ii. 2003 to the Present Day: The European Convention on Human Rights Act 2003

a. Origins

Given the half-century that had passed since ratification without incorporation, one might have been forgiven for imagining in the 1990s that the Convention would never be given domestic effect in Ireland.[132] However, when the impetus

---

[129] Besson (n 112) 61, citing G Hogan, 'Incorporation of the ECHR: Some Issues of Methodology and Process' in U Kilkelly (ed), *ECHR and Irish Law*, 1st edn (Bristol, Jordan 2004) 14.

[130] Of the 18 cases decided against Ireland, 10 have involved violations of Art 6 ECHR, five of Art 8 ECHR, and five of Art 13 ECHR (with an overlap of six cases involving violations of two of these Articles).

[131] See *Report of the Inquiry into Child Sexual Abuse in the Diocese of Ferns* (Ferns Report, October 2005), available at: www.lenus.ie/bitstream/handle/10147/560434/thefernsreportocto-ber2005.pdf; *Report of Dr Kevin McCoy on the Western Health Board Inquiry into Brothers of Charity Services in Galway* (McCoy Report, November 2007), available at: www.hse.ie/eng/services/publications/disability/mcoy-boc.pdf; *Report of the Commission to Inquire into Child Abuse* (Ryan Report, 20 May 2009), available at: www.childabusecommission.ie/rpt/pdfs; *Report of the Commission of Investigation into the Catholic Archdiocese of Dublin* (Murphy Report, 29 November 2009), available at: www.justice.ie/en/JELR/Pages/PB09000504; *Report of the Inter-Departmental Committee to Establish the Facts of State Involvement with the Magdalen Laundries* (McAleese Report, 5 February 2013), available at: www.justice.ie/en/JELR/Pages/MagdalenRpt2013; *Independent Review of Issues Relating to Symphysiotomy* (Murphy Report, 13 March 2014), available at: health.gov.ie/blog/publications/independent-review-of-issues-relating-to-symphysiotomy-by-judge-yvonne-murphy; M Enright, 'Ireland, Symphysiotomy and the UNHRC' (*Inherently Human*, 21 July 2014), available at: inherentlyhuman.wordpress.com/2014/07/21/ireland-symphysiotomy-and-the-unhrc/.

[132] Note also that the ECtHR had by the 1980s declared that there was no legal obligation on states to incorporate the Convention into domestic law: N Krisch, 'The Open Architecture of European Human Rights Law' (2008) 71 *Modern Law Review* 183, 208, citing, in particular, *James and Others v United Kingdom* App no 8793/79 (judgment, ECtHR, 21 February 1986) para 84.

The Irish Legal Order and the European Convention on Human Rights 93

to incorporate did come, it came neither from Dublin, nor from Strasbourg, but from Belfast. The Belfast Agreement of 1998[133] contained a number of commitments by the governments of both the UK and Ireland regarding human rights in general, and the Convention in particular. The UK Government committed itself, inter alia, to completing the incorporation in Northern Ireland of the ECHR (which was ongoing across the UK in any case, having been a manifesto commitment of the New Labour Government in 1997)[134] and to establishing a Northern Irish Human Rights Commission.[135] Though the Irish Government agreed that it would establish a Human Rights Commission 'with a mandate and remit equivalent to that within Northern Ireland', it committed itself only to 'further examining' the question of the incorporation of the ECHR.[136]

This 'further examination' led, after five years, to the enactment of the ECHR Act 2003, which finally incorporated the Convention, but did so in a sub-constitutional, indirect, interpretive and residual fashion. There is a large and growing literature on the origins, provisions and effects of the ECHR Act.[137] Accordingly, only the Act's major features will be mentioned here, in order to ground a discussion of the implications the Act may have for a polyarchic conception of the relationship between the Irish and ECHR legal orders.

b. The Act's Provisions

The Act's most controversial feature was the chosen method of incorporation. In its 1996 report, the Constitution Review Group considered, but ultimately rejected, the constitutional incorporation of the Convention – whether by wholesale replacement of the Constitution's own fundamental rights provisions, or by something along the lines of Sweden's incorporation by reference, forbidding any enactment contrary to the Convention.[138] The rejection of total replacement is unsurprising, given that it would have involved jettisoning decades of

---

[133] *Agreement Reached in the Multi-party Negotiations*, 10 April 1998 (also known as the Good Friday or Stormont Agreement), available at: peacemaker.un.org/sites/peacemaker.un.org/files/IE%20GB_980410_Northern%20Ireland%20Agreement.pdf.

[134] ibid Part 6.2.

[135] ibid Parts 6.3–6.8.

[136] ibid at Part 6.9.

[137] See U Kilkelly (ed), *ECHR and Irish Law*, 1st edn (Bristol, Jordan, 2004); U Kilkelly (ed), *ECHR in Irish Law*, 2nd edn (Bristol, Jordan 2009); Besson (n 112); A Connelly, 'Implications of the ECHR Act 2003' (2004) 98 *Law Society Gazette* 7; D O'Connell, S Cummiskey, E Meeneghan and P O'Connell, *ECHR Act 2003: A Preliminary Assessment of Impact* (Dublin, Law Society of Ireland, 2006); TE O'Donnell, 'The Constitution, the European Convention on Human Rights Act 2003 and the District Court – A Personal View from a Judicial Perspective' (2007) 7 *Judicial Studies Institute Journal* 137; PA McDermott and MW Murphy, 'No Revolution: The Impact of the ECHR Act 2003 on Irish Criminal Law' (2008) 30 *Dublin University Law Journal* 1; F de Londras and C Kelly, *European Convention on Human Rights Act: Operation, Impact and Analysis* (Dublin, Round Hall, 2010); F de Londras, 'Declarations of Incompatibility Under the ECHR Act 2003: A Workable Transplant?' (2014) 35 *Statute Law Review* 50.

[138] Constitution Review Group *Report* (Stationery Office, Dublin, 1996) 216–19.

94   *The Vertical Frame*

home-grown rights jurisprudence. The rejection of the Swedish model is more difficult to understand, particularly given the scant attention the Group paid to the possibility. Instead, the Group's recommendation was for piecemeal incorporation, as part of a wider project of constitutional reform, drawing on the Convention where:

i.   The right is not expressly protected by the Constitution;
ii. The standard of protection of such rights is superior to those guaranteed by the Constitution; or
iii. The wording of a clause of the Constitution protecting such right might be improved.[139]

While an interesting proposal, it was, along with most of the Group's other recommendations, quietly shelved.

Instead, the ECHR Act 2003 followed a model not contemplated by the Group, the interpretive approach of the UK Human Rights Act 1998 (HRA). It is perhaps rather odd that this approach was chosen in the Irish context, given that it was developed with specific reference to the UK's tradition of parliamentary supremacy and a concomitantly weak role for the judiciary in the vindication of fundamental rights. Though the UK and Ireland share a dualist approach to international law, the legal, political and social experience of judicial rights-enforcement in Ireland would have made some form of constitutional or quasi-constitutional incorporation both politically possible and normatively desirable.[140]

Section 2 of the ECHR Act 2003 contains the core interpretive obligation, requiring the judiciary to interpret and apply statutes and rules of (common) law in a manner compatible with the Convention 'in so far as is possible'. However, there is an important proviso: that this obligation is 'subject to the rules of law relating to such interpretation and application'. Section 3 obliges every 'organ of the State' to act in accordance with the Convention. Significantly, the courts are specifically excluded from the definition of an 'organ of the State'.[141] Section 4 obliges the courts to 'take due account' of the jurisprudence of the Strasbourg bodies in considering the Convention's provisions. Section 5 furnishes the High Court, the Court of Appeal and the Supreme Court with the jurisdiction to make 'declarations of incompatibility' against legislation it finds to be incompatible with the Convention, but only 'where no other legal remedy is adequate and available'. These declarations do not affect the 'validity, continuing operation or enforcement' of the incompatible legislation. The Taoiseach is required to bring such a declaration to the attention of both the Dáil and the Seanad,[142] but there is no legal obligation on the political organs

---

[139] ibid 219.
[140] See further de Londras, 'Declarations of Incompatibility' (n 137).
[141] ECHR Act 2003, s 1.
[142] ibid s 5(3).

The Irish Legal Order and the European Convention on Human Rights 95

to rectify the incompatibility. Finally, section 5(4) authorises the government, at its own discretion, to make an ex gratia payment of compensation in the event of a declaration being made, with the amount linked to the ECtHR's practice relating to 'just satisfaction' under Article 41 ECHR.

B. The ECHR Act 2003 and Polyarchy

The method of incorporation adopted in the ECHR Act 2003 is residual, interpretive and sub-constitutional. Certain provisions, particularly the exclusion of the courts from the definition of 'organs of the State', render the claim by the Minister for Justice who oversaw the Act's passage that 'its provisions have exploited, to the utmost sinew and limit, the capacity of our legal system'[143] rather suspect. The well-known limitations of the UK HRA can at least be explained by the constraints in the United Kingdom of the doctrine of parliamentary sovereignty, an idea long rejected in Ireland as unsound.[144] Viewed in this light, the HRA was indeed a revolutionary development in the UK context, as evidenced by the ongoing political controversy surrounding it. The former minister's claim that the British conception of parliamentary sovereignty has 'different, but no less fundamental, echoes in the context of popular sovereignty and the sole and exclusive law-making role of Parliament'[145] in Ireland sheds little light on the issue. Given the long-standing judicial role of parliamentary oversight – which was suggested in section II above to be less offensive to the idea of democracy and popular sovereignty than might be thought given the system of penultimate judicial supremacy – resistance to giving the judiciary a supplementary set of rights provisions to consider, and a supplementary jurisprudence to take into account at a constitutional level, must be explained and justified by more than simple and simplistic analogy to the constitutional configuration of a (very) different jurisdiction. The most likely answer, I suggest, refers us back to the twin shibboleths of pride in the domestic constitutional order, and prejudice as to the abilities and intentions of a 'foreign' supervisory body.[146]

The traditional, dualist approach to the Convention in Ireland therefore has finally and somewhat grudgingly given way to a form of domestication – and

---

[143] M McDowell 'The European Convention on Human Rights Act 2003: What the Act Will Mean' paper delivered at the Law Society of Ireland/Irish Human Rights Commission Conference on New Human Rights Legislation (18 October 2003) at 3 of the typescript.

[144] In this regard, see the extra-curial comment of Sir Igor Judge LCJ, where he argues that 'tyranny' was surmounted in Britain by the establishment of the sovereignty of Parliament, whereas in the US 'a sovereign Parliament was the problem. It could therefore not be the solution'. The parallels with Ireland are obvious. (I Judge, '"No Taxation without Representation": A British Perspective on Constitutional Arrangements' (2010) 88 *Denver University Law Review* 325, 334).

[145] McDowell (n 143) 2.

[146] Though note Besson (n 112) 96: 'Generally speaking, and contrary to the attitude of the British (tabloid) press, "international" standards are well regarded by the Irish media'.

96 The Vertical Frame

this only as the necessary and possibly unfortunate price of peace, stability and a 'levelling-up' of rights protection in Northern Ireland. It was not necessarily for any intrinsic usefulness or goodness in the internalisation of long-standing international standards of human rights; nor a recognition of the numerous deficiencies in Ireland's own constitutional order; nor a desire to aid in the progressive realisation of the Convention's aspirations across Europe by way of the Irish judiciary finally engaging in the kind of dialogic mutual engagement envisaged by constitutional pluralists. However, what the ECHR Act 2003 does do is make quite credible a heterarchical and polyarchical analysis of Irish and ECHR law, for dualism, by definition, is not pluralism: it is *plural*, in that it recognises the concurrent validity, in different spheres, of more than one legal system; but this is not the same thing. As O'Connell noted above, dualism emphasises the 'otherness' of international law, the idea that it is of relevance only to experts and senior politicians, and not to the ordinary business of legislation, administration, adjudication and rights vindication. By making the Convention part of Irish law, even if only residually ('where no other legal remedy is adequate and available'), the Act has opened the door to a conception of the Irish and Convention legal orders as being, in MacCormick's foundational words, 'interactive, rather than hierarchical'.[147] It enables the Irish judiciary to engage with the reasoning of the ECtHR on its own terms, and within the sphere of its own jurisdiction. Moreover, despite the limitations of the interpretive obligation under section 2, the tortious action under section 3 and the declaration of incompatibility under section 5, these remedies do present an important means by which this sense of 'otherness' surrounding the Convention can be undone, and to regard it as an essential component of the Irish and European constitutional polyarchy.

i. Otherness and Embeddedness

Leaving aside for the moment the particular provisions and provisos of the ECHR Act, it is worth further examining, in the round, the overall effect of the Act on the Convention's place in the domestic legal order. We saw above how the ECA 1972 is the legislative vehicle through which EU law became effective in Ireland. The ECA provides that the Treaties as well as the existing and future acts adopted by the Union 'shall be binding on the State and part of the domestic law thereof under the conditions laid down in [the] Treaties'.[148] The ECA 1972 is therefore the provision from which Union measures draw legislative force in Ireland, but the ECA 1972 is not their *origin*. EU legal norms still originate from outwith the domestic order but are automatically made effective by a

---

[147] N MacCormick, 'Risking Constitutional Collision in Europe?' (1998) 18 *Oxford Journal of Legal Studies* 517, 528.
[148] ECA 1972, s 2.

The Irish Legal Order and the European Convention on Human Rights 97

domestic legislative provision.[149] Significantly, this is *not* the approach employed with respect to the Convention by the ECHR Act 2003. Instead of providing that – to borrow the ECA's language – the Convention 'shall be binding on the State and part of the domestic law thereof' (and thus maintaining the external origin of the Convention provisions), the ECHR Act 2003 imposed a specific set of obligations on domestic institutional actors, set out in the Schedules to the Act.[150] This may seem to be a rather nice distinction, but it has important consequences for the 'externality' of human rights discourse, described above by O'Connell. The idea is that rather than being external imports, the rights protected under the ECHR Act 2003 can be seen as being *as domestic in their origin as any other national legislative provision*, while simultaneously being norms of international law to which the State has committed itself. Their interpretation is therefore a matter for the domestic courts, taking judicial notice of (but not necessarily being strictly bound by) the jurisprudence of the ECtHR.[151] Though not strictly required by the legislation, this arrangement would logically seem to imply that attention should be paid to the interpretation given to the Convention by similarly-situated domestic courts in other European jurisdictions, echoing Maduro's contrapunctual principle of horizontal coherence.

This requirement to take judicial notice of Convention provisions and the jurisprudence of the ECtHR has necessarily changed the world-view and terms of reference of the domestic judiciary. The days when the domestic judiciary was precluded from taking into account obviously relevant judgments of the ECtHR, as in *Norris*, are gone. Cases such as *Carmody, Doherty v South Dublin County Council (No 2)*,[152] and *Leonard v Dublin City Council*[153] all provide instances of detailed and sophisticated engagement with external jurisprudence to a degree previously foreclosed by the lack of incorporation. The cases of *Foy v an t-Árd Chláraitheoir (No 1)*[154] and *(No 2)*[155] demonstrate the integrative, pluralising effect of domestication particularly well. Just days after the High Court had upheld Ireland's lack of provision for updated birth certificates for post-operative transgendered people as compatible with the Convention with

---

[149] This is the case even with regulations. Though self-executing as a matter of EU law, they derive their legal force in Ireland from the ECA 1972.

[150] In this regard, it is worth noting the statement of Laffoy J in *Lelimo v Minister for Justice* [2004] 2 IR 178 that '[i]t is not correct to say that the Convention has been incorporated into domestic law. What the Act of 2003 has done is to give effect to rights recognised in the Convention in Irish law'. (at 186); and also O'Neill J's description of the ECHR Act 'importing' Convention law into Ireland in *Dada v Minister for Justice* [2006] IEHC 166. See further, F de Londras, 'Using the ECHR in Irish Courts: More Whisper than Bang?' (Public Interest Law Association Seminar, Dublin, 13 May 2011), available at: www.pila.ie/download/pdf/pilaechrseminar130511fdelondras.pdf. These comments notwithstanding, the standard term 'incorporation' is used here.

[151] ECHR Act 2003, s 4.

[152] *Doherty v South Dublin County Council (No 2)* [2007] 2 IR 696.

[153] *Leonard v Dublin City Council* [2008] IEHC 79.

[154] *Foy v an t-Árd Chláraitheoir (No 1)* [2002] IEHC 116.

[155] *Foy v an t-Árd Chláraitheoir (No 2)* [2007] IEHC 470.

98   *The Vertical Frame*

reference to the ECtHR's jurisprudence, the European Court handed down judgment in *Goodwin v UK*,[156] reversing its previous holdings on the matter and finding the UK in breach of the Convention for its similar refusal to accommodate the wishes of transgendered people. Accordingly, in *Foy (No 2)*, Mrs Foy was successful in seeking a declaration of incompatibility under section 5 in view of this change in the interpretation of the Convention. No trip to Strasbourg was necessary in order to procure a judgment against the State under international law, for the ECHR Act's provisions had allowed for the ECtHR's jurisprudence to be applied domestically. Moreover, the fact that the domestic courts followed the new line of European jurisprudence does not privilege the ECtHR over the domestic judiciary, nor the Convention over the Constitution. Instead, it was merely that one source of authority in the polyarchy had reconsidered its jurisprudence, and the resultant conflict was resolved by the domestic adoption of this new jurisprudence, enabled by the domestic legislature and thus respectful of the autonomy of the domestic order.

Furthermore, the interpretive obligation imposed by section 2 and elaborated by section 4 of the ECHR Act 2003 is phrased in such a way that it is not confined to cases where Convention rights have been specifically pleaded. In this regard, Oran Doyle and Desmond Ryan note that:

> In the context of a declaration of unconstitutionality being sought in the absence of any ECHR-related claim, the Court has a statutory obligation pursuant to [section 2 ECHR Act] to have regard to any of the pertinent ECHR-related authorities listed in section 4. This point underscores the potential for section 4 to create an enhanced impetus for the already-developed practice of the infusion of Convention protection into domestic constitutional analysis.[157]

However, for all the integrative effects of the ECHR Act 2003, its long title is clear that it is intended 'to enable further effect to be given, *subject to the Constitution*, to certain provisions of the [ECHR]'. The question of priority must therefore be considered.

ii. Unconstitutionality and Unconventionality: A Question of Priority

The question of priority is most relevant with reference to the declaration of incompatibility under section 5. The case of *Carmody v Minister for Justice*[158] concerned the compatibility of the State's criminal legal aid arrangements with both the Constitution and the Convention, and whether an indigent defendant facing trial in the District Court on a complex set of charges was entitled to be

---

[156] *Goodwin v UK* (2002) 35 EHRR 18.
[157] O Doyle and D Ryan, 'Judicial Interpretation of the European Convention on Human Rights Act 2003: Reflections and Analysis' (2011) 33 *Dublin University Law Journal* 369, 380, citing de Londras and Kelly (n 137) 6–44.
[158] *Carmody v Minister for Justice* [2005] 1 JIC 2103 (HC), [2010] 1 IR 635 (SC).

The Irish Legal Order and the European Convention on Human Rights 99

provided with both a solicitor and a barrister. Carmody had simultaneously sought a declaration that section 2 of the Criminal Justice (Legal Aid) Act 1962 was repugnant to the Constitution and a declaration of incompatibility with the Convention under Section 5 of the ECHR Act 2003. In the High Court, Laffoy J applied the long-standing (but not absolute) rule that 'a court should not enter upon a question of constitutionality unless it is necessary for the determination of the case before it'.[159] This is a sensible precautionary principle, in that the 'nuclear option' of finding a legislative provision or state action contrary to the Constitution should be avoided if the plaintiff's rights can be vindicated by less drastic measures. However, Hogan points out that to decide the question of conventionality before that of constitutionality may result in:

> [A] practice that the exhaustion of constitutional remedies [is] the exception, not the norm. If that were so, we might well [reach] the point whereby the ECHR would *de facto* have replaced the Constitution as the principal legal instrument of protection so far as the protection of fundamental rights is concerned.[160]

Such an approach would therefore be inconsistent with the ECHR Act's stated intention that Convention rights be protected subject to the Constitution.

Having made the decision that it was most appropriate to begin by investigating the 1962 Act's compatibility with the Convention prior to deciding the constitutional issue, Laffoy J engaged in a wide-ranging and nuanced consideration of the ECtHR's jurisprudence on Articles 6 and 14 ECHR, and relevant decisions of the Judicial Committee of the Privy Council in the UK exercising its former Scottish jurisdiction, before eventually holding, on the facts, that section 2 of the 1962 Act was not incompatible with the requirements of the Convention. A similar finding was made in relation to section 2's compatibility with the Constitution. Accordingly, Carmody lost his case, and then appealed.

Before considering the Supreme Court's reversal of *Carmody*, it is important to note the High Court judgment of O'Neill J in *Law Society of Ireland v Competition Authority*,[161] handed down shortly after Laffoy J's judgment in *Carmody*. Rather than expressly prioritising Convention arguments over constitutional arguments, or vice versa, O'Neill J employed what might be called an 'exhaustive' or 'concurrent' approach: the case was ultimately decided on constitutional grounds, and the order for certiorari sought by the applicants was granted on account of the respondents' breach of Article 40.3 of the Constitution, but the Court nevertheless went on to evaluate the Convention arguments. In the event, the respondents' actions were held also to amount to a breach of Article 6(1) ECHR. However, because a constitutional remedy had already been

---

[159] *The State (Woods) v Attorney General* [1969] IR 385, 400 (Henchy J).

[160] G Hogan, 'The Value of Declarations of Incompatibility and the Rule of Avoidance' (2006) 28 *Dublin University Law Journal* 408, 418.

[161] *Law Society of Ireland v Competition Authority* [2006] 2 IR 262.

100 *The Vertical Frame*

granted, 'it is impermissible to make the declaration of incompatibility envisaged in s 5, there being another adequate legal remedy available'.[162]

The approaches of the High Court in *Carmody* and *Law Society* differ in important respects. In *Carmody*, Laffoy J set out a clear progression, where arguments under the ECHR Act 2003 are dealt with before any constitutional arguments are entertained; whereas O'Neill J in *Law Society* considered both sets of claims as alternatives, only preferring the constitutional remedy because of section 5's requirement that there be no other adequate remedy available.[163] The Supreme Court's judgment in *Carmody* reveals, however, a different approach. The Court held that the ordinary, Constitution-last approach was inappropriate for cases in which both constitutional arguments and a claim under section 5 ECHR Act 2003 are advanced. This was predicated on the fact that, in the present case, a declaration of incompatibility would not have the effect of 'determining the issue'[164] without recourse to the Constitution. Because section 5 specifically states that a declaration 'shall not affect the validity, continuing operation or enforcement of the statutory provision or rule of law in respect of which it is made',[165] Carmody would still have faced trial without the assistance of a barrister and, as the Court held, 'any such declaration in this case would leave the plaintiff in the same position with regard to his claimed constitutional right ... as he was prior to the commencement of proceedings'.[166] This combined with section 5(1)'s requirement that 'no other legal remedy [be] adequate or available' led the Court to conclude that in any case where both declarations of unconstitutionality and incompatibility with the Convention are sought, the constitutional arguments must be decided first.

It is therefore clear from the Supreme Court's judgment in *Carmody* that for all the integrative effect of the ECHR Act 2003, the Constitution remains the supreme law of the land within the epistemology of the Irish constitutional order; and while the judgment still allows for domestic application and interpretation of the Convention, and thus for a growth in domestic Convention jurisprudence over time, Convention remedies are still of a residual nature.

C. Conclusion: *Legislative* Interface Norms

As was stated at the outset of this section, the relationship between the Irish legal order and that of the Convention is fundamentally different from that

---

[162] ibid 290.

[163] This can be contrasted with O'Neill J's decision to grant a declaration of incompatibility in *Dublin City Council v Liam Gallagher* [2008] IEHC 354, where no constitutional arguments had been raised, and the alternative remedy of judicial review would not have been adequate given that the facts of the case were in dispute.

[164] *Carmody* (SC) (n 158) 648, quoting *Murphy v Roche* [1987] IR 106, 110 (Finlay CJ).

[165] ECHR Act 2003, s 5(2)(a).

[166] *Carmody* (SC) (n 158) 650.

between the Irish order and that of the Union. This is to be expected, both because of the very different natures of the two European legal orders per se, and because of the very different means by which the entry of these orders to the Irish system is regulated. Outlining the terms of engagement between Irish and EU law necessarily involved discussion of cases of actual and potential conflict between the legal orders, especially *Crotty* and *Grogan*, and thus the interface norms involved, whether constitutional or metaconstitutional. This was particularly the case given the remarkable nature of Article 29.4.6°, and the orthodoxy surrounding it. The relationship between Irish law and the Convention contains no equivalent to the exclusion clause; and, unlike the judicially formulated constitutional interface norms discussed in section II, the ECHR Act 2003 provides a set of *legislative* norms regulating the interaction between legal systems. Again, these norms are internal to the Irish legal system, and not metaconstitutional. Accordingly, the focus of this section has been on outlining the means by which the Convention has been incorporated in Ireland and demonstrating the polyarchic nature of the resultant relations, and *not* on the approach of the Irish judiciary in cases of conflict. As we have seen with reference to the cases of *Foy (No 1)* and *Foy (No 2)*, conflict between the two legal orders is ordinarily resolved by the adaptation of the domestic order to the norms of the Convention. There are, however, examples of altogether more difficult cases of conflict between the orders, and these will be discussed in greater detail, in the context of the 'triangular' frame, in chapter four.

III. CONCLUSION

This chapter has set out in detail the means by which the legal orders of the EU and the Convention have been received in the Irish legal order. It has demonstrated, first, that, in both cases, the relationship between the systems is best regarded as being heterarchical and, second, that the three systems form part of a tripartite polyarchy: the triangular constitution. There are three systems of valid law in Ireland: national, Union, and Convention. From the national perspective, both European orders depend on the national for their validity and applicability but are subject to the interpretive authority ('final' within their own domain) of the organs established by the European orders themselves. In the ordinary run of things, this arrangement can well be conceived of hierarchically: the Irish order dutifully and loyally applies the law of the European orders, as interpreted by the CJEU and the ECtHR. But the means of reception and integration of both systems leave open the *possibility* – more explicitly in the case of the ECHR, but no less possibly in the case of the EU – of resistance to and departure from the interpretations of the European courts. Whether and when this possibility should be availed of is a question of a different order, to be dealt with in the normative analysis of chapter five, once the picture of the triangular constitution and its interactions is complete.

102　*The Vertical Frame*

With reference to the Irish–EU side of the triangle, the interface norms invoked by the domestic judiciary when dealing with cases of constitutional conflict – whether before or after the coming into force of EU norms – are *constitutional* in nature. That is, they are conflict-of-laws rules internal to the national legal system. Whether and how they can be metaconstitutionalised, and what resemblance they bear to the interface norms posited by Kumm and others is a question that will be addressed further in the chapters to follow, but we can come to the preliminary conclusion that the attempt to universalise norms developed with reference to a particular national configuration is beset with difficulty, and that the external norms posited by Kumm do not quite reflect what has happened in actual practice.

Turning to the Irish–ECHR side of the triangle, we saw that a standard unincorporated dualist relationship between national and international law has given way to the partial internalisation of the international system within the national by virtue of the ECHR Act 2003. That Act itself provides substantive norms for regulating the relationship between the orders, but it does so at the legislative, and therefore sub-constitutional, level. Be that as it may, the Act provides convincing evidence for the polyarchical arrangement of the two legal systems. Discussion of instances of seemingly irresolvable conflict between the orders, and the interface norms adopted therein, will be engaged in chapter four. Before this can be done, however, the third side of the triangle must be outlined: the relationship between the EU and the ECHR. This will be the subject of the next chapter.

3

The Horizontal Frame

INTRODUCTION

THIS CHAPTER EXAMINES the relationship, and the interface norms at work, on the 'horizontal' side of the triangular constitution: the interplay between the Union and Convention legal orders. Though the relationship can be characterised as 'horizontal' within the specific Member State–EU–ECHR configuration, this is subject to two important provisos. First, there is a 'triangular' aspect inherent to the relationship, in that nation states have historically served as the intermediaries through which the two European legal orders have articulated their relationship with and attitudes to each other, given the historic lack of a direct institutional link between them. As we shall see, the coming into force of the Charter of Fundamental Rights of the European Union[1] has partially provided the institutional link that was previously missing, and this link may yet be solidified by the now delayed – though still legally required – accession of the EU to the Convention. Secondly, these two developments, the Charter and accession, raise serious questions about how best to conceptualise the EU–ECHR relationship, and whether heterarchy is giving way – and ought to give way – to hierarchy.

The examination proceeds in three parts. Section I sets out the institutional relationship between the European Union (EU) and the European Convention on Human Rights (ECHR) as it currently stands, without accession, from the perspective of each in turn, and analyses the interface norms employed by the Court of Justice of the European Union (CJEU) and the European Court of Human Rights (ECtHR) in developing the relationship. Section II then outlines and analyses both the means by which the EU was to accede to the ECHR under the Draft Accession Agreement (DAA)[2] negotiated between the EU and the

---

[1] Charter of Fundamental Rights of the European Union [2016] OJ C 202/2.

[2] 'Fifth Negotiation Meeting between the CDDH ad hoc Negotiation Group and the European Commission on the Accession of the European Union to the European Convention on Human Rights: Final Report to the CDDH' (Council of Europe, 47+1(2013)008rev2), available at: www.echr.coe.int/Documents/UE_Report_CDDH_ENG.pdf. For academic comment on this and earlier drafts, and more generally, see C Eckes, 'EU Accession to the ECHR: Between Autonomy and Adaptation' (2013) 72 *Modern Law Review* 254; M Kuijer, 'The Accession of the European Union to the ECHR: A Gift for the ECHR's 60th Anniversary or an Unwelcome Intruder at the Party?' (2011) 3 *Amsterdam Law Forum* 17; T Lock, 'EU Accession to the ECHR: Implications for Judicial Review

104 *The Horizontal Frame*

Council of Europe (CoE), and the CJEU's rejection of the DAA as incompatible with the Treaties in Opinion 2/13.[3] This Opinion has been subject to serious criticism on a range of grounds,[4] but the focus here will be on the Opinion as an adaptation to the EU–ECHR context of Maduro's ex ante national constitutional review of EU norms,[5] similar to those discussed in the Irish context in chapter two, and on what the Opinion can tell us about the CJEU's conception of the pre- and post-accession relationship between the legal orders. In section III, the focus shifts and zooms in to a specific, ongoing case of conflict between the orders regarding labour rights, investigating how it arose and offering suggestions based on precedent, and in the light of Opinion 2/13, as to how it may yet be resolved.

The chapter concludes that though there are similarities with the 'vertical' frame, the specific nature of the EU and the ECHR as non-state legal orders complicates any attempt to simply transpose interface norms developed in the context of the EU–Member State relationship. Moreover, EU accession to the ECHR would shift a large part of the work of managing the interface between the orders from the realm of the *meta*constitutional to that of the *constitutional*, which poses further difficulties for the ostensible universality of metaconstitutional interface norms.

I. THE PRE-ACCESSION TERMS OF ENGAGEMENT BETWEEN THE EU AND THE ECHR

A. The ECHR from the CJEU's Viewpoint

We saw in chapter one how the CJEU's initial disavowal of any jurisdiction in matters of human rights gradually gave way, following pressure from judicial

---

in Strasbourg' (2010) 35 *European Law Review* 777; T Lock, 'Walking on a Tightrope: The Draft ECHR Accession Agreement and the Autonomy of the EU Legal Order' (2011) 48 *Common Market Law Review* 1025.

[3] Opinion 2/13 *Accession of the European Union to the European Convention for the Protection of Human Rights and Fundamental Freedoms* ECLI:EU:C:2014:2454.

[4] L Besselink, M Claes and J-H Reestman, 'Editorial: A Constitutional Moment: Acceding to the ECHR (or Not)' (2015) 11 *European Constitutional Law Review* 2; T Lock, 'The Future of the European Union's Accession to the European Convention on Human Rights after Opinion 2/13: Is it Still Possible and is it Still Desirable?' (2015) 11 *European Constitutional Law Review* 239; S Peers, 'The EU's Accession to the ECHR: The Dream Becomes a Nightmare' (2015) 16 *German Law Journal* 213. Even defences of the Opinion tend to be partial and modest: D Halberstam, '"It's the Autonomy, Stupid!" A Modest Defense of Opinion 2/13 on EU Accession to the European Convention on Human Rights' (2015) 16 *German Law Journal* 105; P Gragl, 'The Reasonableness of Jealousy: Opinion 2/13 and EU Accession to the ECHR' in W Benedek, F Benoît-Rohmer, MC Ketteman, B Kneihs and M Nowak (eds), *European Yearbook on Human Rights 2015* (Vienna, Neuer Wissenschaftlicher Verlag, 2015); M Scheinin, 'CJEU Opinion 2/13 – Three Mitigating Circumstances' (*Verfassungsblog*, 26 December 2014), available at: www.verfassungsblog.de/cjeu-opinion-213-three-mitigating-circumstances/.

[5] MP Maduro, 'Contrapunctual Law: Europe's Constitutional Pluralism in Action' in N Walker (ed), *Sovereignty in Transition* (Oxford, Hart Publishing, 2003) 506–08.

The Pre-Accession Terms of Engagement 105

actors at the state level, to the development of an expansive EU human (or 'fundamental') rights jurisprudence. Judge Allan Rosas of the CJEU describes his Court's attitude to the Convention during this process as progressing through five stages:[6] the initial denial of fundamental rights competence;[7] acceptance of fundamental rights as part of the general principles of Community law (since 1969);[8] explicit reference to the ECHR (since 1974);[9] characterisation of the ECHR as having 'special significance' (since 1991);[10] and reference to the jurisprudence of the ECtHR (since 1996).[11] However, these developments came about quite separately from the institutional machinery of the Convention. Indeed, the CJEU held in 1996 that EU accession to the Convention would be outwith the conferred competences of the Union,[12] being a change which would:

> [E]ntail the entry of the Community into a distinct international institutional system as well as integration of all provisions of the Convention into the Community legal order[,] [s]uch a modification of the system for the protection of human rights in the Community ... would be of constitutional significance and would therefore be such as to go beyond the scope of Article 235 [EC]. It could only be brought about by Treaty amendment.[13]

In a foreshadowing of the later response to Opinion 2/13, this decision was criticised on the ground that although the matter was framed as one of competence, the Court had an ulterior motive in the protection of its own jurisdiction and autonomy from external interference, leading to a decision that was 'needlessly restrictive and diffident towards the ECHR'.[14] In the words of Giorgio Gaja: '[W]hat is here at stake is the conservation by the Court of Justice of its present functions, although understandably the Court has not stressed this point in order not to emphasize its concern with its own prerogatives'.[15]

---

[6] A Rosas, 'The European Union and Fundamental Rights/Human Rights' in C Krause and M Scheinin (eds), *International Protection of Human Rights: A Textbook* (Turku, Åbo Akademi University Institute for Human Rights, 2009) 457.

[7] Case 1/58 *Stork v High Authority* ECLU:EU:C1959:4, [1959] ECR 17; Joined Cases 36, 37, 38 & 40/59 *Geitling v High Authority* ECLI:EU:C:1960:36, [1960] ECR 423; Case 40/64 *Sgarlata and others v Commission* ECLI:EU:C:1965:36, [1965] ECR 215.

[8] Case 29/69 *Stauder v City of Ulm* ECLI:EU:C:1969:57, [1969] ECR 419.

[9] Case 36/75 *Rutili* ECLI:EU:C:1975:137, [1975] ECR 1219.

[10] Case C-260/89 *ERT* ECLI:EU:C:1991:254, [1991] ECR I-2925.

[11] Case C-13/94 *P v S* ECLI:EU:C:1996:170, [1996] ECR I-2143.

[12] Opinion 2/94 *Accession by the Community to the European Convention for the Protection of Human Rights and Fundamental Freedoms* ECLI:EU:C:1996:140, [1996] ECR I-1759.

[13] ibid paras 34–35.

[14] B de Witte, 'The Use of the ECHR and Convention Case Law by the European Court of Justice' in P Popelier, C Van de Heyning and P Van Nuffel (eds), *Human Rights Protection in the European Legal Order: The Interaction Between the European and National Courts* (Cambridge, Intersentia, 2011) 17.

[15] G Gaja, 'Case-note on Opinion 2/94' (1996) 33 *Common Market Law Review* 973 at 988. See, further, N Burrows, 'Question of Community Accession to the European Convention Determined' (1997) 22 *European Law Review* 58, 62, suggesting that: 'Perhaps the Court is jealous of its jurisdiction and will not lightly give way to an international court which may stand above it'. But compare C Franklin, 'The Legal Status of the EU Charter of Fundamental Rights After the Treaty of Lisbon'

106 The Horizontal Frame

While this may well have been the case, the Opinion was still highly supportive of the Convention's general relevance to the EC legal order. The Court repeated its long-standing assertion that 'fundamental rights form an integral part of the general principles of law whose observance the Court ensures',[16] and recalled the further holding from *ERT*[17] that the Convention is of 'special significance' in the context of the Court's consistent statement that it 'draws inspiration from the constitutional traditions common to the Member States and from the guidelines supplied by international treaties for the protection of human rights on which the Member States have collaborated or of which they are signatories'.[18] As a result, the general attitude of the CJEU towards the ECtHR in the period between Opinion 2/94 and Opinion 2/13 was one of comity in the face of potentially overlapping jurisdictions, coupled with (and perhaps tempered by) a desire to preserve its own autonomy and interpretive pre-eminence within the Union – the very substance of Charles Sabel's and Oliver Gerstenberg's deliberative polyarchy. The purpose of this subsection is, therefore, to examine two related consequences of this generally accommodating attitude in the pre-accession era in order to reveal the interface norms – constitutional and metaconstitutional – regulating the relationship: first, the normative status of the Convention within the Union legal order, and, second, how the CJEU uses the ECtHR's jurisprudence.

i. The Normative Status of the Convention Within the EU

As we have seen, the CJEU's case law on the general principles of EU law has followed a three-step formula in respect of the relevance of the Convention to the EU legal order. First, fundamental rights are general principles of Union law; secondly, international treaties between the Member States and others supply 'guidelines' from which the Court 'draws inspiration' in its decisions on these general principles; and thirdly, the Convention has 'special significance' in this regard.[19] This formula leaves the formal relationship between Convention rights and the general principles somewhat unclear, and does not, of itself, give any

---

(2010–11) 15 *Tilburg Law Review* 137, 158, fn 84: '[T]he stance adopted in Opinion 2/94 was in fact no different to that taken in other well-known cases where the Court refused to open the door for other international courts, tribunals or bodies to rule on issues covered by Community law' (citing Opinion 1/91 *Draft Agreement Between the Community and the Countries of EFTA Relating to the Creation of the EEA* ECLI:EU:C:1991:490, [1991] ECR I-6079 and Case C-459/03 *Commission v Ireland* ECLI:EU:C:2006:345, [2006] ECR I-4635).

[16] Opinion 2/94 (n 12) para 33. For a critical view, describing the EU's fundamental rights narrative as an instance of political mythology, see S Smismans, 'The European Union's Fundamental Rights Myth' (2010) 48 *Journal of Common Market Studies* 45.

[17] *ERT* (n 10).

[18] Opinion 2/94 (n 12) para 33.

[19] In addition to the case law cited in section I.A above, see Case C-479/04 *Laserdisken ApS v Kulturministeriet* ECLI:EU:C:2006:549, [2006] ECR I-8089, para 61 for a simple, one-paragraph condensation of this approach.

The orthodox view is that, the EU not being a signatory to the Conven-

particular indication as to the normative status of Convention rights within the EU. It cannot therefore be classified as an interface norm, even in the loosest sense: rather, it is a broad, general statement of relative openness towards the norms of another legal order, leaving more than enough room for those norms to be applied or departed from in a given case.

The orthodox view is that, the EU not being a signatory to the Conven-tion, the Convention is not binding within the EU legal order (at least not as part of the general principles). This is the clear and repeated position of the General Court (GC): '[T]he Court has no jurisdiction to assess the lawfulness of an investigation under competition law in light of the provisions of the ECHR, inasmuch as those provisions do not as such form part of Community law'.[20] However, the Court of Justice has never explicitly endorsed the exclusionary approach of the GC, and Bruno de Witte advances a different interpretation, one based on the actual text of Article 6(3) TEU: 'Fundamental rights, *as guaranteed by the [ECHR]* and as they result from the constitutional traditions common to the Member States, shall constitute general principles of the Union's law'.[21] For de Witte, this wording, present in the Treaties since Maastricht and justicia-ble since Amsterdam,[22] 'indicates that the rights of the Convention *are* general principles of EU law and not just *a source of inspiration* for those principles'.[23] This argument is persuasive: the fact that fundamental rights merely *result from* national constitutional traditions implies a kind of filtration and adaption entirely absent from the bald statement that the fundamental rights contained in the general principles are those *as guaranteed by* the Convention. If this is so, then the relationship between the EU and the ECHR is rather tighter and more formal than the orthodoxy imagines, and can be described as a relationship of 'reverse dualism'. By this I mean that the relationship is the precise converse of that which existed between Ireland and the ECHR prior to the coming into force of the European Convention on Human Rights Act 2003 (ECHR Act 2003), outlined in chapter two. Whereas Ireland is a signatory to the Convention, and is thus bound by it as a matter of international law, the Convention itself was not a part of the Irish legal system, and could not be relied on directly in Irish courts. Conversely, the EU, not being a signatory to the Convention, is neither bound by it under international law nor are its institutions directly subject to the jurisdiction of the ECtHR, but Article 6(3) TEU, by its own clear and specific

---

[20] Case T-99/04 *AC-Treuhand v Commission* ECLI:EU:T:2008:256, [2008] ECR II-1501, para 45. See also, Case T-112/98 *Mannesmannröhren-Werke v Commission* ECLI:EU:T:2001:61, [2001] ECR II-729, para 59; and Case T-347/94 *Mayr-Melnhof Kartongesellschaft v Commission* ECLI:EU:T:1998:101, [1998] ECR II-1751, para 311.

[21] Emphasis added.

[22] Treaty on European Union (Treaty of Maastricht) [1992] OJ C 191, Art F(2) and Treaty on European Union (Treaty of Amsterdam) [1997] OJ C 340, Art 6(2): 'The Union shall respect funda-mental rights, as guaranteed by the [ECHR] ... as general principles of Community law'.

[23] de Witte (n 14) 22, emphasis in original.

108 The Horizontal Frame

terms, *has the effect of incorporating the Convention into the EU order*. This reverse dualism finds some support in a number of judgments of the Court of Justice. In *Elgafaji*, for instance, the Court stated simply, and without more, that 'the ECHR forms part of the general principles of Community law'.[24] However, this tendency is not universal, and the 'inspiration; guidelines; special significance' filtration formula still features in the Court's reasoning in other recent cases, most notably in *Kadi*[25] and in Opinion 2/13 itself,[26] revealing a certain ambivalence on the part of the Court of Justice as to the precise nature of the relationship between the general principles and Convention rights, despite the wording of Article 6(3) TEU. The GC's absolute denial that the Convention is itself a part of Union law, however, is still not quite reflected in Opinion 2/13: rather, the Court of Justice stated that 'as the EU has not acceded to the ECHR, [it] does not constitute a legal instrument which has been *formally* incorporated into the legal order of the EU'.[27] The word 'formally' here is key, and seems to indicate a quiet acknowledgement that the 'inspiration; guidelines; special significance' incantation does not quite capture the specific nature of the relationship. While Opinion 2/13 does not go so far as to overrule the GC's denial of the force of the Convention within the Union, nor does it approve it: instead, we get an acknowledgement that the Convention has not been *formally* incorporated into the Union order, which leaves open exactly the kind of *informal* incorporation described by the reverse dualism thesis.[28]

This view of the direct applicability of Convention rights within the EU is lent further weight since the entry into force of the Lisbon Treaty,[29] and with it the elevation of the Charter to a status equal to that of the Treaties.[30] The general principles of EU law have been supplemented with a written

---

[24] Case C-465/07 *Meki Elgafaji, Noor Elgafaji v Staatsecretaris van Justitie* ECLI:EU:C:2009:94, [2009] ECR I-921, para 28. de Witte also cites Joined Cases C-482/01 and C-493/01 *Georgios Orfanopoulos v Land Baden-Württemberg* ECLI:EU:C:2004:262, [2004] ECR I-5257, para 98 and Case C-450/06 *Varec SA v Etat belge* ECLI:EU:C:2008:91, [2008] ECR I-581, para 44 ff (de Witte (n 14) 23).

[25] Joined Cases C-402/05 P and C-415/05 P *Kadi and Al Barakaat v Council and Commission* ECLI:EU:C:2008:461, [2008] ECR I-6351, para 283, citing Case C-305/05 *Ordre des barreaux francophones et germanophone and Others* ECLI:EU:C:2007:383, [2007] ECR I-5305, para 29.

[26] Opinion 2/13 (n 3) paras 37–45, emphasis added.

[27] ibid para 179, citing Case C-571/10 *Kamberaj* EU:C:2012:233, para 60 and Case C-617/10 *Åkerberg Fransson* EU:C:2013:105, para 44.

[28] See further the statement of AG Jacobs in his Opinion in Case C-84/95 *Bosphorus Hava Yolları Turizm ve Ticaret Anonim Şirketi v Minister for Transport, Energy and Communications and others* ECLI:EU:C:1996:179, [1996] ECR I-3953, para 53: 'Although the Community itself is not a party to the Convention, and ... although the Convention may not be *formally* binding upon the Community, nevertheless for practical purposes the Convention can be regarded *as part of Community law* and can be invoked as such both in this Court and in national courts where Community law is in issue' (emphasis added, citations omitted).

[29] Treaty of Lisbon amending the Treaty on European Union and the Treaty establishing the European Community [2007] OJ C 306.

[30] Art 6(1) TEU: 'The Union recognises the rights, freedoms and principles set out in the [Charter], which shall have the same legal value as the Treaties'.

bill of rights,[31] containing its own provisions as to how these rights relate to those of the Convention. Article 52(3) of the Charter states that:

> Insofar as this Charter contains rights which correspond to rights guaranteed by the [ECHR], the meaning and scope of those rights shall be the same as those laid down by the [ECHR]. This provision shall not prevent Union law providing more extensive protection.

Accordingly, even if one does not accept de Witte's interpretation of Article 6(3) TEU, the combined effect of Article 6(1) TEU and Article 52(3) of the Charter, taken in tandem, is to incorporate into the EU order *at least those Convention rights which correspond to rights in the Charter.* Whether through the general principles (on de Witte's view) or through the Charter, Convention rights *may* therefore be relied on directly by litigants – and applied directly by the courts – within the EU, even without EU accession to the Convention, and notwithstanding the CJEU's recurrent filtering of the Convention through the 'inspiration; guidelines; special significance' formula. This view of the Convention's status within the EU fits well with the notion of polyarchy, with two non-state courts interpreting and applying the same rights within their own jurisdictional spheres, though with only the interpretations of one of these courts being authoritative. This being the case, two questions then arise relating to the interpretation of these rights: the normative force of Strasbourg jurisprudence within the EU, and how this jurisprudence is used by the CJEU.

ii. ECtHR Case Law Before the CJEU

The CJEU made no reference to the case law of the ECtHR until *P v S*,[32] a decision handed down a month after Opinion 2/94. Having ruled out the possibility of EU accession without Treaty amendment, the CJEU appears to have begun citing Strasbourg jurisprudence in a compensatory effort to demonstrate its commitment to human rights protection.[33] Sionaidh Douglas-Scott notes that:

> While the earlier references made to Strasbourg tended to be brief and unexpansive, more recent references engage more with Strasbourg jurisprudence and tend to be more reliant on it as a ground of justification, especially if they are made by Advocates General.[34]

---

[31] On the relationship between the general principles and the rights set out in the Charter, see HCH Hofmann and BC Mihaescu, 'The Relation Between the Charter's Fundamental Rights and the Unwritten General Principles of EU Law: Good Administration as the Test Case' (2013) 9 *European Constitutional Law Review* 73 (and references therein). See also, K Lenaerts, 'Exploring the Limits of the EU Charter of Fundamental Rights' (2012) 8 *European Constitutional Law Review* 375, especially at 384–86.

[32] *P v S* (n 11). Note, however, that references to Strasbourg jurisprudence began appearing in the Opinions of Advocates General in the 1980s: see S Douglas-Scott, 'A Tale of Two Courts: Luxembourg, Strasbourg and the Growing European Human Rights *Acquis*' (2006) 43 *Common Market Law Review* 629, 645.

[33] See de Witte (n 14) 24.

[34] Douglas-Scott (n 32) 645.

110 *The Horizontal Frame*

Despite this development, the CJEU in its use of ECtHR case law tends not to enter into discussion of the case law's normative force, and has never described it as *binding*.[35] Instead, the CJEU has historically restricted itself to an obligation to take Strasbourg jurisprudence into account.[36] This attitude – of maintaining autonomy on one hand, while demonstrating comity on the other – is well illustrated by two sets of cases where the CJEU interpreted the Convention in a manner subsequently contradicted by the ECtHR.

The CJEU held in *Hoechst* – in the absence of ECtHR case law on the point – that the right to inviolability of the dwelling under Article 8 ECHR could not be applied to a business premises.[37] Subsequently, the ECtHR established in *Niemitz*[38] and in *Colas Est*[39] that Article 8 did indeed cover business premises – a finding later acknowledged by the CJEU in *Roquette Frères*,[40] reversing *Hoechst*.

Similarly, the CJEU held in *Orkem* that Article 6 ECHR did not encompass a right against self-incrimination.[41] Again, this was later contradicted by the ECtHR in *Funke*,[42] and again, the CJEU corrected itself in light of this development in *Limburgse Vinyl Maatschappij*.[43] In both of these instances, though Luxembourg ultimately followed the lead set by Strasbourg, it was careful to do so by analogy and on its own terms, rather than to suggest that it was under any strict obligation to correct itself.

However, these cases concerned general principles of Union law, and predated the coming into force of the Charter. As was the case with the status of the Convention within Union law, the Charter in the post-Lisbon era has altered the status of Strasbourg jurisprudence. Article 6(1) TEU, having given the Charter the same legal value as the Treaties, goes on to provide that the Charter is to be interpreted in accordance with its own provisions on interpretation, and with 'due regard' to the explanations referred to in the Charter, which set out the sources of its provisions.[44] These explanations make clear that:

> The reference [in Article 52(3) of the Charter] to the ECHR covers both the Convention and the Protocols to it. The meaning and scope of the guaranteed rights are

---

[35] ibid 651.

[36] See, eg, Joined Cases C-238/99 P, C-244/99 P, C-245/99 P, C-247/99 P, C-250/99 P to C-252/99 P and C-254/99 P *Limburgse Vinyl Maatschappij NV and Others v Commission* ECLI:EU:C:2002:582, [2002] ECR I-8375, para 274.

[37] Joined Cases 46/87 and 227/88 *Hoechst v Commission* ECLI:EU:C:1989:337, [1989] ECR 2859, para 18. Note, however, that the Court held at para 19 that such protection *was* available under the legal systems of the Member States.

[38] *Niemitz v Germany* (1992) 16 EHRR 97, paras 27–33.

[39] *Société Colas Est v France* (2004) 39 EHRR 373, paras 28–39.

[40] Case C-94/00 *Roquette Frères SA v DGCCRF* ECLI:EU:C:2002:603, [2002] ECR I-9011, para 29.

[41] Case 374/87 *Orkem v Commission* ECLI:EU:C:1989:387, [1989] ECR 3283, para 30.

[42] *Funke v France* (1993) 16 EHRR 297, paras 41–44.

[43] *Limburgse Vinyl Maatschappij* (n 36) paras 258–80.

[44] The general provisions governing interpretation of the Charter are set out in Title VII, and the explanations referred to by Art 52(7) are found in Explanations Relating to the Charter of Fundamental Rights [2007] OJ C 303/17.

The Pre-Accession Terms of Engagement   111

determined not only by the text of those instruments, *but also by the case-law of the [ECtHR] and by the [CJEU]*. The last sentence of the paragraph is designed to allow the Union to guarantee more extensive protection. In any event, the level of protection afforded by the Charter may never be lower than that guaranteed by the ECHR.[45]

Although this provision, and the other provisions of the Charter regarding its interpretation, do not make ECtHR case law binding on the CJEU in specific terms, the combined effect is to make the Strasbourg Court's interpretation of the meaning and scope of the Convention rights – and thus many of the Charter's provisions – an authoritative baseline, below which the CJEU's standards of protection may not fall. Furthermore, it is important that this part of the explanations to the Charter *also* charges the CJEU with the interpretation of the Convention as a matter of EU law, as emphasised in the extract above, and thus provides the institutional means by which this interpretation may lead to a higher – but emphatically not lower – level of rights protection. In the post-Lisbon era, therefore, judgments of the ECtHR have greater normative force within the EU itself (at least in the interpretation and application of the Charter) than they do in the Irish legal order under the ECHR Act 2003, which, as we saw in chapter two, requires the Irish judiciary only to 'take due account' of the ECtHR's decisions.[46] In this context, having reviewed the CJEU's Charter case law since Lisbon, Filippo Fontanelli states that: 'It is clear that reference to the ECtHR and its case-law is no longer a matter of nicety and comity but an actual precondition for the application of the Charter'.[47]

The ECHR's status within the EU, and that of the ECtHR's jurisprudence, is therefore based on much more than mere comity between the Luxembourg and Strasbourg courts, although this was previously the case. The EU is not only empowered but *obliged* to accede to the Convention (Opinion 2/13 notwithstanding);[48] Convention rights are stated to *be* general principles of Union law (though the CJEU has been somewhat reluctant to concede this point); and, in a very real sense, the Convention and the case law surrounding it are incorporated into the EU legal order, and made a baseline or floor below which human rights standards may not fall, by means of the Charter. This therefore raises the question of whether hierarchy or heterarchy best characterises the relationship between the two legal orders; and it is at least arguable that (some form of) hierarchy has the upper hand in the post-Lisbon era. Before this question can properly be addressed, however, we must examine the relationship from the other side.

---

[45] Charter Explanations (n 44) 303/33, emphasis added.
[46] ECHR Act 2003, s 4.
[47] F Fontanelli, 'The European Union's Charter of Fundamental Rights: Two Years Later' (2011) 3 *Perspectives on Federalism* 22, 39. See also de Witte (n 14) 24–32, where he describes the CJEU's use of Strasbourg jurisprudence as 'eclectic and unsystematic'.
[48] Art 6(2) TEU.

112 *The Horizontal Frame*

B. The EU from the ECtHR's Viewpoint

The CJEU's development of an EU human rights jurisprudence has been broadly well received by the ECtHR. A relatively early, and somewhat tentative, example is the case of *Goodwin v UK*,[49] where the ECtHR referred to the *P v S* judgment of the CJEU, in which that Court had held that discrimination arising from gender reassignment constituted discrimination on grounds of sex under (and contrary to) EU law. Though the ECtHR did not go into detail in its analysis of the Luxembourg case in this instance, and did not specifically adopt its reasoning, it seems fair to regard the ECtHR's attitude to the case as one of general approval, given that both cases had the effect of upholding a complaint of discrimination against transgendered people. It is also significant that the ECtHR made reference to the Charter in the course of its judgment, which, at the time, the CJEU itself had not yet done.[50]

But there was a significant jurisdictional problem that the ECtHR had to resolve. The majority of the States that are party to the Convention are also Member States of the EU, and are therefore subject to the requirements of the Treaties and the jurisdiction of the CJEU. However, as we know, the EU itself is not a signatory to the Convention and therefore is not directly subject to the jurisdiction of the ECtHR in the same way that its Member States are. What then is to be done in a case where a state subject to both the Convention and the Treaties is found to have acted in breach of the Convention, but this was only done in order to fulfil obligations under the Treaties? The case law on this point can be divided into two categories: review of primary EU law, and review of secondary EU law. There is then a more difficult third category, where it is the actions of the Union institutions themselves, quite separately from the Member States, that are impugned. Each of these categories will be dealt with in turn.

i. Review of Primary EU Law

As early as 1958, the former European Commission of Human Rights (ECmHR) held in *X & X*[51] that if a State's international obligations prevented it from living up to its obligations under the Convention, the State would still be responsible for the latter. Later, the ECmHR held in *M & Co*[52] that this responsibility would not apply if the international organisation to which a State had delegated power provided 'equivalent protection' of human rights, a decision which Douglas-Scott notes has obvious parallels with the *Solange* jurisprudence outlined in chapter one,[53] and thus with the interface norm of conditional recognition. Notwithstanding this development, the ECtHR still

---

[49] *Goodwin v UK* (2002) 35 EHRR 18.
[50] ibid, paras 58 and 100.
[51] *X & X v Germany* App no 342/57 (decision, ECmHR, 4 September 1958).
[52] *M & Co v Germany* [1990] 64 Decisions and Reports 138.
[53] Douglas-Scott (n 32) 636.

The Pre-Accession Terms of Engagement 113

indirectly reviewed a norm of EU law for compliance with the Convention in *Matthews*.[54] The applicant, a Gibraltar resident, alleged that Annex II of the (EC) Direct Elections Act 1976,[55] by which the UK declared that it would apply the Act only in respect of the UK itself (and not the territories for whose foreign affairs the UK is responsible), was in breach of Article 3 of Protocol 1 ECHR. In holding for the applicant, the ECtHR noted that:

> [A]cts of the EC as such cannot be challenged before the Court because the EC is not a Contracting Party. The Convention does not exclude the transfer of competences to international organisations provided that Convention rights continue to be 'secured'. Member States' responsibility therefore continues even after such a transfer.[56]

Crucially, both the 1976 Act and the Maastricht Treaty – which enhanced the powers of the European Parliament, giving it for the first time the characteristics of a 'legislature' within the meaning of the Convention[57] – were not ordinary EC (secondary) legal acts, such as regulations or directives, but rather were primary law instruments, and thus immune from challenge before the CJEU.[58] Accordingly, the Convention rights could not be 'secured' in this instance, there being no method by which the law could be challenged on human rights grounds at EU level, 'equivalent' or otherwise. Clearly not content to allow such a lacuna, the Court held the UK directly responsible for the failure to hold elections to the European Parliament in Gibraltar.[59] *Matthews* demonstrates that the ECtHR is not averse to reviewing primary EU law for conformance with the Convention, provided that responsibility for this law can be attributed to a State party to the Convention. The case thereby demonstrates the partially 'triangular' nature of the EU–ECHR relationship, in that the ECtHR *can* have jurisdiction over primary EU law despite the EU not being a signatory to the Convention, but this jurisdiction is *indirect*, mediated through the responsibility of states as signatories to the Convention, the UK serving in this case as the necessary intermediary to engage the supervision of Strasbourg over norms that would otherwise be outwith its jurisdiction. In other words, rather than proceeding by the shortest (direct) route, the link between EU law and the ECHR travels along two sides of the triangle, a particular EU Member State/State party to the Convention serving as the necessary intermediary.

ii. Review of Secondary EU Law

But there still remains the issue of secondary EU law, which *can* be challenged before the CJEU on human or fundamental rights grounds. In this regard, the

---

[54] *Matthews v UK* (1999) 28 EHRR 361.

[55] Act Concerning the Election of the Representatives of the Assembly by Direct Universal Suffrage [1976] OJ L 278.

[56] *Matthews* (n 54) para 32.

[57] ibid paras 45–54.

[58] ibid para 33.

[59] ibid paras 60–65.

114   *The Horizontal Frame*

most explicit support from the ECtHR for the human rights turn in the CJEU's jurisprudence is found in *Bosphorus v Ireland*.[60] Echoing the much earlier ECmHR decision in *M & Co*, the ECtHR held that:

> State action taken in compliance with [legal obligations deriving from membership of an international organisation] is justified as long as the relevant organisation is considered to protect fundamental rights, as regards both the substantive guarantees offered and the mechanisms controlling their observance, in a manner which can be considered at least equivalent to that for which the Convention provides.[61]

If the ECtHR considers that the organisation at issue does in fact offer an equivalent[62] level of rights-protection to the Convention, state action taken on foot of an international obligation is presumed to be in compliance with the requirements of the Convention, though this presumption can be rebutted if, in a given case, 'it is considered that the protection of Convention rights was manifestly deficient'.[63] In the case at hand, the ECtHR first set out the evolution of human rights protection within the Union, with particular reference to the 'special significance' given to the Convention in *ERT*, and Opinion 2/94's statement that respect for human rights is 'a condition for the lawfulness of [Union] acts'.[64] The Court went on to analyse the procedures by which Union acts can be challenged under the Treaties – whether by way of direct action before the CJEU or by action before a national court making use of the Article 267 TFEU preliminary reference procedure – and held that, at the relevant time, the EU had in fact offered an 'at least equivalent' level of protection of human rights in general, and that in the particular case at hand case there was no deficiency or dysfunction in this protection.[65] Accordingly, the presumption that Ireland's actions on foot of its EU obligations – which, in turn, were on foot of action required by the UN Security Council – were compliant with the Convention was not rebutted, and Bosphorus' application failed. As was the case in *Matthews*, it is important to note the triangularity of this interaction: it was *state* action that was being judged directly. The (potential and, in this case, unnecessary) review of secondary EU norms would still be indirect in a case finding 'manifestly deficient' protection of human rights, mediated through the responsibility of the state at issue.

---

[60] *Bosphorus Hava Yolları Turizm ve Ticaret Anonim Şirketi v Ireland* (2005) ECHR 440 (*Bosphorus*). See generally, T Lock, 'Beyond *Bosphorus*: The European Court of Human Rights' Case Law on the Responsibility of Member States of International Organisations under the European Convention on Human Rights' (2010) 10 *Human Rights Law Review* 529; S Peers, '*Bosphorus* – European Court of Human Rights' (2006) 2 *European Constitutional Law Review* 443.

[61] *Bosphorus* (n 60) para 155.

[62] Note that: 'By "equivalent" the Court means "comparable"; any requirement that the organisation's protection be "identical" could run counter to the interest of international cooperation pursued ... However, any such finding of equivalence could not be final and would be susceptible to review in the light of any relevant change in fundamental rights protection' (ibid).

[63] ibid para 156.

[64] Opinion 2/94 (n 12) para 34.

[65] *Bosphorus* (n 60) paras 156–66.

The Pre-Accession Terms of Engagement 115

The ECtHR has never had the opportunity fully to get to grips with the issue of apportioning responsibility in a case where the EU Member State retained some discretion in applying an EU norm. Though it held in *Bosphorus* that a state 'would be fully responsible under the Convention for all acts falling outside its strict international legal obligations',[66] the presumption of EU conventionality was held not to apply in the more recent case of *Michaud v France*[67] (concerning a directive rather than a regulation), due to the fact that, in the domestic proceedings, the Conseil d'Etat had not requested a preliminary reference from the CJEU, and so that Court had had no opportunity to scrutinise the directive in question on human rights grounds. This distinguished the case from *Bosphorus* and brought it more into line with the situation in *Matthews*, where the CJEU could never have scrutinised the laws in question in the first place, being primary norms of EU law. The essential factor in the ECtHR's decision to review the impugned legislation on the merits in *Michaud* therefore seems not to have been the fact that France had discretion in its transposition of the directive, but rather the fact that the CJEU had not yet been heard on the matter.[68] In the event, the Court held that the French implementing legislation was not in breach of the Convention; but the way in which the Court approached the issue illustrates a certain amount of reluctance, first, to get involved in the apportioning of responsibility between the EU and its Member States, and, secondly, to rule on the substantive compliance of Union measures with the Convention without first having heard the CJEU on the matter.

Two points can be made about the ECtHR's *Bosphorus* approach to human rights protection at EU level. First – and as Douglas-Scott noted with reference to its ancestor, *M & Co* – it is strikingly similar to the *Solange* jurisprudence, a point also emphasised by Sabel and Gerstenberg[69] who note that the decision 'reconciles two conflicting aspects: the recognition of the accommodation of human rights concerns by the ECJ *and* recognition of the specificity and autonomy of the Community law system'.[70] As we have seen in chapter one, in *Solange II*, the Bundesverfassungsgericht (BVerfG) committed itself not to exercise – but did not renounce – its claimed jurisdiction to review norms of EU law for rights-compliance, so long as the level of protection offered by the CJEU was not less than that offered by the BVerfG in Germany. The *Bosphorus* approach is similarly accommodating, recognising as it does the ostensible progress made in terms of the attention paid by the EU to issues of human rights, while still reserving to the ECtHR the right to intervene if it considers such intervention necessary for the vindication of the rights protected by the Convention.

---

[66] ibid para 157.

[67] *Michaud v France* [2012] ECHR 2030.

[68] An earlier example of the ECHR not fully engaging with the issue is *MSS v Belgium and Greece* (2011) 53 EHRR 2.

[69] CF Sabel and O Gerstenberg, 'Constitutionalising an Overlapping Consensus: The ECJ and the Emergence of a Coordinate Constitutional Order' (2010) 16 *European Law Journal* 511, 519 and 547.

[70] ibid 519, footnote omitted.

116   *The Horizontal Frame*

However, the *Bosphorus* principle is unique in the ECtHR's jurisprudence, in that the Court specifically *privileges* the jurisprudence of the CJEU in a way that it does not in relation to the High Contracting Parties to the Convention. No national legal system under the ECHR enjoys a presumption, rebuttable or otherwise, that its whole system of law is compliant with the Convention. Quite the contrary: the very raison d'être of the ECtHR is to supervise national legal systems party to the ECHR, and the existence of such supervision logically implies a certain suspicion (though this may be too strong a word) that the Convention will not always be upheld at the domestic level. Such supervision is, by the very fact of its existence, an 'undermining' of the autonomy of the domestic system, regardless of the fact that this was done voluntarily, deliberately and for very good reasons. Moreover, to borrow terms from software development, this 'intrusion' is not a *bug* in the system, but a *feature*. The doctrine of the margin of appreciation, whereby the ECtHR allows states a certain leeway in their interpretation and application of some of the rights under the Convention, may seem comparable to the rule in *Bosphorus* at first glance, but the two notions are fundamentally different: a supervised leeway is not the same thing as a (rebuttable) presumption of compatibility. This discrepancy (margin of appreciation for states; presumption of compliance for the Union) may well have been justified at the time by the specific nature of the EU as an autonomous legal order not yet party to the Convention, with which the ECtHR had to come to terms within the structural confines of its own jurisdiction. However, as we shall soon see in section II, the sometimes suspect reasoning of the CJEU in its rejection of the negotiated means of EU accession to the ECHR raises questions as to whether the presumption should now be narrowed at the very least, if not lifted altogether. Moreover, in *Bosphorus* the ECtHR gave 'the interest of international cooperation' as justification for requiring mere *equivalence*, rather than *identity*, between the systems of human rights protection.[71] While international cooperation can certainly be a worthy interest, it is questionable whether it is sufficient to legitimise a breach of the Convention. This issue of the justifiability and appropriateness of the *Bosphorous* presumption, particularly in the aftermath of Opinion 2/13, is one to which we will return.

iii. Review of Actions of the Union's Institutions

We now turn to situations where it is difficult or impossible to engage an EU Member State as the intermediary through which ECtHR jurisdiction over Union law can be channelled, described by Lock as the '*Connolly* gap'.[72] In both

---

[71] *Bosphorus* (n 60) para 155.

[72] Lock, 'The Future of the European Union's Accession to the European Convention on Human Rights after Opinion 2/13' (n 4) 268, referring to *Connolly v 15 Member States of the EU* App no 73274/01 (decision, ECtHR, 9 December 2008).

Matthews and *Bosphorus*, the existence of discretionary state action was crucial for engaging the jurisdiction of the ECtHR: while the challenged action was in fulfilment of the State's international obligations, the facts that the actions could be attributed to a Contracting State, and that the State had some residual discretion in how to fulfil its obligations, were the necessary hooks on which the applicants could hang the allegation of a breach of the Convention. However, in *Connolly*, the applicant was a former employee of the European Commission, dismissed for having published a book critical of his employers without having first received permission to do so. Connolly had challenged his dismissal on procedural grounds and as an infringement of his right to freedom of expression before the Union's courts, and had failed.[73]

The ECtHR's decision in the case was exceedingly terse. The Court noted that at no time did any of the Member States intervene in the litigation, directly or indirectly; and that it was the actions of the Union institutions themselves – whether the Court of Justice or Commission – which were being challenged, with no state action or omission coming into question. Accordingly, the case was inadmissible *ratione personae*: the alleged violations could not be (directly) attributed to a Contracting State, and the Union itself is not a party to the Convention. The ECtHR did refer to the *Bosphorus* presumption, but it did so in passing, and held that there was nothing in the case to demonstrate a 'manifestly deficient' protection of the applicant's rights. However, this conclusion was reached without reasoning, and without any analysis of the cases Connolly had lost before the Union courts. It is therefore not clear from the decision how the application of the *Bosphorus* presumption related to the two separate bases for the finding of inadmissibility (lack of state action; lack of Union responsibility under the Convention). Was the Union's 'passing' of the *Bosphorus* 'test' in the case a necessary prior factor in the finding of inadmissibility, or a separate, additional reason for this inadmissibility? *Connolly* provides an insufficient basis to attempt any answer to this question. Its application of the *Bosphorus* presumption (an instance of the interface norm of conditional recognition) and its associated test provides no insight into the mechanics of how *Bosphorus* is applied: it serves rather more as a rhetorical and jurisprudential flourish than as a clearly reasoned interface norm for the working out of the relationship of the two legal orders.

This issue is fundamental for our understanding of the ECtHR's conception of the relationship between the two orders: let us imagine for the moment that there *had* been some glaring and incontrovertible defect in the Union's treatment of Connolly, sufficient to trigger the 'manifestly deficient' exception to the

---

[73] Case T-203/95 *Connolly v Commission* ECLI:EU:T:1999:101, [1999] ECR II-443; Joined Cases T-34/96 and T-163/96 *Connolly v Commission* ECLI:EU:T:1999:102, [1999] ECR II-463; Case T-214/96 *Connolly v Commission* ECLI:EU:T:1999:103, [1999] ECR II-517; Case C-273/99 P *Connolly v Commission* ECLI:EU:C:2001:126, [2001] ECR I-1575; Case C-274/99 P *Connolly v Commission* ECLI:EU:C:2001:127, [2001] ECR I-1611.

118   *The Horizontal Frame*

Bosphorus doctrine. Certainly, the fact remains that the ECtHR has no direct jurisdiction over the actions of the Union and its institutions. But is this enough for the ECtHR to regard itself as impotent in the face of a clear breach of the Convention by the Union? Let us bear in mind the temporal context in which *Connolly* was decided: after the finalisation of the Lisbon Treaty, but before its coming into force. It is not idle to speculate that the ECtHR was prepared to tolerate the existence of the *Connolly* gap on a temporary basis, pending EU accession to the Convention. As we shall see in sections II and III below, there may well now be sound reasons for arguing for the gap to be bridged: for the ECtHR to drop the requirement of a Member State 'link' for its juris-diction over the actions of the Union to be engaged. If this is the case, then *Connolly* provides exactly the institutional mechanism by which this indirect jurisdiction might be engaged: a challenge would not be made against the Union itself, but rather against the Member States as joint respondents – not *Applicant v EU* (which is legally impossible), but *Applicant v 28 Member States of the EU* (which emphatically is not, *Connolly* notwithstanding).[74]

iv. Institutional Matters: The CJEU's Advocates General and Article 6 ECHR

Before moving on to the details of accession, Opinion 2/13 and its aftermath, there is one further matter that warrants examination: the potential – but averted – conflict between the ECtHR and the CJEU on the question of the compatibility of the role of the CJEU's Advocates General with Article 6 ECHR. The *Hoechst* and *Orkem* series of cases discussed above at section I.A.ii revealed a divergence in the approaches of the two European courts, which was ulti-mately resolved, uncontroversially and without difficulty, by the CJEU adopting the ECtHR's jurisprudence and correcting its own – an archetypal example of 'good behaviour' under the Convention, and an instance where the relation-ship between the orders can well be conceived of hierarchically. However, these cases concerned the manner in which the EU, and in particular the Commission, went about enforcing EU competition law, and did not call into question the substantive nature of that enforcement. Though the right to inviolability of the dwelling (or business premises) and the right against self-incrimination are important in their own right, they do not – and did not in these cases – pose constitutional or institutional difficulties for the EU or offend against that legal order's self-image of autonomy and autochthony. The divergence in the case law outlined in this subsection had the potential to pose an altogether more serious threat to the autonomy of EU law, and its ultimate resolution demon-strates the sheer extent of the ECtHR's deference to that autonomy under the

---

[74] On shared responsibility before the ECtHR, see M den Heijer, 'Shared Responsibility Before the European Court of Human Rights' (2013) 60 *Netherlands International Law Review* 411; M den Heijer, 'Procedural Aspects of Shared Responsibility in the European Court of Human Rights' (2013) 4 *Journal of International Dispute Settlement* 361.

Bosphorus presumption; the power of the presumption itself; and illustrates the questionable justifiability of privileging the Union above its Member States.

The ECtHR had held in *Vermeulen*[75] that the impossibility of the defence replying to the observations of the Procureur Général before the Belgian Cour de cassation constituted a breach of the right to adversarial proceedings under Article 6 ECHR, a right that:

> Means in principle the opportunity for the parties to a criminal or civil trial to have knowledge of and comment on all evidence adduced or observations filed, even by an independent member of the national legal service, with a view to influencing the court's decision.[76]

The breach had been aggravated by the Procureur Général's participation in the Court's deliberations, albeit in an advisory capacity.[77] Similar decisions were made regarding equivalent officers in the courts of Portugal, the Netherlands and France.[78] *Vermeulen* was subsequently relied on before the CJEU by the applicants in *Emesa Sugar*,[79] who had been refused leave to reply to the Advocate General's Opinion in the course of a preliminary reference, since neither the Statute of the CJEU nor the Court's Rules of Procedure made provision for such a reply.[80] Emesa argued that in the light of the ECtHR's decision in *Vermeulen*, the impossibility of replying to the AG's Opinion was in breach of Article 6 ECHR. In its decision, the CJEU recounted the 'general principles; guidelines; special significance' formula regarding the Convention,[81] but distinguished *Vermeulen* on the grounds that the CJEU's Advocates General are full members of the Court, equal in rank to the Judges, and are subject to no external authority.[82] Moreover, the Court can reopen the oral procedure after the delivery of the AG's Opinion 'if it considers that it lacks sufficient information, or that the case must be dealt with on the basis of an argument which has not been debated between the parties'.[83] Accordingly, the decision in *Vermeulen* was not 'transposable'[84] to the position of the Luxembourg AGs, and on its own – autonomous – interpretation of the requirements of the Convention, the CJEU held that its structure and procedures did not constitute a breach of Article 6 ECHR.

Later, the decision in *Emesa* was relied on before the ECtHR by the French Government in *Kress*,[85] in respect of an Article 6 ECHR challenge against the

---

[75] *Vermeulen v Belgium* (2001) 32 EHRR 15.

[76] ibid para 33.

[77] ibid para 34.

[78] *Lobo Machado v Portugal* (1996) 23 EHRR 79; *JJ v the Netherlands* (1999) 28 EHRR 168; *KDB v the Netherlands* [1998] ECHR 20; *Reinhardt and Slimane-Kaïd v France* (1998–II) 28 EHRR 59.

[79] Case C-17/98 *Emesa Sugar (Free Zone) NV v Aruba* ECLI:EU:C:2000:70, [2000] ECR I-675.

[80] ibid para 2.

[81] ibid para 8.

[82] ibid paras 10–15.

[83] ibid para 18.

[84] ibid at para 16.

[85] *Kress v France* (2001) ECHR 382 (*Kress*).

120   *The Horizontal Frame*

impossibility of replying to the Opinion of the Commissaire du Gouvernement at the Conseil d'Etat, who, like the Luxembourg AGs – and unlike the Belgian officials in *Vermeulen* – are members of the Court, and not subject to any external authority. Moreover, the Community's archives show the office of the AG at the CJEU to have been inspired in particular by the Commissaire du Gouvernement.[86] The French Government argued that to find a breach of Article 6 ECHR with respect to the Commissaire would be to call into question the system in operation at the CJEU since its inception. The ECtHR again found a breach of Article 6 ECHR, but this time specifically on the ground of the Commissaire's participation in the trial bench's deliberations – something which the Luxembourg AGs do not do, though the ECtHR did not mention this – and not on the basis of his or her being subject to external authority. Such participation – *after* having submitted an Opinion to the Court – may seem unfair under the 'doctrine of appearances' (that is, in the eyes of a layperson 'not familiar with the mysteries of administrative proceedings').[87] The ECtHR reproduced the relevant part of the CJEU's decision in *Emesa* at length as part of the 'relevant domestic law and practice', but did not engage substantively with the decision in its judgment. *Kress* accordingly left the issue of the compatibility of the CJEU's structure and practice with Article 6 ECHR open. In *Kaba II*,[88] the CJEU 'failed to reconsider the matter ... when presented with a chance'.[89] The CJEU's silence on the issue – deciding the case on different grounds – was particularly noteworthy given AG Ruiz-Jarabo Colomer's highly critical overview of the *Kress* jurisprudence, stating that:

> It seems that what was being sought was not so much the protection of a fundamental right as the imposition of a uniform conception of the organisation of the procedure [across disparate legal traditions] without explaining the need for it in terms going beyond the doctrine of appearances.[90]

The ECtHR having set itself on a collision course with the CJEU on this issue, the *dénouement*, when it came, was somewhat surprising. In *Kokkelvisserij*,[91] the applicants, in the course of an Article 267 TFEU reference, had been denied leave to reply to the AG's Opinion, and the CJEU had refused to reopen the oral procedure. The ECtHR held that because the national court had actively sought a preliminary ruling from Luxembourg, national responsibility for a potential

---

[86] C Ritter, 'A New Look at the Role and Impact of Advocates-General – Collectively and Individually' (2005–06) 12 *Columbia Journal of European Law* 751, 751.

[87] *Kress* (n 85) paras 81–83.

[88] Case C-466/00 *Arben Kaba v Secretary of State for the Home Department (Kaba II)* ECLI:EU:C:2003:127, [2003] ECR I-2219.

[89] Douglas-Scott (n 32) 648, fn 83.

[90] Case C-466/00 *Arben Kaba v Secretary of State for the Home Department (Kaba II)* (Opinion) ECLI:EU:C:2002:447, [2003] ECR I-2219, para 105.

[91] *Cooperatieve Producentenorganisatie van de Nederlandse Kokkelvisserij UA v the Netherlands* App no 13645/05 (decision, ECtHR, 20 January 2009).

The Pre-Accession Terms of Engagement   121

breach of the Convention by the EU institutions was engaged.[92] The Court recalled the *Bosphorus* presumption of equivalent protection and proceeded to an examination of whether the EU's protection of human rights was 'manifestly deficient' in this instance. Intriguingly, in finding that the presumption of equivalent protection was *not* rebutted by the impossibility of replying to the AG's Opinion, the ECtHR adopted an approach entirely different from that adopted with respect to the national systems in its previous case law. It did not focus on the institutional position of the AG (his or her independence; the fact that AGs do not take part in the CJEU's deliberations) or on the doctrine of appearances. Rather, it focused somewhat narrowly on the specific nature of the Article 267 TFEU procedure.[93] The Court noted that the protection offered did not need to be *identical* to that of Article 6 ECHR, and focused in particular on the possibility of reopening the oral procedure, which it held to be realistic and not merely theoretical.[94] In the case at hand, the CJEU had reviewed the request for a reopening of the oral procedure on the merits, and had found that the applicants had submitted no precise information suggesting that a reopening would be useful or necessary. Accordingly, the *Bosphorus* presumption was not rebutted, and the case was declared inadmissible.

The decision in *Kokkelvisserij* is a reaffirmation of the *Bosphorus* presumption of equivalent protection and demonstrates just how difficult it may be to prove 'manifestly deficient' protection of fundamental rights in the EU legal order. Despite having made a series of judgments with respect to national legal systems which called into question the very structure and procedures of the CJEU – and in the face of a refusal by the CJEU to accept that its structure and procedures were in conflict with Article 6 ECHR – when the matter came to a head, the ECtHR 'scrutinized the ECJ's procedures with considerable restraint in comparison to the national procedures'.[95] The ECtHR accepted, without investigation, the CJEU's finding of 'no precise information' warranting a reopening of the oral procedure, and though it had previously characterised the right to adversarial proceedings under Article 6 ECHR as requiring the possibility of responding to 'all evidence adduced or observations filed, even by an independent member of the national legal service',[96] it accepted the possibility of the CJEU (at its sole discretion) reopening the oral proceedings as sufficient to safeguard that right, with no investigation of the proportionality of the possible restriction. Accordingly, the *Bosphorus* presumption – an application of the

---

[92] ibid, section B(3) of the decision as to the law (no paragraph numbers in the decision).

[93] ibid.

[94] ibid. The Opinion of AG Sharpston in Case C-212/06 *Gouvernement de la Communauté française and Gouvernement wallon v Gouvernement flamand* ECLI:EU:C:2007:398, [2008] ECR I-1683 was particularly influential in the ECtHR so deciding.

[95] C Van de Heyning, 'PO Kokkelvisserij v the Netherlands' (2009) 46 *Common Market Law Review* 2117, 2124.

[96] *Kress* (n 85) para 65.

122 *The Horizontal Frame*

interface norm of conditional recognition – was employed to avoid a head-on collision between the two European courts on a matter of central importance. It may well be the case that AG Colomer's complaint – that the ECtHR's jurisprudence on the issue was not really geared towards the protection of the right to a fair trial, but rather towards the imposition of a uniform system – is valid. However, this does not explain or justify the ECtHR's refusal in *Kokkelvisserij* to hold the EU to the same standards – rightly or wrongly – it had held various states.

C. Conclusions: Metaconstitutional Interface Norms

The terms of engagement described above are complex, have changed over time, and this process of change is ongoing. As things stand, I argue that the EU has progressed to a situation where the Convention is binding within the EU order (notwithstanding the lack of formal incorporation, and notwithstanding the CJEU's reluctance to concede the point), and the ECtHR's case law provides an authoritative baseline below which EU standards may not fall, but beyond which they may go. In recognising this progress, the ECtHR has attempted to reconcile its own duties and prerogatives as the overseer of the Convention with the EU's autonomy and specificity as a legal order. As the *Connolly* gap and the saga (anti-)climaxing in *Kokkelvisserij* illustrate, the ECtHR – at least prior to Opinion 2/13 – has been very accommodating of the EU legal order, and has been willing to tie itself into knots to avoid finding the *Bosphorus* presumption to have been rebutted.

How does Mattias Kumm's conception of the universal metaconstitutional interface norms regulating the relationships between legal orders relate to the specific context of the relationship between the EU and the ECHR? Though Kumm's procedural principle of democracy – which I characterised in chapter two rather as a means for the protection of national specificity on democratic grounds – may have certain parallels in the supranational space with the protection of a supranational organisation's autonomy and uniformity, these are still very different things. Most notably, though the protection of the EU's autonomy may be justified on many different grounds, democracy is almost certainly not one of them. As we have seen, neither the CJEU nor the ECtHR have employed a principle along these lines in their jurisprudence.

The formal principle of legality may, however, have some relevance here. Recall that this involves a strong presumption that '[national courts] are required to enforce EU law, national constitutional provisions notwithstanding'.[97] Transposing this to the supranational domain, such a principle would require the

---

[97] M Kumm, 'The Jurisprudence of Constitutional Conflict: Constitutional Supremacy in Europe Before and After the Constitutional Treaty' (2005) 11 *European Law Journal* 262, 299.

CJEU to enforce the Convention, EU law notwithstanding. This being the case, the acquiescence of the CJEU to the ECtHR's divergent interpretation of the Convention in the context of the inviolability of business premises and the right against self-incrimination is nothing more than the correction of an erroneous interpretation of the Convention in light of a subsequent clarification by the body charged with interpreting that document authoritatively. It does not threaten the EU legal order's autonomy, or that of the CJEU as the authoritative interpreter of that legal order, and fits well with Kumm's principle of legality.

The jurisdictional principle of subsidiarity has little relevance to the EU–ECHR relationship, predicated as it is on the particular nature of the relationship between the EU and its Member States, and it finds no reflection in the non-state context. However, the substantive principle of the protection of basic rights finds an almost exact reflection in the ECtHR's *Bosphorus* presumption of equivalent protection, the similarity of which to the *Solange* jurisprudence being what led Sabel and Gerstenberg to characterise the EU–ECHR relationship as being part of a deliberative polyarchy in the first place. As a result, while there are certain aspects of Kumm's interface norms which are reflected in the case law surrounding the EU–ECHR relationship, the specificity of these two legal orders, and the resultant specificity of their relationship, means that Kumm's metaconstitutional interface norms cannot be directly transposed from their statist origins. Instead, the less prescriptive notion of deliberative polyarchy, epitomised not just by the *Bosphorus* principle but also, more specifically, by its application in the judicial interaction regarding Article 6 ECHR and the structure and procedures of the CJEU with respect to the Advocates General, better captures the nature of the relationship.

However, important changes to this relationship will be (or rather may yet be) effected by EU accession to the Convention, and it is to the specifics of this accession, and the difficulty it has encountered, to which we must now turn.

II. THE DRAFT ACCESSION AGREEMENT AND OPINION 2/13

On 5 April 2013, the Council of Europe and EU negotiators finalised a Draft Accession Agreement (DAA), by which the Union was to accede to the Convention, as is required, since Lisbon, by Article 6(2) TEU. However, when asked by the European Commission, under the procedure laid out in Article 218(11) TFEU, for its opinion on the compatibility of the DAA with the Treaties, the Court of Justice responded emphatically in the negative. We saw in chapter one how Miguel Poiares Maduro posits ex ante and ex post national constitutional review of EU norms as two of the main types of national constitutional challenge to the claim to ultimate authority made by EU constitutionalism;[98] and in

---

[98] Maduro (n 5) 506–08.

124   *The Horizontal Frame*

chapter two how *Crotty v An Taoiseach*[99] was a particularly instructive example of ex ante review in the Irish–EU context. In that case, the Supreme Court employed the interface norm of conditional recognition in the form of a 'scope and objectives' test for determining whether amendments to the Treaties could be ratified without further constitutional authorisation by referendum. Though the ECHR does not make the same kind of claims to primacy in cases of conflict with national law that EU law does, the parallels between *Crotty* and Opinion 2/13 are nevertheless significant: the apex court within a given ('domestic')[100] legal system (Ireland in *Crotty*; the EU in Opinion 2/13) was asked to rule on the constitutionality of an attempt to make the norms of another legal system (EU; ECHR), interpreted by another apex court (CJEU; ECtHR), effective within the domestic system, and responded with a judgment that sought, at bottom, to protect the autonomy and integrity of the domestic system. In *Crotty*, the changes brought about by the European Communities (Amendment) Act 1986 were held to be within the 'scope and objectives' of the Treaties, and thus had already been constitutionally authorised. The one exception to this was the attempt to ratify Title III of the Single European Act by parliamentary vote, which was held to be an unconstitutional surrender of sovereignty in the sphere of foreign policy: such a change would require specific authorisation by way of constitutional amendment, which in Ireland can be achieved only by referendum. In Opinion 2/13, the CJEU's objections to the DAA can be grouped into two major categories: the first, more general – and less easily remedied – category concerns the specificity of EU law in general and the autonomy of EU fundamental rights law in particular. The second, more particular, and less difficult category concerns the specific institutional and procedural machinery set out in the DAA, and whether these comply with the Treaty conditions for EU accession to the ECHR.[101] Each of these categories, and the CJEU's specific objections to the DAA within each category, will be examined in turn, before analysing the Opinion as a whole in terms of its use of interface norms.

A. Specificity and Autonomy

Though the Union is required to accede to the Convention, this requirement is not unconditional. Article 6(2) TEU requires, in its second sentence, that '[s]uch accession shall not affect the Union's competences as defined in the Treaties'. Protocol No 8 TEU imposes further conditions, most notably a requirement that any accession agreement must 'make provision for preserving the specific characteristics of the Union and Union law', particularly with regard to the EU's

---

[99] *Crotty v An Taoiseach* [1987] IR 713.
[100] This is almost certainly the wrong word in the Union context but will be used regardless for the sake of the analogy.
[101] See Opinion 2/13 (n 3) para 178.

participation in the ECHR's control bodies and to the correct addressing of applications against Member States and/or the Union itself.[102] Finally, the Intergovernmental Conference's Declaration on Article 6(2), annexed to the TEU, states that accession 'should be arranged in such a way as to preserve the specific features of Union law'.[103] However, the CJEU held in Opinion 2/13 that the DAA failed to meet these requirements in four respects.

i. Article 53 ECHR and Article 53 of the Charter

Article 53 of the Charter and Article 53 of the ECHR are both 'floor' provisions, intended to make clear that nothing in either document is to be interpreted as *lowering* the standard of human rights protection in the High Contracting Parties (in the case of the ECHR) or in the Member States, the Union and international law (in the case of the Charter). Though the explanations to the Charter do not say so, it is clear from the numbering and the language used that Article 53 of the Charter was based on Article 53 ECHR.[104]

However, in *Melloni*,[105] the CJEU (re-?)interpreted Article 53 of the Charter as being both a 'floor' *and* a 'ceiling', at least in cases where EU law completely determines Member State action,[106] such as in the field of the European Arrest Warrant at issue in the case. In such a situation, higher national standards of human rights protection cannot be justified under Article 53 and must give way to the EU standard in accordance with the principle of primacy. This being the case, the Court held in Opinion 2/13 that Article 53 ECHR should be 'coordinated' with Article 53 of the Charter. However, 'coordination' here is a euphemism, the CJEU making clear that it means that

> the power [to lay down higher standards] granted to Member States by Article 53 of the ECHR [should be] limited – with respect to the rights recognised by the Charter

---

[102] Protocol (No 8) relating to Article 6(2) of the Treaty on European Union on the Accession of the Union to the European Convention on the Protection of Human Rights and Fundamental Freedoms [2016] OJ C 202/273, Art 1.

[103] Declaration on Article 6(2) of the Treaty on European Union [2016] OJ C 202/337.

[104] Daniel Sarmiento notes parallels also with Art 5.2 of the International Covenant on Civil and Political Rights; Art 5.2 of the International Covenant on Economic, Social and Cultural Rights; and Art 29 of the American Convention on Human Rights: D Sarmiento, 'Who's Afraid of the Charter? The Court of Justice, National Courts and the New Framework of Fundamental Rights Protection in Europe' (2013) 50 *Common Market Law Review* 1267, 1288, fn 88, citing R Alonso García, 'The General Provisions of the Charter of Fundamental Rights of the European Union' (2002) 8 *European Law Journal* 492, 507 and JB Liisberg, 'Does the EU Charter of Fundamental Rights Threaten the Supremacy of Community Law?' (2001) 38 *Common Market Law Review* 1171, 1183–88.

[105] Case C-399/11 *Melloni* ECLI:EU:C:2013:107.

[106] The situation is slightly different where EU law only partially determines Member State action, as in Case C-617/10 *Åkerberg Fransson* ECLI:EU:C:2013:105. See generally Sarmiento, Who's Afraid of the Charter?' (n 104); J-H Reestman and LFM Besselink, 'Editorial: After *Åkerberg Fransson* and *Melloni*' (2013) *European Constitutional Law Review* 169; F Fontanelli, '*Hic Sunt Nationes*: The Elusive Limits of the EU Charter and the German Constitutional Watchdog' (2013) 9 *European Constitutional Law Review* 315.

126 *The Horizontal Frame*

that correspond to those guaranteed by the ECHR – to that which is necessary to ensure that the level of protection provided for by the Charter and the primacy, unity and effectiveness of EU law are not compromised.[107]

This is a remarkable proposal, in that it regards 'the level of protection provided for by the Charter' and the 'primacy, unity and effectiveness of EU law' as a (single) standard which the ECHR must be amended to accommodate, rather than the other way around. Moreover, it is worth mentioning that the judgment in *Melloni* was handed down on 26 February 2013, just over a month before the DAA was concluded, after almost three years of negotiations. It is therefore hardly surprising that the DAA made no effort to 'coordinate' Article 53 ECHR and Article 53 of the Charter, even if such a 'coordination' were desirable, or indeed acceptable to the Union's negotiating partners in the Council of Europe.

ii. Article 344 TFEU

Under Article 344 TFEU, 'Member States undertake not to submit a dispute concerning the interpretation or application of the Treaties to any method of settlement other than those provided for therein'. Article 3 of Protocol No 8 TEU specifically requires that nothing in any Accession Agreement should affect Article 344 TFEU. However, Article 55 ECHR contains a similar exclusion clause, prohibiting signatories from submitting disputes regarding the interpretation of the Convention to any extra-Convention settlement system.

The DAA therefore attempted to reconcile these two provisions, and meet Protocol No 8 TEU's requirements, by making clear in Article 5 DAA that proceedings before the CJEU do not constitute dispute settlement within the meaning of Article 55 ECHR. However, the CJEU in Opinion 2/13 held this to be insufficient, in that it leaves open the possibility of the EU or a Member State submitting an application to the ECtHR alleging a violation of the Convention by a Member State or the EU.[108] According to the CJEU, Article 344 TFEU 'is specifically intended to preserve the exclusive nature of the procedure for settling ... disputes within the EU ... and thus precludes any prior or subsequent external control'.[109] However, this is almost impossible to reconcile with the very concept of EU accession to the Convention, which by its nature involves the EU submitting its legal system to 'subsequent external control' (albeit of a subsidiary and supervisory nature), a point which the CJEU did not acknowledge. Moreover, the CJEU contradicts itself at this point in the Opinion. On the one hand, it accepts that 'as a result of accession, the ECHR would form an integral part of EU law'[110] (though I have argued above that this is already the case in

---

[107] Opinion 2/13 (n 3) para 189.
[108] ibid para 207.
[109] ibid para 210.
[110] ibid para 204, citing para 180.

any event, though in a less formal way). Yet on the other hand, it states that 'the very nature of EU law ... requires that relations between the Member States be governed by EU law to the exclusion, if EU law so requires, of any other law'[111] as justification for its objection to the possibility of the EU or its Member States being able to challenge each other in Strasbourg. But if the ECHR is an *integral* part of EU law, then the Convention machinery is not something *external* to EU law in any meaningful sense and does not breach the requirement that relations between the Member States be governed by EU law exclusively.

It is undoubtedly the case that EU accession to the ECHR must not affect the workings of Article 344 TFEU: Article 3 of Protocol No 8 TEU makes this clear. What is not at all clear is whether the solution can only be that proposed by the CJEU: the total exclusion of the ECtHR's jurisdiction to hear disputes between the EU and its Member States regarding the interpretation of the Convention within the (ever-widening) scope of EU law. Rather, such total exclusion would go some way towards defeating the whole point of EU accession.

iii. Mutual Trust

The principle of mutual trust between Member States, which was one of the factors underlying the decision in *Melloni* regarding the meaning of Article 53 of the Charter, requires that Member States presume that fundamental rights have been observed by other Member States, and only in the most exceptional cases can a Member State actually enquire into the specifics of a given case in order to determine whether fundamental rights have been breached.[112] However, the DAA contained no provisions intended to reflect or accommodate the principle of mutual trust, leading the CJEU to hold that accession would be 'liable to upset the underlying balance of the EU and undermine the autonomy of EU law'.[113] Here, the CJEU repeats the same error noted above, in that it regards Convention control mechanisms as something external to EU law, rather than, following accession, an integral part thereof.[114] Moreover, the Court identifies as the root of this problem '[t]he approach adopted in the [DAA], which is to treat the EU as a State and to give it a role identical in every respect to that of any other Contracting Party', which 'specifically disregards the intrinsic nature of the EU'.[115] But this is clearly and specifically *not* the approach taken in the DAA: rather than having to become *more state-like* in order to accede to an international agreement between states, the EU had instead succeeded in having that international agreement modified in order to accommodate the EU's specifically

---

[111] ibid para 212.
[112] ibid para 192.
[113] ibid para 194.
[114] ibid para 193.
[115] ibid.

128   *The Horizontal Frame*

non-state legal nature. The fact that this accommodation was necessary is noted in the explanatory report accompanying the DAA:

> The EU should, *as a matter of principle*, accede to the Convention on an equal footing with the other Contracting Parties, that is, with the same rights and obligations. It was, however, acknowledged that, because the EU is not a State, some adaptations would be necessary.[116]

Among the adaptations are the new procedural and institutional mechanisms with which the CJEU also found fault, discussed in section II.B below. But putting the Union 'on an equal footing' with other signatories to the ECHR 'as a matter of principle' is emphatically not the same thing as 'giv[ing] it a role identical in every respect to that of any other [signatory]', as the CJEU would have it.

iv. The Common Foreign and Security Policy (CFSP)

The CJEU's jurisdiction over CFSP matters is limited.[117] Whatever else can be said about this fact,[118] it is not constitutionally unusual: whether by specific constitutional exclusion or by unwritten convention, some form of limitation of judicial control over matters of foreign relations is the rule, rather than the exception, in state constitutional orders, as we saw in chapter two with reference to Ireland. For the CJEU, the fact that it lacks jurisdiction to review most CFSP matters in the light of fundamental rights means that the ECtHR must also lack this jurisdiction.[119] As the DAA did not propose to oust Strasbourg's jurisdiction in this way, it had 'fail[ed] to have regard to the specific characteristics of EU law'.[120] This argument is difficult to sustain in light of the fact that the jurisdiction of the ECtHR has never been dependent on the (varying) jurisdictions of the courts of the signatories. To take a simple example, the fact that United Kingdom courts were precluded until the coming into force of the Human Rights Act 1998 from engaging in any human rights review of Acts of Parliament never meant that Strasbourg was similarly forbidden from doing so. Rather, when a state (or indeed a non-state) signs and ratifies the Convention, it puts its entire legal system under the jurisdiction of the ECtHR, with the exception of any specific (and not sectoral) reservations or derogations it made upon

---

[116] Art (I)(6) of Annex V to the DAA (n 2), emphasis added.

[117] See Art 24(1) TEU, limiting the Court's jurisdiction to monitoring compliance with Art 40 TEU and reviewing the legality of certain decisions under Art 275 TFEU; see further L Šaltinytė, 'Jurisdiction of the European Court of Justice Over Issues Relating to the Common Foreign and Security Policy Under the Lisbon Treaty' [2010] *Jurisprudencija/Jurisprudence* 261.

[118] For contemporaneous criticism of the modest extension of the CJEU's jurisdiction over the CFSP by the Lisbon Treaty and of the fact of this limited jurisdiction in the first place, see L Pech, '"A Union Founded on the Rule of Law": Meaning and Reality of the Rule of Law as a Constitutional Principle of EU Law' (2010) 6 *European Constitutional Law Review* 359, 393–96 and references therein.

[119] Opinion 2/13 (n 3) paras 254–57.

[120] ibid para 257.

accession. For Luxembourg to argue that where it lacks jurisdiction, Strasbourg must too, ignores the very nature and purpose of the Convention system.

B. Institutional and Procedural Mechanisms

i. The Co-Respondent Mechanism

As we saw in section I.B above, one problem stemming from the interplay between EU and ECHR law is that of the allocation of responsibility between the EU and its Member States for (alleged) breaches of the Convention. For the ECtHR to involve itself in deciding precisely where responsibility lies in cases involving EU law would involve the Strasbourg Court in determining issues of substantive EU law, rather than the compatibility of such law with the Convention, which is precisely the sort of threat to the autonomy of EU law which so concerned EU actors during the accession negotiations,[121] but which ultimately proved fatal in Opinion 2/13. The DAA's solution was termed the co-respondent mechanism, and was set out in Article 3:

> Where an application is directed against one or more member States of the European Union, the European Union may become a co-respondent to the proceedings in respect of an alleged violation notified by the Court if it appears that such allegation calls into question the compatibility with the Convention rights at issue of a provision of European Union law, including decisions taken under the TEU and under the TFEU, notably where that violation could have been avoided only by disregarding an obligation under European Union law.[122]

Particularly important is the last sentence: that the mechanism was to be engaged '*notably*' (and not '*only*') where the Member State had no discretion in its application of EU law. As we have seen, the *Bosphorus* presumption of equivalent protection that the ECtHR affords to the EU – which was to be extinguished upon accession – arose in circumstances where the Member State was acting on foot of a Council regulation, and so had no discretion in its actions. The co-respondent mechanism provided a neat way of circumventing this first problem in such cases, allowing the ECtHR to treat both the Union and its Member States as jointly liable without getting into specifics,[123] particularly because the mechanism was to be used 'notably' but *not* 'only' when the Member State had no discretion.

---

[121] See Eckes (n 2); and Lock, 'EU Accession to the ECHR' and Lock, 'Walking on a Tightrope' (n 2) passim.

[122] Art 3(2) DAA (n 2). Art 3(3) goes on to provide for the reverse case, whereby a Member State may become a co-respondent in an action against the Union.

[123] See Art 3(7) DAA (n 2): 'If the violation in respect of which a High Contracting Party is a co-respondent to the proceedings is established, the respondent and the co-respondent shall be jointly responsible for that violation, unless the Court, on the basis of the reasons given by the respondent and the co-respondent, and having sought the views of the applicant, decides that only one of them be held responsible'.

130　*The Horizontal Frame*

However, the CJEU in its Opinion objected to the design and structure of the mechanism. It had no complaint with the situation where the ECtHR *invites* a Contracting Party to become a co-respondent, because the invitation is not binding, thus leaving the EU and its Member States free to assess whether use of the co-respondent mechanism is appropriate in the given case.[124] However, in the situation where a Contracting Party *requests* to be made a co-respondent, it is for the ECtHR to assess whether the conditions for the use of the mechanism have been met. For Luxembourg, this would involve Strasbourg in making binding decisions regarding the division of powers between the EU and its Member States. This, along with the ECtHR's power to decide to hold only one co-respondent responsible for a violation, fails to account for the specific characteristics of EU law.[125]

There is much less to criticise in this objection than in those outlined in section II.A above. Whereas those issues revealed at best questionable and at worst worrying conceptions on the part of the CJEU as to what EU accession to the ECHR would and should entail, the objection to the design and structure of the co-respondent mechanism is largely a matter of technicality (in the non-pejorative sense); asks for no exemptions, ousters or unjustifiable special treatment under the Convention; and could be remedied in any future accession agreement without doing violence to the very concept of subsidiary oversight by Strasbourg.

ii. The 'Prior Involvement' of the CJEU

Article 3(6) DAA provided as follows:

> In proceedings to which the European Union is a co-respondent, if the Court of Justice of the European Union has not yet assessed the compatibility with the Convention rights at issue of the provision of European Union law ..., sufficient time shall be afforded for the [CJEU] to make such an assessment, and thereafter for the parties to make observations to the Court.

The practical effect of this provision is to introduce to the law of the Convention an entirely new mechanism, comparable – though different – from the Article 267 TFEU preliminary reference procedure in EU law. Though the action is not formally framed as a 'reference' from Strasbourg to Luxembourg, the result would be similar: proceedings would be stayed in order to allow the CJEU to give its interpretation of norms of EU law, specifically in relation to conformance with the Convention. Though the ECtHR would be obliged to accept the correctness of the CJEU's interpretation of EU law as a matter of EU law itself, it would be under no obligation to accept the CJEU's assessment of this law's

---

[124] Opinion 2/13 (n 3) paras 219–22.
[125] ibid para 235.

compatibility with the Convention. Gaja noted that 'members of the Court of Justice have clearly expressed their strong wish that [this] procedure of "prior involvement" be introduced'[126] as part of any accession agreement. It is interesting to note how well the procedure dovetails with the decision in *Michaud*, where the lack of a previous Opinion from the CJEU was decisive in rebutting the *Bosphorus* presumption. However, again the design of procedure was found wanting by the CJEU. First, nothing in the DAA precludes the ECtHR from itself determining the question of whether the CJEU has yet assessed the compatibility of the provision of EU law in question with the Convention, and thus from interpreting the case law of the CJEU. For the CJEU, such a question can only be determined by the competent EU institution.[127] Secondly, the DAA provides for the prior involvement procedure to be used in order for the CJEU to have the opportunity to rule on the *interpretation* of a provision of primary law but only on the *validity* (and not the interpretation) of a provision of secondary law.[128] This, in theory, leaves open the possibility of the ECtHR providing its own interpretation of EU secondary law, and thus intruding on the exclusive jurisdiction of the CJEU.[129]

As was the case with the co-respondent mechanism, this aspect of Opinion 2/13 is relatively unproblematic, and in the case of the interpretation/validity distinction appears to result from an oversight in drafting, rather than from any fundamental difference in conception as to the meaning and substance of EU accession to the ECHR.

iii. Protocol No 16 ECHR

The final objection discussed here relates to Protocol No 16 ECHR, which is not part of the DAA, and indeed post-dates it, having been signed on 2 October 2013. Under Protocol No 16 (which has not yet entered into force, and to which the DAA did not envisage the EU acceding), the highest courts of the High Contracting Parties may request advisory opinions on the interpretation of the Convention from the ECtHR. However, the CJEU noted that there is the possibility of the Article 267 TFEU preliminary reference procedure being circumvented if a Member State of the EU were to request an Opinion from the ECtHR under Protocol No 16 ECHR, where that request triggered the procedure for the prior involvement of the CJEU. In such a case, communication between national courts and the CJEU would be mediated through the involvement of Strasbourg, rather than via a direct line, with potential adverse effects for the autonomy and effectiveness of EU law.[130]

---

[126] G Gaja, 'The "Co-Respondent Mechanisms" According to the Draft Agreement for the Accession of the EU to the ECHR' (2013) 2 *European Society of International Law Reflections* 1.

[127] Opinion 2/13 (n 3) paras 238–41.

[128] ibid para 242.

[129] ibid paras 246–47.

[130] ibid paras 196–99.

132   *The Horizontal Frame*

Again, there is little in this criticism to which we can object, and the difficulty could be remedied by careful revision of the DAA.

C. Conclusions: Constitutional and Metaconstitutional Interface Norms

As we have seen, the second tranche of objections to the DAA in Opinion 2/13 is much less problematic than the first. The second set is focused on the specifics of the procedures and mechanisms provided for in the DAA to take account of the unique and specifically non-state nature of the EU legal order, and identifies genuine (or at least arguable) problems with their design. These problems may have been fatal to the DAA as it initially stood, but they could be (and, one hopes, will be) rectified without difficulty or controversy. This aspect of Opinion 2/13 is therefore a relatively unremarkable instance of Maduro's ex ante constitutional review, with the apex court within a given legal order identifying specific constitutional difficulties with the proposal for the formalisation of the links between two distinct legal orders. Importantly, the interface norms employed by the CJEU in this part of the Opinion are specifically *constitutional*, rather than *meta*constitutional, being predicated on distinct, written provisions of the DAA and on their effect on EU law, rather than on more general rules-about-constitutional rules, such as Kumm's interface norms of legality; subsidiarity; democracy; and the protection of basic rights. The institutional objections do however fit well with Maduro's contrapunctual principles of coherence and universalisability, in that though the objections are geared towards the protection of the specificity and autonomy of one legal order, there is nothing in them which is potentially offensive to the nature or *telos* of the other. In this regard, the objections are inherently dialogic, alerting other actors in the polyarchy (most notably the EU and the Council of Europe's accession negotiators) to legal difficulties so that they may be corrected in advance – and thus avoiding greater legal difficulty further down the line – and this in a way that makes sense from any epistemic perspective, whether situated within or outwith the EU legal order.

But the first set of objections is altogether different. What is most important about these objections for present purposes is not the precise legal justifications of each one (though these are of variable and generally questionable quality), but rather the *Gestalt*: the overall picture that emerges from the objections from autonomy and specificity when taken together. Let us recall Gaja's statement made in the aftermath of Opinion 2/94:

> [W]hat is here at stake is the conservation by the Court of Justice of its present functions, although understandably the Court has not stressed this point in order not to emphasize its concern with its own prerogatives.[131]

---

[131] Gaja, 'Case-note on Opinion 2/94' (n 15) 988.

The difference here is that in Opinion 2/13 the Court made much less effort to hide or de-emphasise this aspect of its judgment, with little in the way of compensatory rhetoric. Instead, the CJEU comes out of Opinion 2/13 looking recalcitrant, obstructive and uncooperative – a noticeable shift from the decades of relative harmony in its attitude to the Convention, and an impression that one might more readily expect from the most jealous and least cosmopolitan national constitutional court. There is little of Kumm's principle of legality in the objections, with relatively scant attention being paid to Article 6(2) TEU's *requirement* of EU accession, and much more emphasis placed on the *conditions* of this requirement. My argument here is not that the conditions are unimportant, but rather that the requirement of EU accession is of much greater normative weight than that assigned to it by the CJEU. As noted in section I.C above, Kumm's principle of subsidiarity is geared very much towards the EU–Member State relationship and finds little reflection in the EU–ECHR sphere. However, the principle of democracy, which I have characterised as the protection of national specificity on democratic grounds, is partially reflected in the Opinion: 'partially' because the EU's specificity is of course not 'national' specificity, and because whatever other grounds it may be justified on, democracy is almost certainly not one of them. However, the CJEU's application of the principle is problematic in that it regards the specificity and autonomy of EU law as unqualified goods in their own right, without further principled justification, and – by the Court's focus on the conditions for, rather than the requirement of, accession to the ECHR – elevates them to a normative status commensurate with the protection of human rights. This difficulty is further reflected in the Court's use of the principle of the protection of basic rights: whereas in its *Solange* manifestation this principle allows for the exceptional disapplication of one set of norms in favour of another set *more* protective of fundamental rights, in Opinion 2/13 – and particularly as regards the relationship between Article 53 ECHR and Article 53 of the Charter – the CJEU turns this on its head, and instead openly argues for a potential *reduction* in fundamental rights protection, for the sake of the uniformity, effectiveness and primacy of Union law.

Whereas the institutional and procedural objections employed constitutional interface norms in a way that Maduro would classify as vertically and horizontally coherent and universalisable, the objections from autonomy and specificity employ metaconstitutional interface norms in ways that are highly jurisdictionally contingent, and far from coherent across legal orders. Consider the changes necessary to the DAA and the Convention itself in order to satisfy the objections: the amendment of Article 53 ECHR in order to permit a lowering of human rights standards where the efficacy of Union law requires this; the exclusion of the ECtHR's jurisdiction to hear disputes between EU actors over the application of the ECHR within the scope of EU law; the elevation of the principle of mutual trust between Member States to a status equal to that of the protection of human rights themselves; and the ouster of the ECtHR's jurisdiction over CFSP matters simply because the CJEU lacks jurisdiction in the area.

134   *The Horizontal Frame*

To put it mildly, these proposals are unlikely to find much purchase in any setting removed from the epistemic confines of EU law.

The complexity of the EU–ECHR relationship – both before and after accession; both ignoring Opinion 2/13 and taking it into account – therefore casts further doubt on the possibility of the a priori formulation of universal metaconstitutional interface norms regulating such a relationship. It was suggested in chapter two that to take the *constitutional* interface norms at work in 28 different legal orders and to attempt to boil them down to a single set of universally applicable *metaconstitutional* norms was beset with difficulties, not least the highly contingent way in which such norms are formulated and applied in each system. This observation applies with even greater force with respect to the EU and the ECHR, neither of which are states, both of which differ from states, and both of which differ from each other. If EU accession to the Convention had proceeded smoothly, the terms of engagement between the two orders would mostly have shifted from the metaconstitutional and informal to the constitutional and formal. In halting this process, the CJEU employed both constitutional and metaconstitutional interface norms, in ways alternately generalisable across legal orders and highly jurisdictionally contingent.

In setting out the relationship between the EU and the ECHR, the above discussion highlighted several instances of conflict between the orders, all of which – Opinion 2/13 aside – were ultimately resolved, whether 'in favour' of the CJEU or the ECtHR. However, there is a further instance of conflict to be examined, which is still unresolved, and is of altogether greater constitutional significance, because it concerns the relationship between fundamental rights as protected by the Charter and the Convention, and the fundamental economic freedoms at the very foundations of EU law.

III. LABOUR RIGHTS AND CONSTITUTIONAL CONFLICT

A series of decisions by the CJEU and the ECtHR has revealed a wide, and perhaps unexpected, gap between the two Courts' understandings of a particular subset of human rights – labour rights – and their relative importance vis-a-vis other legal rights and principles. This disconnect in the jurisprudence of the two Courts, which is still unresolved after more than 10 years, poses a fascinating opportunity to analyse further the interface norms at work, and that may yet be employed, in the EU–ECHR relationship, for three reasons. First, it was noted above in section I.B.iv that the potential conflict surrounding the role of the Advocates General of the CJEU was of greater constitutional significance to the EU than the previous conflict concerning Article 6 ECHR and the manner of the Commission's enforcement of EU competition law. The current incompatibility between the two Courts' jurisprudence on labour rights is of still greater constitutional significance to the EU, because it relates to the balance to be struck between the human rights at the heart of the Convention legal order, and

Labour Rights and Constitutional Conflict   135

the fundamental economic freedoms at the heart of that of the EU. Secondly, the conflict relates to labour rights, the precise level and nature of the protection of which varies significantly across Europe, touching on exactly the sort of concerns regarding national specificity and democratic legitimacy which inform Kumm's conception of metaconstitutional interface norms. More generally, the conflict raises questions about the protection of human rights in the social and economic sphere which are of particular relevance given the current situation of multiple, overlapping European crises and the rise of precarious employment. Finally, the ongoing nature of the conflict allows us to analyse the ways in which it may yet (or may not) be resolved.

A. The CJEU, Labour Rights and Market Freedoms: An Indelicate Balance?

i. *The Right to Take Collective Action as a Fundamental Right*

The roots of the controversy are the CJEU's judgments in a series of cases concerning the relationship between the EU's fundamental market freedoms and fundamental labour rights: specifically, freedom of association, the right to collective bargaining, and the right to collective action.[132] Our starting point in analysing these cases is the CJEU's significant recognition of the right to take collective action – including the right to strike[133] – as a fundamental right forming part of the general principles of Union law.[134] In so holding, the Court drew on the recognition of the right in a wide range of international, Council of Europe, and EU documents: the International Labour Organization (ILO) Convention No 87 on Freedom of Association and Protection of the Right to Organise; the European Social Charter (ESC); the Community Charter on the Fundamental Social Rights of Workers (CCFSRW); and the Charter of Fundamental Rights. The attention given to the EU Charter is significant because of its lack of specific enforceability at the time of the judgment, and because of the Court's previous reluctance to make use of it.[135] Grounding the decision more specifically in the Treaties proper, the Court noted that Article 151 TFEU makes express reference to the ESC and to the CCFSRW in its elaboration of the objectives of the Union's social policy.[136] The Court made no mention of the ECHR at this point in its judgments, and with good reason, for the categorisation of

---

[132] Case C-341/05 *Laval un Partneri v Svenska Byggnadsarbetareförbundet* ECLI:EU:C:2007:809, [2007] ECR I-11767 (*Laval*); Case C-438/05 *ITWF & FSU v Viking Line* ECLI:EU:C:2007:772, [2007] ECR I-10779 (*Viking*); Case C-319/06 *Commission v Luxembourg* ECLI:EU:C:2008:350, [2008] ECR I-4323; Case C-346/06 *Rüffert v Land Niedersachsen* ECLI:EU:C:2008:189, [2008] ECR I-1989.

[133] *Viking* (n 132) para 44.

[134] ibid paras 43–44; *Laval* (n 132) paras 90–92.

[135] ACL Davies, 'One Step Forward, Two Steps Back? The *Viking* and *Laval* Cases in the ECJ' (2008) 37 *Industrial Law Journal* 126, 138. The right to collective action, including strike action, is set out in Art 28 of the Charter.

[136] *Viking* (n 132) para 43; *Laval* (n 132) para 90.

136   *The Horizontal Frame*

the right to strike as part of the fundamental right to take collective action went far beyond the (then) much more limited ECtHR jurisprudence on Article 11 ECHR, which had consistently ruled out a right to strike being protected by the Convention since *Schmidt and Dahlström*.[137]

However, the way in which the CJEU went on to balance the right to take collective action with free movement rights under the Treaties raises serious questions as to the depth and quality of the Court's understanding of the right. In their submissions to the CJEU in *Viking* and *Laval*, the Danish and Swedish governments had sought to insulate the right to take collective action and the right to strike (which are constitutionally protected in those jurisdictions) from regulation by EU law in the first place by relying on Article 153(5) TFEU's exclusion of these rights from the scope of Union action; and, secondly, by arguing that the fundamental nature of the right was enough to exempt it from the scope of Article 49 TFEU's protection of freedom of establishment in *Viking* and Article 56 TFEU's protection of freedom to provide services coupled with Directive 96/71/EC[138] on posted workers in *Laval*. The Court disposed of the argument based on Article 153(5) TFEU with ease, relying on its consistent case law that the exclusion of a certain area of the law from the scope of the Treaties does not absolve the Member State from its general obligation to observe the requirements of Union law in its regulation of that area.[139]

The second argument, on the fundamental nature of the rights at issue, was also rejected, on two grounds: first, because Article 28 of the Charter makes clear that the right to take collective action is not absolute but is to be exercised in accordance with national and Union law and practice;[140] and, secondly, by analogy with the decisions in *Schmidberger*[141] and *Omega*.[142] In those cases, the rights to freedom of expression and respect for human dignity – though fundamental – were not held to fall outside the scope of the Treaties, but rather their exercise had to be reconciled with Treaty freedoms and with the principle of proportionality.[143] While it is difficult to argue with the basic premise of this first ground – very few human rights are absolute – the second requires deeper scrutiny, because of what it can tell us about the Court's conception of

---

[137] *Schmidt and Dahlström v Sweden* (1976) 1 EHRR 632 (*Schmidt and Dahlström*) (see below at section III.B).

[138] Parliament and Council Directive 96/71/EC Concerning the Posting of Workers in the Framework of the Provision of Services [1997] OJ L18/1.

[139] *Viking* (n 132) paras 39–41; *Laval* (n 132) paras 86–88, citing, inter alia, Case C-120/95 *Decker* ECLI:EU:C:1998:167, [1998] ECR I-1831 paras 22–23; Case C-158/96 *Kohll* ECLI:EU:C:1998:171, [1998] ECR I-1931 paras 18–19. See further the subsequent Case C-617/10 *Åkerberg Fransson* EU:C:2013:105.

[140] *Viking* (n 132) para 44; *Laval* (n 132) para 91.

[141] Case C-112/00 *Eugen Schmidberger, International Transporte und Planzüge v Austria* ECLI:EU:C:2003:333, [2003] ECR I-5659, para 77 (*Schmidberger*).

[142] Case C-36/02 *Omega Spielhallen- und Automatenaufstellungs-GmbH v Oberbürgermeisterin der Bundesstadt Bonn* ECLI:EU:C:2004:614, [2004] ECR I-9609, para 35 (*Omega*).

[143] *Viking* (n 132) paras 45–47; *Laval* (n 132) paras 93–95.

Labour Rights and Constitutional Conflict 137

the relationship between fundamental – which is to say, human – rights and the fundamental economic freedoms of EU law.[144]

ii. Conceptualising Collective Action

The Court's ostensible reliance on *Schmidberger* and *Omega* in this context is questionable not just because of the differing circumstances of the cases, but also because of the differing nature of the rights and actions at issue. In both the earlier cases, EU law was vertical in its effect: private enterprises were seeking damages from the State for infringing their free movement rights by action or omission. In *Schmidberger*, this was a breach of the right to free movement of goods arising from Austria's failure to ban a demonstration which shut down a motorway; and in *Omega*, the claim was a breach of the right to free movement of services arising from the state authorities' ban on a 'laser tag' game. In seeking to vindicate fundamental human rights (freedom of expression; human dignity), the State had infringed fundamental economic freedoms (free movement of goods; services), and the question was therefore whether the state infringements were justifiable and proportionate. This is in contrast to the situations in *Viking* and *Laval*, where rather than seeking ex post reparations from the State for the damage already caused by state (in)action, the enterprises were seeking to *prevent* other private actors – trade unions – from *continuing to exercise their rights*.

The Court had little difficulty in holding that Articles 49 and 56 TFEU were capable of horizontal direct effect in this manner,[145] and so the trade union action was held to constitute a restriction on Treaty freedoms. However, this reasoning ignores the very same fundamental nature of the right to collective action that the Court had earlier recognised. Though some of the organisations at the centre of the cases cited by the Court in justifying its decision were clearly not state actors, and so are legitimate precedents to draw on in applying Treaty freedoms horizontally, none of them could have claimed in their cases (and none in fact did claim) that the restrictions they had imposed on free movement were the result of their exercise of a fundamental right. UEFA,[146] the Union Cycliste Internationale,[147] and the Netherlands Bar Association[148] may very well have

---

[144] For an early critique of the CJEU's equating fundamental economic freedoms with fundamental rights, see J Coppel and A O'Neill, 'The European Court of Justice: Taking Rights Seriously?' (1992) 12 *Legal Studies* 227, 242–44. Relatively more recently, see J Morijn 'Balancing Fundamental Rights and Common Market Freedoms in Union Law: *Schmidberger* and *Omega* in the Light of the European Constitution' (2006) 12 *European Law Journal* 15.

[145] *Viking* (n 132) paras 56–66, citing, inter alia, Case C-415/93 *Bosman* ECLI:EU:C:1995:293, [1995] ECR I-4921 (*Bosman*); Case C-309/99 *Wouters and Others* ECLI:EU:C:2002:98, [2002] ECR I-1577 (*Wouters*); and *Schmidberger* (n 141); *Laval* (n 132) para 98, citing Case 36/74 *Walrave and Koch* ECLI:EU:C:1974:140, [1974] ECR 1405.

[146] *Bosman* (n 145).

[147] *Wouters* (n 145).

[148] *Walrave and Koch* (n 145).

138   *The Horizontal Frame*

had an *interest* (usually financial) in acting as they did, but they emphatically did not have a *fundamental right to do so*.[149] From the very beginning of the analysis, then, the right to take collective action assumes a position subordinate to the Treaties' economic freedoms: the starting point is the restriction on free movement, and the burden is then on the trade unions to justify their actions. Though this was also the approach taken in *Schmidberger* and *Omega*, those were cases of state liability, where the Court was evaluating whether the State's approach in seeking to vindicate fundamental rights was proportionate with respect to the Treaties. Nowhere in the judgments does the Court address how the horizontal nature of the actions in *Viking* and *Laval* may modify the calculus, despite the fact that the approach taken by a state in seeking to uphold fundamental rights will of necessity be very different from the approach taken by a trade union in deciding whether or not to exercise a fundamental right by engaging in collective action.

iii. *Justifying its Exercise*

Aside from the conceptualisation of the right to collective action as a purely defensive mechanism, rather than a freestanding entitlement in its own right, the Court's reasoning also founders on the question of the justification (or otherwise) of its exercise. In *Omega*, the importance attached to human dignity by the Grundgesetz, coupled with the limited nature of the ban imposed (which was restricted to the variant of the game that involved 'playing at killing' and not, for example, shooting at non-human targets), meant that the State's restriction was a justifiable and proportionate exercise of the public policy derogation envisaged by Articles 62 and 52 TFEU.[150] We saw in chapter two that this was significant from the perspective of the Court's fundamental rights jurisprudence because though the right to human dignity is a right common to the constitutional traditions of the Member States, its particular formulation and expression in the German Constitution differs from that found elsewhere. In this way, the Court in *Omega* was not insisting on the uniformity of Union law at the expense of national specificity, but rather reconciling the two through the acceptance of the specific national rule provided its exercise survived the proportionality test.

In *Schmidberger*, a case dealing with a right which *is* common to all the Member States, the Court allowed the State a wide margin of discretion in determining the proportionality of its actions, and noted the facts, specific to the case at hand, that the demonstration was limited both in time and in

---

[149] The same point is made, but from the reverse angle, in C Joerges and F Rödl, 'Informal Politics, Formalised Law and the "Social Deficit" of European Integration: Reflections after the Judgments of the ECJ in *Viking* and *Laval*' (2009) 15 *European Law Journal* 1, 15: '[T]he right to collective action does not imply the power to regulate market affairs unilaterally. Quite to the contrary, collective action is intended to compensate the absence of such a unilateral regulatory autonomy'. See, further, Davies (n 135) 136–37.

[150] *Omega* (n 142) paras 28–40

Labour Rights and Constitutional Conflict   139

scope, and was widely publicised in advance for the avoidance of inconvenience. Importantly, the Court also noted that though the State *could* have imposed more onerous restrictions on the demonstration – both in terms of location and duration – such restrictions 'could have been perceived as an excessive restriction, depriving the action of a substantial part of its scope'.[151] Finally, the Court recognised that public demonstrations 'usually [entail] inconvenience for non-participants ... but the inconvenience may in principle be tolerated provided that the objective pursued is essentially the public and lawful demonstration of an opinion'.[152] Importantly, so long as this demonstration of opinion is lawful, it does not matter what the opinion actually *is*. The question had been raised whether the environmentalist purpose of the demonstration was relevant, and the Court rightly noted that it was not: the case concerned the liability of the Member State, which arises solely from state action or omission.[153] Whether the purpose and aims of the demonstrators were justifiable in Treaty terms was immaterial.

It is this dual acknowledgement by the Court of the *essentially disruptive intent* of the demonstration and the *irrelevance of the purpose* of this disruption that makes the ostensible application of the *Schmidberger* reasoning to *Viking* and *Laval* so problematic. As Anne Davies writes, '[t]here is more than a little sleight of hand in the Court's use of *Schmidberger* as authority for its application of the proportionality test in *Viking* and *Laval*'.[154] In both cases, the Court placed great emphasis on the ways in which the trade union action was detrimental to the enterprises concerned: action designed to make Laval sign a collective agreement was 'liable to make it less attractive, or more difficult' to take advantage of the freedom conferred by Article 56 TFEU, exacerbated by the prospect of Laval being 'forced' into negotiations 'of unspecified duration'.[155] This plaintive phrasing – drawn in part from *Gebhard*,[156] another case where the contested restriction could never be classified as flowing from the exercise of a fundamental right – signifies a lack of understanding or appreciation on the part of the Court of the nature and purpose of industrial action. In the sphere of free expression, even a non-disruptive demonstration can still serve to highlight a cause, and to attract public and political sympathy for the demonstrators. In this context, an element of disruption may enhance the effectiveness of a demonstration, but its absence does not rob it of all force. But the exercise of the right to collective action, including the right to strike, *requires* this element of disruption. Without it, collective action is 'reduced' to the level of 'mere' expression, and a picket line becomes indistinguishable from an ordinary demonstration.

---

[151] *Schmidberger* (n 141) para 90.
[152] ibid para 91.
[153] ibid paras 65–69.
[154] Davies (n 135) 142.
[155] *Laval* (n 132) paras 99–100; see also *Viking* (n 132) paras 72–73.
[156] Case C–55/94 *Gebhard* ECLI:EU:C:1995:411, [1995] ECR I–4165.

140   *The Horizontal Frame*

With this in mind, consider how the Court applied the proportionality test in *Viking* and *Laval*. In line with the case law on restrictions of free movement, in order to be justified the trade union action would: (a) have to pursue a legitimate aim compatible with the Treaties; (b) be justified by an overriding reason of public interest; (c) be suitable for securing the attainment of the objective pursued; and (d) not go beyond what is necessary to attain it.[157] The focus on the legitimacy or otherwise of the union's aims is in contrast to *Schmidberger*, where the demonstrators' environmentalist aims were immaterial to the question of state liability, but this is a necessary consequence of free movement provisions being applied horizontally without any allowance being made for the difference between a state acting to balance one set of constitutional rights (by which I mean EU constitutional rights), on the one hand, and a group of citizens collectively exercising other constitutional rights, on the other. Additionally, *Viking* and *Laval* diverge at this point of the justification exercise. Whereas in *Viking* the legitimacy of the union's aims was held by the CJEU to be a question of fact to be determined by the national court,[158] in *Laval* the Court pre-empted this traditional division of labour between it and national courts (acting in their capacity as Union courts), holding that the trade union's blockade in the case could not be justified because it was seeking terms which went beyond the 'nucleus of mandatory rules for minimum protection in the host Member State' laid down by Directive 96/71,[159] and because the negotiations on pay sought by the trade union

> form part of a national context characterised by a lack of provisions, of any kind, which are sufficiently precise and accessible that they do not render it impossible or excessively difficult in practice for ... an undertaking to determine the obligations with which it is required to comply as regards minimum pay.[160]

Accordingly, the trade union was effectively being penalised for a legal framework that was beyond its control, being the responsibility of the State and not the trade union.

The CJEU went on to elaborate that even though the aim of protecting workers may be a legitimate and justifiable one, it would cease to be so if the jobs or conditions of the workers in question were not jeopardised or under serious threat.[161] If it were established that the jobs *are* jeopardised, then the collective action would need to be suitable and no more than was necessary in the circumstances.[162] Moreover, the union would need to have exhausted all

---

[157] *Viking* (n 132) para 75, citing *Gebhard* (n 156) and *Bosman* (n 145).
[158] *Viking* (n 132) para 83.
[159] *Laval* (n 132) para 108.
[160] ibid para 110.
[161] ibid para 81.
[162] *Viking* (n 132) para 84.

available alternative avenues for redress.[163] Two final objections can be raised to these considerations. First, the purpose of collective action by trade unions is not necessarily confined to achieving more favourable conditions for the specific workers affected, nor even for the union's broader membership, but rather to enhance the position of labour generally. The Court's view – that only a threat to the position of the workers in question is relevant – employs a highly individualistic approach to an expressly non-individualist right and practice. Secondly, considerations such as suitability, necessity in the circumstances, the exhaustion of alternatives – indeed, the whole question of proportionality – are the stuff of daily life for state agents, with a civil service, legal officers and a national budget at their disposal. Imposing such conditions on the exercise of a fundamental right by individuals acting in concert potentially constitutes a significant restriction on the very essence of the right.

B. The ECtHR and Labour Rights: The Ground Shifts

Whatever criticisms can be made of the CJEU's recent labour rights jurisprudence from the internal perspective of EU law (and as we have seen, there are many),[164] there is a strong argument that, at the time the decisions were handed down, they were at least consistent both with the terms of the ECHR and the jurisprudence of the ECtHR. Historically, the ECtHR had been circumspect in its interpretation of Article 11 ECHR, holding that while it

> safeguards freedom to protect the occupational interests of trade union members by trade union action, the conduct and development of which the Contracting States *must both permit and make possible* … [It] nevertheless leaves each State *a free choice* of the means to be used towards this end.[165]

---

[163] ibid para 87.

[164] See Joerges and Rödl (n 149) and Davies (n 135). See further, R Eklund, 'A Swedish Perspective on *Laval* (2007–08) 29 *Comparative Labor Law & Policy Journal* 551; N Reich, 'Free Movement v Social Rights in an Enlarged Union – The *Laval* and *Viking* Cases before the ECJ' (2008) 9 *German Law Journal* 125; T van Peijpe, 'Collective Labour Law after *Viking, Laval, Rüffert* and *Commission v Luxembourg*' (2009) 25 *International Journal of Comparative Labour Law and Industrial Relations* 81; K Apps, 'Damages Claims Against Trade Unions after *Viking* and *Laval*' (2009) 34 *European Law Review* 141; C Woolfson, C Thörnqvist and J Sommers, 'The Swedish Model and the Future of Labour Standards after *Laval*' (2010) 41 *Industrial Relations Journal* 333; C Kaupa 'Maybe Not Activist Enough? On the Court's Alleged Neoliberal Bias in its Recent Labor Cases' in M Dawson, B de Witte and E Muir *Judicial Activism at the European Court of Justice* (Cheltenham, Edward Elgar, 2013); A Ludlow 'The Right to Strike: A Jurisprudential Gulf Between the CJEU and ECtHR' in K Dzehtsiarou, T Konstadinides, T Lock and N O'Meara (eds), *Human Rights Law in Europe: The Influence, Overlaps and Contradictions of the EU and the ECHR* (London, Routledge, 2014); and L Mason, 'Labour Law, the Industrial Constitution and the EU's Accession to the ECHR: The Constitutional Nature of the Market and the Limits of Rights-Based Approaches to Labour Law' in K Dzehtsiarou, T Konstadinides, T Lock, and N O'Meara (eds), *Human Rights Law in Europe: The Influence, Overlaps and Contradictions of the EU and the ECHR* (London, Routledge, 2014).

[165] *Schmidt and Dahlström* (n 137) para 36, citations omitted, emphasis added.

142 The Horizontal Frame

Accordingly, though Article 11 'presents trade union freedom as one form or a special aspect of freedom of association, [it] does not guarantee any particular treatment of trade unions, or their members, by the State'.[166] Though the members of a trade union have the right that their union be heard,[167] this was held not to extend to a right to be consulted,[168] a right to conclude collective agreements,[169] or to a right to strike.[170] Virginia Mantouvalou has summed up the rationale of *Schmidt and Dahlström* as follows: 'when a right can be classified as social and is protected in the ESC or in instruments of the ILO, it ought to be excluded from the ECHR'.[171] This she dubs the 'exclusive' approach to interpretation of the Convention.[172]

However, two subsequent judgments of the ECtHR – *Demir and Baykara*[173] and *Enerji Yapı-Yol Sen*[174] – expressly departed from this restrictive approach to Article 11 ECHR. In giving an altogether wider interpretation of Article 11's requirements,[175] the judgments also raise serious questions about the compatibility of the CJEU's approach with the Convention. As we shall now see, these judgments are examples of what has been dubbed the 'integrated' approach[176] to interpretation, whereby the ECtHR draws on the work of other institutional actors – particularly the ESC and the ILO – in seeking to determine the contours, requirements and limits of the social and labour requirements of the Convention.[177]

---

[166] *National Union of Belgian Police v Belgium* (1979–80) 1 EHRR 578, para 38.

[167] ibid para 39.

[168] ibid para 38.

[169] *Swedish Engine Drivers Union v Sweden* (1976) 1 EHRR 617, para 39; *Schettini and Others v Italy* App no 29529/95 (decision, ECtHR, 9 November 2000).

[170] *Schmidt and Dahlström* (n 137) para 36, see also *UNISON v UK* App no 53574/99 (decision, ECtHR, 10 January 2002).

[171] V Mantouvalou, 'Labour Rights in the European Convention on Human Rights: An Intellectual Justification for an Integrated Approach to Interpretation' (2013) 13 *Human Rights Law Review* 529, 532, referring also to *van Volsem v Belgium* App no 14641/89 (decision, ECmHR, 9 May 1990).

[172] ibid.

[173] *Demir and Baykara v Turkey* (2009) 48 EHRR 54 (*Demir and Baykara*).

[174] *Enerji Yapı-Yol Sen v Turkey* [2009] ECHR 2251 (French only).

[175] See generally, KD Ewing and J Hendy, 'The Dramatic Implications of *Demir and Baykara*' (2010) 39 *Industrial Law Journal* 2.

[176] The term is Scheinen's: M Schienen, 'Economic and Social Rights as Legal Rights' in A Eide, C Krause and A Rosas (eds), *Economic, Social and Cultural Rights*, 2nd edn (Leiden, Martinus Nijhoff 2001) 29.

[177] The 'integrated approach' is a relatively new departure for the ECtHR and is not universally applied in its case law: see *N v UK* (2008) 47 EHRR 885, para 44, and compare the joint dissenting opinion in the case at para 6. Enthusiastic endorsement of the integrated approach can, however, be found in extra-curial statements of current and former judges of the ECtHR: see, eg, J-P Costa, 'La Déclaration Universelle des Droits de l'Homme (1948–2008): Les Droits Economiques, Sociaux et Culturels en Question' (Strasbourg, 16 October 2008), available at: www.echr.coe.int/Documents/Speech_20081016_OV_Costa_FRA.pdf; and F Tulkens, 'La Convention Européenne des Droits de l'Homme et la Crise Economique: La Question de la Pauvreté' (2013) *Journal Européen des Droits de l'Homme* 8.

i. The 'Integrated' Approach to Interpretation and Article 11

One feature that the judgment in *Demir and Baykara* has in common with the decisions in *Viking* and *Laval* is reference to a wide range of international legal authority, but where *Demir and Baykara* differentiates itself is in the depth and quality of its *engagement* with this authority. In its survey of the right to organise and to bargain collectively, the ECtHR drew on ILO Conventions Nos 87, 98 and 151; the International Covenant on Civil and Political Rights; the International Covenant on Economic, Social and Cultural Rights; the ESC; and the Charter of Fundamental Rights. But in doing so, and in contrast with the CJEU's approach described above at section III.A.i, the ECtHR went beyond merely adverting to the existence of these instruments or the citation of their bare text; it also surveyed the jurisprudence of and literature on the various bodies with responsibility for overseeing their implementation, including the ILO's Committee of Experts, its Committee on Freedom of Association, and the European Committee of Social Rights.[178] Amid such a wide range of sources, the omission of any mention of the CJEU's jurisprudence on Article 28 of the Charter – including the then year-old cases of *Viking* and *Laval* – is telling, and almost certainly deliberate.[179]

The Turkish Government had objected to the ECtHR placing reliance on instruments other than the Convention, and in particular on instruments that Turkey had not ratified, such as Articles 5 and 6 ESC.[180] In rejecting this argument, the Court gave a robust defence of its 'integrated' approach to interpretation, stating that it 'has never considered the provisions of the Convention as the sole framework of reference for the interpretation of the rights and freedoms enshrined therein'.[181] In the light of the ECtHR's previous, 'exclusive' approach to interpretation, this statement ('has *never* considered') may seem somewhat tenuous, but on closer investigation it holds true: even when the Court was in the habit of ruling that a right was not covered by the Convention because of its protection by the ESC or ILO, this did not mean that the Convention was its 'sole framework of reference': quite the opposite, for excluding a right from the scope of the Convention because of its protection elsewhere still counts as placing reliance on instruments external to the Convention. Whether such reliance results in a diminution or an enlargement of the scope of the Convention makes

---

[178] *Demir and Baykara* (n 173) paras 37–52.

[179] There is a parallel here with what Daniel Sarmiento has called the 'silent judgments' of the CJEU, which enable the CJEU 'to avoid delicate points, delay an issue for future occasions, or grant a wider margin of action to the national court'. See D Sarmiento, 'The Silent Lamb and the Deaf Wolves: Constitutional Pluralism, Preliminary References and the Role of Silent Judgments in EU Law' in M Avbelj and J Komárek (eds), *Constitutional Pluralism in the European Union and Beyond* (Oxford, Hart Publishing, 2012) 293.

[180] *Demir and Baykara* (n 173) para 53.

[181] ibid para 67.

144   *The Horizontal Frame*

no difference to the essential point that the Court's epistemic confines are not the four corners of the Convention itself.

It is this epistemic openness – coupled with the ECtHR's long-standing principle of the '"living" nature of the Convention, which must be interpreted in the light of present-day conditions, and … evolving norms of national and international law'[182] – that enabled the Court, in rejecting in particular Turkey's contention that its non-ratification of various instruments should shield it from their effects, to state with confidence that:

> Being made up of a set of rules and principles that are accepted by the vast majority of States, the common international or domestic law standards of European States reflect a reality that the Court cannot disregard … [I]n searching for common ground among the norms of international law [the Court] has never distinguished between sources of law according to whether or not they have been signed or ratified by the respondent State.[183]

Having cleared the preliminary hurdles of reliance on extra-Conventional sources and Turkish non-ratification, the stage was set for a major departure from precedent. The ECtHR surveyed the place of the right to bargain collectively in ILO Convention No 98, the ESC, the EU Charter, and the law and practice of European states,[184] and held that:

> In light of these developments, the Court considers that its case-law to the effect that the right to bargain collectively and to enter into collective agreements does not constitute an inherent element of Article 11 should be reconsidered, so as to take account of the perceptible evolution in such matters, in both international law and domestic legal systems.[185]

A similar approach, relying on the reasoning developed in *Demir and Baykara*, was employed in *Enerji Yapı-Yol Sen v Turkey* with respect to the right to strike, the ECtHR stating that '[l]a grève, qui permet à un syndicat de faire entendre sa voix, constitue *un aspect important* pour les membres d'un syndicat dans la protection de leurs intérêts'.[186] Here, the Court cited paragraph 38 of its judgment in *Schmidt and Dahlström*, but more important is what it left out: the fatal addendum to '*un aspect important*', 'but there are others'.[187] This completed the about-turn in the ECtHR's labour rights jurisprudence and, as Albertine Veldman notes, reveals that the approaches of the two European courts differ in profoundly important respects, not least in the general legal methodology applied and the proportionality required.[188]

---

[182] ibid para 68.

[183] ibid paras 76–78.

[184] ibid paras 147–51.

[185] ibid para 153, citing *Swedish Engine Drivers Union* (n 169) para 39; *Schmidt and Dahlström* (n 137) para 34.

[186] *Enerji Yapı-Yol Sen* (n 174) para 24, emphasis added.

[187] *Schmidt and Dahlström* (n 137) para 38.

[188] A Veldman, 'The Protection of the Fundamental Right to Strike within the Context of the European Internal Market: Implications of the Forthcoming Accession of the EU to the ECHR' (2013)

C. Managing Impending Judicial Conflict in Europe

There is a jarring discordance that runs throughout the CJEU's judgments between the loud noises the Court makes about the fundamental nature of the right to strike and importance to the Union of 'a high level of social protection',[189] on the one hand, and the onerous restrictions that the Court imposes on the exercise of the right to strike, on the other. Though there was no particular reason to suppose that the judgments in *Viking* and *Laval* offended the Convention at the time they were handed down, this is no longer the case, and it is difficult to see how the CJEU's understanding of labour rights, if it persists, can now be seen as anything but contrary to the ECtHR's standard of protection as constructed through *Demir and Baykara* and *Enerji Yapı-Yol Sen*. This provides an opening for discussion of the possible consequences, especially in the aftermath of Opinion 2/13, and what this might tell us about the interface norms by which the European legal orders relate.

It was noted above in section I.A.ii that the CJEU was easily able to adopt subsequent ECtHR jurisprudence in the *Hoechst* and *Orkem* series of cases, as the rights at issue in those cases hardly went to the core of the EU legal order. Conversely, with respect to the rather more jealously guarded role of the Advocates General and the CJEU's Rules of Procedure with respect to Article 6 ECHR, the CJEU was altogether less willing to follow Strasbourg's lead, leaving the ECtHR to settle the matter by finding the *Bosphorus* presumption not rebutted in *Kokkelvisserij*: while the CJEU's structure and procedures may not *equal* the standard of protection demanded by Strasbourg, they were not 'manifestly deficient'. However, the disconnect between Luxembourg and Strasbourg over labour rights examined in this section emphatically falls into this latter category, dealing as it does with the relationship between human rights as protected by the Convention and the free movement rights at the very core of the CJEU's jurisdiction and jurisprudence. How, then, is this disconnect to be resolved?

As we saw in section I.B.i, membership of an international organisation, even one of the scope and breadth of the EU, does not absolve parties to the Convention of their obligations thereunder. Though the EU institutions themselves are not directly subject to the jurisdiction of the Strasbourg Court, the Member States remain so in their application of EU law, regardless of whether they had any discretion or room for manoeuvre in so doing. The question of

---

9 *Utrecht Law Review* 104, 113–15; see further, V Vėlyvytė, 'The Right to Strike in the European Union after Accession to the European Convention on Human Rights: Identifying Conflict and Achieving Coherence' (2015) 15 *Human Rights Law Review* 73.

[189] *Viking* (n 132) para 78, quoting then-Art 2 EC. It is perhaps important, and telling, that this 'high level' of social protection has since been downgraded to a guarantee of merely 'adequate' social protection in Art 9 TFEU and 'proper' social protection in Art 151 TFEU: aims which Alain Euzéby has rightly called 'both more vague and less ambitious' (A Euzéby, 'Economic Crisis and Social Protection in the European Union: Moving Beyond Immediate Responses' (2010) 63 *International Social Security Review* 71, 81).

146   *The Horizontal Frame*

discretion is only relevant to whether the *Bosphorus* presumption of equiva-lent human rights protection applies, but we can deduce from *Michaud* that the more important factor is not necessarily whether the Member State had any discretion, but rather whether the CJEU has yet had an opportunity to scrutinise the norm of EU law at issue on grounds of fundamental rights. This being the case, as things stand, the EU's Member States may find their actions on foot of the judgments in *Viking* and *Laval* subject to the full measure of the ECtHR's scrutiny in an appropriate case. Concerning, as they do, the interpretation of directly effective Treaty norms, such cases will not leave much in the way of discretion to the Member States; but given the disparity between the recent approaches of the CJEU and the ECtHR on the issue of labour rights, it is diffi-cult to see how the ECtHR could justify applying the *Bosphorus* presumption where a state gives precedence to the EU 'version' of labour rights. Of course, at the time of the decisions in *Viking* and *Laval*, the CJEU did not have the benefit of the ECtHR's later Article 11 judgments, and so the ECtHR might prefer first to have the benefit of the CJEU's response to this change in direction under the Convention. But in the current state of relations between the legal orders, the ECtHR cannot itself request such a response, and must await future develop-ments at the CJEU.

This leaves us in an interesting situation. The CJEU is bound under the Charter not to go below the level of rights protection provided by the ECtHR's jurisprudence (*Melloni* notwithstanding). Similarly, the ECtHR has historically expressed both a great deal of confidence in the CJEU's competence as a court with a human rights jurisdiction and a great deal of concern for the auton-omy of EU law as a distinct and unique legal order. Yet this mutual respect and comity cannot allow for clearly divergent approaches towards the meaning and requirements of the Convention: put bluntly, something will have to give. As will be clear from the tenor of the above, I prefer the ECtHR's approach to the issues, but this is for reasons of process as much as for reasons of outcome. The Strasbourg cases engage in a more sophisticated manner with the international jurisprudence on labour rights than their Luxembourg counterparts, and they do so in a way that takes a holistic, evolutionary and interactive view of the protection of labour rights both within the Council of Europe and worldwide – even to the extent of applying (or at least drawing inspiration from) norms of international law to which Turkey was not a party. This openness is rooted in a deep understanding of the Convention as an expressly *constitutional* instru-ment, devoted to the limitation of coercive state power against the individual, and is an exemplar of Maduro's contrapunctual principle of pluralism itself.

On the other hand, there is little such openness in the CJEU judgments: the cases pay scant attention to national specificities in terms of the operation of labour relations (both in the Member States directly concerned and across the Union more widely), and instead are altogether more concerned with the vindi-cation of the EU's fundamental market freedoms. This is an approach that fits well with the CJEU's previous constitutionalising tendencies, and thus what

Labour Rights and Constitutional Conflict   147

Kumm would call European (Union) constitutional supremacy, but it sits uncomfortably with the (limited) deference shown to national specificity in *Omega* and its successors. Moreover, given the quality of the reasoning in the ECtHR cases, the force with which they were phrased, and their status as being subsequent in time to the relevant CJEU judgments, it is the Strasbourg Court's approach that should prevail. Importantly, this is *not* to say that the judgments of the ECtHR are to be preferred to those of the CJEU always and in every case, and thus to be regarded as hierarchically superior. Rather, the point is that, in a deliberative polyarchy, such conflicts will naturally arise and ought to be worked out dialogically, in a way that best realises the shared ideals underlying the overlapping consensus. For the reasons given above, I would argue that in this particular set of circumstances, the ECtHR has the better of the argument.

The critical question is, therefore, how this is actually to happen. Had EU accession to the Convention proceeded as planned, the co-respondent mechanism could have been employed. Rather than the ECtHR having to address the compatibility of EU law with the Convention indirectly through the Member States' implementing measures and actions, both the State and the Union could be joined as co-respondents. This allows the two actors to be regarded as indivisible parts of a whole and relieves the ECtHR of the responsibility of apportioning responsibility between them, this instead becoming a matter for internal resolution within the Union. Moreover, the prior involvement procedure would solve the procedural difficulties adverted to above, providing an institutional mechanism whereby the CJEU could be prompted by the ECtHR to consider the more recent Convention jurisprudence and – ideally – make whatever adjustments it considers necessary to its own.

But as a result of Opinion 2/13, these mechanisms are not available. There are therefore two possibilities: in light of the new turn in the Convention jurisprudence, the CJEU could correct itself in a future case; or, in a different case, the ECtHR could specifically find the CJEU's interpretation of Article 28 of the Charter and Article 11 ECHR to be contrary to the Convention. However, for this latter possibility to occur, a case would have to find its way to the ECtHR, having exhausted domestic remedies, which would include opportunities for the issue to be referred to the CJEU by national courts. Moreover, all of this is predicated on the assumption that the CJEU will in fact acquiesce to the new and previously somewhat unexpected turn in the ECtHR's Article 11 ECHR jurisprudence.

It is important at this point to note that the criticism provoked by Opinion 2/13 has not been confined to the academy. Judges of the ECtHR themselves have expressed scepticism regarding the CJEU's approach to labour rights:

> [*Viking* and *Laval*], although citing Article 28 of the Charter, were delivered when this provision was not yet binding, and before *Demir and Baykara*. In spite of the [CJEU's] laudable statement of principle of the right to strike as a 'fundamental right' … the conclusions of those judgments on the admissibility of extensive restrictions to the right to strike *may* no longer be tenable after the entry into force of

148   *The Horizontal Frame*

[Art 28 Charter], when read in the light of *Demir and Baykara*, which *is not compatible* with a reading giving undue prominence to the employers' economic freedoms over the professional interests of workers, nor with the levelling down of national labour protection standards to the condition of the worst. The more balanced approach of the [CJEU in *Commission v Germany*[190]] comes closer to the *imperative direction* set by the [ECtHR] in *Demir and Baykara*.[191]

This passage is revealing in two respects. First, in terms of its substantive content, the passages emphasised above are indicators of how Judge Pinto de Albuquerque conceives of the relationship between the Charter and the Convention, and between Luxembourg and Strasbourg. He states flatly that the approach in *Demir and Baykara* is not compatible with the that in *Viking* and *Laval*. This being the case, he *suggests* that *Viking* and *Laval* 'may no longer be tenable' when Article 28 of the Charter, now formally binding, is read in the light of the ECtHR's approach, which is an 'imperative direction'. We see here Judge Pinto de Albuquerque carefully distinguishing between the ECtHR's own jurisdiction and that of the CJEU: he was perfectly entitled to declare the incompatibility between the two approaches, in the abstract and as a matter of Convention law, but left the 'final' decision as to how the Article 11 ECHR jurisprudence should filter through to Article 28 of the Charter to the CJEU, albeit with an unsubtle suggestion ('imperative direction') as to how this should be done. His encouraging but non-committal words regarding *Commission v Germany* served as a kind of sweetener, leading us to the second revealing factor in the passage. For all (or perhaps because of) its clarity and bluntness, the passage quoted above appeared only as a footnote to the concurring opinion of a single judge. Hidden away down there, obiter, and not representing the view of the ECtHR as a whole, the passage is a friendly, but somehow still stern, statement of the existence of a conflict, the necessity of its avoidance, and the means by which this could be achieved.

The President of the ECtHR, in his foreword to the Court's annual report for 2014, was rather less shy:

Bearing in mind that negotiations on European Union accession have been under way for more than thirty years, that accession is an obligation under the Lisbon Treaty and that all the member States along with the European institutions had already stated that they considered the draft agreement compatible with the [TEU] and [TFEU], the CJEU's unfavourable opinion is a great disappointment. Let us not forget, however, that the principal victims will be those citizens whom [Opinion 2/13] deprives of the right to have acts of the European Union subjected to the same external scrutiny as regards respect for human rights as that which applies to each member State.

---

[190] Case C-271/08 *Commission v Germany* ECLI:EU:C:2010:426 [2010] ECR I-7091.

[191] *Hrvatski Liječnički Sindikat v Croatia* App no 36701/09 (Judgment, ECtHR, 27 November 2014) para 5, fn 21 of the concurring opinion of Judge Pinto de Albuquerque, emphasis added. On the 'more balanced' approach in *Commission v Germany*, particularly that of AG Trstenjak (ECLI:EU:C:2010:183), see Vėlyvytė (n 188) 84–85, 89–99.

Conclusion   149

More than ever, therefore, the onus will be on the Strasbourg Court to do what it can in cases before it to protect citizens from the negative effects of this situation.[192]

Given the generally cordial relations between Luxembourg and Strasbourg up to this point, these are fighting words, and it cannot be assumed with any safety that the *Bosphorus* presumption and the *Connolly* gap, strong though they may be, will hold without modification in the post-Opinion 2/13 era. Indeed, there are already signs of a shift in Strasbourg's attitude: in *Avotiņš v Latvia*,[193] though the majority of the Grand Chamber held that the *Bosphorus* presumption applied in the case, this was based on a rather more searching analysis of the specific facts than in previous cases, and was accompanied by the Court reiterating that the application of the presumption is subject to the dual conditions that the domestic authorities must have had no discretion in the issue; and the full array of supervisory mechanisms under EU law must have been deployed.[194] Additionally, the dissenting Opinion of Judge Sajó merits attention:

> [E]ven assuming, for the sake of argument, that the EU system provides equivalent protection in terms of its substantive law and also procedurally, through the CJEU, one should not sacrifice Convention rights for the sake of international cooperation,[195] a consideration that is not recognised among the Convention grounds for limitation of rights. I can see good practical reasons for [the *Bosphorus* presumption]. Comity requires a certain respect in this regard. But the requirement of respect for human rights in the legal sources of the EU does not make the role of this Court fundamentally different from its supervisory role *vis-à-vis* national constitutional systems … Otherwise, a system not amenable to Convention review will be created.[196]

In the right circumstances, and given the right case, it is at least an open question whether a challenge to the CJEU's *Viking* and *Laval* conception of the rights protected by Article 11 ECHR would pass the *Bosphorus* test, and whether the less forgiving approach of Judge Sajó would find greater currency among his colleagues.

IV. CONCLUSION

The most obvious feature that emerges from surveying the current and future relationship between the EU and the ECHR is that this relationship is entirely unlike that which exists between the EU and its Member States or between the

---

[192] European Court of Human Rights, *Annual Report 2014* (Registry of the ECtHR, Strasbourg, 2015), available at: www.echr.coe.int/Documents/Annual_Report_2014_ENG.pdf, 6.

[193] *Avotiņš v Latvia* App no 17502/07 (judgment, ECtHR, 23 May 2016).

[194] ibid paras 105–12.

[195] Here Judge Sajó is referring to the justification given in *Bosphorus* (n 60) para 155, which I criticise above in section I.B.ii, text following n 70.

[196] *Avotiņš* (n 193) para 8 of Judge Sajó's dissent.

150   *The Horizontal Frame*

ECtHR and the States party to the Convention. For the CJEU and the ECtHR, both being non-state actors, the norms that regulate their interaction cannot be analogised directly to those developed with reference to the relationship between national and EU law. Certainly, similarities exist, as in the presumption that ECtHR jurisprudence should be followed which informed the CJEU's decisions in *Roquettes Frères* and *Limburgse Vinyl Maatschappij*, as well as the principle of conditional recognition inherent in the *Bosphorus* presumption. However, as the CJEU's reasoning in Opinion 2/13, and the ongoing conflict regarding Article 11 ECHR demonstrate, the EU's nature as a supranational organisation, and the CJEU's status as a court with transnational jurisdiction – particularly, in this instance, in economic matters – means that the polyarchic relationship between the orders cannot be boiled down to a simple set of universal rules or principles. Contrary to the assumption in the metaconstitutional literature, it is only through the actual, case-specific engagement of different legal orders that the norms regulating the relationship emerge, and these themselves are subject to modification and evolution over time. As to whether and how the impasse created by Opinion 2/13 will be resolved, one way or another, we shall have to wait and see.[197]

In any event, the relationship is further complicated by the important and continuing role of the Member States, which, even after EU accession, will continue to be important intermediaries given the specific division of competences within the Union. In the next chapter, this tripartite polyarchy – the triangular constitution – will be looked at in the round.

---

[197] The European Parliament maintains a 'legislative train schedule' website for the process, describing it as 'derailed' and 'on hold'. Most recently updated in July 2018, the site's outline of recent developments suggests we may be waiting on the platform for some time yet: see European Parliament, 'Completion of Accession to the ECHR', available at: www.europarl.europa.eu/legislative-train/theme-area-of-justice-and-fundamental-rights/file-completion-of-eu-accession-to-the-echr and references therein.

4

The Triangular Frame

INTRODUCTION

Aims and Structure of the Chapter

THIS CHAPTER TELLS the story of a particular constitutional controversy: the protection of the right to life of the 'unborn' in the Irish Constitution. Having set out in detail the 'vertical' and 'horizontal' axes of the triangular constitution, we can now examine how this controversy played out along all these axes; how conflict was avoided; how conflict was resolved when it did occur; and how the controversy was ultimately brought to an end. As I will seek to demonstrate throughout, the controversy is a rich source of evidence for the descriptive accuracy of the triangular constitution as an explanatory framework; for the normative preferability of a heterarchical conception of legal orders; and for the importance of paying close attention to jurisdictional specificity, at every point of the triangle.

Article 40.3.3° of the Irish Constitution, as it stood until 2018, provided as follows:

> The State acknowledges the right to life of the unborn and, with due regard to the equal right to life of the mother, guarantees in its laws to respect, and, as far as practicable, by its laws to defend and vindicate that right.
>
> This subsection shall not limit freedom to travel between the State and another state.
>
> This subsection shall not limit freedom to obtain or make available, in the State, subject to such conditions as may be laid down by law, information relating to services lawfully available in another state.

As will immediately be clear, this is a strangely structured provision. It begins with a strong statement of principle (regardless of whether or not one agrees with the principle, on which more below): that the right to life, a right of obviously fundamental importance, inheres not only in those who have been born, but in the foetus also. It commits the State to defending and vindicating this right, which it declares to be equal to the right to life of the 'mother'. And yet the two provisos immediately row back on this declaration of an allegedly fundamental right, partially lessening its claimed imperative normative strength, and allowing for activities which the State would otherwise be required to forbid in fulfilling its mandate to defend and vindicate the right to life of the 'unborn'.

152   *The Triangular Frame*

This peculiar – and internally incoherent – structure is itself the result of interaction within the triangular constitution. The first sentence was added to the Constitution in 1983 by the Eighth Amendment, endorsed by the electorate by a margin of 67 per cent to 33 per cent, on a turnout of 54 per cent.[1] As we shall see below, the two provisos were added in 1992, by the Thirteenth and Fourteenth Amendments,[2] in order to remedy or avoid conflict with the two European legal orders.

Finally, on 25 May 2018, the electorate voted to endorse the Thirty-sixth Amendment, deleting the text of Article 40.3.3° in its entirety, and replacing it with the following statement: 'Provision may be made by law for the regulation of termination of pregnancy'.[3] So ended a constitutional prohibition which, over 35 years, had humiliated, endangered, and occasionally killed women in Ireland.[4]

It was mentioned previously but bears repeating here that this chapter is emphatically not about the substantive issue of abortion rights. The questions of when human life begins; the morality of terminating a pregnancy (or the prior question of the relevance of morality thereto); and the relative strength and importance of the rights of pregnant women as autonomous individual agents and equal citizens bearing equal rights and dignity are not the issues the chapter seeks to address. Nor is it about the broader sociological aspects of the abortion debate in Ireland, touching on issues of religiosity, misogyny and the various sexual and reproductive pathologies of Irish society.[5] However, the chapter is not

---

[1] *Referendum Results 1937–2015* (Dublin, Department of Housing, Planning, Community and Local Government, Dublin 2016), available at: www.housing.gov.ie/sites/default/files/migrated-files/en/Publications/LocalGovernment/Voting/referendum_results_1937-2015.pdf, 37 (throughout this chapter, percentages will be rounded to the nearest whole figure).

[2] ibid 48–51. On a turnout of 68%, the Thirteenth Amendment was passed by a margin of 62% to 38%, and the Fourteenth by 60% to 40%.

[3] Thirty-sixth Amendment of the Constitution Bill 2018, clause 1(b). The referendum was passed by a margin of 66% to 34%, on a turnout of 64%: Referendum Returning Officer, 'Referendum on the Thirty-sixth Amendment of the Constitution Bill 2018: Detailed Results', available at: www.referendum.ie/detailed-results.

[4] The Thirty-sixth Amendment was signed into law, and the Constitution formally amended, on 18 September 2018, following the failure of all legal challenges to the conduct of the referendum taken under the Referendum Acts. The legislation authorised by the new Art 40.3.3°, regulating access to abortion, is pending. See F Kelly, 'President Signs Bill Repealing Eighth Amendment Into Law' *Irish Times* (18 September 2018), available at: www.irishtimes.com/news/politics/president-signs-bill-repealing-eighth-amendment-into-law-1.3633601.

[5] See generally, R Sweetman, *On Our Backs: Sexual Attitudes in a Changing Ireland* (London, Pan, 1979); T Hesketh, *The Second Partitioning of Ireland? The Abortion Referendum of 1983* (Dún Laoghaire, Brandsma, 1990); A Smyth (ed), *The Abortion Papers: Ireland* (Cork, Attic Press, 1992); J Kingston, A Whelan and I Bacik, *Abortion and the Law* (Dublin, Round Hall Sweet & Maxwell, 1997); J Schweppe (ed), *The Unborn Child, Article 40.3.3° and Abortion in Ireland: Twenty-five Years of Protection?* (Dublin, Liffey Press, 2008); A Quilty, S Kennedy and C Conlon (eds), *The Abortion Papers Ireland: Volume 2* (Cork, Cork University Press, 2015); C Hug, *The Politics of Sexual Morality in Ireland*, 2nd edn (London, Springer, 2016); F de Londras and M Enright, *Repealing the 8th: Reforming Irish Abortion Law* (Bristol, Policy Press, 2018); U Mullally (ed), *Repeal the 8th* (London, Unbound, 2018).

Introduction 153

neutral or agnostic on these issues. The near total constitutional prohibition of abortion in Ireland is portrayed here as being a grievous error, but, importantly, it was an error that the Irish electorate was legally and constitutionally entitled to make, at least within the epistemic confines of the Irish constitutional order, given its amendability by referendum, unlimited by any concept of an 'unconstitutional constitutional amendment', or of an unalterable, 'permanent' core. The insertion of the Eighth Amendment in 1983, its clarification or alteration by the Thirteenth and Fourteenth Amendments in 1992, and the final repeal of all three of these amendments by the Thirty-sixth Amendment in 2018 were all constitutional and political decisions made by a particular political community, but, like the constitutional order established in the name of this community and which, self-referentially, bestows sovereignty on this community, these amendments did not occur in a vacuum. The focus of this chapter is therefore specifically *meta*constitutional: it evaluates the process by which the constitutional prohibition of abortion triggered the engagement of the other orders in the triangular constitution, and how this engagement in turn affected the domestic order.

The preceding chapters have set out the nature and workings of the triangular constitution as an explanatory framework and have sought to demonstrate this framework's descriptive accuracy: the Irish, EU and European Convention on Human Rights (ECHR) legal orders do not operate in isolation, but are conditioned by – and in turn condition – the legal orders at the other points of the triangle. Moving from the explanatory frame to the normative, the preceding chapters have suggested that not only *can* these three legal orders be regarded as being arranged heterarchically, rather than hierarchically, but that they *should* be so regarded. Together, in their *Gestalt*, they form a deliberative polyarchy, a simultaneously unified but non-unitary whole, recognising the final authority of each order within its own domain, but each order refusing to subsume itself entirely under the authority of any other. This chapter seeks further to advance both claims, the explanatory and the normative, by examining the manner in which the Irish abortion controversy ricocheted around the triangular constitution, each legal order dealing with the issue within the confines of its own jurisdiction and in accordance with its own *telos*. In what follows, I present this conception as being normatively preferable, in terms of both process and results, to any hierarchical conception or arrangement of the three legal orders. In short, the case study is a stark illustration of the danger of constitutional solipsism described in chapter one, and gives more concrete form to the claim that a heterarchical conception of legal orders, by forcing each order to always bear in mind the claims of its counterparts and to adjust its own claims and self-image in response, is a legitimate and desirable refinement of the traditions of state-based constitutionalism. Moreover, the Irish abortion issue provides an archetypal example of national constitutional specificity (frequently referenced in the literature but rarely properly analysed in concrete form), and, given the means by which it originated and played out, it also engages questions of democratic legitimacy. The case law surrounding it therefore provides an ideal field for

154 *The Triangular Frame*

analysing the issues of specificity and universality at the heart of metaconstitutional pluralisms.

These issues of solipsism, democratic legitimacy, specificity and universality highlight a particular danger that the chapter seeks to avoid: that of ignoring, or, worse, instrumentalising the very real suffering inflicted on Irish women by the prohibition of abortion. The ending of this prohibition, and the suffering it caused, would have been a cause for celebration regardless of whether it had been mandated or achieved judicially or politically, at the national or either European level – and the earlier the better. But as a *strategic* matter, the particular way in which it has now been ended – politically, not judicially; nationally, not supranationally or internationally – is the most emphatic ending possible, endowed with the very same democratic legitimacy that the prohibition itself initially enjoyed. Mere *judicial* vindication of a woman's right to control what does and does not happen to her own body is, by its nature, susceptible to charges of being undemocratic or otherwise somehow tainted. This would be all the more so if this vindication could be portrayed by its opponents as being 'forced' upon a national legal system by some 'external' 'other'. The *political* vindication of abortion rights, particularly at the national level at which the problem began, has the potential to be rather more robust and lasting, as the contrasting histories of the regulation of abortion in the United States and the United Kingdom demonstrate. The victory of 2018 was hard fought and hard won by the diverse coalition of groups and individuals, led by women, that achieved it, and – given the impossibility of permanence in law – must now be sustained by consistent political vigilance. But it is a victory that was aided in part by the fact of the Irish constitutional order's integration within the triangular constitution, by the existence of frames of reference and spaces of contestation beyond the national, as this chapter will seek to demonstrate.

Pending the introduction of the legislation now expressly permitted by the new Article 40.3.3°, abortion remains illegal in Ireland in almost all circumstances. The one exception is when the procedure is carried out in order to save the life (but not the health) of a pregnant woman, including – in certain circumstances – from possible suicide. This narrowly drawn exception, nowadays set out in and governed by the Protection of Life During Pregnancy Act 2013, arose from the Supreme Court judgment in *Attorney General v X*,[6] where it was held to be inherent in Article 40.3.3° of the Constitution as it then stood.

Section I sets out the two pivotal domestic cases through which the regulation of abortion under national constitutional law entered European legal discourse. Section II will outline how the European legal orders and the domestic order interacted regarding three specific aspects of the abortion issue: the right to receive and impart information about abortion services; the right to travel to receive an abortion abroad; and the right to a private and family life.

---

[6] *Attorney General v X* [1992] 1 IR 1 (X).

Introduction 155

Finally, section III will examine what this interaction tells us about the self-images and attitudes of the three legal orders, or at least of their judicial branches; about the nature of the relationships between them; and, therefore, about the particularity or universality of the interface norms regulating the relationship. The chapter concludes that though (very) broad, general metaconstitutional principles can be drawn out from the various judgments, we cannot derive hard and fast, universally applicable norms from them without stripping these norms of the content and meaning which made them capable of guiding judicial action in the first place.

But first, it is important properly to situate the argument by outlining the history of Irish abortion law prior to the addition of Article 40.3.3° to the Constitution by the Eighth Amendment.

Prologue: The Situation Prior to 1983

Though the specific right to life of the 'unborn' was only inserted into the Constitution in 1983, the ban on abortion in Ireland is much older. For centuries an offence at common law, the crime was put on a statutory footing by sections 58 and 59 of the Offences Against the Person Act 1861, an Act of the UK Parliament at Westminster. First 'carried over' to the legal order of the Irish Free State by Article 73 of that State's 1922 Constitution,[7] and again in 1937 by Article 50.1 of the Constitution,[8] these sections of the 1861 Act were not repealed until July 2013.[9] They provided as follows:

58. Every woman, being with child, who, with intent to procure her own miscarriage, shall unlawfully administer to herself any poison or other noxious thing or shall unlawfully use any instrument or other means whatsoever with the like intent, and whosoever, with intent to procure the miscarriage of any woman, whether she be or not be with child, shall unlawfully administer to her or cause to be taken by her any poison or other noxious thing, or shall unlawfully use any instrument or other means whatsoever with the like intent, shall be guilty of a felony, and being convicted thereof shall be liable to be kept in penal servitude for life.

59. Whoever shall unlawfully supply or procure any poison or other noxious thing, or any instrument or thing whatsoever, knowing that the same is intended to be unlawfully used or employed with intent to procure the miscarriage of any woman,

---

[7] Which read: 'Subject to this Constitution and to the extent to which they are not inconsistent therewith, the laws in force in the Irish Free State (Saorstát Éireann) at the date of the coming into operation of this Constitution shall continue to be of full force and effect until the same or any of them shall have been repealed or amended by enactment of the Oireachtas'.

[8] Which reads: 'Subject to this Constitution and to the extent to which they are not inconsistent therewith, the laws in force in Saorstát Éireann immediately prior to the date of the coming into operation of this Constitution shall continue to be of full force and effect until the same or any of them shall have been repealed or amended by enactment of the Oireachtas'.

[9] Protection of Life During Pregnancy Act 2013, s 5.

156   *The Triangular Frame*

whether she be or be not with child, shall be guilty of a misdemeanour, and being convicted thereof shall be liable to be kept in penal servitude.[10]

The recurrence of the word 'unlawfully' in sections 58 and 59 was crucial in Great Britain, where medical opinion came to regard abortion as a legitimate therapeutic practice where the pregnancy posed a danger to the woman's life or mental or physical health. As James Casey notes, there is little evidence that Irish medical practice ever adopted this stance, but this was for moral and religious, not legal, reasons.[11] No one was prosecuted under the 1861 Act between independence in 1922 and the Act's repeal in 2013.[12]

Following the coming into force of the 1937 Constitution, and particularly since the beginning of its judicial exegesis in the 1960s (discussed in chapter two), the ban on abortion both gained a basis in constitutional theory and faced a new – potential – threat. In *Ryan v Attorney General*,[13] it was held that the rights guaranteed to the citizen by the Constitution were not limited to those specifically mentioned in the text of the document itself. Instead, Article 40.3.1°'s statement that '[t]he State guarantees in its laws to respect, and, as far as practicable, by its laws to defend and vindicate the personal rights of the citizen' was held to include 'all those rights which result from the Christian and democratic nature of the State'.[14] These 'unenumerated' constitutional rights were later held, in *McGee v Attorney General*,[15] to include a right to marital privacy. The statutory ban on the sale, manufacture or importation of contraceptives at issue in that case was struck down for breaching this right, at least with respect to married couples. The Supreme Court in *McGee* made clear that the unenumerated right to (marital) privacy could not trump the State's abortion laws, Walsh J in his judgment holding that:

> [A]ny action on the part of either the husband and wife or of the State to limit family sizes by endangering or destroying human life must necessarily not only be an offence against the common good but also against the guaranteed personal rights of the human life in question.[16]

Accordingly, even prior to the insertion of Article 40.3.3°, the constitutional right to life contained in Article 40.3.2° had been interpreted as applying equally

---

[10] Offences Against the Person Act 1861, ss 58–59, as amended by the Statute Law Revision Act 1892 and the Statute Law Revision (No 2) Act 1893.

[11] J Casey *Constitutional Law in Ireland*, 3rd edn (Dublin, Round Hall Sweet & Maxwell, 2000) 433–34, citing J Keown, *Abortion, Doctors and the Law* (Cambridge, Cambridge University Press, 1988) ch 3.

[12] Though Casey notes that charges of murder have been brought where women have died following an abortion: ibid 434, citing *People (Attorney General) v Cadden* (1956) 91 ILTR 97.

[13] *Ryan v Attorney General* [1965] IR 294.

[14] ibid 312 (Kenny J).

[15] *McGee v Attorney General* [1974] IR 284.

[16] ibid 312.

Introduction 157

to the born and the unborn. This was made explicit in *G v An Bord Uchtála*,[17] an adoption case, where it was held (again by Walsh J) that:

> [All children have] the right to life itself and the right to be guarded against all threats directed to [their] existence whether before or after birth ... The right to life necessarily implies the right to be born, [and] the right to preserve and defend (and have preserved and defended) that life ... It lies not in the power of the parent who has the primary, natural rights and duties in respect of the child to exercise them in such a way as intentionally or by neglect to endanger the health or life of the child or to terminate its existence. The child's natural right to life and all that flows from that right are independent of any right of the parent as such.[18]

Given these strong judicial statements of support for the idea that the constitutional right to life extended to the foetus, what happened next was perhaps surprising. The 'potential threat' to the 1861 Act adverted to above arose from the doctrine of unenumerated rights itself. Despite the Supreme Court's assurances on the issue, there was thought to be nothing in theory *definitively* to preclude a future Supreme Court – or, 'worse', a future European court – from liberalising the law on abortion. The US experience was crucial here. The US Supreme Court's striking down of a statute criminalising contraception in *Griswold v Connecticut*[19] was seen as a stepping stone towards its later finding, in *Roe v Wade*,[20] that the right to privacy (unenumerated, but held to flow from the due process clause of the Fourteenth Amendment to the US Constitution) extended to a woman's choice as to whether to have an abortion, within gestational limits. The parallels between *Griswold* and *McGee*, and what this might mean for the future of abortion in Ireland,[21] unnerved anti-abortion campaigners, who – not content either with judicial statements confirming a pre-natal right to life or with the specific invocation and reaffirmation of sections 58 and 59 of the 1861 Act in the statute enacted to regulate contraception on foot of *McGee*[22] – began to campaign for a constitutional amendment to settle the issue conclusively. A referendum on the Eighth Amendment was held on 7 September 1983, and passed by a majority of 67 per cent to 33 per cent, on a turnout of 54 per cent.[23] Accordingly, Article 40.3.3° (or rather, what later became its first paragraph) was added to the Constitution.

---

[17] *G v An Bord Uchtála* [1980] IR 32.
[18] ibid 69.
[19] *Griswold v Connecticut* 381 US 479 (1965).
[20] *Roe v Wade* 410 US 113 (1973).
[21] This also raises interesting questions about judicial 'borrowing' and the interaction of legal orders beyond the European, which is beyond the scope of the present study. For a (now dated) account of the US influence on Irish constitutional jurisprudence, see PD Sutherland 'The Influence of United States Constitutional Law on the Interpretation of the Irish Constitution' (1984) 28 *St Louis University Law Journal* 41.
[22] Health (Family Planning) Act 1979, s 10.
[23] *Referendum Results* (n 1) 37.

158 *The Triangular Frame*

I. AVOIDANCE, ENGAGEMENT AND CONDITIONAL RECOGNITION

This section will set out the High Court and Supreme Court judgments in the cases which triggered the engagement of the European legal orders on the question of abortion regulation in Ireland: *AG (Society for the Protection of Unborn Children) (SPUC) v Open Door Counselling and Dublin Well Woman*[24] and *Society for the Protection of Unborn Children (SPUC) v Grogan*.[25] As we shall see, the reasoning in the cases is diverse, and there is a variety of interface norms at work – from a principle of avoidance, through to a (threatened) application of the *Solange* principle of conditional recognition – depending on the circumstances and the position of the court in the domestic hierarchy.

A. *AG (SPUC) v Open Door Counselling and Dublin Well Woman*

The first case to call for judicial interpretation of Article 40.3.3° was *Open Door*. The defendants were organisations offering non-directive counselling services to pregnant women; critically, both organisations were prepared, in the course of this counselling, to discuss with clients the possibility of travel to England to procure an abortion in accordance with English law. If the client wished to consider this option further, they would make arrangements to refer her to a medical clinic in England (with which the counselling organisations had no formal relationship, financial or otherwise). SPUC sought a declaration that the activities of the defendants were unlawful having regard to Article 40.3.3°, and an injunction prohibiting the defendants from continuing to counsel, advise or assist pregnant women regarding the procurement of an abortion abroad.[26]

The first defendant, Open Door, denied that its activities were unlawful having regard to Article 40.3.3°, and further claimed that it was entitled to engage in these activities 'by virtue of the provisions of the Constitution'.[27] Oddly, in making this defence, it did not claim reliance on any *specific* provision of the Constitution, such as Article 40.6.1°i's guarantee of freedom of expression,[28]

---

[24] *Attorney General (Society for the Protection of Unborn Children) v Open Door Counselling and Dublin Well Woman* [1988] IR 593 (*Open Door*).

[25] *Society for the Protection of Unborn Children v Grogan (No 1)* [1989] IR 753 (*Grogan*).

[26] The plaintiffs also sought a declaration that the defendants' activities amounted to the common law offence of conspiracy to corrupt public morals. Hamilton P, in the High Court, held that the activities *could* amount to the commission of such an offence, but that to make such a declaration would be to usurp the authority of the criminal courts, the offence being a misdemeanour triable on indictment before a judge and jury. Hamilton P was not prepared to run the risk of 'treating conduct as criminal when a jury might consider otherwise' (at 615). This leg of the case will not, therefore, be discussed.

[27] *Open Door* (n 24) 604.

[28] Though note the proviso at Art 40.6.1° itself, that such right is 'subject to public order and morality'.

Avoidance, Engagement and Conditional Recognition 159

or on the unenumerated right to privacy established in *McGee*. Additionally, no provision of EU law or of the ECHR was raised.[29]

The second defendant, Well Woman, also denied that it had acted unlawfully, and raised in its defence the constitutional rights to privacy, to freedom of expression, to freedom of communication, and to freedom of access to information in the course of counselling and generally.[30] Importantly for present purposes, however, Well Woman also claimed reliance on certain rights arising from EU law, made effective in Ireland by the European Communities Act 1972 and, as we have seen in chapter two, allegedly immunised from constitutional challenge by the 'exclusion clause' then to be found at Article 29.4.3°.[31]

i. Avoidance of Triggering Engagement: The High Court Judgment

Hamilton P, for the High Court, found for the plaintiff and granted the declaration and injunction sought. In the course of his judgment, he noted that Article 40.3.3° of the Constitution, like any other constitutional provision granting or recognising rights, is self-executing and thus requires no subsequent legislation to give it effect. Accordingly, the fact that there had been no legislation on foot of Article 40.3.3° in the years since the passage of the Eighth Amendment was neither here nor there.[32] Hamilton P evaluated the history and present position of the right to life in Ireland, and invoked the dicta of Walsh J in *McGee* and *G v An Bord Uchtála* (quoted in the prologue above), along with the plain text of Article 40.3.3° and the following statement of McCarthy J in *Norris v Attorney General*:

> [T]he provisions of the preamble [to the Constitution] ... would appear to lean heavily against any view other than [that] the right to life of the unborn is a sacred trust to which all the organs of government must lend their support.[33]

On the strength of this, the High Court held that:

> [T]he judicial organ of government is obliged to lend its support to the enforcement of the right to life of the unborn, to defend and vindicate that right and, if there is a threat to that right from whatever source, to protect that right from such threat, if its support is sought.[34]

---

[29] The ECHR was not part of domestic law at this time, as discussed in ch 2.

[30] Though note that this last right had never been 'discovered' by the courts as being inherent in the Constitution.

[31] Now Art 29.4.6°.

[32] *Open Door* (n 24) 605–07, relying on the traditionally very strong judicial authority to vindicate constitutional rights: *Educational Company of Ireland v Fitzpatrick (No 2)* [1961] IR 345; *Byrne v Ireland* [1972] IR 241; *Meskell v CIÉ* [1973] IR 121; and *Mead* (Supreme Court, unreported, 26 July 1972).

[33] *Norris v Attorney General* [1984] IR 36, 103.

[34] *Open Door* (n 24) 597–99.

160   *The Triangular Frame*

The High Court went on to find that the defendants' activities amounted in fact 'to counselling and assisting pregnant women to travel abroad to obtain further advice on abortion and to secure an abortion',[35] and that such activities must be unlawful with regard to Article 40.3.3°:

> Obedience to the law is required of every citizen and there exists a duty on the part of the citizens to respect that right [to life of the unborn] and not to interfere with it. The court is under a duty to act so as not to permit any body of citizens to deprive another of his constitutional right, to see that such rights are protected and to regard as unlawful any infringement or attempted infringement of such constitutional right as constituting a violation of the fundamental law of the State.
>
> The qualified right to privacy, the rights of association and freedom of expression and the right to disseminate information cannot be invoked to interfere with such a fundamental right as the right to life of the unborn, which is acknowledged by the Constitution of Ireland.[36]

Finally, the High Court dealt with the issues of EU law raised by Well Woman: the effect of the Constitution's EU 'exclusion clause'; of then Articles 59 and 60 EEC with regard to services; and of the provisions of Council Directive 73/148/EEC,[37] dealing with free movement and residence within the Community for Member State nationals with regard to establishment and the provision of services.[38] In a brief passage at the end of his judgment, Hamilton P took pains to point out how seriously he had taken and studied these submissions, but concluded that all of the activities at issue in the case had occurred within Ireland, and, there being no cross-border element, that no issue of EU law therefore arose.[39] Because such questions might be considered in a future case, he made no finding as regards the interaction or relationship between the EU law rights relied on and the provisions of Article 40.3.3°.

The possible relevance of EU law having been ruled out, the High Court judgment in this case is an ordinary instance of domestic constitutionalism. While arguments based on EU law had been advanced – and the trial judge tried to stress his *communautaire* credentials in stating that the submissions on EU law 'warranted [full and careful] consideration',[40] echoing, to a limited extent, Miguel Poiares Maduro's contrapunctual principle of pluralism itself – the reasoning behind his finding that EU law had not been triggered was threadbare, contained no reference to the jurisprudence of the Court of Justice of the European Union (CJEU) and, as we shall see in section II.A.i, was later indirectly

---

[35] ibid 617.

[36] ibid.

[37] Council Directive 73/148/EEC of 21 May 1973 on the abolition of restrictions on movement and residence within the Community for nationals of Member States with regard to establishment and the provision of services [1973] OJ L 172.

[38] *Open Door* (n 24) 618.

[39] ibid.

[40] ibid

contradicted by that Court. The view of the relationship between the domestic and EU legal systems arising from the judgment is not one where the two are interwoven in any particular way, but where they are imagined to be neatly separable. There being no cross-border issue, this must therefore be a purely national issue, and was treated as one. However, this approach ignores the extensive case law of the CJEU on *potential* restrictions of free movement rights.[41] Accordingly, the only metaconstitutional interface norm that can be derived from the High Court judgment is one which plays no part in the theories of Mattias Kumm or Miguel Poiares Maduro or Charles Sabel and Oliver Gerstenberg: a principle of *avoidance*, whereby matters are kept firmly within the domain of the national constitution, and within the jurisdiction of the national courts.

ii. Engagement Avoided Again, More Narrowly: The Supreme Court Judgment

On appeal to the Supreme Court, the defendants were similarly unsuccessful. In a brief, unanimous judgment delivered by Finlay CJ, the Supreme Court held that it was 'satisfied beyond doubt that ... the defendants were assisting in the ultimate destruction of the life of the unborn by abortion'.[42] As a result:

> [T]here could not be an implied and unenumerated constitutional right to information about the availability of a service of abortion outside the State, which, if availed of, would have the direct consequence of destroying the expressly guaranteed constitutional right to life of the unborn.[43]

Furthermore, the argument that Article 40.6.1°i's guarantee of freedom of expression implied an ancillary right to receive information was also unsuccessful, the Court holding that 'no right could constitutionally arise to obtain information the purpose of the obtaining of which was to defeat the constitutional right to life of the unborn child'.[44]

As part of their appeal, the defendants asked the Supreme Court to make a preliminary reference to the CJEU under then Article 177 EEC in order to determine whether a pregnant woman resident in Ireland had the right, under Articles 59 and 60 EEC, to travel to another Member State 'for the purpose of being the recipient of a service consisting of the performing of an abortion upon her', and whether 'a necessary corollary to that right ... was the right to

---

[41] See, with reference to the trade in goods, Case 8/74 *Dassonville* ECLI:EU:C:1974:82, [1974] ECR 837, para 5: 'All trading rules enacted by Member States which are capable of hindering, directly or indirectly, actually or potentially, intra-community trade are to be considered as measures having an effect equivalent to quantitative restrictions'. This approach has long been extrapolated beyond goods to services: for an overview, see the Opinion of AG Sharpston in Case C-34/09 *Ruiz Zambrano* ECLI:EU:C:2010:560, [2011] ECR I-1177, paras 69–74.
[42] *Open Door* (n 24) 624.
[43] ibid 625.
[44] ibid.

162   *The Triangular Frame*

information about the availability of that service'.[45] However, the reference was not made, for a reason different from that of the High Court, but similarly narrow. Counsel for the defendants had conceded that the corollary right 'was confined to the obtaining of *information* about the availability or existence of the service' and 'could not be extended to the obtaining of *assistance* to avail of or receive the service'.[46] The order of the High Court was not confined to the question of information, and nor did it seek to 'prevent a pregnant woman from becoming aware of the existence of abortion outside the jurisdiction'.[47] Instead, it sought to restrain '*assistance* to a pregnant woman to travel abroad and obtain the service of abortion'.[48] Because the defence had made no claim that *this* was a right flowing from the Treaty, the Supreme Court held on this very narrow ground that no question of the interpretation of the Treaty arose, and the Court was therefore not obliged to make a reference to Luxembourg. Accordingly, the Court expressed no opinion on three issues which had arisen in argument: whether the Treaty grants pregnant women a right to travel for the purpose of having an abortion; whether the defendants would be entitled to rely on such a right despite it being vested in pregnant women and not in them as counselling services; and the general nature of the right to travel to receive services under then Articles 59 and 60 EEC.

Again, the only metaconstitutional interface norm at work in the judgment is a principle of avoidance. However, there is an important difference between the reasoning of the High Court and the Supreme Court as to why EU law had not been engaged in the case, and thus how the principle of avoidance was applied: whereas for the High Court the lack of actual cross-border activity was decisive, the Supreme Court made no mention of this finding, depending instead on the rather nice distinction between providing 'assistance' and providing 'information'. The EU law arguments therefore failed because of the defendants' concession that the EU rights they claimed were narrower than the restrictions that had been placed upon them. This concession is rather strange, in that it can at least be argued that providing assistance to someone to avail of a service must necessarily include the provision of information about that service: indeed, the defendants would have failed in their primary duty as counsellors had they not provided this information. On this analysis, the fact that the injunction's restrictions were *broader* than the right claimed should have been no bar to a finding that EU law had been engaged. Assistance *encompasses* information, and a right to impart and receive that information having been claimed, this went to the heart of the validity of the injunction with respect to EU law. The question then arises of the extent to which fear of the possible consequences of engagement with EU law on this issue played a part in the Court's reasoning.

[45] ibid 622.
[46] ibid 626, emphasis added.
[47] ibid.
[48] ibid, emphasis added.

Dissatisfied with their defeat, the defendants applied to the European Court of Human Rights in Strasbourg (ECtHR). That Court's judgment, in *Open Door and Dublin Well Woman v Ireland*,[49] will be discussed at section II.A.ii below.

B. *SPUC v Grogan*

In chapter two, the decision in *Grogan* was discussed as part of a preliminary analysis of the relationship between Irish and EU law and the 'torpedo' or 'ripple' effect of what is now Article 29.4.6°, and the Supreme Court's application of the principle of conditional recognition. These features will be elaborated upon in this section.

i. *Engagement Begins: The High Court Judgment*

As will be recalled, the facts were quite similar to *Open Door*, but whereas in that case SPUC had sought an injunction preventing *assistance* in procuring an abortion abroad by means of one-to-one counselling, the defendants in *Grogan* were the officers of various students' unions who had published the contact *information* of licensed English abortion clinics in their annual students' welfare guides. The defendants relied on this difference to distinguish their case from *Open Door* and claimed a right to distribute the impugned information under EU law, the right to receive information in relation to services provided in another Member State giving rise to a corresponding right to impart such information. Carroll J, for the High Court, agreed with the distinction between these two cases, and exercised her discretion under then Article 177 EEC to refer questions on the issue to the CJEU. Having done this, and considering that an answer from the CJEU was required in order for her to dispose of the case, she made no formal order in relation to the interlocutory injunction that had been sought by SPUC.[50]

As with the High Court and Supreme Court decisions in *Open Door*, this judgment is an ordinary instance of national constitutionalism, but in a different way. A national judge was faced with a case that she felt required an authoritative interpretation of EU law and duly referred the question to Luxembourg, as she was entitled to do under the national constitution and under the Treaty. We cannot make any distinction here between *EU*-constitutionalism and *national*-constitutionalism – at least in this case and at this stage – as the two amount to the same thing, particularly in light of the constitutional status afforded to EU law in Ireland. Kumm's terms, 'European Constitutional Supremacy' and

---

[49] *Open Door and Dublin Well Woman v Ireland* (1992) 15 EHRR 244 (*Open Door* (ECtHR)).
[50] *Grogan* (n 25) 758–59.

164   *The Triangular Frame*

'National Constitutional Supremacy',[51] are inapplicable here, the case not (yet) being one of conflict between legal orders, and the question of primacy therefore not yet being called into question. The principle of avoidance, employed in different ways by the High Court and Supreme Court in *Open Door* in an attempt to avoid even the possibility of precipitating a conflict between the Irish and EU orders, played no part in the High Court judgment in *Grogan*. The decision exhibits none of the wariness of engaging EU law that permeates the judgments in *Open Door*; in fact, Síofra O'Leary suggests that 'the national judge was eager to introduce the case to the European forum given the continuous flow of litigation at national level'.[52]

ii. Solange *in Ireland: The Supreme Court Judgment*

On appeal by SPUC to the Supreme Court, the interlocutory injunction it had sought – and on which the High Court had made no formal decision – was granted. The Supreme Court was unanimous that regardless of the form of her order, Carroll J had effectively made *two* decisions: first, to refer questions to the CJEU; and, secondly, not to grant the injunction sought.[53] The Supreme Court did not question or seek to review the propriety of Carroll J's having sought a reference under then Article 177 EEC (an option unavailable to the Supreme Court by its own jurisprudence),[54] but noted that it was entirely open to her to have made this reference while still granting the interlocutory injunction, which is the course that, for the Supreme Court, should have been followed.[55]

As noted in chapter two, the justices of the Supreme Court were critical of Carroll J's distinction between the facts of *Open Door* and the present case, Finlay CJ rejecting the distinction as unsound, and noting that:

> It is clearly *the fact that such information is conveyed* to pregnant women, and not *the method of communication* which creates the unconstitutional illegality, and the judgment of this Court in [*Open Door*] is not open to any other interpretation.[56]

---

[51] M Kumm, 'The Jurisprudence of Constitutional Conflict: Constitutional Supremacy in Europe Before and After the Constitutional Treaty' (2005) 11 *European Law Journal* 262, 266.

[52] S O'Leary, 'Freedom of Establishment and Freedom to Provide Services: The Court of Justice as a Reluctant Constitutional Adjudicator: An Examination of the Abortion Information Case' (1992) 17 *European Law Review* 138, 143.

[53] *Grogan* (n 25) 762 (Finlay CJ).

[54] *Campus Oil v Minister for Industry* [1983] IR 82, 86 (Walsh J): 'A request by a national judge to [the CJEU] for an interpretation of articles of the Treaty is not, in any sense, an appeal to a higher court. It is an exercise of a right ... to request an interpretation of the Treaty from the Court of Justice which itself is the only one having jurisdiction to give such binding interpretations ... The power is conferred upon [the national judge] by the Treaty without any qualification, express or implied, to the effect that it is capable of being overruled by any other national court ... The national judge has an untrammelled discretion as to whether he will or will not refer questions for a preliminary ruling under article 177. In doing so, he is not in any way subject to the parties or to any other judicial authority'.

[55] *Grogan* (n 25) 762 (Finlay CJ).

[56] ibid 764, emphasis added.

This seems difficult to reconcile with the importance that the Supreme Court had attached in *Open Door* to the distinction between the provision of *information* and the provision of *assistance*, and I suggest that this difficulty arises from the Supreme Court's losing sight of another important distinction: between *legality* (under Irish law) and the *necessity of a reference*. With respect to the former, both information *and* assistance in the circumstances were illegal under Irish law, and the Supreme Court was perfectly correct that this was clear from *Open Door*. Accordingly, Carroll J should indeed have granted the injunction pending the return of the answers from Luxembourg: no real distinction could be made between the two cases as regards legality. However, a close reading of the judgment in *Open Door* shows that the information/assistance distinction in that case related only to the question of whether an issue of EU law arose – and thus the necessity of a reference to the CJEU – and *not* to the substantive question of whether the impugned action was illegal. Thus, the Supreme Court confused the issue by seeming to regard the two cases as entirely indistinguishable: they were not, at least as regards the necessity of a reference.

The remainder of the judgments in the *Grogan* case concern the interpretation to be given to the constitutional 'exclusion clause' in relation to EU law, the paramount duty of the national judge to vindicate constitutional rights, and, as we saw in chapter two, a clear application of the principle of conditional recognition in the *Solange*-style warning that the Supreme Court's obedience to the CJEU could not be guaranteed in the event of that Court deciding that EU law was in conflict with the Supreme Court's Article 40.3.3° jurisprudence. However, there is one further important aspect of the judgment, linked to the Supreme Court's warning shot, which was not discussed in chapter two. Let us bear in mind that this case, and its counterpart in the CJEU's jurisprudence which will be discussed in sections II.A.i and II.A.i below, were procedurally unusual: a case was brought before the High Court and a reference made to the CJEU, but the Supreme Court heard the plaintiff's appeal *prior* to the CJEU having answered the questions asked. This was not, however, an attempt by the Supreme Court to pre-empt the decision of the CJEU: the appeal related only to the question of the interlocutory injunction, and not the substance of the issues. We have already seen the Supreme Court's warning that:

> *If and when* a decision of the [CJEU] rules that some aspect of European [Union] law affects the activities of the defendants impugned in this case, the consequence of that decision on these constitutionally guaranteed rights and their protection by the courts will then fall to be considered *by these courts*.[57]

Crucially, however, Finlay CJ also expressly granted both parties liberty to apply to the High Court to have the injunction varied in light of the CJEU's judgment once it was handed down.[58] This essential fact had two effects, one legal and one theoretical. Legally, it was instrumental in the CJEU's determination that the

---

[57] ibid 765 (Finlay CJ), emphasis added.
[58] ibid 766.

166 *The Triangular Frame*

questions referred to it were not moot, and that it could therefore accept juris-diction in the case.[59] Theoretically, it lends weight to the argument made initially in chapter two that the Supreme Court's judgment in *Grogan* is an example of the metaconstitutional principle of conditional recognition in action: having made its point regarding the particular importance attached in Ireland to the right to life of the 'unborn' and how obedience to an adverse judgment from the CJEU could not be guaranteed, the Supreme Court did not go so far as to *preclude* either the CJEU from delivering its judgment or that judgment from being given legal effect by the High Court. Seen in this light, what the Supreme Court 'took away' with one hand (automatic and unquestioning obedience to Luxembourg), it 'gave' with the other (the very real possibility of the loyal appli-cation of the Luxembourg judgment).

We can therefore see reflected in the Supreme Court's decision the first of Kumm's metaconstitutional interface norms, the formal principle of legality.[60] For Kumm, 'legality' means that 'national courts should start with a strong presumption that they are required to enforce EU law, national constitutional provisions notwithstanding'.[61] That this is the *starting* position of the Supreme Court in *Grogan* is evident from both its language in the case and its general praxis of loyal application of EU law. But Kumm's countervailing principles of subsidiarity, democracy and the protection of basic rights would all seem to weigh strongly in the present case against the automatic enforcement of that presumption: subsidiarity because abortion is not something regulated at the EU level; democracy (which I categorised in chapter two as a means of defend-ing national specificity) because the right recognised by Article 40.3.3° (whether rightly or wrongly) was a democratically endorsed, specific expression of the values of a self-determining political community; and the protection of rights because that is what the entire controversy boils down to, with the right to life – and its particular formulation in Ireland – being considered decisive, at least from the domestic perspective, rather than the rights of women. However, the fact that Kumm's interface norms mesh well with the decision in *Grogan* does not lend too much weight to the claim as to their universality, bearing in mind that they were formulated by Kumm with precisely such a situation in mind. As we shall see below in section III, their applicability to the decision in *Grogan* is the exception, and not the rule.

II. POLYARCHIC DELIBERATION

The national decisions in *Open Door* and in *Grogan* triggered a series of responses at each point in the triangular constitution, which can be grouped

---

[59] Case C-159/90 *SPUC (Ireland) v Grogan* ECLI:EU:C:1991:378, [1991] ECR I-4685, paras 11–13 (*Grogan* (CJEU)).

[60] Kumm (n 51) 299.

[61] ibid.

thematically into three areas: the right to receive and impart information; the right to travel; and the right to private and family life. The first of these, the right to receive and impart information, will be further divided into two subsections, reflecting the different natures of the two European orders: the right as a corollary to the EU freedom to provide services; and the right as an inherent part of the right to freedom of expression under Article 10 ECHR.

A. The Right to Receive and Impart Information

i. The Right as a Corollary to the Freedom to Provide Services

The CJEU's response[62] to the reference requested by the High Court in *Grogan* was the first opportunity for a European court to rule on the compatibility of Irish abortion law with a European legal order. Before dealing with the questions raised in the reference, the Court summarised the law in Ireland as it arose from *Open Door*:

> According to the Irish Courts ... to assist pregnant women in Ireland to travel abroad to obtain abortions, *inter alia* by informing them of the identity and location of a specific clinic or clinics where abortions are performed and how to contact such clinics, is prohibited under Article 40.3.3° of the Irish Constitution.[63]

We can see straightaway that the distinction between providing *information* and providing *assistance*, which had been decisive in the Supreme Court's refusal to make an Article 177 reference in *Open Door*, and which had been the cause of confusion between the High Court and Supreme Court in *Grogan*, did not appear to be important to the CJEU. Instead, the two were elided: the act of providing information subsumed under the rubric of giving assistance generally, the former being an obviously essential part of the latter. This is an altogether more logical approach, lacking the casuistry of attempting to make a nice distinction between the two.

The questions submitted by the High Court to the CJEU were as follows:

> Does the organized activity or process of carrying out an abortion or the medical termination of pregnancy come within the definition of 'services' provided for in Article 60 [EEC]?

> In the absence of any measures providing for the approximation of the laws of Member States concerning the organized activity or process of carrying out an abortion or the medical termination of pregnancy, can a Member State prohibit the distribution of specific information about the identity, location and means of communication with a specified clinic or clinics in another Member State where abortions are performed?

> Is there a right at Community law in a person in Member State A to distribute specific information about the identity, location and means of communication with

---

[62] *Grogan* (CJEU) (n 59).
[63] ibid para 5.

168   *The Triangular Frame*

a specified clinic or clinics in Member State B where abortions are performed, where the provision of abortion is prohibited under both the Constitution and the criminal law of Member State A but is lawful under certain conditions in Member State B?[64]

SPUC objected to the CJEU accepting jurisdiction in the case on the grounds, first, that the distribution of information in question was not done in the context of any economic activity and, secondly, that the distribution of information had taken place entirely within Ireland, with no cross-border element. However, the Court held that while these objections may be relevant to the substantive answers to be provided, they were no bar to the Court accepting jurisdiction in the matter.[65] By this logic, it must also then be accepted that Hamilton P's decision that no issue of EU law had arisen in the High Court in *Open Door* due to the lack of a cross-border element was incorrect, as was suggested above in section I.A.i.

The Court's answer to the first question was both brief and affirmative. The plain text of then Article 60 EEC provides that a 'service' within the meaning of the Treaty is any service 'normally provided for remuneration, in so far as [it is] not governed by the provisions relating to freedom of movement for goods, capital and persons'.[66] Then as now, Article 60 went on to include, at indent (d), activities of the professions. Because abortion is a medical activity which is lawfully practised and provided for remuneration in several Member States, it must be regarded as a service within the meaning of the Treaties, especially in light of the finding in *Luisi and Carbone*[67] that medical activities fell within the scope of then Articles 59 and 60 EEC.[68] As against this, SPUC alleged that abortion could not be regarded as a service due to its 'gross immorality' and because it involves the destruction of the life of an unborn child, which, on SPUC's analysis, and by Irish constitutional law, is a human being.[69] The CJEU's response to this objection was as follows:

> Whatever the merits of those arguments on the moral plane, they cannot influence the answer to the national court's first question. It is not for the Court to substitute its assessment for that of the legislature in those Member States where the activities in question are practiced legally.[70]

The converse of this statement must also be true, that it is not for the Court to substitute its assessment for that of the legislature (still less that of the electorate) in those Member States where abortion is *not* legal. We must bear in mind

---

[64] ibid para 9.

[65] ibid paras 14–15, citing Case 180/83 *Moser v Land Baden-Württemberg* ECLI:EU:C:1984:233, [1984] ECR 2539.

[66] Art 60 EEC, now Art 57 TFEU.

[67] Joined Cases 286/82 and 26/83 *Luisi and Carbone v Ministero del Tesoro* ECLI:EU:C:1984:35, [1984] ECR 377, para 16.

[68] *Grogan* (CJEU) (n 59) paras 17–18.

[69] ibid para 19.

[70] ibid para 20.

that the CJEU was emphatically not called upon to rule substantively whether EU law required abortion to be legal, and the manner in which the CJEU resisted SPUC's attempt to enlist the Court in its campaign by asking it to declare abortion 'grossly immoral' demonstrates the Court's total lack of desire (and lack of jurisdiction) to engage with the substance of the issue.

The second and third questions were similarly easily disposed of on the facts of the case as the CJEU found them. For the Court:

[T]he link between the activity of the [defendants] and medical termination of pregnancies carried out in clinics in another Member State is *too tenuous* for the prohibition on the distribution of information to be capable of being regarded as a restriction within the meaning of Article 59 [EEC].[71]

Accordingly, the defendants' allegation that the restriction on the distribution of information fell foul of the 'no-backsliding' provision of then Article 62 EEC[72] did not need to be considered by the Court: Article 62 was complementary to Article 59, and the Court having already decided that the 'restriction' at issue was not a 'restriction' within the meaning of Article 59, no further legal issues arose.

Taken together, all this meant that the second and third questions had to be answered negatively. It was:

[N]ot contrary to Community law for a Member State in which medical termination of pregnancy is forbidden to prohibit students' associations from distributing information about the identity and location of clinics in another Member State where voluntary termination of pregnancy is lawfully carried out and the means of communicating with those clinics, where the clinics in question have no involvement in the distribution of the said information.[73]

Before analysing the judgment further, it is worthwhile to note the Opinion of the Advocate General on the case, which differed substantially from the Court's judgment. Though the Advocate General's Opinion is not law, it provides a useful foil for the discussion to follow.

a. A Less Reticent Approach

For Advocate General van Gerven, the tenuous link between the defendants and the English clinics was no barrier to a finding that there had been a restriction within the meaning of Article 59. He had little difficulty in deriving from

---

[71] ibid para 24; Case C-362/88 *GB-INNO-BM v Confédération du Commerce Luxembourgeois* ECLI:EU:C:1990:102, [1990] ECR I-667 distinguished, emphasis added.

[72] Which has since been repealed, and read: 'Save as otherwise provided in this Treaty, Member States shall not introduce any new restrictions on the freedom to provide services which have in fact been attained at the date of the entry into force of this Treaty'.

[73] *Grogan* (CJEU) (n 59) para 32.

170　*The Triangular Frame*

Luisi and Carbone[74] and *Cowan*[75] the existence of a right to go to another Member State to receive a service provided there. This is the same logic that was later adopted by the Court itself. However, the Opinion differs in its answer to the next question: whether this gives rise to an ancillary right 'to receive, unimpeded, information in one's own Member State about providers of services in the other Member State and about how to communicate with them'.[76] This the Advocate General answered in the affirmative. He noted the importance that the Court attached to consumer information with respect to goods in *GB-INNO-BM*,[77] argued that this logic applied with no less force to trade in services, and then stated that the right to receive information:

> [A]lso holds good where the information comes from a person who is not himself the provider of the services and does not act on his behalf ... *As a fundamental principle of the Treaty, the freedom to supply services must ... be respected by all, just as it may be promoted by all, inter alia* by means of the provision of information, whether or not for consideration, concerning services which the provider of information supplies himself or which are supplied by another person.[78]

As we have seen, this analysis was not taken up by the Court, without much in the way of explanation as to why not. The Court distinguished *GB-INNO-BM* on the ground that that case concerned restrictions on advertising by the foreign economic operators themselves, but this does not go to the substance of the portion of the Opinion emphasised above, that a fundamental principle of the Treaty must be respected by all and may be promoted by all, regardless of whether they have a personal economic stake in its promotion.[79] However, even if the Court had applied AG van Gerven's recommendations in full, this still would have been of little avail to the defendants. The Advocate General went on to confirm that the objective behind the restriction of information in question – the protection of the 'unborn' enshrined in the Irish Constitution – was an imperative requirement of public interest within the meaning of Community law,[80] and that the restriction itself was not disproportionate.[81] What is notable, however, is the *erga omnes* nature of the Advocate General's reasoning: the

---

[74] *Luisi and Carbone* (n 67) para 10.

[75] Case 186/87 *Cowan v Trésor Publique* ECLI:EU:C:1990:102, [1989] ECR 195, para 15.

[76] Case C-159/90 *SPUC (Ireland) v Grogan* ECLI:EU:C:1991:249, [1991] ECR I-4685, para 18 (*Grogan* (CJEU Opinion)).

[77] *GB-INNO-IM* (n 71) para 8.

[78] *Grogan* (CJEU, Opinion) (n 76) para 19, emphasis added.

[79] ibid.

[80] ibid para 26, citing, inter alia: Case 30/77 *R v Bouchereau* ECLI:EU:C:1977:172, [1977] ECR 1999; Case 279/80 *Webb* ECLI:EU:C:1981:314, [1981] ECR 3305; Joined Cases 110 and 111/78 *Van Wesemael* ECLI:EU:C:1979:8, [1979] ECR 35; Case 205/84 *Commission v Germany* ECLI:EU:C:1986:463, [1986] ECR 3755; Joined Cases 60 and 61/84 *Cinéthèque and Others v Fédération Nationale des Cinémas Français* ECLI:EU:C:1985:329, [1985] ECR 2605; and Case C–145/88 *Torfaen Borough Council v B&Q* ECLI:EU:C:1989:593, [1989] ECR 3851.

[81] *Grogan* (CJEU, Opinion) (n 76) paras 27–29.

Polyarchic Deliberation   171

expansive – indeed, theoretically horizontal in its application – interpretation he gave to the freedom to provide services is quintessentially constitutionalist reasoning, but its breadth is tempered by the recognition of the legitimacy of the imperative requirement of public interest pursued. In this sense, the Opinion in *Grogan* (CJEU) is a precursor to the later decision in *Omega*[82] and its successors, which similarly sought to reconcile the requirements of free movement law with national specificities, and contrasts with the much more limited reasoning of the CJEU in its judgment in *Grogan* (CJEU), which, by its focus on the individual economic links between actors, is more contractual in its nature, casting EU law in this instance as a sort of quasi-private law. Such an approach is in marked contrast to the CJEU's well-known constitutionalising tendencies in other cases, and shows the extent of the Court's reluctance to involve itself, and wariness of triggering constitutional conflict.

ii. The Right as Part of Freedom of Expression

The CJEU did not confine itself in *Grogan* (CJEU) to viewing the case from the perspective of the freedom to provide services. Because of the 'tenuous' link between the defendants and the English clinics, the Court regarded the contested restrictions on information as 'constitut[ing] a manifestation of freedom of expression and of the freedom to impart and receive information which is independent of the economic activity carried on by clinics established in another Member State'.[83] However, this too did not avail the defendants, who had claimed that the restriction was a breach of fundamental rights, and in particular of Article 10 ECHR,[84] triggering engagement on the 'horizontal' axis of the triangle – though mediated, as has so often been the case, by the State as an interstitial actor. The Court noted that its jurisdiction as regards determining the compatibility of national legislation with fundamental rights is limited to cases where that national legislation falls within the scope of Community law.[85] Though the Court repeated its (by 1991) familiar dictum that fundamental rights, as laid down in particular in the ECHR, set standards the observance of which the Court must ensure, it made no mention of the 'inspiration; guidelines; special significance' formula discussed in chapter three. In parallel with the argument based on free movement, the lack of an economic link – meaning that no 'restriction' arose under Article 59 – was fatal to the fundamental rights argument too,[86] and the finding that Ireland's actions were therefore outwith the scope of Community law foreclosed any further analysis of the issue.

---

[82] Case C-36/02 *Omega Spielhallen- und Automatenaufstellungs-GmbH v Oberbürgermeisterin der Bundesstadt Bonn* ECLI:EU:C:2004:614, [2004] ECR I-9609.
[83] *Grogan* (CJEU) (n 59) para 26.
[84] ibid para 30.
[85] ibid paras 28–32, citing Case C-260/89 *ERT* ECLI:EU:C:1991:254, [1991] ECR I-2925, para 42.
[86] *Grogan* (CJEU) (n 59) paras 28–32.

172   *The Triangular Frame*

Again, the Opinion of AG van Gerven went further than the Court's judgment. As we saw in section II.A.i, he suggested that there had been a restriction within the meaning of Article 59, though this restriction was motivated by an imperative requirement of public interest and was therefore justified. However, this brings the Member State's actions within the scope of Union law, and thus subjects them to review for conformance with fundamental rights as general principles of Union law.[87] The Advocate General discussed the restriction in light of the Union's obligation to uphold fundamental rights and freedoms, and, as was the case with the right to impart and receive information as a corollary of the freedom to provide services, found that the aim behind the restriction was legitimate and the restriction itself was not disproportionate.[88] His analysis on this issue was extensive, and included detailed consideration of the case law of the European Commission of Human Rights (ECmHR) and the ECtHR that existed at that time.[89]

However, while AG van Gerven's attempt to interpret the Convention was done in good faith, the ECtHR itself would soon take a different view. In *Open Door and Dublin Well Woman v Ireland*,[90] as well as the two counselling organisations against which the original injunctions had been issued in *Open Door*, there were four other applicants: two women who had worked as trained counsellors for Well Woman, and two women – Mrs X and Ms Geraghty – who joined in Well Woman's application 'as women of child-bearing age'.[91] Despite the Irish Government's objections, these four women were accorded 'victim' status within the meaning of the Convention by the Court by a 15:8 split, the same 15:8 split which went on to uphold the applicants' complaint that there had been a violation of Article 10 ECHR, contrary to AG van Gerven's assessment.

The complaint under Article 10 was that the Supreme Court injunction restraining the applicants from assisting pregnant women to travel abroad to obtain abortions infringed the rights of Open Door and Well Woman and the two counsellors to impart information, as well as the rights of Mrs X and Ms Geraghty to receive information. The complaint was confined to that part of the injunction restraining the provision of information to pregnant women,

---

[87] *Grogan* (CJEU, Opinion) (n 76) para 31. This remains the legal position today, after the Lisbon Treaty and the elevation of the Charter to Treaty status: see Case C-617/10 *Åkerberg Fransson* ECLI:EU:C:2013:105, paras 19–22.

[88] *Grogan* (CJEU, Opinion) (n 76) paras 30–38.

[89] ibid, citing the ECmHR decisions in *X v UK* (1980) 19 *Decisions and Reports* 244 and *Brüggemann and Scheuten v Germany* (1981) 3 EHRR 244; and the ECtHR cases of *Sunday Times v UK* (1979–1980) 2 EHRR 245; *Markt Intern and Beerman v Germany* (1990) 12 EHRR 161; and *Silver and Others v UK* (1983) 5 EHRR 347. Recall Sionaidh Douglas-Scott's observation, quoted in ch 3, that the Advocates General took to referencing Strasbourg jurisprudence long before the CJEU began to do so in its judgments: S Douglas-Scott, 'A Tale of Two Courts: Luxembourg, Strasbourg and the Growing European Human Rights *Acquis*' (2006) 43 *Common Market Law Review* 629, 645.

[90] *Open Door* (ECtHR) (n 49).

[91] ibid para 9.

Polyarchic Deliberation   173

and not the part restraining the making of travel arrangements or referral to clinics.[92] The government contested these claims, and argued that Article 10 should be interpreted in the light of Article 2's protection of the right to life, Article 17's prohibition on the Convention being interpreted so as to permit the destruction or limitation of the rights it guarantees, and Article 60's 'floor' provision, that the Convention shall not be construed so as to limit or derogate from any rights or freedoms additionally ensured by the Contracting States or by other agreements to which they are party.[93]

The government did not contest that the injunction constituted an interference with the counselling services' freedom to impart information, and the Court noted that given the plain terms of the injunction, which restrained the 'servants and agents' of the counselling services from assisting 'pregnant women', there must also have been an interference with the rights of the individual counsellors to impart information, and with the rights of Mrs X and Ms Geraghty to receive information should they become pregnant.[94]

As to whether the interference had been 'prescribed by law' within the meaning of Article 10(2) ECHR, the Court noted the broad powers of the Irish judiciary to vindicate constitutional rights; the horizontal effect given to the Irish Constitution in certain circumstances whereby the infringement of a constitutional right by an individual may be actionable as a constitutional tort; and the interpretation given by the Irish judiciary to the word 'laws' in Article 40.3 of the Constitution[95] so as to include judge-made law.[96] These factors, coupled with the fact that 'the possibility that action might be taken against the corporate applicants must have been, with appropriate legal advice, reasonably foreseeable',[97] led the Court to conclude that the interference had been prescribed by law, a decision reinforced by the fact that Well Woman had in fact received legal advice as to its vulnerability to legal action following the coming into force of Article 40.3.3° of the Constitution.[98]

The Court went on to hold that the restriction had aims that were legitimate under Article 10(2) ECHR, and did so in terms very similar to Advocate General van Gerven's Opinion in *Grogan* (CJEU):[99]

> [I]t is evident that the protection afforded under Irish law to the right to life of the unborn is based on profound moral values concerning the nature of life which were reflected in the stance of the majority of the Irish people against abortion as

[92] ibid para 53.
[93] ibid para 54.
[94] ibid para 55.
[95] Which reads, at Art 40.3.1: 'The State guarantees in its laws to respect, and, as far as practicable, by its laws to defend and vindicate the personal rights of the citizen'.
[96] *Open Door* (ECtHR) (n 49) paras 59 and 35, citing *State (Quinn) v Ryan* [1965] IR 70; *Meskell v CIÉ* (n 32); and *The People v Shaw* [1982] IR 1.
[97] *Open Door* (ECtHR) (n 49) para 60, citing *Sunday Times v UK* (n 89).
[98] *Open Door* (ECtHR) (n 49) para 60.
[99] *Grogan* (CJEU, Opinion) (n 76) para 26.

174   *The Triangular Frame*

> expressed in the 1983 referendum. The restriction thus pursued the legitimate aim of the protection of morals of which the protection in Ireland of the right to life of the unborn is one aspect.[100]

However, the government's contention that the relevant provisions of Irish law were intended for the prevention of crime was rejected, seeing as neither the provision of the information in question nor the procurement of an abortion abroad were criminal offences.[101] In light of the finding that the aim of the protection of morals was legitimate, the Court held that it was unnecessary to examine the government's further contention that the contested Irish law was intended for the protection of the rights of others, which the government had argued included the 'unborn'. Thus, the Court avoided expressing a view as to whether the use of the term 'others' in Article 10(2) ECHR extends to the 'unborn'.[102]

The final question to be decided in relation to the Article 10 complaint was whether the interference was 'necessary in a democratic society' as required by Article 10(2). The government contended that the Court's approach to this question should be guided by the combined effects of Articles 2, 17 and 60 ECHR, as outlined above, and added that a test of proportionality must be inadequate in a case where the rights of the 'unborn' were in issue.[103] According to the government, '[t]he right to life could not, like other rights, be measured according to a graduated scale. It was either respected or it was not'.[104] The government also argued that in granting the injunction, the Supreme Court 'was merely sustaining the logic of Article 40.3.3° of the Constitution. The determination by the Irish courts that the provision of information ... assisted in the destruction of unborn life was not open to review by the Convention institutions'.[105]

The Court dismissed the argument with respect to Article 2 because no question arose in the case as to whether the foetus is encompassed by that provision's guarantee of a right to life, and the Court had not been asked to determine whether a right to abortion is guaranteed under the Convention.[106] The government's argument against the use of a proportionality test with respect to the right to life was also dismissed, the Court rightly disagreeing with the assertion that 'the State's discretion in the field of the protection of morals is unfettered and unreviewable'.[107] While 'national authorities enjoy a wide margin of appreciation in matters of morals, particularly in an area such as the present which touches on matters of belief concerning the nature of human life',[108] this margin

---

[100] *Open Door* (ECtHR) (n 49) para 63.
[101] ibid para 61.
[102] ibid para 63.
[103] ibid para 64.
[104] ibid para 67.
[105] ibid.
[106] ibid para 66.
[107] ibid para 68, citing *Norris v Ireland* [1991] 13 EHRR 186, para 45.
[108] *Open Door* (ECtHR) (n 49) para 68.

Polyarchic Deliberation   175

is not unlimited and is still subject to supervision by the Court. For the Court to accept the government's argument as to the inappropriateness of a proportionality test 'would amount to an abdication of the Court's responsibility under [Article 19 ECHR] "to ensure the observance of the engagements undertaken by the High Contracting Parties"'.[109]

Before moving on to the Court's application of the proportionality test, something must be said about its verdict as regards the injunction's 'legitimate aim' and about the application of the margin of appreciation in the case. I suggest that the (preliminary) deference shown to a democratically expressed moral choice on the part of a (theoretically) sovereign people – similar in form to the previous statements of a national judge[110] and a member of the CJEU – is emblematic of both what Nico Krisch meant when he described the margin of appreciation as a 'central political tool in a pluralist order',[111] and also of the conception of 'overlapping consensus' employed by Sabel and Gerstenberg, whereby 'the parties to an overlapping consensus know that they have reached agreement on essentials ... through differing, only partially concordant interpretations of ... comprehensive ideas'.[112] The right to life is protected under both the Irish Constitution and the ECHR, and is a right of basic and foundational importance in the legal orders of both. But the interpretation given to it by each order was 'differing, [and] only partially concordant'. In Ireland, the right extended to the 'unborn' (although the precise meaning of this would not be defined until 2013) and was, after *Attorney General v X*, almost absolute. The ECtHR, being a court with supervisory jurisdiction over a diverse array of 'differing, only partially concordant' constitutional orders, was never going to come down on one side of the argument or the other, and had not been asked to do so. But, *contra* Krisch, the fact that the ECtHR's jurisdiction and jurisprudence in this sense is *pluralist* does not make it non-*constitutional*, particularly in light of its strong statement, above, that a state's discretion in the field of morals cannot be unfettered or unreviewable – that state power and discretion must be fettered and reviewable is, rather, a fundamental aspect and hallmark of constitutionalism. For the Court to have given Ireland, or any other state, free reign in the way the government argued for would have been neither constitutionalist nor pluralist but *unconstitutional*: an (illegal) dereliction of the Court's (legal) duty.

In applying the proportionality test, the Court recalled its long-standing *Handyside*[113] doctrine that freedom of expression extends to information or

---

[109] ibid para 69.

[110] See the judgment of Costello J in *Attorney General v X* (n 6) 15, discussed below at section III.B.

[111] N Krisch, 'The Open Architecture of European Human Rights Law' (2008) 71 *Modern Law Review* 183, 210.

[112] CF Sabel and O Gerstenberg, 'Constitutionalising an Overlapping Consensus: The ECJ and the Emergence of a Coordinate Constitutional Order' (2010) 16 *European Law Journal* 511, 513.

[113] *Handyside v UK* [1976] 1 EHRR 737.

176 *The Triangular Frame*

ideas which may offend, shock or disturb; noted that it was not a criminal offence in Ireland to travel abroad for an abortion; and noted further that the information restricted in the case concerned activities which were lawful in other Convention countries.[114] In this regard, the absolute nature of the injunction was striking, in that it was perpetual and took no account of a woman's age, state of health, or reasons for seeking counselling about abortion. This was even more striking in light of the subsequent decision in *Attorney General v X*[115] (to be discussed in the next section) and, at the oral hearing in *Open Door* (ECtHR), the government conceded that the injunction could no longer apply to the limited class of women who could in theory receive an abortion within Ireland under the X criteria.[116] These reasons alone were sufficient for the ECtHR to find the injunction overbroad and disproportionate,[117] a finding compounded by the facts that the link between the provision of information and the actual procurement of an abortion was not definite;[118] similar information was available in British magazines and phone books freely circulating in Ireland;[119] the injunction was ineffective in that it did not prevent large numbers of women from obtaining abortions abroad;[120] it created a risk to the health of women who, because of a lack of information were seeking abortions later in their pregnancies and were not availing themselves of proper aftercare;[121] and these effects would be worse in the case of poorer and less well-educated women.[122] The government's arguments regarding Articles 17 and 60 ECHR were of no use in light of the injunction's ineffectiveness in preventing abortion and the availability of information by means other than counselling.[123]

The restriction of information about abortion services available abroad having been found – at least in this case – in violation of the Convention, it was clear that Irish law on the matter was in need of revision or the two legal orders would remain in a state of conflict. However, judgment in *Open Door v Ireland* was handed down on 29 October 1992, and the process of bringing Irish constitutional law into line with Convention norms was in motion even before it had become certain that the two were in conflict, as we shall now see.

---

[114] *Open Door* (ECtHR) (n 49) para 72.

[115] *Attorney General v X* (n 6).

[116] *Open Door* (ECtHR) (n 49) para 73.

[117] ibid para 74. In light of the finding of a violation under Art 10, the Court held that it did not need to examine the applicants' privacy and discrimination arguments under Arts 8 and 14, in particular because these arguments had not been raised in the domestic proceedings (ibid paras 81–83).

[118] ibid para 75.

[119] ibid para 76.

[120] ibid.

[121] ibid para 77.

[122] ibid.

[123] ibid paras 78–79.

iii. Political Resolution: The Fourteenth Amendment

Less than a month[124] after the verdict in *Open Door v Ireland*, three referendums were held, on the Twelfth, Thirteenth and Fourteenth Amendments to the Constitution. The Twelfth and Thirteenth Amendments will be discussed below at sections II.B.iii and II.C. With respect to the Fourteenth Amendment, the Irish electorate was asked whether it agreed with the following text being inserted as a proviso to Article 40.3.3°: 'This subsection shall not limit freedom to obtain or make available, in this State, subject to such conditions as may be laid down by law, information relating to services lawfully available in another state'. The Amendment was endorsed by a margin of 60 per cent to 40 per cent, on a turnout of 68 per cent,[125] and the conflict between the Irish and ECHR legal orders was therefore resolved by the adaptation of the Irish order.[126] What is remarkable about the Fourteenth Amendment is that in its origins and by its express text, it constitutes a chink in the solipsistic armour of the national constitution. As was noted in the introduction to this chapter, the main body of Article 40.3.3° is a bold statement of principle, imbued with the authority of specific popular endorsement. And yet the very next clause – itself also popularly endorsed – rows back on this principle, recognising the existence of *other* legal orders; the legitimacy, within those orders, of *other* principles; and limiting (though not denying) the power of the national order to restrict the free flow of information from and about those orders. Moreover, this adjustment to the national order was itself brought about specifically as a result of legal engagement with other orders forming part of the triangular constitutional whole. This, then, is a practical demonstration of the normative claim of constitutional pluralism: that heterarchy *can* be (not necessarily *must* be) preferable to hierarchy. The adoption of the Eighth Amendment in the first place may have been a catastrophic error, but it was an error that the electorate was entitled to make, at least from the perspective of the Irish constitutional order. But given that this constitutional order does not exist in a vacuum, the ancillary consequences of the Eighth Amendment triggered the engagement of the other vertices of the triangular constitution. The issue of the right to receive and impart information, whether as a corollary of the economic freedom to provide services under EU law or of the human right to freedom of expression under the Convention, was one element of the process by which the Irish constitutional order's claims were adjusted in light of the input of the European legal orders. Moreover, this adjustment to the national order was made autonomously and voluntarily by

---

[124] On 25 November 1992.

[125] *Referendum Results* (n 1) 51.

[126] Though the genesis of the Amendment predated the ECtHR's judgment in *Open Door* (ECtHR), that judgment and subsequent public comment thereon cannot have harmed the Amendment's chances of finding public acceptance.

178   *The Triangular Frame*

the national order itself and was not *ordered* in a hierarchical sense. This claim, of the normative preferability of leaving open the question of the final say, and having multiple, concurrent spheres of jurisdiction in which constitutional claims can be advanced, rebutted and adjusted, will be pursued further below, once the picture has been completed regarding the other ancillary consequences of the Eighth Amendment: on the right to travel and on the right to private and family life.

B. The Right to Travel

In the course of his Opinion in *Grogan* (CJEU), AG van Gerven had noted that 'Ireland does not prohibit or seek to prevent a pregnant woman from exercising her right to travel and receive services of termination of pregnancy abroad'.[127] However, this is precisely what Ireland sought to do in the later case of *Attorney General v X*.[128] The discussion of this case here needs to be explained, in that it was not part of any formal 'interaction' or 'dialogue' between Ireland and the EU. However, the verdict in the case had important repercussions as regards EU law, which, as we shall see, ended up being resolved politically rather than legally (or, better, politically *and* legally, rather than *judicially*), in the same manner as the conflict between the Irish and ECHR orders with respect to the availability of information. Moreover, the X case is the proximate cause of the subsequent ECtHR judgment regarding the right to private and family life under Article 8 ECHR, to be discussed below at section II.C. The X case remains as controversial as ever, both because of the way in which the case came before the courts in the first place, and because of the way in which it was ultimately resolved. Notwithstanding two political attempts to have its meaning restricted, on which more below, the Supreme Court verdict in the case was the law in Ireland until the Thirty-sixth Amendment entered into force in 2018.

   X was a 14-year-old girl, pregnant as a result of having been raped by her schoolfriend's father in December 1991. When her parents learned of this in late January 1992, they and their daughter decided to go to England for an abortion. The parents told the Gardaí of this decision and asked if it would be possible to have tests performed on the foetus in order to prove the rapist's paternity, and therefore automatically his guilt, the victim being a minor. An officer explained that such evidence may not be admissible in Ireland but said that he would make enquiries. Legal advice was sought from the Director of Public Prosecutions, who advised that the evidence would not be admissible, and who then, of his own volition, informed the Attorney General of the intentions of the girl and her parents. On the morning of 6 February, the Attorney General applied ex

[127] *Grogan* (CJEU, Opinion) (n 76) para 13.
[128] *Attorney General v X* (n 6).

parte to the High Court for an interim injunction restraining X and her parents from interfering with the right to life of the 'unborn'; restraining X from leaving Ireland for nine months and restraining her parents from assisting her to leave; and restraining X from procuring or arranging an abortion, whether within or outwith the jurisdiction. The injunctions were granted. That same day, the family had travelled to London for the procedure, but when they learned of the orders of the High Court, they cancelled the procedure and returned to Ireland to challenge the orders, which the Attorney General sought to make permanent.

Crucial to the final outcome of the case was the oral and documentary evidence of the parents, Gardaí and a clinical psychologist regarding X's mental and emotional state. X had 'coldly expressed a desire to solve matters by ending her life',[129] which in the psychologist's opinion 'she was capable [of doing], not so much because she is depressed but because she could calculatingly reach the conclusion that death is the best solution'.[130] The psychologist testified that continuing with the pregnancy would be devastating to X's mental health.[131]

i. 'A Spurious and Divisive Uniformity'? The High Court Judgment

In the High Court, the defence objected to the grant of the orders on four grounds. First was a jurisdictional issue, that because there had been no legislation regulating the manner in which the equal rights to life of the 'unborn' and pregnant women under Article 40.3.3° should be reconciled, the Court could make no order in a case such as this where such a reconciliation was necessary.[132] The second objection related to the substance of X's guaranteed right to life: for the Court to make the order sought would be to prejudice X's right to life because of the very real danger that she would commit suicide if she was unable to procure an abortion.[133] Third was an argument based on Article 40.4 of the Constitution, and the guarantee contained therein that 'no citizen shall be deprived of his personal liberty save in accordance with law'.[134] The final objection was based on EU law, that the plain text of then Articles 59 and 60 EEC, coupled with the CJEU's interpretation of these provisions in *Luisi and Carbone* and *Grogan* (CJEU) – which had been handed down just months earlier – guaranteed a right to travel to another Member State to avail of services (now definitely including abortion) legally available there. In view of the urgency of the case, the defence did not request an Article 177 EEC reference.[135]

---

[129] ibid 8.
[130] ibid.
[131] ibid.
[132] ibid 10–11.
[133] ibid 11.
[134] ibid 12–13.
[135] ibid 13. Note that the expedited and urgent preliminary ruling procedures now available under Arts 105–14 of the CJEU's Rules of Procedure ([2012] OJ L 265/1) did not exist at this time.

180   *The Triangular Frame*

The first objection quickly fell, Costello J invoking the clear ruling in *Open Door* that Article 40.3.3° was self-executing, and required no enabling or explanatory legislation: '[c]omplicated and difficult issues of fact may, of course, arise in individual cases but that does not inhibit the court from applying the clear rule of law laid down in [Article 40.3.3°]'.[136]

As regards the second objection, Costello J distinguished the present case from those that arise in the ordinary practice of medicine

> [i]n which surgical intervention, necessary to save the life of the unborn, may involve risk to the mother's life, or in which the surgical invention necessary to save the life of a mother may involve risk to the life of the unborn.[137]

In this case, in which the threat to the life of the pregnant woman arose from the state of mind of the woman herself, Costello J held that he was

> quite satisfied that there is a real and imminent danger to the life of the unborn and that if the court does not step in to protect it by means of the injunction sought its life will be terminated. ... [T]he *risk* that the defendant may take her own life if an order is made is much less and is of a different order of magnitude than the *certainty* that the life of the unborn will be terminated if the order is not made.[138]

This distinction between risk on the one hand and certainty on the other was sufficient for Costello J to regard it as his constitutional duty to protect the life of the 'unborn', while still claiming to have had 'due regard for the equal right to life of the mother' as required by Article 40.3.3°.[139]

Costello J rejected the third objection as being based on a misunderstanding. The defence had based their argument on cases decided under Article 40.4, where the Supreme Court had held unlawful the refusal of bail in criminal cases on the mere suspicion that the accused would commit further crimes if left at liberty.[140] Costello J distinguished these cases in that '[t]hey did not decide that the court cannot order a defendant to refrain from doing an unlawful act, if necessary by restraining his or her constitutional right to liberty'.[141]

The fourth objection, the argument based on EU law, also failed. Costello J noted that he was required to determine the issue of EU law raised, and that no request for a preliminary reference had been made, before stating (without reference to CJEU or Irish jurisprudence on the point) that '[o]ur courts must enforce Community law; and if that law conflicts with Irish law, including Irish constitutional law, then Community law will prevail'.[142] There was no mention of the altogether more ambiguous, *Solange*-style statements of the Supreme Court in *Grogan*. The Attorney General argued, without disputing the general principles

---

[136] *Attorney General v X* (n 6) 11, citing *Open Door* (n 24) 623 (Finlay CJ).

[137] *Attorney General v X* (n 6) 11.

[138] ibid 12, emphasis added.

[139] ibid.

[140] ibid 12, citing *Ryan v DPP* [1989] IR 399 and *The People v O'Callaghan* [1966] IR 501.

[141] *Attorney General v X* (n 6) 12.

[142] ibid 13.

of Community law on which X relied, that Article 40.3.3° of the Constitution and its legal consequences – including the jurisdiction of the Court to prohibit travel abroad to procure an abortion – constituted a derogation from Directive 73/148/EEC on grounds of public policy within the meaning of Article 8 of that Directive.[143] Costello J quoted at length from *Bouchereau*,[144] where the CJEU had expounded on the meaning of a 'public policy' derogation in the context of Article 48 EEC's provisions on the free movement of workers; he accepted as valid the Attorney General's argument that the reasoning in that case could be legitimately transplanted to the context of the Article 59 EEC freedom to provide and receive services; and he held accordingly that

> I can find no provision or principle of Community law which would prohibit the exercise of the discretionary power to derogate in the manner contained in the Eighth Amendment. On the contrary, Community law already recognises that within the Community wide cultural differences exist and has permitted derogations which flow from such differences. I can see no reason why it should refuse to do so when the derogation by a Member State arises because of deeply held convictions on moral issues. *Indeed, I think the attainment of the fundamental objectives of the Treaty is enhanced by laws which assist in the development of a Community in which legitimate differences on moral issues are recognised and which does not seek to impose a spurious and divisive uniformity on its members on such issues.*[145]

Finally, Costello J noted that '[i]n considering certain issues of public policy in Community law it may be relevant to consider the jurisprudence of the [ECtHR]'.[146] This is perhaps surprising, given the historically rather sceptical attitude of the Irish judiciary to the Convention and its lack of incorporation into Irish law at the time (outlined in chapter two); the fact that the CJEU itself had yet to refer to the jurisprudence of the ECtHR at this point (outlined in chapter three); and the fact that no Convention argument had been raised by the defence. However, Costello J's analysis on the point was terse and made no reference to any specific case decided by the ECtHR. Instead, he merely noted that 'the case law of that court has allowed ... national authorities a margin of appreciation in relation to laws dealing with moral issues',[147] and stated (but did not expand on this) that he did not think that the power to stop a woman going abroad for an abortion was disproportionate to the aim of Article 40.3.3°. On the contrary, without such a power, the right to life afforded to the 'unborn' 'would in many cases be worthless'.[148]

---

[143] ibid 13–14.

[144] *Bouchereau* (n 80) 2013–14, citing Case 41/74 *Van Duyn v Home Office* ECLI:EU:C:1974:133, [1974] ECR 1337 at 1350. Note that *Bouchereau* had also formed the basis of AG van Gerven's finding in his Opinion in *Grogan* (CJEU) that the aim of Art 40.3.3° constituted an imperative requirement of public interest within the meaning of Community law (see above at section II.A.i.a).

[145] *Attorney General v X* (n 6) 15, emphasis added.

[146] ibid 16.

[147] ibid.

[148] ibid.

182   *The Triangular Frame*

Having ruled against all the defendants' objections, Costello J held in favour of the Attorney General and made permanent the interim injunction.

As was suggested in chapter two, if we leave aside the context in which it was employed and look at it in the abstract, Costello J's fundamental point about the objectives of the Treaty being endangered by the imposition of a 'spurious and divisive uniformity' is not unfounded, particularly in the subsequent light of the CJEU's decisions in *Omega*, *Sayn-Wittgenstein*,[149] and *Runevič-Vardyn*[150] and the requirements of the modern Article 4(2) TEU. We can also discern within it something of Maduro's requirements of vertical and horizontal coherence. Though it is essentially an argument from national specificity (and therefore potentially appealing 'horizontally' to the courts of other Member States, for better or for worse), it is also vertically coherent, couched as it is in the CJEU's own language of the fundamental objectives of the Treaty, and thus of the integrity and efficacy of EU law. However, the decision also contains a very strong and unqualified statement of the primacy of EU law, and this without reference to authority. The nature of this statement fits well with the Luxembourg understanding of that principle, but it is odd with regard to the Supreme Court's more qualified, unanimous, and at the time very recent, pronouncements in *Grogan*. The High Court judgment in *X* therefore demonstrates a certain inconsistency in terms of interface norms. The effect of the judgment was to limit an individual's freedom to travel to another Member State to avail of a service, something which AG van Gerven had indirectly warned against in his Opinion in *Grogan* (CJEU),[151] and yet the High Court made no attempt to shield its decision from the rigours of EU law by invoking the Supreme Court's application of the principle of conditional recognition in *Grogan*. In this instance, at least, it would seem that quite aside from not being universal across the Union, the interface norms at work were not even universal within the domestic jurisdiction.

ii. Conflict Avoided, for Now: The Supreme Court Judgment

On appeal to the Supreme Court, the judgment of the High Court was reversed by a 4:1 split decision. The Court was unanimous on three points: that the Attorney General had acted properly in bringing the matter before the courts;[152] that the provisions of Article 40.3.3° were self-executing and required no enabling legislation;[153] and that the Constitution must be interpreted harmoniously,

---

[149] Case C-208/09 *Ilonka Sayn-Wittgenstein v Landeshauptmann von Wien* ECLI:EU:C:2010:806, [2010] ECR I-13693.

[150] Case C-391/09 *Malgožata Runevič-Vardyn and Łukasz Paweł Wardyn v Vilniaus Miesto Savivaldybės Administracija* ECLI:EU:C:2011:291, [2011] ECR I-3787.

[151] *Grogan* (CJEU, Opinion) (n 76) para 13.

[152] *Attorney General v X* (n 6) 47 (Finlay CJ); 62 (Hederman J); 77–78 (McCarthy J); 88 (O'Flaherty J), upholding the finding of Costello J at 9. This was almost certainly done in view of the considerable public opprobrium the AG's actions in the case had attracted, at least in certain sections of the media. Only Egan J was silent on the issue.

[153] ibid 50–51 (Finlay CJ); 62 (Hederman J); 80–81 (McCarthy J); 88 (O'Flaherty J); 90–91 (Egan J).

Polyarchic Deliberation   183

involving a changing hierarchy of rights in a case of conflict between them, generally (but not always) headed by the right to life, the violation of which is irreversible.[154] The most important aspect of the Supreme Court judgments is the interpretation given to Article 40.3.3°, and specifically its statement that the State's guarantee to respect, defend and vindicate the life of the 'unborn' extended only 'as far as practicable' and must be 'with due regard to the equal right to life of the mother'. For the majority of the Court (Finlay CJ, McCarthy, O'Flaherty and Egan JJ; Hederman J dissenting), these two aspects of Article 40.3.3° meant that, in the words of Finlay CJ:

> [T]he proper test to be applied is that if it is established as a matter of probability that there is a real and substantial risk to the life, as distinct from the health, of the mother, which can only be avoided by the termination of her pregnancy, such termination is permissible, having regard to the true interpretation of [Article 40.3.3°].[155]

Because the thrust of the judgments was such as to authorise a lawful abortion *even within* the jurisdiction – the risk to X's life flowing from her suicidal state – it therefore followed that no order could be sustained which purported in any way to prohibit or inhibit X from obtaining an abortion, whether at home or abroad. As a result, the previously central question of the right to travel, whether under the Constitution or the Treaty, was no longer relevant. X and her parents now being free to deal with her situation as they saw fit, their arguments based on Union law, which had been offered in the alternative to their constitutional arguments, did not need to be considered.

While the Supreme Court in X did clarify the meaning of Article 40.3.3°, in particular that it permitted abortion in Ireland under very narrowly drawn circumstances – to the surprise and horror of many of those who had campaigned for the Eighth Amendment in the first place – it left the law in relation to the freedom to travel abroad to procure an abortion (or services more generally) less clear than it had found it. For Finlay CJ and Hederman and Egan JJ, the right to travel could *never* trump the right to life of the 'unborn' if the two rights were in conflict.[156] This was not the case for O'Flaherty J, who held that an injunction restraining travel from the jurisdiction interfered to an 'extraordinary degree with the individual's freedom of movement', and also constituted – in the present case – an unwarranted interference with the authority of the family.[157] McCarthy J went even further, holding that the right to travel could *never* be curtailed because of a particular intent, going so far as to state that 'if I proclaim my intent to explode a bomb or shoot an individual in another

---

[154] ibid 53 (Finlay CJ); 73 (Hederman J); 78–79 (McCarthy J); 87–88 (O'Flaherty J); 92 (Egan J).
[155] ibid 54.
[156] ibid 57–59 (Finlay CJ); 73 (Hederman J); 92 (Egan J).
[157] ibid 87–88. The Constitution at Art 41.1.1° 'recognises the Family as the natural primary and fundamental unit group of Society, and as a moral institution possessing inalienable and imprescriptible rights, antecedent and superior to all positive law'.

184   *The Triangular Frame*

country, I cannot lawfully be prevented from leaving my own country for that purpose'.[158] Although – or perhaps because of the fact that – all of these conflicting statements were obiter dicta,[159] their combined effect was to leave Irish law on the freedom to travel, both under the Constitution and with respect to EU law, in a very confused state indeed.

Taking these statements together, and although no aspect of EU law was discussed in any detail, the fact remains that a majority of the Court was of the opinion that the right to travel (logically under both Irish law as an aspect of the liberty of the individual and under EU law as a right ancillary to the freedom to provide services) must *always* be subordinated to the Irish constitutional conception of the right to life. The fact that these comments were obiter was scant comfort, in that they set up the distinct possibility that in a future case, where the life of the pregnant woman seeking an abortion abroad was held *not* to be in danger (or that the risk to her life was not 'probable' or 'real' or 'substantial' enough, under the test enunciated by the Court), then her right to travel could be curtailed in order to prevent the abortion taking place. Of course, in such a case, it is unlikely that the woman's reason for travelling would ever become known to any organ of the State in the first place, particularly considering that, in light of the State's actions in X, pregnant women travelling abroad would not be inclined to *let* their intentions become known. The unlikeliness of the situation arising does not, however, lessen the potential incompatibility between the laws of Ireland and of the EU. In this sense, this aspect of the judgments in X owes rather more to Kumm's national constitutional supremacy or democratic statism than to any other conception of European constitutionalism, and bears little resemblance to the ostensibly *communautaire* – but still, I argue, pluralist in the limited sense of being vertically and horizontally coherent – reasoning of the High Court. Moreover, it makes only partial use of the principle of avoidance. While the resolution of the case on grounds of national law meant that the arguments based on EU law did not have to be considered – and thus conflict in this specific instance was avoided – the general tenor of the majority's opinions regarding the subordination of the right to travel to the right to life of the 'unborn' left the door open for conflict in a future case.

iii. Potential Conflict Resolved Politically: The Thirteenth Amendment

The uncertainty surrounding a woman's right to leave the jurisdiction – and Ireland's conformance with EU law with respect to services – did not last long. As noted above in section II.A.iii, three referendums were held on 25 November 1992. The Thirteenth Amendment proposed to insert the following text as a proviso to Article 40.3.3°: 'This subsection shall not limit freedom to travel between the State and another state'. The electorate accepted this proposal, by

---

[158] *Attorney General v X* (n 6) 84–85.
[159] ibid 57 (Finlay CJ).

Polyarchic Deliberation   185

a margin of 62 per cent to 38 per cent, on a turnout of 65 per cent,[160] and thus the uncertainty caused by the X case, and Ireland's potential breach of EU law, was ended. As was the case with the right to receive and impart information, the potential for conflict between legal orders was resolved by political means. It would be a stretch, however, to imagine that removal of the potential incompatibility between Irish and EU law was the sole reason for the Amendment's endorsement by the electorate. Public concern with the treatment of the victim in X – including from those opposed to abortion as a general, abstract matter, but not, it turned out, in the specific circumstances of X herself – and with the idea of pregnant women being effectively detained within the jurisdiction were more likely explanations. But just as with the Fourteenth Amendment, this political resolution of the issue regarding the right to travel substantiates the normative preferability of a heterarchical conception of the legal orders in the triangular constitution. A potential inconsistency between the national and Union legal orders having been revealed, the national order was amended to remove the inconsistency voluntarily, and in accordance with its own logic, rather than being formally required or ordered to do so by the normative command of a hierarchically superior legal order. Moreover, this 'retreat' from law into politics need not necessarily undermine the integrity of the legal order or the claim of constitutional pluralism to be a specifically legal theory, particularly given that the metaconstitutional pluralisms under discussion here are specifically institutional, rather than pure, theories of law.

C. The Right to Private and Family Life

Along with the Thirteenth and Fourteenth Amendments, the Twelfth Amendment proposed to insert the following additional text as a proviso to Article 40.3.3°:

> It shall be unlawful to terminate the life of an unborn unless such termination is necessary to save the life, as distinct from the health, of the mother where there is an illness or disorder of the mother giving rise to a real and substantial risk to her life, not being a risk of self-destruction.[161]

As is clear, the aim of this amendment was to keep the essence of the Supreme Court's judgment in X – that abortion was permissible in Ireland in order to save the life (but not the health) of the pregnant woman – but to restrict it by removing the risk of suicide as a ground justifying such a procedure. On a turnout of 68 per cent, the amendment was rejected by a margin of 65 per cent to 35 per cent.[162] Accordingly, the rule in X would remain the law. A further attempt

---

[160] ibid.
[161] Referendum (Amendment) (No 2) Act 1992, Appendix, Part II(1).
[162] *Referendum Results* (n 1) 47.

186   *The Triangular Frame*

was made similarly to restrict the circumstances under which abortion is legal in Ireland on 6 March 2002, which also failed, but by the much narrower margin of 50.4 per cent to 49.6 per cent, on a turnout of 43 per cent.[163]

Despite the failure of these two attempts to reverse the decision in X at least insofar as the threat of suicide is concerned, no legislation was enacted to regulate the availability of abortion to protect the life of pregnant women. Though the Supreme Court in X had held that Article 40.3.3° provided for such a right, narrow and limited though it may be, the lack of legislation meant that the right remained largely theoretical. It is this failure to legislate which led to the ECtHR case of *A, B & C v Ireland*.[164] The case differs substantially from those discussed above in that the applicants were not claiming that state *action* had breached their rights under the Convention, but rather state *inaction*. Moreover, the case did not arise from any domestic legal proceedings but was instead entirely freestanding. As was the case with X, it is therefore not part of any formal (judicial) dialogue. However, the judgments of the majority and a partly dissenting minority of the Grand Chamber in the case reveal an interesting disconnect between the institutional self-images of the two sets of judges which is of particular relevance to the present discussion, because it may lead us to prefer the more nuanced (and, in this sense, heterarchical) approach of the majority over the more constitutionally ambitious (and, in this sense, hierarchical) approach of the dissent.

All the applicants had travelled from Ireland to England in order to procure abortions, A for what the ECtHR termed reasons of health and wellbeing (in view of her history of alcohol addiction, post-natal depression, and difficult family and financial circumstances); B for reasons of wellbeing (she did not feel ready to have a child); and C because she feared that her pregnancy put her life at risk, having previously undergone three years of chemotherapy for a rare form of cancer.[165]

A and B complained that the prohibition of abortion on health and wellbeing grounds in Ireland was a violation of their rights not to be subject to inhuman and degrading treatment under Article 3 ECHR; to private and family life under Article 8; to an effective remedy under Article 13; and not to be discriminated against under Article 14. C's complaint was that the failure to implement legislation under Article 40.3.3° of the Constitution following the X case – and the failure of the referendums to narrow its implications – meant that she had no appropriate means of establishing her right to a lawful abortion in Ireland on the grounds of a risk to her life, and thus she alleged violation of the same rights as A and B, along with a further violation of her right to life under Article 2.

It was mentioned above that the case was freestanding and did not arise from any domestic legal proceedings. The Irish Government therefore objected to the

---

[163] ibid 71.
[164] *A, B & C v Ireland* (2010) 53 EHRR 13.
[165] ibid paras 13–26 and 125.

Polyarchic Deliberation   187

ECtHR hearing the case on the ground that the applicants had not exhausted their domestic remedies as required by Article 35 ECHR. As regards A and B, the Court rejected this argument, it being abundantly clear from the judgment in *X*, and the lack of a change in the law since then, that any domestic constitutional challenge to the unavailability in Ireland of abortion for reasons of health or wellbeing had no chance of success.[166] Furthermore, the Court noted the residual, subsidiary and sub-constitutional nature of the incorporation of the Convention into Irish law under the ECHR Act 2003, which, as shown in chapter two, places no legal obligation on the State to amend domestic law in the event of a declaration of incompatibility being granted. This being the case, a request for such a declaration would not constitute an effective remedy.[167] As regards C, the Court joined the objection to the merits of her complaint.[168]

C's Article 2 complaint was held to be manifestly ill-founded for lack of evidence, and her associated complaint under Article 13 fell with it.[169] All three applicants' Article 3 complaints were also held to be manifestly ill-founded on account of the treatment complained of not reaching the minimum level of severity required by the Court's case law, and again the linked Article 13 complaints also fell.[170] The case was therefore decided on the basis of the Article 8 complaints. Because of the differing reasons of A and B, on the one hand, and C on the other for having had their abortions (and thus for their complaints under the Convention), the Court addressed the two situations separately.

With respect to A and B, it was found that there had been an interference with their rights under Article 8's private life component, but that this was 'in accordance with law' under Article 8(2).[171] Furthermore, the interference was held to have been in pursuit of a legitimate aim, the Court confirming its earlier finding on the same point in *Open Door v Ireland*, and reiterating its subsequent statement in *Vo v France*[172] that it was not just undesirable but also impossible to answer the question of whether the 'unborn' was a person within the meaning of Article 2.[173] The applicants' argument – based on opinion polls they had submitted in evidence – that the views of the Irish people had significantly changed since the passage of Article 40.3.3° in its original form in 1983 was held not to be sufficient to rebut this finding.[174]

---

[166] ibid paras 142–49.

[167] ibid para 150, recalling the Court's similar judgments in relation to the UK Human Rights Act 1998: *Hobbs v UK* App no 63684/00 (decision, ECtHR, 18 June 2002); *Burden v UK* (2008) 47 EHRR 38, paras 40–44.

[168] *A, B & C v Ireland* (n 164) para 156.

[169] ibid paras 157–59.

[170] ibid paras 160–64, citing *Ireland v UK* (1978) 2 EHRR 25, para 162; *Lotarev v Ukraine* App no 29447/04 (judgment, ECtHR, 8 April 2010) para 79.

[171] *A, B & C v Ireland* (n 164) paras 216–21.

[172] *Vo v France* (2005) 40 EHRR 259.

[173] *A, B & C v Ireland* (n 164) paras 222–28.

[174] ibid para 226.

188   *The Triangular Frame*

In the final leg of the analysis – the proportionality test of whether the interference was 'necessary in a democratic society' – the majority held that owing to the 'acute sensitivity'[175] of the moral and ethical issues at stake, a broad margin of appreciation should, in principle, be accorded to the Irish State. However, the Court went on to note that the question of whether there was consensus as to how rights should be reconciled in a particular area was essential to determining the breadth of the margin of appreciation in such matters, and that the question of a developing consensus had long played a role in the development and evolution of the Convention's protections, and its interpretation as a 'living instrument',[176] which Krisch has described as another of the 'central political tools in a pluralist order'.[177] The Court then held that there *is* a consensus among a substantial number of the States of the Council of Europe towards allowing abortion on grounds wider than those in Irish law: indeed, only three of the 47 Contracting States had more restrictive abortion laws than Ireland.[178] However, the consensus in this case did *not* decisively narrow the margin of appreciation to be afforded to Ireland:

> Since the rights claimed on behalf of the foetus and those of the mother are inextricably interconnected ..., the margin of appreciation accorded to a State's protection of the unborn necessarily translates into a margin of appreciation for that State as to how it balances the conflicting rights of the mother. It follows that, even if it appears ... that most Contracting Parties may in their legislation have resolved those conflicting rights and interests in favour of greater legal access to abortion, this consensus cannot be a decisive factor in the Court's examination of whether the impugned prohibition ... struck a fair balance between the conflicting rights and interests, notwithstanding an evolutive interpretation of the convention.[179]

It therefore followed that, in light of the right to travel for an abortion and the availability of travel and suitable medical care in Ireland, the interference was not disproportionate, and A's and B's Article 8 rights were held not to have been violated. The very different reasoning of a minority of the Grand Chamber on this issue will be discussed below.

i. (Temporary?) Reverse Conditional Recognition: The Judgment of the Majority

With respect to C, matters were different. Because her argument was that her rights had been violated by the State's failure to legislate with respect to the Supreme Court's judgment in *X*, her complaint fell to be examined under the State's positive obligations under Article 8.[180] Reiterating that there was a broad

---

[175] ibid para 233.
[176] ibid para 234.
[177] Krisch (n 111) 210.
[178] *A, B & C v Ireland* (n 164) para 235.
[179] ibid para 237.
[180] ibid paras 244–46.

Polyarchic Deliberation 189

margin of appreciation for states to decide the circumstances under which abortion should be permissible, the Court stated that:

> [O]nce that decision is taken the legal framework devised for this purpose should be 'shaped in a coherent manner which allows the different legitimate interests involved to be taken into account adequately and in accordance with the obligations deriving from the Convention'.[181]

However, despite the decision having been taken as long ago as 1992, no legal framework had been devised at all, 'shaped in a coherent manner' or otherwise. Returning to her alleged non-exhaustion of domestic remedies, the government claimed that C could have sought mandatory orders in the High Court requiring doctors to terminate her pregnancy.[182] The ECtHR did not consider this an effective remedy, quoting a judgment of McCarthy J in another abortion case (not directly relevant for present purposes) that it would be wrong to turn the High Court into a 'licensing authority' for abortions.[183] Accordingly, the uncertainty caused by the lack of legislation following *X*, and especially the lack of effective and accessible procedures to establish the right to an abortion, led the Court to conclude that the State had failed in its positive obligations to C, and found a violation of Article 8.[184]

The Court held fast to its *Open Door* (ECtHR) finding of a legitimate aim (the protection of morals as decided domestically) and the relevance of a broad margin of appreciation, and this even in the face of a finding of a broad European consensus on the issue of abortion with which Ireland is at odds. This, I suggest, can be taken as a warning. European and Irish developments in the time between *Open Door* (ECtHR) and *A, B & C* were not, in this case, sufficient to dislodge the legitimacy finding in *Open Door* (ECtHR), but it would be going too far to suggest that this is going to be the case for all time coming. As a court of subsidiary and supervisory jurisdiction, the ECtHR (or rather, a majority of the Grand Chamber) was not prepared to pre-empt the future domestic development of the law but was perfectly prepared to put domestic actors on notice, even if not expressly and specifically. Further evidence of this is the way in which the Court repeated a finding of McCarthy J in *X*:

> In the context of the eight years that have passed since [Article 40.3.3°] was adopted and the two years since [*Grogan*] the failure by the legislature to enact the appropriate legislation is no longer just unfortunate; it is inexcusable.

If a failure to legislate with respect to Article 40.3.3°, adopted in 1983, was 'inexcusable' in 1992, what word could adequately describe such persistent inertia in 2010? Perhaps wisely, the Grand Chamber did not offer one, but the

---

[181] ibid para 249, quoting the Court's judgment in *SH and Others v Austria* [2011] ECHR 1879.
[182] *A, B & C v Ireland* (n 164) para 256.
[183] ibid para 258, citing *A and B v Eastern Health Board, Judge Mary Fahy and C* [1998] 1 IR 464.
[184] *A, B & C v Ireland* (n 164) paras 259–68.

190 *The Triangular Frame*

specific invocation by an international court of a domestic Supreme Court judge's damning indictment of state failure to act furthers the argument that *A, B & C* constitutes a dialogic warning to the State, articulating the ECtHR's own position while still leaving room for the (voluntary) adjustment of domestic preferences. The Court was not (yet) prepared to find the lack of provision for abortion on health and wellbeing grounds in breach of the Convention, but was perfectly prepared to find the lack of implementation of a right pronounced by the State's *own* highest judicial actors, 18 years previously, to be so. Maduro's principle of vertical coherence is relevant here: what could be more vertically coherent than pointing out that the 'inexcusable' nature of a state's failure to act was initially pronounced by a domestic actor?

Of course, *dialogue* requires two voices, so it is important to note the results of the ECtHR's prompting of the Irish legislature with respect to C, and the effective operationalisation of the very limited right to an abortion outlined in X. Both the Fine Gael and Labour political parties committed in their manifestos for the 2011 Irish general election to act on the ruling, and the coalition government they subsequent formed announced the establishment of an expert group to examine how to proceed in June 2011.[185] The group reported on 27 November 2011.[186] This would have been a significant moment in itself, but events conspired to push the issue to the very top of the agenda. One month previously, Savita Halappanavar had died of septicaemia while miscarrying in hospital in Galway, having requested, and been denied, an abortion.[187] The expert group's report led to the enactment of the Protection of Life During Pregnancy Act in July 2013, which established specific, highly restrictive means by which a woman may procure an abortion within the State in accordance with the X criteria, that is, in case of risk to her life, including from the threat of suicide, but not of risk to her health.[188] Though the relevant sections of the Offences Against the Person Act 1861, outlined above in section I.B, were repealed,[189] the 2013 Act went on to create a new offence, that of intentional destruction

---

[185] Jamie Smyth, 'Expert group on abortion to be set up by November' *Irish Times* (17 June 2011), available at: www.irishtimes.com/news/expert-group-on-abortion-to-be-set-up-by-november-1.598305.

[186] *Report of the Expert Group on the Judgment in A, B and C v Ireland* (Dublin, Department of Health, 2012), available at: health.gov.ie/wp-content/uploads/2014/03/Judgment_ABC.pdf.

[187] Details are to be found in Health Service Executive, *Investigation of Incident 50278 from Time of Patient's Self-Referral to Hospital on the 21st of October 2012 to the Patient's Death on the 28th of October 2012* (2013), available at: cdn.thejournal.ie/media/2013/06/savita-halappanavar-hse-report.pdf, and the subsequent Health Information and Quality Authority, *Investigation into the Safety, Quality and Standards of Services Provided by the Health Service Executive to Patients, Including Pregnant Women, at Risk of Clinical Deterioration, Including those Provided in University Hospital Galway, and as Reflected in the Care and Treatment Provided to Savita Halappanavar* (2013), available at: www.hiqa.ie/sites/default/files/2017-01/Patient-Safety-Investigation-UHG.pdf.

[188] Protection of Life During Pregnancy Act 2013, ss 7–9.

[189] ibid, s 5.

Polyarchic Deliberation   191

of unborn life,[190] punishable by a fine, up to 14 years' imprisonment, or both.[191] Though the Act did at least attempt to make effective the previously entirely theoretical right to an abortion in *X* case circumstances, whether it would pass muster at Strasbourg (or even in the Irish courts) is a question that will never be answered. The death of Dr Halappanavar and other grievous injustices[192] proved the catalysts for a concerted and ultimately successful feminist-led social and political campaign against the constitutional prohibition of abortion, culminating in the 2018 referendum. The 2013 Act will be repealed and replaced by the forthcoming legislation.[193]

ii. Unconvincing Constitutionalism: The Dissent Regarding A & B

The Grand Chamber of the ECtHR was unanimous in finding a violation of Article 8 with respect to C, but a significant minority of eight judges dissented with respect to A and B, holding that there had in fact been a violation of Article 8 in their cases. The dissent's argument centred on the relationship between European consensus and the margin of appreciation, the minority disagreeing with the majority's assessment of the issue, and I argue that their reasons for doing so lean very heavily – indeed, openly so – towards the constitutional and hierarchical, rather than pluralist and heterarchical, end of the spectrum.

The dissent repeated the majority's finding that there was a broad consensus among a substantial majority of Contracting States that abortion should be legal in circumstances much wider than in Ireland, and stated that:

> According to the Convention case-law, in situations where the Court finds that a consensus exists among European States on a matter touching upon a human right, it usually concludes that the consensus decisively narrows the margin of appreciation which might otherwise exist if no such consensus were demonstrated. This approach is commensurate with the 'harmonising' role of the Convention's case-law: indeed, one of the paramount functions of the case-law is to gradually create a harmonious application of human rights protection, cutting across the national boundaries of the Contracting States and allowing the individuals within their jurisdiction to enjoy, without discrimination, equal protection regardless of their place of residence.[194]

As should immediately be obvious, this is quintessentially constitutionalist reasoning, with its focus on the universality and integrity of the Convention

---

[190] Itself defined legislatively for the first time, as 'such a life during the period of time commencing after implantation in the womb of a woman and ending on the complete emergence of the life from the body of the woman' (ibid, s 2(1)).

[191] ibid, s 22.

[192] See de Londras and Enright (n 5) 13–14 and references therein.

[193] See Department of Health, 'General Scheme of a Bill to Regulate Termination of Pregnancy' (27 March 2018), available at: health.gov.ie/wp-content/uploads/2018/03/General-Scheme-for-Publication.pdf, in particular at Head 20(d).

[194] *A, B & C v Ireland* (n 164) para 5 of the partial dissent.

192 The Triangular Frame

system within the territories of the Contracting States. The minority went on to note that this harmonising role is not unlimited, and that one limit upon it is in cases where there is, first, no clear European consensus on how (or whether) to protect a particular human right from state violation and, second, the alleged Convention violation concerns a relative right which can be balanced against 'other rights or interests also worthy of protection in a democratic society'.[195] In such cases, the Court allows a (limited) margin of appreciation to the states to make this balance for themselves, 'preferring not to become the first European body to "legislate" on a matter still undecided at European level'.[196] The broad European consensus in favour of less restrictive abortion laws was therefore sufficient for the minority to find Ireland's restrictions beyond the limits of its margin of appreciation. In so finding, the minority was critical of the majority's rather more complex analysis regarding the issue of consensus, calling it 'the first time that the Court has disregarded the existence of a European consensus on the basis of "profound moral views"'.[197]

There are three serious flaws with the analysis of the minority, which may lead us to prefer the more nuanced (and less rigidly 'constitutionalist') approach of the majority. First, the dissenters were of the opinion that:

> [The question of when life begins] was not the issue before the Court, and undoubtedly the Court is not equipped to deal effectively with it. The issue before the Court was whether, regardless of when life begins – before birth or not – the right to life of the foetus can be balanced against the right to life of the mother, or her right to personal autonomy and development, and possibly found to weigh less than the latter rights or interests.[198]

This is emphatically not the issue that was before the Court. What is more, the question as formulated here makes little sense. The rights to life of the foetus and of the woman *cannot* be weighed and balanced against each other 'regardless of when life begins – before birth or not', because the answer to the balancing question will differ greatly depending on one's answer to the question of when life begins. The question of whether the rights of the foetus can *possibly* be found to weigh less than the competing rights of the pregnant woman leads us inexorably to a particular answer: yes, of course they can, as the laws of a number of Contracting States make clear. However, for this possibility to be sufficient to narrow the margin of appreciation in the case ignores the *reasons* behind the differing abortion laws of the states forming part of the consensus, and thus whether the consensus is relevant.[199]

---

[195] ibid.
[196] ibid.
[197] ibid para 9 of the partial dissent.
[198] ibid para 2 of the partial dissent.
[199] This idea of a *relevant* consensus is the essential thrust of Judge Finlay Geoghegan's brief concurring opinion in the case.

The analysis of the European consensus in both the majority and minority judgments was restricted to the bare text and effect of the laws currently in force, with no evidence before the Court regarding their relevant context: do they recognise, even in a contingent or limited way, a right to life vested in the foetus? Are they the result of some balancing exercise under national law, by which the relative strength of the rights of the foetus (if any) and of the pregnant woman can be determined? Do they flow from some specific and fundamental constitutional choice on the part of the electorate or their representatives, or do they flow instead or in addition from ordinary (non-constitutional) politics; or medical and scientific opinion; or some particular aspect of the State's political or social history; or from a multitude of such sources and factors? The answers given to these questions will differ in each national context, considerably lessening the strength of the dissent's assertion that the existence of a general consensus regarding the circumstances under which abortion should be permissible necessarily narrows the particular margin of appreciation to be afforded to Ireland in the case. Accordingly, a more nuanced, contingent approach, such as that of the majority, is preferable, and this leads directly to the question of the universality of interface norms. Just as the way abortion is regulated across Europe is jurisdictionally specific, so too must be the norms applied in regulating the interactions between legal orders on the issue.

Secondly, and related to the foregoing, is the fact that the dissenting judgment does not attempt seriously to engage with the majority's reasoning as to *why* the consensus identified should not narrow Ireland's margin of appreciation. This reasoning is worth recalling:

> Since the rights claimed on behalf of the foetus and those of the mother are inextricably interconnected ..., the margin of appreciation accorded to a State's protection of the unborn necessarily translates into a margin of appreciation for that State as to how it balances the conflicting rights of the mother.[200]

This is an altogether more justifiable view. The whole Court was in agreement that the question of when life begins was not in issue. In any event, the Convention neither requires nor prohibits that the State should afford a right to life to the foetus. It therefore follows, particularly in light of the moral element of the argument, that a wide margin of appreciation should be afforded to how the State resolves the question. If this is the case, by what logic may we then move the goalposts by narrowing the margin of appreciation, not at the level of principle itself (the right to life of the foetus), but at the level of the *application* of that principle (how this balances with the rights of the pregnant woman)? Contrary to the dissenting argument, the mere fact that the law in most Contracting States with respect to abortion was wider than in Ireland – and regardless of the prior question of whether this consensus is a relevant consensus – does not change

---

[200] *A, B & C v Ireland* (n 164) para 237.

194 *The Triangular Frame*

the essential fact that if a state is to be afforded a wide margin of appreciation in determining the extent to which the life of the foetus ought to be protected, then it must logically also be afforded a similarly wide margin in any subsequent balancing or reconciliation exercise, the rights of the two entities at issue (both human persons within the logic of Irish law, and this without offence to the Convention) being interconnected. Again, the specificity of the law and practice at issue leads us away from a universal conception of interface norms.

While the first and second objections to the majority's reasoning relate to their conception of European consensus and its effect on the margin of appreciation (and are thus procedural or metaconstitutional), the third relates more directly to the substantive question of the rights and wrongs of abortion. That is not the focus of this chapter, but this third difficulty must be discussed in the present context because of the way in which it relates to the institutional self-image of the dissenting minority. The minority did not confine itself to noting the European consensus with respect to abortion, but went on to justify it, holding that:

> This seems to us a reasonable stance for European legislation and practice to take, given that the values protected – the rights of the foetus and the rights of a living person – are, by their nature, unequal: on the one hand there are the rights of a person already participating, in an active manner, in social interaction, and on the other hand there are the rights of a foetus within the mother's body, whose life has not been definitively determined as long as the process leading to the birth is not yet complete, and whose participation in social interaction has not even started.[201]

This sentence makes a point which is entirely valid, even if we allow for the fact that the minority's use of language in the juxtaposition of the rights of the 'foetus' and the rights of a 'living person' is question-begging in light of the specific earlier finding that the case was *not* about when 'life' begins.[202] What is much more difficult to understand is the sentence which immediately follows:

> In Convention terms, it can also be argued that the rights enshrined in that text are mainly designed to protect individuals against State acts or omissions while the former participate actively in the normal everyday life of a democratic society.[203]

This is a bizarre statement. Quite aside from being entirely without precedent (the prefix '[i]n Convention terms' thereby being rendered meaningless), it is about as far from being vertically coherent as one could imagine. The idea that the rights protected by the Convention are 'mainly designed to protect individuals ... while [they] participate actively in the normal everyday life of a democratic society' is highly suspect, and is potentially dangerous in terms

---

[201] *A, B & C v Ireland* (n 164) para 2 of the partial dissent.

[202] The exact same point had been made by McCarthy J in the course of his judgment in *Attorney General v X* (n 6): '[t]he right of the girl here is a right to a life in being; the right of the unborn is to a life contingent; contingent on survival in the womb until successful delivery' at 79.

[203] *A, B & C v Ireland* (n 164) para 2 of the partial dissent.

Polyarchic Deliberation 195

of how it could be abused. Taken to its conclusion, it would not be difficult to use such a conception to argue that, among others, the sick, the disabled, and the imprisoned are somehow deserving of less protection under the Convention against state acts or omissions because they may not 'participate actively in the normal everyday life of a democratic society', which itself is left undefined. Even if not taken to the extreme of being applied to these categories of people, and only used as a justification for weighing the foetus's right to life less heavily than the pregnant woman's competing rights, it is not an argument that makes any sense from within the internal perspective of Irish constitutional law, or from the perspective of a Convention which is agnostic as to the right to life of the foetus. Put simply, the above-quoted passages went too far: rather than confining themselves to making the important and valid observation that the life of a foetus (if it is a human life) is necessarily contingent and the life of a woman is a life in being, and drawing justifiable conclusions from this, the minority went on to make a bold yet highly suspect statement as to the purpose of the Convention and the characteristics of those it protects.

The reason this is important for the present analysis is because of the resultant gap between the dissent's *constitutional ambitions* and the *quality of its constitutional reasoning*. In their (entirely understandable) eagerness to enhance the protection of abortion rights within the Convention system and to increase the pressure on Ireland to reform its laws, the minority of the Grand Chamber fell into precisely the trap of constitutional solipsism in which we have previously seen the Irish courts (*Open Door*, the High Court in *X*) and the CJEU (*Viking*, *Laval*) become ensnared. The major issue of the case was formulated by the dissent in a way that permits of only one answer: there was no investigation as to whether the European consensus was a relevant consensus; there was no attempt to engage with the majority's reasoning on the margin of appreciation; and the dissent contained exactly the sort of crass and unthinking generalisation that apex courts ought to avoid because of the potential to create problems in cases beyond the present. The judgment was couched in the language of constitutionalism, of 'gradually creat[ing] a harmonious application of human rights protection'[204] across Europe. But with a view gradually to creating this harmonious application of human rights protection, which decision as regards A and B is preferable? I suggest that the decision of the majority, which I have categorised above as being dialogic, pluralist, and non-solipsistic, is superior. By its application of the margin of appreciation doctrine – what Sabel and Gerstenberg have called reverse conditional recognition[205] – it seeks to engage, rather than impose, and prefers to postpone conflict in the hope that it can be properly avoided by other means (particularly by politics), rather than ensuring conflict – both constitutional and political – by means of reasoning which is of doubtful

---

[204] ibid para 5 of the partial dissent.
[205] Sabel and Gerstenberg (n 112) 519–20.

196 *The Triangular Frame*

rigour, of doubtful justifiability to the national legal order, and of doubtful coherence with respect to the Convention itself.

III. THE NATURE OF THE RELATIONSHIPS AND THE UNIVERSALITY OF INTERFACE NORMS

The foregoing has described in detail the means by which an issue of human rights under national constitutional law entered the European legal discourse; the responses and reactions of the different sites of constitutional authority within the deliberative polyarchy of the triangular constitution; and the means by which conflict, when it arose or could have arisen, was resolved. In the light of this experience, let us consider again the whole evolution of Article 40.3.3°. In its original form, the Article inserted by the Eighth Amendment stated that:

> The State acknowledges the right to life of the unborn and, with due regard to the equal right to life of the mother, guarantees in its laws to respect and, as far as practicable, by its laws to defend and vindicate that right.

As was outlined in the introduction, the insertion of this Article was arguably unnecessary even on its own terms, given that abortion was already a criminal offence, and the chances at that time of judicial or political alteration of this prohibition were close to nil. However, its proponents advocated for the change in an effort to copper-fasten the prohibition, elevating a mere legislative ban to the status of a constitutional norm, which, they argued at the time, would be absolute. We can disagree strenuously with the content and purposes and principle of the Eighth Amendment, but the fact remains that it was the specific and deliberate choice of the electorate on a matter of constitutional and moral principle, under a constitutional system that allows for the expression and entrenchment of such principles without limitation. Any argument against that principle must be at the level of principle itself: that it *should* not have been done, and *must* be undone, not that it *could* not have been done.

And yet, given the triangular, rather than self-contained, nature of the Irish constitutional order, matters did not end there, and Ireland's place within the triangular constitution allowed for the space of contestation within which those arguments of contrary principle could be advanced. The State's attempt to prevent a suicidal 14-year-old rape victim from leaving the jurisdiction would never have been compatible with EU law. Quite aside from any question of (non-economic) fundamental rights (and given the less explicit and concrete nature of these rights in the then Community, rather than Union, legal order), abortion is a medical service legally available in other Member States. In the event, the threat to X's life from the risk of suicide was enough for the Supreme Court to avoid the issue of compatibility with the Treaties, holding that X was entitled to an abortion within the jurisdiction, revealing the (slightly) less-than-absolute nature of the prohibition contained in the Eighth Amendment. But the question of the right to travel in a different case, not involving a risk of suicide, remained.

The Nature of the Relationships 197

When offered the opportunity, on two occasions, to remove the risk of suicide as a relevant factor in balancing the right to life of the foetus and the pregnant woman, the Irish electorate declined to do so, demonstrating that at the level of fundamental principle, the electorate's opposition to abortion was rather less absolute and all-encompassing than the initial endorsement of the Eighth Amendment might have suggested.

But the Thirteenth Amendment, expressly granting the right to travel to procure an abortion, was endorsed, adding Article 40.3.3's first proviso: 'This subsection shall not limit freedom to travel between the State and another state'. Thus, the potential for conflict between the Irish and EU orders was averted by the autonomous, but not autochthonous, decision of the Irish order itself. Similarly, the State's endorsement of the attempts of anti-abortion groups to restrain the publication of information about abortion services available abroad brought the national constitution into potential conflict with the EU legal order, and actual conflict with that of the ECHR. Again, this conflict was resolved by the popular endorsement of a further proviso to Article 40.3.3: 'This subsection shall not limit freedom to obtain or make available, within the State, subject to such conditions as may be laid down by law, information relating to services lawfully available in another state'.

Finally, and following a further judgment from Strasbourg decrying the State's failure to legislate even for the very narrow grounds on which abortion would be permissible, the whole ordeal was brought to an end in 2018, with the deletion of all these provisions, and their replacement with the statement that: 'Provision may be made by law for the regulation of termination of pregnancy'. This democratic volte-face illustrates the only-ever relative nature of the final say, and the impossibility of permanence in law. What was once argued to be an insuperable, entrenched statement of fundamental moral principle by a sovereign democratic community came, over time, to be adjusted, limited and eventually undone entirely by that exact same sovereign democratic community (or, rather, its successor in title, given the passage of time). The fundamental principle that abortion was a moral wrong was replaced by another fundamental principle: that pregnant women have the right to determine what does and does not happen to their own bodies. What all this demonstrates is the important normative value inherent in pluralism: in a legal and constitutional system which is not – and does not ultimately regard itself as – the be-all and end-all of the articulation and vindication of rights, justice and the common good, but is instead structurally open, by its own express terms, to contestation, adjustment and reinterpretation, judicially or politically, in light of the claims of other legal actors and individuals, whether these be expressed in an internal or external forum. The triangular constitution as a deliberative polyarchy describes precisely such a constitutional configuration. When we look back over the whole 35-year saga detailed above, it is clear that the constitutional events and relations being described do *not* match any monist or particularist conception of the European constitutional space. None of the apex courts involved insisted, in these instances, that they and they alone enjoyed hierarchical superiority over the

198   *The Triangular Frame*

whole constitutional panoply. In dealing with an issue of political sensitivity, the Irish Supreme Court, the CJEU and the ECtHR limited themselves to insisting on their interpretive authority over only the constitutional order that each oversees. This is not to say that the actions of any of these courts were at all times beyond reproach, or that any of them reached an objectively 'right' answer. The absence of an all-encompassing overarching normative frame means that such an answer is elusive. Moreover, each of the apex courts, in various ways and at various stages, rendered judgments which were not always coherent with the rest of their jurisprudence, or conflicted with the jurisprudence of their counterparts, as is revealed by an analysis of the metaconstitutional interface norms employed in regulating the relationships between legal orders.

I suggest that the universality of these norms – a claim made openly by Kumm and inherent in the work of Maduro – is seriously called into question by the evidence presented. As was noted in section I.B.ii, Kumm's interface norms of legality, subsidiarity, democracy and the protection of rights fit well with the Irish Supreme Court's decision in *Grogan*. However, as was also noted above, this is hardly surprising given that Kumm's norms were formulated with specific reference to the relationship between the EU and its Member States, citing in particular the Irish Constitution's provisions on abortion.[206]

With respect to the right to receive and impart information, the Irish courts repeatedly subordinated this right – whether under the national constitution or under European law of either species – to the Constitution's particular formulation of the right to life. Whether or not one agrees with the right's particular application to the 'unborn', this subordination is justifiable on its own terms – or at least within the terms of reference of the Irish courts and their self-image as guardians of the national constitutional order – because of the foundational nature of the right to life, both under the Constitution and the Convention. The Irish courts privileged the Irish conception of the right to life over the right to receive and impart information *not* merely because the domestic right was domestic, or democratically endorsed, but precisely because of its fundamentality. This is a vertically coherent argument, using the language and logic of the European legal orders, transposed to the national frame, to argue for the partial subordination of those orders to the national. But in metaconstitutional terms, what is notable is the role played by what I have termed the 'principle of avoidance'. While reticence to involve the EU legal order is clear from both the High Court and Supreme Court judgments in *Open Door*, we can also see the principle employed by the CJEU itself in *Grogan* (CJEU). Whereas AG van Gerven had been willing to deal with the substance of the issue – and this in a way which would still have accommodated national concerns – the CJEU adopted a less ambitious approach in its finding that the economic link between the Irish counselling services and the English providers of abortion services was 'too tenuous'.

---

[206] Kumm (n 51) 297.

The Nature of the Relationships   199

Restrictions on free movement go to the very core of the EU's constitutional order, as expounded and defended by the CJEU. In a contemporaneous assessment of the judgment, O'Leary wrote that:

> Beyond the recognition of abortion as a service, the progressive approach forged by the Court in the area of services was forgotten. Furthermore, recent developments expanding the power of the Court in its assessment of national legislation in the light of the Community's fundamental rights principles sit uneasily with the refusal to engage in any such analysis in *Grogan* ... Taken unawares by the nature and the subject matter of the preliminary ruling requested, the Court was unwilling to act as arbiter in such an unfriendly arena. No doubt it was aware of the Irish Supreme Court's barely restrained protest in *Grogan*. Content to assert a role for Community law, it left the resolution of the case to national law. This judicial restraint is legally and logically acceptable, particularly given the delicate and controversial nature of the issue. What is not acceptable is the legal method employed by the Court and its failure substantively to dispose of the case ... on the grounds of Community law at its disposal.[207]

There is the obvious difficulty that we cannot know what the Court's judgment might have been if the Supreme Court had adopted a less assertive stance in *Grogan*, but nonetheless, by far the most important factor for the CJEU was the first question referred, whether abortion constitutes a service within the meaning of the Treaty. As is plain from the judgment, and from the Court's previous decisions, the ruling that it does could never have been otherwise without undermining the integrity of the Court's jurisprudence. Moreover, the Court's refusal to take into account SPUC's moral objection to classifying abortion as a service demonstrates an awareness of its own institutional limitations as regards the many Member States where abortion was regulated more liberally than in Ireland. But the CJEU, in attempting to recognise the limits of its own authority, ability and legitimacy, managed to do so in a manner which undermined its own jurisprudence on free movement. It is true that the importance to the CJEU – and to the Union and its law more generally – of the second and third questions referred was of a much lesser degree. The questions were narrowly phrased, focusing specifically on the question of abortion, and not services generally, and the attempt to frame the third question in the abstract, with talk of travelling between 'Member State A' and 'Member State B', surely fooled no one. It was specifically noted in the Advocate General's Opinion that Ireland was not (yet, as it turned out) seeking to prevent pregnant women from travelling to avail of services lawfully available abroad[208] – something which would rightly have exercised the Court – and neither were criminal sanctions threatened. Accordingly, it is no great leap of the imagination to see the restriction at the heart of the case – on the provision of information regarding the location and contact

---

[207] O'Leary (n 52) 156.
[208] *Grogan* (CJEU, Opinion) (n 76) para 13.

200   *The Triangular Frame*

details of foreign abortion clinics in a jurisdiction where abortion is illegal – as a local matter of minor importance, at least from the perspective of the freedom to provide and receive services.

However, this does not justify the CJEU's 'ducking'[209] of the issue. The approach of AG van Gerven, which I characterised above in section II.A.i.a as a precursor to the later judgment in *Omega* – itself a modified application of the principle of conditional recognition – would have allowed the Court to have regard to its own limited competence and jurisdiction while still safeguarding the core of its jurisprudence. Let us bear in mind the triangularity of the dispute: the restriction of information in *Grogan* was already subject to challenge in Strasbourg (a fact of which the CJEU would have been aware), and the ECtHR had yet to rule on the issue. Given the dark tone of what Ireland's Supreme Court had to say about the potential for conflict with EU law; given the very limited impact of the restriction on the provision of services throughout the Union; and given the CJEU's (at least then) limited experience and expertise as regards non-economic fundamental rights, the approach of AG van Gerven would still have safeguarded the 'uniformity and efficacy'[210] of EU law, as the CJEU requires itself and others to do, without precipitating inter-order conflict *and* without undermining the jurisprudence on free movement with the finding that a 'too tenuous' economic link was fatal to the engagement of EU law.

This point can be extended to the right to receive and impart information as protected by Article 10 ECHR. Though the CJEU did not enter into any discussion of the issue, AG van Gerven entered into the 'horizontal' side of the triangle and offered his own interpretation of the requirements of the Convention. He found that the fundamental right to freedom of expression *had* been breached, but that this breach was necessary and proportionate. Problematically, this is *not* the decision arrived at by the ECtHR a short time later in *Open Door* (ECtHR), where that Court found the restriction over broad and disproportionate on several grounds. But this disconnect between the two Courts could easily have been remedied: as conflicts between Luxembourg and Strasbourg go, the constitutional difficulties it would have raised were rather more similar to the cases following *Hoechst*[211] and *Orkem*[212] than to the much more serious disconnect following *Demir and Baykara*[213] and *Enerji Yapı-Yol Sen*,[214] discussed in chapter three. The CJEU's application of a principle of avoidance in *Grogan* (CJEU), therefore, may have had the effect of staving off constitutional conflict both with a Member State and with the ECtHR, but unlike the approach of

---

[209] O'Leary (n 52) 156.

[210] See, inter alia, Case 11/70 *Internationale Handelsgesellschaft mbH v Einfuhr- und Vorratsstelle für Getreide und Futtermittel* ECLI:EU:C:1970:114, [1970] ECR 1125, para 3.

[211] Joined Cases 46/87 and 227/88 *Hoechst v Commission* ECLI:EU:C:1989:337, [1989] ECR 2859.

[212] Case 374/87 *Orkem v Commission* ECLI:EU:C:1989:387, [1989] ECR 3283.

[213] *Demir and Baykara v Turkey* (2009) 48 EHRR 54.

[214] *Enerji Yapı-Yol Sen v Turkey* (2009) ECHR 2251.

AG van Gerven, it did so at the expense of the integrity of the CJEU's own jurisprudence and its own self-image as interpreter of the Treaties.

In rejecting the government's claim in *Open Door* (ECtHR) that the State's discretion in moral matters was unfettered and unreviewable, the ECtHR's decision was quintessentially constitutionalist, and demonstrates that Court's institutional self-image as the guardian of the Convention. However, this was tempered by the ECtHR's emphasis that Ireland's (broad) margin of appreciation in the area was restricted by the breadth, permanence, practical ineffectiveness and socially unequal effects of the restriction on information about abortions available abroad – concerns which were as vertically coherent as they were coherent within the Convention legal order itself. A similar approach was employed nearly 20 years later in *A, B & C*, with the Court being unwilling to go so far as to find Ireland's (lack of) abortion laws in breach of the Convention with respect to A and B. However, with respect to C, the Court effectively put Ireland on notice that this sensitivity to national specificity was neither definitive nor permanent. This approach, applying the margin of appreciation doctrine as a principle of reverse conditional recognition, is in sharp contrast to the approach of the minority dissent in the case, which relied on questionable assumptions about the nature of European consensus and a questionable interpretation of the purpose of the Convention to reach an altogether more rigid conclusion than that of the majority. Indeed, the minority dissent casts the ECtHR as exactly the kind of European Supreme Court which it would be under a hierarchical construction of the Convention legal order, not as a court of subsidiary and supervisory jurisdiction, playing its part in polyarchic deliberation, which is what emerges from the majority judgment, and from the general thrust of the Court's jurisprudence.

What emerges from the decisions taken together is a distinctively constitutional – yet emphatically pluralist – legal universe, well captured by the notion of overlapping consensus. With respect to the different fundamental rights in question – information, travel and private and family life – we have seen that conflict between the legal orders, both actual and potential, was ultimately resolved by Ireland modifying its Constitution or its laws. However, this emphatically does not cast Ireland as being in any way *subordinate* to the two European legal orders. Rather, the citizens (in the case of constitutional amendment) and the legislature (in the case of law reform) were modifying domestic arrangements in light of (but *not* at the behest of) the positions of legal orders beyond the domestic.

Like the Irish Constitution's protection of the right to life of the 'unborn', much of this is nationally specific and historically contingent. The Constitution's amendability only by referendum is unusual in Europe (and worldwide), and the way in which the Irish courts, the CJEU and the ECtHR interacted in their decisions is predicated not just on the legal relationships that these institutions share (which can be at least partially generalised across the Union), but also on the specific ways in which the cases came before the courts, the specific ways

202 *The Triangular Frame*

in which the courts dealt with the issues at hand, and the general historic praxis of interaction and cooperation between the courts. It was noted in chapter two that there are probably at least as many instances of specific national constitutional provisions – jealously guarded by national courts – as there are Member States of the Union. The above has demonstrated that with respect to one of these – abortion in Ireland – the norms employed by courts at each site in the European polyarchy were contingent and specific to the case at hand. Certainly, some major threads can be drawn out – the principle of avoidance for one. But though this is a principle that courts can employ in seeking to avoid conflict in balancing the claims of overlapping legal orders, it is altogether looser and more general than the tightly formulated interface norms proposed by Kumm. Avoidance and (reverse) conditional recognition are exactly the sorts of tools that can be employed within a deliberative polyarchy to constitutionalise an overlapping consensus, but they are not a ready-made, step-by-step, a priori guide for the resolution of constitutional conflict.

IV. CONCLUSION

Having looked at the 'vertical' relationships between Ireland and both European legal orders in chapter two, and at the 'horizontal' (but frequently in practice 'triangular') relationship between the EU and the ECHR in chapter three, this chapter sought to examine the way in which all three legal orders have interacted with respect to one specific national constitutional provision. The way that this interaction played out – encompassing the right to receive and impart information both under the Treaties and under the Convention, the right to travel, and the right to a private and family life – demonstrates the contingent nature of such interaction, which in another case, in another country, at another time, may well have involved different rights or gone a different way. Though (very) general metaconstitutional principles can be drawn out from the various judgments, we cannot derive hard and fast, universally applicable norms from them.

However, the main series of cases under discussion above occurred 20 years ago, and the CJEU's case law as regards fundamental rights has developed significantly since then, *Kadi*[215] being a seminal example. Recall that Sabel and Gerstenberg have noted that this extension of the CJEU's jurisdiction may 'overlap and potentially compete with that of Member States in matters of visceral concern'.[216] We can easily add to this that it may overlap and potentially compete with that of the ECtHR, as we saw with respect to labour rights in chapter three. If the 1986–92 dialogue – from *Open Door* to the amendment

---

[215] Joined Cases C-402/05 P and C-415/05 P *Kadi and Al Barakaat v Council and Commission* ECLI:EU:C:2008:461, [2008] ECR I-6351.

[216] Sabel and Gerstenberg (n 112) 512.

of Article 40.3.3° of the Constitution with respect to the rights to travel and to information – had in fact not occurred until, say, 2006–12, the outcome of the cases may have been very different indeed, especially in light of the more expressly political, rather than economic, basis of the Union as opposed to the Community; the growth of the CJEU's fundamental rights jurisprudence; and the rather more rigidly constitutionalist dissent in *A, B & C*.

The purpose of the next chapter is, therefore, to take what we have learned from chapters two, three and four, and analyse it holistically, with respect to the three legal orders as they relate and interact today, and with respect to the whole array of national constitutional orders in the Union.

5

Towards Triangular Constitutionalism: Universalising the Triangular Constitution

INTRODUCTION

I N THIS BOOK, I have posited Irish constitutional law, the law of the European Union (EU) and the law of the European Convention on Human Rights (ECHR) as a single, composite, polyarchic constitutional order: a triangular constitution, where each legal order reserves the final say to itself within its own domain, and no legal order has the final say from an external perspective. The individual components of the triangular constitution – the triangle's points – are certainly severable for analytical purposes: each has its own origins, text, *telos* and tendencies, and none depends on any of the others for its authority. However, each of these constitutional orders is so deeply embedded in each of the others that it is only in their composite whole, the *Gestalt* of the triangular constitution, that we can fully understand them. Such is the explanatory claim that has been advanced throughout the preceding chapters. There has also been a further, normative claim, that this state of affairs is in fact preferable to any monist, particularist, or hierarchical conception of the relationship between the three legal orders. This claim has been advanced most frequently by reference to what I have described as the trap or danger of constitutional solipsism: of any legal order failing to internalise the reality of the polyarchy in which it is situated. There has then been the final, doctrinal claim, for which the explanatory and normative claims are background requirements: in each of the previous three chapters, I have suggested that the specific interface norms employed by the judicial actors at each site in the polyarchy in regulating the relationships between the different systems vary in their nature, from the legislative, through to the constitutional, to the metaconstitutional. While we might well expect sub-constitutional and constitutional interface norms – being creatures of their own legal systems – to lean away from the universal, and towards the historically contingent and jurisdictionally specific, this tendency has also been evident with respect to the metaconstitutional interface norms employed.

Chapter two and chapter three focused on the three 'sides' of the triangular constitution in turn and illustrated the nature of the relevant relationships and

The Triangular Constitution Assessed   205

the interface norms thereunder with reference to a wide range of cases over a long period of time. Chapter four broadened the focus jurisdictionally, dealing simultaneously with all three sides of the triangle, and narrowed the focus jurisprudentially, dealing with the specific issue of the regulation of abortion and its various manifestations across different sites in the polyarchy.

The purpose of this final chapter is twofold. First, it seeks to tie all these threads together by assessing the particular triangular constitution of Ireland, the EU and the ECHR as it currently stands, and finally proving the hypothesis of the non-universality of metaconstitutional interface norms. Section I will briefly restate the structure of the polyarchy in order to ground the discussion of the particular interface norms at work. The section will then conclude that the specific norms at work in regulating the relationships between legal orders are necessarily contingent, and that the attempt to universalise them results not in specific, universally applicable norms, but merely in broad categories that must be concretised in given cases and circumstances to offer any guidance. This then leads to the discussion in section II, where I examine whether and to what extent the lessons learned from this book's evaluation of a specific triangular constitution can be generalised across the Union, notwithstanding the non-universality of interface norms. In brief, the metaconstitution may not be universal, but I suggest that as a basic framework it is *universalisable*, provided we continue to pay close attention to jurisdictional specificity. In so doing, I attempt to lay the foundations for a theory of national and European constitutionalism that is fully committed to the normative ideals of European integration while still paying due respect to the continuing relevance, authority and importance of national constitutional orders, and is appropriately sceptical of the desirability and legitimacy of an entirely vertically integrated, hierarchical conception of the European constitutional space, where any one legal order has ultimate primacy. In these times of trial for constitutionalism at every level in Europe, triangular constitutionalism provides a way through and beyond the antediluvian monisms of national, supra-national or international primacy.

I. THE TRIANGULAR CONSTITUTION ASSESSED

It was noted in chapter one that the idea that constitutionalism and pluralism are irreconcilable is perfectly true if we take the classical, documentary constitutionalism of the State as our sole point of reference for what counts as constitutionality. As an organisation of (still) sovereign states based on (reversibly) conferred powers, the EU could never claim to be constitutional in this sense; and as an international treaty – even one overseen and interpreted by an autonomous international court – the ECHR's claim to constitutionality would be even weaker. However, when we broaden our concept of constitutionalism to include the evolutionary, as I have argued we must, the claims to the constitutional nature of their respective jurisdictions and their respective legal orders

206 *Towards Triangular Constitutionalism*

made by the Court of Justice of the European Union (CJEU) and the European Court of Human Rights (ECtHR) are perfectly plausible. These orders are not constitutional in *exactly the same way* in which the legal orders of Ireland and other European states are, but this is precisely because the two European orders are not states. The evolutionary nature of these non-state constitutional orders is further reflected in the evolutionary nature of the tripartite deliberative polyarchy of which they form two parts. The relationships between Ireland, the EU and the ECHR have changed over time, due to Treaty and constitutional amendment, judicial (re)interpretation of the constitution(s), and legislative changes.

Ireland is a Member State of the EU, and this membership is specifically authorised by a provision of the Irish Constitution, inserted and repeatedly updated by referendum.[1] From within the internal perspective of Irish law, norms of EU law derive their legal force from an Act of the Oireachtas,[2] and these norms are ostensibly immunised from challenge on national constitutional grounds by a constitutional 'exclusion clause'.[3] The widespread orthodoxy is that this exclusion clause has a 'torpedo' effect on the rest of the Constitution, 'whereby [it] destroy[s] the effect of every other provision'.[4] However, it was suggested in chapter two that this interpretation is unprincipled; is at odds with a unanimous decision of the Supreme Court, which has never been reversed;[5] and therefore does not reflect what has actually happened – and should happen – in constitutional practice. It is more principled, more justifiable, and more accurate to regard the exclusion clause as having a 'ripple effect', 'whereby [it] temporarily displace[s], without destroying the effect, of the other provisions'.[6]

Ireland is also a signatory to the ECHR. Not only is the Convention binding on Ireland as a matter of international law, but, since 2003, Convention rights are themselves also enforceable (legislative, sub-constitutional) norms of domestic law,[7] and Irish courts are obliged to take 'due account of the principles laid down' in the jurisprudence of the ECtHR.[8]

The Irish constitutional order is not, therefore, self-contained, but rather intricately linked with the European orders. A vast swathe of what we can properly call *Irish* law (that is, law having effect within Ireland) has its origin outwith the domestic legal order. Moreover, though the Irish High Court, Court of Appeal and Supreme Court retain their interpretive authority over the Irish Constitution, interpretive authority over the other two sources of what we can properly call Irish *constitutional* law rests with the CJEU and the ECtHR.

---

[1] See, now, Arts 29.4.3°–10°.

[2] European Communities Act 1972, as amended.

[3] Art 29.4.6°.

[4] M Cahill, 'Constitutional Exclusion Clauses, Article 29.4.6°, and the Constitutional Reception of European Law' (2011) 18 *Dublin University Law Journal* 74, 90.

[5] *Society for the Protection of Unborn Children v Grogan (No 1)* [1989] IR 753 (*Grogan*).

[6] Cahill (n 4) 90.

[7] European Convention on Human Rights Act 2003.

[8] ibid, s 4.

In short, the Irish legal system does not operate, and cannot be analysed, in isolation.

Similarly, the legal order of the EU cannot be looked at in isolation from its Member States. Regardless of whether we regard EU law as being autochthonous or dependent on national law for its legitimacy, it is on the authorities and institutions – including the courts – of the Member States that the CJEU depends for the actual enforcement of its jurisprudence. This division of labour between the CJEU and national judiciaries occupies a central role in the constitutional development of the Union, as the CJEU has attempted to reconcile its own autonomy and prerogatives with those of the national judiciaries with which it is in a dialogic and symbiotic relationship.

Moreover, the ECHR is a part of the law of the EU (whether imported through the medium of the general principles of Union law[9] or the Charter);[10] the EU is obliged to accede to the ECHR, notwithstanding the delay in this process; and, even without this accession, the CJEU's level of protection of fundamental rights may not fall below that of the ECtHR.[11] Accordingly, the jurisprudence of the ECtHR is of greater normative force within the EU under the Charter than it is within Ireland under the European Convention on Human Rights Act 2003 (ECHR Act 2003).

Finally, the ECtHR has subsidiary and supervisory jurisdiction over all 28 EU Member States, 19 other members of the Council of Europe, and, eventually, the EU itself, whether this is achieved by accession of the EU to the ECHR or by the ECtHR closing the '*Connolly* gap'[12] and adjusting its application of the *Bosphorus*[13] presumption. As the court with supreme interpretive authority over the Convention – which is itself enforceable and of constitutional *significance*, if not *status*, within Ireland and the EU – the ECtHR's judgments form an integral part of the constitutional make-up of both.

Such is the deliberative polyarchy of the triangular constitution. But a fundamental and distinctive feature of this polyarchy is its asymmetry. First, each of the three constitutional sites in the polyarchy partially differs from the others and also partially overlaps: in their nature, structure, origins, functions, and purpose. Secondly, and as a result of this, each order within the polyarchy relates to the others in different ways. The metaconstitutional interface norms posited by Mattias Kumm and Miguel Poiares Maduro are ostensibly universal criteria that can be employed in regulating these relationships. The two sets of interface norms differ among themselves, with Kumm's, for example, being a prescriptive

---

[9] Art 6(3) TEU.

[10] Art 52(3) of the Charter.

[11] Explanations Relating to the Charter of Fundamental Rights [2007] OJ C 303/17 at 303/33.

[12] T Lock, 'The Future of the European Union's Accession to the European Convention on Human Rights after Opinion 2/13: Is it Still Possible and is It Still Desirable?' (2015) 11 *European Constitutional Law Review* 239, 268, referring to *Connolly v 15 Member States of the EU* App no 73274/01 (decision, ECtHR, 9 December 2008).

[13] *Bosphorus Hava Yolları Turizm ve Ticaret Anonim Şirketi v Ireland* [2005] ECHR 440.

208   *Towards Triangular Constitutionalism*

set of substantive criteria, and Maduro's being rather looser sets of epistemic requirements. However, the preceding chapters have seriously called into question their ostensible universality, and it is to this question that we now turn.

A. Interface Norms Within the Triangular Constitution: Universal Categories, Particular Norms

It was noted in chapter one that Kumm's 'cosmopolitan constitutionalism' serves a dual purpose. It provides a set of ostensibly universal metaconstitutional principles that allow us to determine, first, when heterarchy is preferable to hierarchy in the relations between legal orders, and, secondly, how that heterarchy should be structured in those cases where heterarchy is, in fact, preferable.[14] Accordingly, the first – and keystone – of Kumm's metaconstitutional interface norms is the principle of legality, whereby 'national courts should start with a strong presumption that they are required to enforce EU law, national constitutional provisions notwithstanding'.[15] The priority accorded to this principle, and its normative strength, demonstrates the heavily *constitutionalised* nature of Kumm's pluralism, and its structural preference for the stability and certainty of the orthodox account of the primacy of EU law in cases of conflict. However, for all its strength, the principle of legality is not absolute, and is potentially rebuttable through the application of three further interface norms: the principles of subsidiarity, democracy, and the protection of basic rights. Of these three, the principle of subsidiarity is the most tightly embedded in – and therefore most difficult to extricate from – the Member State–EU relationship with reference to which it was developed by Kumm. Moreover, it played no part in any of the instances of interaction and (potential) conflict discussed in this book and will therefore form no part of the discussion to follow. In chapter two, I characterised the principle of democracy (or democratic legitimacy) as a means of protecting national specificity, and this is the title under which it will be analysed here. Similarly, in chapter one, I noted that the principle of the protection of basic rights is essentially a recitation of the *Solange* principle of conditional recognition. Again, this is the nomenclature that will be used below.

B. The Principle of Legality

Though phrased with specific reference to EU law, it is not difficult to generalise the principle of legality to take into account the relationship between the

---

[14] M Kumm, 'Rethinking Constitutional Authority: On the Structure and Limits of Constitutional Pluralism' in M Avbelj and J Komárek (eds), *Constitutional Pluralism in the European Union and Beyond* (Oxford, Hart Publishing, 2012) 65.

[15] M Kumm, 'The Jurisprudence of Constitutional Conflict: Constitutional Supremacy in Europe Before and After the Constitutional Treaty' (2005) 11 *European Law Journal* 262, 299.

The Triangular Constitution Assessed   209

EU and the ECHR. Kumm himself adopts such a generalised version of the principle in his account of *Kadi*,[16] where he sees the principle of legality considered, and departed from, in the CJEU's review of the UN's lack of judicial protection for those subject to sanctions regimes mandated by the Security Council.[17] The evidence adduced in the preceding chapters allows us to draw two major conclusions regarding the principle of legality as an ostensibly universal metaconstitutional interface norm. First, it *is*, in fact, capable of universal application. But, secondly, this is only because at the level of application, it is *not*, in fact, *meta*constitutional at all. These seemingly but not contradictory conclusions must be explained in greater detail.

None of the cases of actual and potential conflict considered in this book were instances of open rebellion on the part of the Irish or EU courts with respect to the law of the Union or the Convention, along the lines of the Czech Constitutional Court's *Holubec* decision[18] (or at least how that decision was initially received and interpreted).[19] Quite the contrary: in each case, the courts were careful to stress the weight that must be attached to the norms of the more encompassing system as a preliminary matter, quite aside from whether these norms were ultimately to be followed, departed from, or such a departure threatened. But importantly, when we find the principle of legality being applied by the Irish courts with respect to the EU or the ECHR, this is only because *it is a norm specifically commanded by the Irish legal system*. In the case of the Irish–EU relationship, the principle of legality finds legislative expression in section 2 of the European Communities Act 1972 (ECA 1972):

> From the 1st day of January, 1973, the treaties governing the European Communities and the existing and future acts adopted by the institutions of those Communities shall be binding on the State and shall be part of the domestic law thereof under the conditions laid down in those treaties.

Sections 2 and 3 of the ECHR Act 2003 perform a similar function in the Irish–ECHR relationship, requiring courts to interpret the law in accordance with the Convention 'in so far as possible', and requiring organs of the State to perform their functions in a Convention-compatible manner. With respect to the EU and the ECHR, the Convention is nowadays part and parcel of EU law at a constitutional level, whether through Article 6(3) TEU or Article 52(3) of the Charter.

The principle of legality, therefore, rather than being an external, freestanding constitutional-norm-about-constitutional-norms, is better regarded as being

---

[16] Joined Cases C-402/05 P and C-415/05 P *Kadi and Al Barakaat v Council and Commission* ECLI:EU:C:2008:461, [2008] ECR I-6351.

[17] Kumm, 'Rethinking Constitutional Authority' (n 14) 62–63.

[18] Judgment of 31 January 2012, Pl ÚS 5/12, *Slovak Pensions XVII (Holubec)*.

[19] See the reassessment of the *Holubec* and *Landtová* decisions in M Bobek, '*Landtová, Holubec*, and the Problem of an Uncooperative Court: Implications for the Preliminary Rulings Procedure' (2014) 10 *European Journal of Constitutional Law* 54, discussed at section II.B below.

210   Towards Triangular Constitutionalism

merely the generalised and delocalised expression of the particular legislative or constitutional mandate by which the norms of a more encompassing legal order become applicable within a less encompassing order. The precise nature and normative strength of this applicability will necessarily vary from order to order, particularly given the asymmetry of the polyarchy adverted to above. This then poses a further difficulty for the principle's ostensible universality: the principle of legality is a *rebuttable* presumption and, for Kumm, the criteria justifying its rebuttal are 'countervailing concerns of sufficient weight that suggest [that the more encompassing norm should not be applied]'.[20] But whether the 'countervailing concerns' are of 'sufficient weight' or not will again differ according to jurisdictional circumstance. In the case of EU law in Ireland, the interpretation one gives to Article 29.4.6° – 'torpedo' or 'ripple' – will be determinative. If the 'exclusion clause' really does have a 'torpedo' effect on the rest of the Constitution, then the principle of legality expressed in the ECA 1972 is not, in fact, rebuttable, but definitive. As we have seen, in *Grogan* – the sole decided case where the matter came to a head – the Irish Supreme Court opted for a 'ripple' interpretation, signalling its (potential) refusal to subordinate the Constitution's protection of the right to life of the 'unborn' to the 'exclusion clause', and, through the 'exclusion clause', to the requirements of EU free movement law.

The Irish courts have never refused to follow the jurisprudence of the ECtHR since the coming into force of the ECHR Act 2003, but that Act's incorporation of the Convention 'subject to the Constitution', its requirement for the courts merely to take 'due account' of Strasbourg jurisprudence, and its requirement that the law be interpreted in accordance with the Convention only 'in so far as possible' leave open the possibility of disagreement, and thus the rebuttal of the principle of legality. But as with EU law in *Grogan*, in such a case, the criteria establishing what constitutes a 'countervailing concern' of 'sufficient weight' will be criteria *internal* to Irish constitutional law, and not the freestanding exceptions – democratic legitimacy, fundamental rights – posited by Kumm.

There is one area where the application of the principle of legality in a properly *meta*constitutional sense is evident: the CJEU's case law with respect to the Convention. However, this only held true prior to the elevation of the Charter to the status of primary EU law. The presumption that ECtHR jurisprudence should be followed – evident in the CJEU's reversal of its *Hoechst*[21] and *Orkem*[22] jurisprudence in the light of subsequent developments at Strasbourg[23] – did not, at that stage in the development of the EU–ECHR relationship, arise from primary

---

[20] Kumm, 'Rethinking Constitutional Authority' (n 14) 65.

[21] Joined Cases 46/87 and 227/88 *Hoechst v Commission* ECLI:EU:C:1989:337, [1989] ECR 2859.

[22] Case 374/87 *Orkem v Commission* ECLI:EU:C:1989:387, [1989] ECR 3283.

[23] Case C-94/00 *Roquette Frères SA v DGCCRF* ECLI:EU:C:2002:603, [2002] ECR I-9011, following *Niemitz v Germany* (1992) 16 EHRR 97 and *Société Colas Est v France* (2004) 39 EHRR 373, reversing *Hoechst* (n 21); Joined Cases C-238/99 P, C-244/99 P, C-245/99 P, C-247/99 P, C-250/99 P to C-252/99 P and C-254/99 P *Limburgse Vinyl Maatschappij NV and Others v Commission* ECLI:EU:C:2002:582, [2002] ECR I-8375, following *Funke v France* (1993) 16 EHRR 297, reversing *Orkem* (n 22).

The Triangular Constitution Assessed 211

EU law, but rather from the CJEU's own metaconstitutional jurisprudence on the relations between the orders, specifically the 'inspiration; guidelines; special significance' formula. Despite the cogency of de Witte's argument that Article 6(3) TEU specifically imports the norms of the Convention as general principles of EU law,[24] this interpretation has only recently – and partially – made its way into the CJEU's judgments. The closest that the CJEU has come to disagreement with the ECtHR as to the requirements of the Convention is with respect to the compatibility of its procedures and the role of the Advocates General with Article 6 ECHR, an issue which was again resolved prior to the elevation of the Charter to Treaty status. In *Kaba II*,[25] though Advocate General Ruiz-Jarabo Colomer's Opinion had expressed serious concerns regarding the cogency of the relevant ECtHR case law in a manner redolent of Kumm's criteria justifying rebuttal of the presumption of legality,[26] the CJEU did not engage with this reasoning, and instead avoided outright conflict (but maintained its possibility) by deciding the case on different grounds. The ECtHR subsequently defused the potential conflict between the orders through the application of the *Bosphorus*[27] presumption of equivalent protection in *Kokkelvisserij*.[28]

Following the elevation of the Charter to Treaty status, the principle of legality with respect to the relationship between EU and ECHR law is no longer metaconstitutional in nature, but is rather the logical result of the Charter's own provisions regarding the status of the Convention and Strasbourg jurisprudence in EU law. This alteration to the terms of engagement between the two European orders may yet have important repercussions for the manner in which the current disconnect between the jurisprudence of the CJEU and the ECtHR on labour rights is resolved. However, as was made clear in chapter three, the resolution of this conflict could take a number of forms, and may yet be further influenced by the EU's accession to the ECHR. What is clear, however, is that whether rebutted or not, the principle that the CJEU should apply the law of the Convention and the jurisprudence of the ECHR, notwithstanding its own prior, conflicting articulation of the requirements of the Convention and of EU law, will derive from the primary law of the EU, and not from a freestanding metaconstitutional principle.

Taken together, all this implies that Kumm's metaconstitutional principle of legality *is in fact capable of universal application*, but only because it is a

---

[24] B de Witte, 'The Use of the ECHR and Convention Case Law by the European Court of Justice' in P Popelier, C Van de Heyning and P Van Nuffel (eds), *Human Rights Protection in the European Legal Order: The Interaction Between the European and National Courts* (Cambridge, Intersentia 2011) 19–24.

[25] Case C-466/00 *Arben Kaba v Secretary of State for the Home Department (Kaba II)* ECLI:EU:C:2003:127, [2003] ECR I-2219.

[26] Case C-466/00 *Arben Kaba v Secretary of State for the Home Department (Kaba II)* (Opinion) ECLI:EU:C:2002:447, [2003] ECR I-2219, para 105.

[27] *Bosphorus Hava Yolları Turizm ve Ticaret Anonim Şirketi v Ireland* (n 13).

[28] *Cooperatieve Producentenorganisatie van de Nederlandse Kokkelvisserij UA v the Netherlands* App no 13645/05 (decision, ECtHR, 20 January 2009).

212   Towards Triangular Constitutionalism

generalised statement of *what is already the law*. This universal applicability is therefore *at the expense of what makes the principle metaconstitutional*. The CJEU's obligation to provide a standard of protection of Convention rights at least equivalent to that of the ECtHR is an obligation imposed by the terms of primary EU law itself. Similarly, each Member State of the EU has its own jurisdictionally specific means by which norms of EU law and the Convention become effective within the legal order. In the particular case of Ireland, this is achieved by legislation, strengthened in the case of EU law by a constitutional 'exclusion clause', however we interpret it. As a result, neither the substantive presumption of legality, nor the (possible, differing) means by which that presumption might be rebutted, is external or freestanding in nature. Rather, they are historically contingent and intimately connected with jurisdictional circumstance. Kumm's principle of legality is therefore caught in a trap: when viewed as universally applicable, it is not in fact metaconstitutional. When viewed as metaconstitutional, it is too general and abstract in its statement and requirements to be universally applicable. This problem with the first and keystone of Kumm's interface norms then filters down through the others, as we shall now see.

C. The Protection of National Specificity

In elaborating what he describes as the principle of democracy or democratic legitimacy, Kumm states that:

> Given the persistence of the democratic deficit on the European level ... national courts continue to have good reasons to set aside EU Law *when it violates clear and specific constitutional norms that reflect essential commitments of the national community.*[29]

The attempt to generalise this interface norm so that it might be applied also to the relationship between the EU and the ECHR is rather more difficult than was the case with the principle of legality, but it is not impossible. As was suggested in chapter three, concern for national specificity in the Member State–EU relationship has parallels on the EU–ECHR side of the triangle with concern for the autonomy, uniformity and specificity of Union law as a specifically non-state legal system. Though this concern may be justified on many grounds, democracy is almost certainly not one of them, for precisely the reasons of democratic deficit identified by Kumm. However, this is not necessarily fatal for the potential universal applicability of the principle, provided that we recast it in these specific circumstances as a method of protecting specifically '*post*national specificity'.

In this regard, the CJEU's filtering of the Convention through its (metaconstitutional) 'inspiration; guidelines; special significance' formula allowed room for

---

[29] Kumm, 'The Jurisprudence of Constitutional Conflict' (n 15) 300, footnote omitted, emphasis in original.

The Triangular Constitution Assessed   213

manoeuvre in a potential case where a provision of the Convention or its interpretation by the ECtHR might strike at the heart of the EU legal order. However,
until Opinion 2/13, concern for the specificity of the EU found its strongest
expression not in the jurisprudence of the CJEU, but rather in the jurisprudence
of the ECtHR. The *Bosphorus* presumption of equivalent protection (itself an
application of the principle of conditional recognition, to be discussed below
in section I.D) is the means by which the ECtHR operationalises its concern for
EU specificity prior to EU accession. The sheer strength of this presumption
is demonstrated by the highly deferential approach of the ECtHR to matters
of EU law in applying the presumption in *Kokkelvisserij*. While this presumption
of equivalence was to be lifted upon EU accession to the Convention, the terms of
the Accession Agreement tried to accommodate the autonomy and specificity
of EU law – though arguably to a lesser extent, and to an extent that the CJEU
found to be deficient in Opinion 2/13. The co-respondent mechanism tried to
absolve the ECtHR of the need to apportion responsibility for breaches of the
Convention between the Member States and the EU, and thus effectively decide
questions of substantive EU law, leaving this instead to be worked out within
the Union. The 'prior involvement' mechanism sought to ensure that the CJEU
would first have the opportunity to remedy breaches of the Convention, or to (re)
interpret EU law in accordance with the Convention. However, in its rejection
of the Accession Agreement as incompatible with the Treaties, the CJEU found
both mechanisms to be insufficiently protective of the autonomy and specificity of EU law, for reasons ranging from the entirely justifiable to the arguably
solipsistic and recalcitrant. Therefore, while it is not theoretically impossible
to generalise the principle of the protection of 'postnational specificity' so that
it can encompass the relationship between the EU and the ECHR, the evidence
suggests that it may be unnecessary to do so: the ECtHR's application of the
(metaconstitutional) principle of conditional recognition already provides for
such protection, and this protection would shift from the metaconstitutional and
jurisprudential to the constitutional and institutional following successful ratification of a future Accession Agreement, should it pass muster at Luxembourg.

Generalising the principle to the relationship between Ireland and the ECHR
is less difficult, but as was the case with the principle of legality, Kumm's principle of democracy attempts to serve a purpose that is in fact already served
by domestic law and practice. The sub-constitutional status of the Convention
in Irish law not only permits but also obliges the domestic judiciary to prefer
constitutional norms to those of the Convention in cases of conflict. As the
case of *Foy (No 2)*[30] demonstrates, where developments in ECtHR jurisprudence render previously compatible Irish law or practice now incompatible
with the Convention's requirements, the domestic law or practice can be – and

---

[30] *Foy v an t-Árd Chláraitheoir (No 2)* [2007] IEHC 470.

214 *Towards Triangular Constitutionalism*

will be – remedied judicially, provided that this is possible within the terms of the Constitution. Where such judicial remedy is impermissible, three possibilities arise. First, the legislature can amend the law, as eventually happened following the adverse judgment with respect to C in *A, B & C v Ireland*.[31] Secondly, the Constitution can be amended by referendum, as happened with the adoption of the Fourteenth Amendment following the adverse judgment in *Open Door v Ireland*.[32] Thirdly, the incompatibility between Irish law and the ECHR might simply continue unresolved, leaving Ireland in breach of its international obligations and subject to the Council of Europe's diplomatic enforcement (or, better, 'monitoring') mechanisms. This would have been the case had the Fourteenth Amendment been rejected by the electorate, and would almost certainly have been the case if the dissenting minority of the Grand Chamber with respect to A and B in *A, B & C* had, in fact, been in the majority. But in each of these three cases, the domestic judiciary has no need of a *metaconstitutional* principle justifying the rebuttal of the (legislative) presumption of legality: its own domestic terms of reference not only permit but oblige such a rebuttal where conflict between the orders cannot be resolved judicially, whether this is on grounds of democratic legitimacy, national specificity, both, or neither.

With respect to the Irish–EU relationship, matters are more complex, but no more promising for the ostensible universality of the interface norm. First, by focusing his interface norm of democratic legitimacy on issues of national specificity, Kumm elides two separate, though related, issues into one. In imposing the requirement, in *Crotty*,[33] that any Treaty amendment which would alter the 'scope and objectives'[34] of the Union be put to a further referendum, the Supreme Court was clearly concerned with democratic legitimacy, but *not* with national specificity. Though the Irish Constitution's precise provisions regarding the locus of constituent power and the means by which the Constitution may be amended are specific to that state, there is nothing nationally specific about the idea of popular sovereignty.

Secondly, even on the abortion issue – where democratic legitimacy and national specificity *did* overlap – the way in which the issue came to a head and the way in which the Supreme Court phrased and structured its decision in *Grogan* bear little resemblance to the interface norm as Kumm presents it, despite the fact that the Irish constitutional provision on the right to life of the 'unborn' specifically informed Kumm's development of the principle, and despite the further fact that this development post-dated the decision in *Grogan*. The orthodox, 'torpedo' interpretation of Article 29.4.6° would have rendered the presumption of legality absolute, and no interface norm would justify its rebuttal. But by holding fast to its obligation to uphold and vindicate

---

[31] *A, B & C v Ireland* (2010) 53 EHRR 13.
[32] *Open Door and Dublin Well Woman v Ireland* (1992) 15 EHRR 244.
[33] *Crotty v An Taoiseach* [1987] IR 713.
[34] ibid 767 (Finlay CJ).

The Triangular Constitution Assessed   215

constitutional rights, even in the face of a conflicting constitutional norm which seemed to exempt EU law from the requirement of compatibility with these rights, the Supreme Court in *Grogan* was *not disapplying EU law*, but rather *indicating the possibility* – but no more than this – that it *might* do so. Though the particular constitutional norm that the Supreme Court sought to insulate from the potential rigours of EU free movement law – Article 40.3.3°'s protection of the right to life of the 'unborn' – *is* an example of national specificity, it is the *fundamentality* of the right, rather than the specificity of its formulation, which motivated the Court: if the constitutional norm at issue had been nationally specific but had also been capable of being limited in certain circumstances, the Supreme Court's approach may well had been less assertive. Being a constitutionally guaranteed *absolute* right, it 'must be fully and effectively protected by the courts'.[35] Moreover:

> [I]t cannot be one of the objectives of the European Communities that a member state should be obliged to permit activities which are clearly designed to set at nought the constitutional guarantees for the protection within the State of a fundamental human right.[36]

Seen in the light of *Crotty* and *Grogan*, Kumm's interface norm of democracy, rather than being a universally applicable, a priori metaconstitutional principle, is instead cast as a somewhat inaccurate ex post rationalisation of difficult circumstance, which not only confuses two separate issues – democratic legitimacy and national specificity – but also cannot account for historical constitutional practice.

As was the case with the ECtHR's *Bosphorus* presumption with respect to EU law, it is also the case that the CJEU's jurisprudence is in fact capable of taking national specificity into account and reconciling its exigencies with those of Union law, particularly since the coming into force of Article 4(2) TEU. The divergence between the judgment of the CJEU and the Opinion of the Advocate General in *Grogan* (CJEU)[37] predated *Omega*,[38] *Sayn-Wittgenstein*[39] and *Runevič-Vardyn*[40] and illustrates the advantages for both legal orders of the latter approach. Advocate General van Gerven had considered that the restriction of information at issue fell within the scope of Union law, but that the restriction was justified because its objective qualified as an imperative requirement of

---

[35] *Grogan* (n 5) 764–65.
[36] ibid 769.
[37] Case C-159/90 *SPUC (Ireland) v Grogan* ECLI:EU:C:1991:249, [1991] ECR I-4685 (*Grogan* (CJEU, Opinion)).
[38] Case C-36/02 *Omega Spielhallen- und Automatenaufstellungs-GmbH v Oberbürgermeisterin der Bundesstadt Bonn* ECLI:EU:C:2004:614, [2004] ECR I-9609.
[39] Case C-208/09 *Ilonka Sayn-Wittgenstein v Landeshauptmann von Wien* ECLI:EU:C:2010:806, [2010] ECR I-13693.
[40] Case C-391/09 *Malgožata Runevič-Vardyn and Łukasz Paweł Wardyn v Vilniaus Miesto Savivaldybės Administracija* ECLI:EU:C:2011:291, [2011] ECR I-3787.

216 *Towards Triangular Constitutionalism*

public interest within the meaning of Union law.[41] However, the CJEU went on to avoid the issue altogether by holding that the 'tenuous' link between the Irish students' unions and the English abortion providers took matters outside the scope of Union law.[42] While clearly motivated by a desire to avoid precipitating constitutional conflict, this decision rode roughshod over the Court's previous jurisprudence on potential restrictions on freedom of movement, a consequence that could have been avoided by the adoption of the Advocate General's rather more nuanced approach. The CJEU subsequently developed precisely such an approach: though the effective and uniform application of EU law is of foundational importance to the CJEU's jurisprudence, it is going too far to argue that it is *the* most important constitutional norm in Europe. AG van Gerven's Opinion in *Grogan* (CJEU) and the subsequent judgments following *Omega* illustrate the CJEU's recognition of this fact. Certainly, in attempting to reconcile national specificity with the requirements of the Treaties, the CJEU will not always get it 'right' from a national perspective – as the reaction to *Viking*[43] and *Laval*[44] demonstrates – but the point is that rather than being the sole responsibility of national courts, reconciling national specificity with EU law is now, like so much else in EU law, a shared enterprise between the national and Union judiciaries. Such a vision of relations between legal orders leaves little room for the universal applicability of Kumm's principle of democracy.

D. The Principle of Conditional Recognition

The last of Kumm's metaconstitutional interface norms is the protection of fundamental rights, by which he means that the principle of legality can be rebutted if the enforcement of a norm of EU law would violate a basic right guaranteed by a Member State constitution.[45] However, if 'the guarantees afforded by the EU amount to structurally equivalent protections, then there is no more space for national courts to substitute the EU's judgment on the rights issue with their own'.[46] The principle is therefore essentially a recitation of the *Solange* principle of conditional recognition. Whereas Kumm posits the principle as a substantive interface norm that can be applied in order to protect fundamental rights, Charles Sabel's and Oliver Gerstenberg's conception is less prescriptive and somewhat more subtle. Though their 'coordinate constitutionalism' is a species of metaconstitutional pluralism, Sabel and Gerstenberg

---

[41] *Grogan* (CJEU, Opinion) (n 37) para 26.

[42] Case C-159/90 *SPUC (Ireland) v Grogan* ECLI:EU:C:1991:378, [1991] ECR I-4685, para 24.

[43] Case C-438/05 *ITWF & FSU v Viking Line* ECLI:EU:C:2007:772, [2007] ECR I-10779.

[44] Case C-341/05 *Laval un Partneri v Svenska Byggnadsarbetareförbundet* ECLI:EU:C:2007:809, [2007] ECR I-11767.

[45] Kumm, 'The Jurisprudence of Constitutional Conflict' (n 15) 294.

[46] ibid 299.

expressly discount the possibility of substantive interface norms being posited in the abstract.[47] Rather than being a substantive norm, the principle of conditional recognition on this account is a *jurisgenerative mechanism*, allowing for the dialogic articulation, re-articulation and adjustment of requirements and perspectives in a deliberative polyarchy. In light of the evidence adduced in this thesis, Sabel and Gerstenberg's conception of the principle is to be preferred, but is itself not without difficulty.

The major problem with conceiving of the principle of conditional recognition as a freestanding metaconstitutional interface norm capable of universal application is that it begs the most important question: *conditional on what?* The answer 'conditional on the protection of fundamental rights' only begs the question further, because, given the asymmetries of the triangular constitution and the only partially overlapping nature of their conceptions and articulations of fundamental rights, what one order regards as sufficiently fundamental to justify the withholding of legal recognition may not arouse similar concerns in another order, even one situated similarly in the polyarchy.

Though the principle is capable of being phrased or posited in the abstract, it is devoid of meaningful content at this stage and offers us no guidance in the resolution of conflict. It is only when the principle is concretised in a particular case that it becomes capable of fulfilling the role of an interface norm, but – as was the case with the principle of legality – this can only come at the expense of the principle's metaconstitutionality. The problem is therefore one of epistemology, and brings us back to chapter one's camp fire metaphor: it is only from an epistemic vantage point situated *within* a constitutional order, looking out, that the principle becomes meaningful. Kumm partially recognises this problem in his admission that the weakness of the claim to universality 'lies in the fact that it does not guarantee that the results [the application of an interface norm] leads to will be the same in every legal order'.[48] However, this is much more than a weakness of the claim. Rather, it is fatal to it. Consider the application of the principle of conditional recognition by the Irish Supreme Court in *Crotty*. The 'scope and objectives' test is one that is particularly within the interpretive domain of the Irish courts, and any Treaty amendment which broadened the 'scope and objectives' of the Union would require popular authorisation by referendum. But this is only because of the specific nature and provisions of the Irish Constitution: in another jurisdiction, other methods of Treaty ratification – usually parliamentary – might suffice. Similarly, in *Grogan*, the effect of the judgment was to hold open the possibility of the loyal application of Luxembourg jurisprudence so long as that jurisprudence does not 'set at nought the constitutional guarantees for the protection within the State of a

---

[47] CF Sabel and O Gerstenberg, 'Constitutionalising an Overlapping Consensus: The ECJ and the Emergence of a Coordinate Constitutional Order' (2010) 16 *European Law Journal* 511, 550.
[48] Kumm, 'The Jurisprudence of Constitutional Conflict' (n 15) 300.

218   *Towards Triangular Constitutionalism*

fundamental human right'.[49] A statement such as this is only *meta*constitutional in the very thin sense that it concerns the relationships between legal orders. It is substantively situated within the constitutional order and, accordingly, its frame of reference is limited to that order.

The same problem presents itself in the 'horizontal' frame: the ECtHR's *Bosphorus* presumption, though an application of an ostensibly universal principle, is necessarily specific to the particular – unique – relationship it has with the CJEU. It is the means by which the ECtHR reconciles the triply conflicting requirements of maintaining its own interpretive authority over the Convention, respecting the autonomy of EU law, and still ensuring that the Convention rights continue to be guaranteed in the face of EU action. The doctrine of the margin of appreciation, as applied by the majority judgment in *A, B & C*, sees the principle applied in reverse: the ECtHR reconciling state autonomy with the requirements of the Convention by means of a conditional, supervised, temporally contingent leeway. In both cases, the substantive principles being applied – the presumption of equivalence or the margin of appreciation – are much more than the mere application of a universal metaconstitutional interface norm. Instead, they are substantive doctrines in their own right, with their own specific case law, based within the epistemic confines of the Convention.

Accordingly, we can well regard the principle of conditional recognition as a jurisgenerative *mechanism* in Sabel and Gerstenberg's sense, a framework the particular application of which will differ depending on jurisdiction, subject matter and much else. What we cannot do is posit it in the abstract, as a universally applicable norm-about-constitutional-norms, because when stated so generally, the principle is stripped of the action-guiding potential that it only acquires at the level of site-specific application.

In light of the evidence presented, we must conclude that none of Kumm's interface norms are in fact universal. It is perfectly permissible and possible to posit broad, freestanding *categories* into which the various norms applied in regulating the relationships between legal orders in a polyarchy may fall. Such taxonomies are important and useful in helping us to analyse these inter-order relationships. However, the fundamental problem is that these categories are just that: categories, rather than substantive action-guiding rules or principles. For the actual rules or principles that regulate the relationships between legal orders – the substantive interface norms at work – we must sit around the camp fire, assuming a viewpoint internal to the legal system in question, and take into account its own constitutional text and its own particular *telos*. But when we do this, the norms cease to be metaconstitutional, and are so far evolved from their abstract description that they are incapable of universal application. When we retreat to the forest, zooming back out of a particular legal order, and attempt

---

[49] *Grogan* (n 5) 769.

to metaconstitutionalise the particular constitutional interface norms at work, we lose precisely what it was that made those norms useful in the first place, and are left back with mere categories, not norms.

II. FROM THE PARTICULAR TO THE UNIVERSAL

The above analysis has clarified the inherent and ever present tension between the particular and the universal in European constitutionalism. The specific ways in which the Irish, EU and ECHR legal orders combine into a holistic constitutional polyarchy has been shown to be jurisdictionally contingent and highly context sensitive. The temptation may therefore be to conclude, as far as the particular is concerned, that the triangular constitution might be an apt framework for understanding the constitutional configuration in the far northwestern corner of the Union, but is of little relevance elsewhere. Similarly, as regards the universal, it may seem that any kind of metaconstitutional pluralism, no matter how attractive at a theoretical level, falls apart at the level of application. However, let us recall the reiterative universalism of Michael Walzer, described by Neil Walker as 'a continuous and progressive process of recontextualization in which the universal is not just realized by also reshaped by the particular'.[50] This section seeks to illustrate what the particular experiences of constitutional interaction and integration outlined in the preceding chapters may tell us about the nature of European constitutionalism in the present day, across the Union. Equipped with the evidence presented throughout this book, we can return to metaconstitutional pluralism at the theoretical level, and better equip it to account for the vagaries of jurisdictional and temporal specificity, enabling its application throughout the Union.

Let us begin by departicularising the triangular constitution as it has been presented throughout this book, stripping it of all reference to the specifics of any one Member State. When we adopt the broadest, evolutionary, discursive and socio-political conception of constitutionalism outlined in chapter one, 'the constitution' in each Member State consists of the national constitution, the law of the Treaties, and the law of the Convention, taken together both on their own individual terms and in their relations with one another. Each of these constitutional parts of the constitutional whole have their own claims to normative authority and legitimacy. For all the development and importance of the non-state and supra-state legal orders, it is an observable reality that the domestic constitutional order remains the primary locus of political and legal discourse within each state, and the primary repository of citizens' loyalties and feelings

---

[50] N Walker, 'The Idea of Constitutional Pluralism' (2002) 65 *Modern Law Review* 317, 380, citing M Walzer, 'Nations and Universe' in D Miller (ed), *Thinking Politically: Essays in Political Theory* (New Haven, CT, Yale University Press, 2007).

220 Towards Triangular Constitutionalism

of group identity and commonality within the polity.[51] Whatever we wish to call it, this constitutional loyalty, or patriotism, or identity, must be taken seriously and not immediately dismissed as mere chauvinism or xenophobia. It certainly can (and should) be so dismissed in certain circumstances, and part of the task of triangular constitutionalism is to provide a normative framework by which we can determine these circumstances. But whether it was developed over centuries as a series of gradual victories over the whims of monarchs and various elites, or was enacted in the aftermath of the collapse of an authoritarian order or the overthrow of an imperial power, there is nothing *inherently* unsound in national constitutionalism, and quite a bit that is entirely sound: a fact recognised by the language of the Treaties and of the CJEU themselves, whether in Article 4(2) TEU's requirement of respect for the national identities and fundamental political and constitutional structures of the Member States, or the CJEU's consistent restatement of the inspiration it draws from the constitutional traditions common to the Member States. But the dangers of the valorisation of the nation, its identity, its traditions and its distinctiveness are all too well known: it is precisely to minimise these dangers, in differing ways, that the Union and the Convention were created in the first place. The two European legal orders are voluntary limitations on the authority of the national orders: normative systems which supplement the national systems, without supplanting them entirely. The Union's claim to normative authority rests on the voluntary accession of each Member State; each State's acceptance and implementation of Union law as part of the domestic legal system; and the values and aims expressed in the Treaties, which are no more or less merely theoretical than those expressed by national constitutions. Similarly, the Convention's claim rests on its voluntary and mutual nature, the promise each Contracting Party has made to each other, and the common system of adjudication that they have set up between themselves to see that these promises are kept. But the European orders are incomplete systems of normative authority, and, as was the case with national constitutionalism, also suffer from certain defects, whether in terms of their relative 'distance' from the citizen; comparative lack of democratic accountability; or possible tendency, which they share with the states, to regard their own perspective and approach as the only one. It is in the nature of institutions, and, by extension, institutional orders, that they will seek to preserve their own authority, and, if possible, extend it.

Triangular constitutionalism, therefore, refuses *as a matter of principle* to regard any one of the vertices of the constitution as supreme. There is no entirely insuperable, a priori reason why any one legal order should prevail in cases of conflict: at least not when the triangle is viewed from an external perspective. When we zoom in to any one order, the logic of that order (depending on the

---

[51] This is to say nothing of the vagaries of schemes of federalism or regionalism or devolution within individual Member States: my analysis here stops at the state level.

specifics of that order) *may* require us to accept its final say, but this is only true internally, and even then only as a truly last resort. But triangular constitutionalism does not itself in the abstract provide a comprehensive framework for the resolution of conflict. It does not because it cannot: the individual orders will vary so greatly in their own internal conflict rules, and the individual events of conflict will vary so greatly in their circumstances, reasons and context, that no toolkit of overarching, hard-and-fast rules can be supplied. Rather, the approach of triangular constitutionalism is every bit as evolutionary as the concept of constitutionalism on which it is built: it is only by analysis of the events, outcomes, agreements, disagreements and resolutions *themselves* that we can determine the proper result, and this only *after the fact*. Triangular constitutionalism, like constitutionalism before it and indeed like the concept of law itself, is temporally open-ended. There is no *finalité*, no point at which we can declare the task complete and expect matters to rest thus for all time coming. Once we acknowledge this, we can acknowledge that any 'final' say is only ever final in a relative sense, subject to short-, medium- or long-term contestation, reinterpretation, or reversal. This is not to say that we are entirely at a loss: there is a large common 'bank' of shared principles we can use in avoiding, guiding and resolving conflict, and, given the evolutionary nature of the discourse and framework, the accumulation of experience and precedents will provide an ever-growing 'bank' on which to draw for further guidance. Moreover, the triangular conception of constitutionalism is intended itself to have an integrative effect on all the individual legal orders. In the case of the national orders, both the popular and elite discourse, whether sceptical of or enthusiastic about 'Europe', tends to see European integration as something bolted on to the national constitution, rather than something baked in. In the case of the European orders, something similar could be said about the CJEU's 'othering' of the ECHR in Opinion 2/13, where it regarded the Convention machinery as something external to the legal order, rather than something – both before and after accession – deeply embedded within it. The looser nature of the Convention order and the explicitly subsidiary nature of the ECtHR's jurisdiction makes that order less prone to this solipsism, but even in Strasbourg we have seen examples of a privileging of uniformity over justifiability, as in the jurisprudence on the 'doctrine of appearances' and the role of the CJEU's Advocates General, or in the minority dissent in *A, B & C v Ireland*. A triangular conception of the arrangement encourages constant recognition of the incompleteness of any one point of the triangle, and internalises the mutuality and symbiosis of the legal orders.

Triangular constitutionalism therefore attempts, in the first place, to wean constitutional thought off the solipsism that imagines that particular legal orders in Europe can be thought of and engaged with in isolation, cut off from the counterparts with which they are embedded. Secondly, it seeks to provide a theoretically sound framework for the application of constitutional pluralist thought *within* a given legal order, rather than only from an unmoored and freestanding epistemic perspective. Finally, it offers an account of the interactions

222 *Towards Triangular Constitutionalism*

between legal orders in Europe that does not depend only on isolated cases of conflict between powerful actors (though these can be important), but also on the daily workings of constitutionalism, at the periphery as much as at the centre.

This, then, is triangular constitutionalism in its most abstract form, ready for adaptation to the specificities of any one Member State and its relations with the European legal orders. But there still remain the objections noted in chapter one: the legitimation of dissent from the primacy of EU law threatens the rule of law; and the problems of trying to particularise a universal conception of relations between the legal orders. Equipped with the evidence adduced in chapters two, three and four, let us engage with these objections afresh.

A. The Rule of Law in Dangerous Times

We saw, in chapter one, the objection that constitutional pluralism, by contemplating even the possibility, let alone the legitimacy, of national courts disapplying norms of EU law, undermined legal certainty, stability and integrity: in short, the rule of law itself. However, the empirical evidence of chapters two, three and four suggest that this concern is overstated in its insistence that any real or even potential deviation from the CJEU's primacy principle is always, in every circumstance, detrimental to the integrity of the European legal order. Certainty and stability are core components of legal integrity, but they are not the only ones: countervailing principles exist, most notably justifiability and democratic legitimacy, which may, in certain circumstances, trump the important but not absolute ideal of certainty. The Irish Supreme Court's warning to the CJEU in *Grogan* and the ongoing disconnect between the CJEU and the ECtHR's conception of the consequences of the right to strike both undermine(d) the coherence and certainty of the law in their respective areas, but the potentially deleterious effects of these disconnects must be taken in their specific contexts; relativised by the strength of competing concerns; and not become subject to overreaction. Even in the context of a clear and explicit disconnect between legal orders, matters can (and should) be remedied by legal or political means, as evidenced by the amendment of the Irish Constitution guaranteeing the right to travel, notwithstanding Article 40.3.3°'s other provisions. It is undoubtedly true that a shared constitutional order of almost 30 Member States requires a high level of consistency and uniformity, but this level must of necessity differ from that possible in a Union of six, nine, 12 or 15 Member States, for both practical and normative reasons. In practical terms, the diversity of polities and jurisdictions in Europe makes absolute consistency a goal which we can only ever fail to achieve, unless we are to give up on the European project as it has developed to date and embrace a truly integrated, explicitly federalised Union state. This then leads to the normative reason: European integration within the Union as it currently exists is an explicitly *non*-totalising project, aiming for 'ever closer union between the peoples of Europe' (which itself is subject to a range of interpretations) over an indefinite, ideally permanent period, in which the Member States maintain their independence and sovereignty from the perspective of public international law. To create the kind of super-state in which absolute uniformity might (and only might) be possible would be to merely recreate, this time at a level further abstracted from the citizenry, the exact same constitutional structures which, at state level, are subject to the 'unprecedented range and intensity of attack' noted by Walker.[52] Unless and until the current Union is replaced with a vertically integrated federal pan-European state, for the Union legal system to be able to accommodate certain non-ideal but tolerable deviations and disconnects in the short term, at least, would be a sign of its commitment to *overall* consistency and integrity, and its focus on the long-term goals of integration, rather than the short-term goal of absolute consistency. There is a certain legal and constitutional fetishism at work in the assumption that any and every conflict between constitutional orders in a constitutional polyarchy must *necessarily* pose an existential threat to the integrity of the combined legal order: an assumption that is not borne out by the evidence presented here.

Moreover, stability, certainty and integrity are only some of the aspects of the rule of law. There are also the thicker and more concrete requirements of institutional independence and interdependence within the constitutional order; the observance of substantive democratic norms; and the protection of human rights.[53] It is on this ground that Daniel Keleman mounts a recent attack, writing that:

> The inherent dangers of constitutional pluralism and its unsustainability as an approach to resolving conflicts over supremacy were somewhat obscured while the [BVerfG] and the handful of others who challenged the supremacy of European law practiced self-restraint and sincere cooperation. But those days are gone, and today we are seeing increasing signs of 'rebelliousness' among national constitutional courts.[54]

But self-restraint and sincere cooperation are not optional extras. They are *requirements* of triangular constitutionalism. They are constitutive elements of the discourse, and are important threshold indicators which dialogic counterparts can use in assessing the validity and seriousness of any given challenge, calibrating their response accordingly, as has been exemplified in the case law recounted in the preceding chapters. The kind of rebelliousness described by Keleman, which I have characterised elsewhere as backsliding and free-riding, is

---

[52] Walker (n 50) 318.

[53] See N Krisch, *Beyond Constitutionalism: The Pluralist Structure of Postnational Law* (Oxford, Oxford University Press, 2010) 276–85 and references therein.

[54] RD Keleman, 'The Dangers of Constitutional Pluralism' in G Davies and M Avbelj (eds), *Research Handbook on Legal Pluralism and EU Law* (Cheltenham, Edward Elgar, 2018) 402, footnote omitted.

224 *Towards Triangular Constitutionalism*

not constitutional pluralism of any kind: it is solipsistic constitutional particularism. It fails to take seriously the nature of the domestic constitutional order as part of the European polyarchy, and fails to adjust its own orthodoxy and praxis in light of this, instead privileging the domestic order over all others, whatever the cost, and whether or not this privileging is horizontally and vertically coherent in Maduro's sense, justifiable in terms going beyond those comprehensible only to the domestic order. Alternatively (and worse), it could be that this backsliding is in fact *not* solipsistic, and *does* take the polyarchic situation seriously: it is then so appalled by the 'erosion' of national sovereignty that it sees in the polyarchy that it actively seeks to undermine this polyarchy by confrontation, making ill-tempered and unjustifiable demands that it knows can never be met by its interlocutors, in a cynical attempt to precipitate conflict and hasten either a significant downgrade in the normative strength of competing orders, or a reversion to some 'lost' insular particularism. In such a case, it is not that there is an incompletely theorised agreement in Sabel and Gerstenberg's sense: there is no agreement in the first place, incompletely theorised or otherwise.

Keleman focuses his analysis specifically on the context of Hungary, where the autocratic government of Viktor Orbán's Fidesz party is engaged in a systematic and deliberate programme of 'illiberalising' the State, concentrating power in its own hands, demonising internal and external opponents, and undermining the constitutional foundations of political and social pluralism in the Hungarian Rechtsstaat. As part of this wider programme, the concept of the constitutional identity of the nation state has been employed in political and legal efforts to circumvent the EU's refugee quota scheme, culminating in the Hungarian Constitutional Court's declaration in 2016 that it had the power to declare a Council decision ultra vires on grounds of fundamental rights, state sovereignty, or constitutional identity.[55] In this context, Keleman declares that:

> [Constitutional pluralism] should be abandoned by all those who value of the survival of the EU legal order and of the European Union itself. Scholars should embrace the CJEU's straightforward and compelling approach to the question of supremacy: For those states that voluntarily choose to join and voluntarily choose to remain members of the Union, EU law, and the Court of Justice as the ultimate guardian of that law, must enjoy unconditional supremacy.[56]

It was noted above that self-restraint and sincere cooperation are requirements of constitutional pluralism, but it is also true that they are inherent in the very idea of constitutionalism itself, at the domestic or any other level. Constitutionalism by its nature requires a certain minimum level of 'buy-in' from all competing actors within the constitutional order, and, as is well known, constitutional democracy itself leaves open the possibility of its own destruction,

---

[55] G Halmai, 'National(ist) Constitutional Identity? Hungary's Road to Abuse Constitutional Pluralism' EUI Working Papers LAW 2017/08, 12–14.

[56] Keleman (n 54) 403.

in that it provides a path to power for those who do not share or respect the principles underlying the system, and have no intention of abiding by them. The Hungarian situation which so rightly concerns Keleman is not merely an abuse of constitutional pluralism (though it certainly is that). It is barely even *constitutional*.[57] In this regard, constitutionalism itself is no less 'dangerous' or 'unsustainable' than its postnational extension into constitutional pluralism, and the fact that constitutional pluralism is open to abuse is unsurprising and even obvious, given that the very same is true of domestic constitutionalism. Constitutionalism's susceptibility to rhetorical abuse was one of the failings that Walker outlined in 2002 in suggesting constitutional pluralism as a possible, partial remedy,[58] yet for Keleman and Gábor Halmai, the abuse of constitutional pluralism in Hungary is sufficient reason for its total abandonment as an idea. But as has so often been the case throughout this book, what is initially cast as a binary reveals itself on closer inspection to be a relative matter, a question of degree. Constitutionalism is fragile and contains within it the circumstances of its own collapse. A 'captured' constitutional court of ruling-party apparatchiks, operating in an increasingly authoritarian domestic environment characterised by restrictions on the media, the vilification of dissent, and the state-sponsored inculcation of a climate of tension and fear of the other does not qualify as an interlocutor worthy of respect. Like a chess player moving her rook diagonally, it has ceased to play by the rules of the game, and its moves do not need to be accepted or respected. With very little effort, the argument that the Hungarian State's behaviour requires us to abandon constitutional pluralism could be extended to an argument that this behaviour requires us to abandon democratic constitutionalism itself.

Keleman goes on to state that '[i]f the legal demands of membership present an unacceptable violation of the state's national constitutional identity, the exit door is always open'.[59] This is entirely true, and the voluntary nature of Union membership and the continuous possibility of exit is always the ultimate method of resolving truly irreconcilable conflict between the national and Union constitutional orders. But Keleman's approach is far too keen to show objectors the door. Triangular constitutionalism is not so quick to regard every case of actual or potential conflict as an existential issue, and an approach that elevates each and every disagreement to existential status is a recipe for a relationship that is at best sullen and at worst fractious, a relationship all too easily characterised by its opponents as one of 'domination' by the Union of the State: precisely the kind of arrangement of legal orders falsely propagated by the Hungarian Government.

---

[57] On the use of constitutional mechanisms to undermine the constitutional order, see D Landau, 'Abusive Constitutionalism' (2013) 47 *University of California Davis Law Review* 189.

[58] Walker (n 50) 328–33.

[59] Keleman (n 54) 403.

226 *Towards Triangular Constitutionalism*

What is more, the speedy-exit approach depends on a rather binary conception of affairs, where the EU is 'good' (cosmopolitan, socially and politically pluralist, just, protective of rights, progressive, democratic etc) and where states are 'bad' (narrow-minded, parochial, unjust, exclusionary, racist, oppressive, undemocratic etc). This binary may accurately describe the current situation as regards Hungary's relations with the EU, but it is not *inherently* true. The Hungarian abuse of constitutional pluralism, far from being *caused* by 'contagion from Karlsruhe',[60] simply takes its opportunities where it can find them and is happy to dress unsound conduct in sound language. This is symptomatic of a much broader European crisis. The disingenuous mutilation of a pluralist jurisprudence built on an ethically sound basis in the service of unethical ends is not sufficient reason for this jurisprudence to be abandoned. Orbán and his reactionary counterparts on the new European right, like the anti-Midas, have the uncanny knack of turning gold to base lead at the slightest touch. History can be raided in the service of ahistorical grievance-mongering. The biological sciences can be perverted towards racist ends. Theology can be debased to justify all manner of murderousness. The rule of law, appropriately framed, is a favoured defence of autocrats justifying baton-charges. Why, then, should we sacrifice a sound idea because of its misuse by the worst among us? Moreover, even if we were to jettison the concept of constitutional pluralism entirely and insist always and in every circumstance on the primacy of EU law, this would not solve the problem of the continent's reactionary turn. We would not be throwing the baby out with the bathwater but throwing the baby out and keeping the bathwater. Orbán's Fidesz party is a member in good standing of the European People's Party, the largest group in the European Parliament, which has treated Fidesz with kid gloves.[61] Orbán himself is a member with full voting rights in the European Council. His ministers sit and vote (for now) in the Council, and it is his government which appoints Hungary's Commissioner and member of the Court of Justice. Joseph Weiler once observed that 'a democracy of vile people will be vile',[62] and it therefore follows that a Union of vile Member States will also be vile. The shortcomings of the Article 7 TEU mechanism in defence of the rule of law, even when deployed to its full extent, are well known,[63] and with the electoral rise of a whole array of reactionary forces right across the Union nothing can be taken for granted. The all-or-nothing, European-supremacy-or-exit approach advocated by Keleman may well be perfectly sound in the isolated context of a single recalcitrant Member State,

---

[60] ibid 398.

[61] Anna Maria Corazza Bildt, 'This Time, Viktor Orbán Has Gone Too Far' *Politico.eu* (3 August 2018), available at: www.politico.eu/article/viktor-orban-parliament-epp-hungary-has-gone-too-far/.

[62] JHH Weiler, 'Europe: The Case Against Statehood' (1998) 4 *European Law Journal* 43, 60.

[63] D Kochenov and L Pech, 'Monitoring and Enforcement of the Rule of Law in the European Union: Rhetoric and Reality' (2015) 11 *European Constitutional Law Review* 512; D Kochenov and L Pech, 'Better Late Than Never?' (2016) 24 *Journal of Common Market Studies* 1062; D Kochenov, 'Busting the Myths Nuclear: A Commentary on Article 7 TEU' EUI Working Papers LAW 2017/10.

captured by an autocratic government. It is entirely unsound in the context of a Union-wide crisis of constitutionalism, where entire Member States are vulnerable to capture by democratically elected nativist authoritarians who regard democracy as an event, rather than as a process.

How much longer before the rot spreads from the national level to the European? And what do we do then? The principled, normative resistance of triangular constitutionalism to according all-purpose primacy to either the national or Union legal orders arises, in part, from its constitutionalist suspicion of concentrated public power. Just as a well-functioning state constitution distributes state power among various institutions in varying and jurisdictionally contingent ways, and just as the Union itself is architected towards 'institutional balance' in the make-up and powers of its institutions, so too does constitutional pluralism seek to provide the space for a balance between the Union and its Member States: a balance going beyond that already set out in the Treaties and overseen by the CJEU alone. Triangular constitutionalism specifically, in its delocalised and departicularised form, provides a conception of the national and EU legal orders that is cooperative and symbiotic, rather than fractious and domineering, and then widens the field of this inter-order balancing act and the space for principled contestation by including the Convention in the analysis. This is not to say that any form of constitutional pluralism on its own can provide a final bulwark against some future Union captured by autocratic Member States. Rather, the point is that just as it is unwise to place all one's faith in any single institution within a state constitutional order, it is similarly unwise to place all one's faith in any single constitutional order in the triangle.

As was the case with the general objection in chapter one, the specific objection that any theory that legitimises national resistance to the absolute primacy of EU law poses a threat to the rule of law cannot stand. Rather, the importance of legal certainty heightens the general strength that we must accord to the doctrine of primacy, but does not render it absolute. In the specific context of a Hungarian-style situation of the abuse of the language of pluralism, the background requirements of coherence and universalisable justification, and the nature of the shared principles undergirding the order enable us to recognise solipsistic recalcitrance for what it is.

B. Jurisdictional Specificity

Let us recall Alexander Somek's indictment that '[i]t is indeed a quite remarkable fact about European constitutional theory that in its most visible form it scarcely amounts to more than a series of glosses on lengthy opinions by the German Federal Constitutional Court'.[64] While perhaps a little too dismissive, it

---

[64] A Somek, 'Monism: A Tale of the Undead' in M Avbelj and J Komárek (eds), *Constitutional Pluralism in the European Union and Beyond* (Oxford, Hart Publishing, 2012) 346.

228　*Towards Triangular Constitutionalism*

is undeniable that the entire discourse of constitutional pluralism in all its forms has built a rather top-heavy edifice on some quite narrow foundations, drawing far-reaching, ostensibly universal conclusions from a small number of jurisdictionally specific and temporally contingent premises. A major motivation behind the present work has been to broaden the field, focusing in particular on a jurisdiction which has been peripheral to the pluralist debate so far, and, according to what I have suggested is the mistaken orthodoxy, is infertile ground for such a debate in the first place, given the received 'torpedo' interpretation of the Irish Constitution's EU exclusion clause.

Chapter two's analysis of this exclusion clause suggested that it may, in certain circumstances, be rather less exclusionary than might be thought. But let us bear in mind Ana Bobić's categorisation of Ireland, along with Austria, Belgium, Croatia, Luxembourg and Malta, as jurisdictions that have 'expressly accepted the primacy of EU law … be it by way of a constitutional provision, or based upon the binding nature of the ECJ's case law'.[65] The fact that the Irish situation, on close inspection, is rather more complicated than Bobić alleges is no criticism of her analysis: she was relying on the express wording of an extra-curial publication of the Supreme Court. It simply reveals that the possibility of Irish judicial resistance to absolute EU primacy in every circumstance is not the starting point of the Supreme Court's analysis, nor is it a possibility it wishes to emphasise in its relations with other courts. Rather, it results from taking seriously the Court's own jurisprudence over the decades on its own isolated terms. This then raises the question as to whether similar re-examination of the jurisprudence in Austria, Belgium and the rest may result in a picture rather more complicated than is usually admitted in those jurisdictions. Perhaps it would not: under triangular constitutionalism, this is perfectly acceptable. Every point in the triangle reserves to itself the means of resolving conflict between the legal orders, and if a given jurisdiction does so in the case of conflict with the EU by accepting unconditionally the CJEU's reading of the primacy doctrine, then so be it. This is simply the metaconstitutional interface norm of legality given an uncompromising and irrebuttable concretisation within a given jurisdiction, as each jurisdiction is free to do if it so chooses and if this is consistent with the logic of the domestic order. The further lessons of triangular constitutionalism, such as the political, legal and social internalisation of polyarchy, remain on offer, as do the advantages of including the Convention in the analysis in order to provide a full understanding of the relations of the three orders and the nature of the constitutional scheme as a whole. But even within an order that willingly embraces the absolute primacy of EU law, the impossibility of temporal closure raises the ultimate 'what if' question, whereby we

---

[65] A Bobić, 'Constitutional Pluralism Is Not Dead: An Analysis of Interactions Between Constitutional Courts of Member States and the European Court of Justice (2017) 18 *German Law Journal* 1395, 1413–14.

ask whether there are *any* circumstances that might justify the disapplication of EU norms in that jurisdiction. Importantly, no matter how we structure the 'what if' question, at the level of concretisation within a jurisdiction it results in a question not of conflict between the norms of *different* orders, but rather of conflict between competing norms of the *same* order. The national constitution provides – along with the usual state structures; their powers; their limits; the rights they must respect and so forth – the means by which EU law becomes effective and is given primacy within the legal order. If a supreme or constitutional court, for whatever reason, feels that any given norm of EU law poses some truly enormous threat to an important norm of the national constitution, the question of priority between these norms is a question of national law which must be resolved by the national court. Perhaps it will be resolved in favour of the application of the EU norm: this may result in legal and political acceptance of the norm within the national order, or in legal and political attempts to undo this application, up to and including exit from the EU. Perhaps it will be resolved in favour of the national norm: again, this may result in the exact same consequences, except in reverse. Either way, a triangular conception of the workings of 'the constitution' (here broadly conceived) provides a far more useful 'doctrinal instrumentarium'[66] then the bland assumption that real conflict will simply never happen, and the accompanying absence of jurisprudential tools to manage this conflict in the event, no matter how unlikely, that it does arise. Even within the jurisdictions with the most seemingly uncomplicated relationship with EU law, therefore, triangular constitutionalism has its advantages, advantages which are no less useful and important for being held in reserve.

As regards the jurisdictions which expressly do not accept the CJEU's precise reading of the primacy doctrine, the pluralist discourse's historic (over)reliance on German jurisprudence poses two possible dangers. First, there is the difficulty adverted to throughout this book, of attempting to generalise a jurisprudence with deep roots in the specificities of the Federal Republic, its particular structures and institutions, and its historic relations with the Union. But there is also the flipside of this: the danger of overcompensating for the Germanocentrism of the discourse, which could manifest itself as a kind of hasty neo- or xenophilia, where every new scrap of what may be, or seems to be, raw material for a pluralist analysis is either fêted as proving the pluralists' point, or, conversely, as another nail in the coffin of the idea, and justification for the exit of a Member State. We have already seen attempts to argue that the behaviour of the Hungarian Constitutional Court justifies the wholesale embrace of the CJEU's conception of primacy by all national legal orders, and my counter-argument that the jurisdictional specificities of that situation render the entire affair categorically separate from constitutional pluralism, and strip it of any defensibility or legitimacy. Similarly, though occurring in entirely different jurisdictional and political

---

[66] Krisch (n 53) 286.

230 *Towards Triangular Constitutionalism*

circumstances, the *Slovak Pensions* saga of the Czech Constitutional Court may have seemed at first glance as a rare instance of a national court actually 'biting', rather than merely 'barking'.[67] However, as Michal Bobek's careful contextual and sociological analysis demonstrates, a whole array of historical contingencies, jurisdictional specificities, and inter-institutional rivalries complicate the picture enormously.[68] The situation outlined by Bobek encourages us not to become too enchanted with the notion of judicial dialogue: not every actor will always be honest, cooperative, informed, attentive or diplomatic. But it also encourages us not to catastrophise every incident of seeming breakdown in relations, and not to be too quick to show dissenters the door. Rather, close attention must be paid not only to jurisdictional specificities and historical contingencies, but to the very nature and architecture of the European legal order(s) themselves, as Bobek makes clear in his analysis of the preliminary reference procedure and its tendency to subvert and undermine domestic court hierarchies.[69]

Therefore, just as an abstract and universalised conception of triangular constitutionalism requires us to take seriously the intricacies of each Member State, their advantages and disadvantages, so too must we take seriously the specificity of the Union and Convention legal orders: the complex system of systems we have built for ourselves in Europe does not allow for simple answers. It requires a theoretical framework equally attentive to the part as to the whole, one that can zoom in and back out at will. Triangular constitutionalism attempts to do just this.

III. CONCLUSION

The analysis in this book has sought to demonstrate that a constitutionally pluralist conception of the relationship between the legal orders of Ireland, the EU and the ECHR as a deliberative polyarchy – a triangular constitution – is descriptively accurate and normatively desirable. However, in drawing on the literature on metaconstitutional conceptions of pluralism, the analysis revealed a significant problem: the non-universal nature of the interface norms by which the relations between the orders are regulated. It is perfectly possible to place the various means – metaconstitutional, constitutional, and legislative – by which polyarchically arranged legal orders manage their interrelations in broad categories, but these categories are then so loose and general in their formulation that they cannot serve as action guiding rules and principles. When concretised

---

[67] See JHH Weiler, 'The "Lisbon *Urteil*" and the Fast Food Culture' (2009) 20 *European Journal of International Law* 505, 505; N Petersen, 'Karlsruhe Not Only Barks, But Finally Bites – Some Remarks on the *OMT* Decision of the German Constitutional Court' (2014) 15 *German Law Journal* 321.
[68] Bobek (n 19).
[69] ibid 73–87.

in actual cases, these interface norms then become too jurisdictionally specific to regeneralise across the European legal sphere.

Therefore, while it is indeed possible to constitutionalise the plural or to pluralise the constitutional, under such a reconciled, polyarchic legal regime, the universal and the particular seem to remain stubbornly separate. This finding highlights the importance of continued, close, careful analysis of the intricacies of the individual cases that make up the jurisprudence of the European polyarchy, and the intricacies of the individual jurisdictions from which they arise. The polyarchy is not an indivisible whole and cannot be analysed as one. Rather, to the extent that the universal exists, it must be shaped by reference to the particular. A generalised theory of triangular constitutionalism, equally respectful of the legitimacy and authority of all three constitutional orders that make up the constitutional whole, may therefore be able to provide both a free-standing perspective by which to assess the entire polyarchy, and to epistemically anchor itself within each legal order, and within each order to aid in the institutional, political, legal and social internalisation of the world that we have built.

Bibliography

Books

Alexy, R, *A Theory of Legal Argumentation* (Oxford, Clarendon Press, 1989).
—— *A Theory of Constitutional Rights* (Oxford, Oxford University Press, 2002).
Avbelj, M, Fontanelli, F and Martinico, G (eds), *Kadi on Trial: A Multifaceted Analysis of the Kadi Trial* (Abingdon, Routledge, 2014).
Casey, J, *Constitutional Law in Ireland*, 3rd edn (Dublin, Round Hall Sweet & Maxwell, 2000).
Cass, DZ, *The Constitutionalization of the World Trade Organization* (Oxford, Oxford University Press, 2005).
Craig, P and de Búrca, G, *EU Law: Text, Cases, and Materials* 6th edn (Oxford, Oxford University Press, 2015).
de Londras, F and Enright, M, *Repealing the 8th: Reforming Irish Abortion Law* (Bristol, Policy Press, 2018).
de Londras, F and Kelly, C, *European Convention on Human Rights Act: Operation, Impact and Analysis* (Dublin, Round Hall, 2010).
del Mar, M and Bańkowski, Z (eds), *Law as Institutional Normative Order* (Farnham, Ashgate, 2009).
Drzemczewski, AZ, *European Human Rights Convention in Domestic Law: A Comparative Study* (Oxford, Oxford University Press, 1983).
Dworkin, R, *Taking Rights Seriously* (Cambridge MA, Harvard University Press, 1977).
—— *Law's Empire* (London, Fontana, 1986).
Estella, A, *The EU Principle of Subsidiarity and its Critique* (Oxford, Oxford University Press, 2002).
Grimm, D, *Sovereignty: The Origin and Future of a Political and Legal Concept* (New York, Columbia University Press, 2015).
Hesketh, T, *The Second Partitioning of Ireland? The Abortion Referendum of 1983* (Dún Laoghaire, Brandsma, 1990).
Hirschman, A, *Exit, Voice, and Loyalty* (Cambridge, MA, Harvard University Press, 1970).
Hogan, G and Whyte, G, *JM Kelly: The Irish Constitution* 4th edn (Dublin, Tottel, 2003).
Hug, C, *The Politics of Sexual Morality in Ireland* (London, Springer, 2016).
Jackson, RH, *The Struggle for Judicial Supremacy* (New York, Knopf, 1941).
Jaklič, K, *Constitutional Pluralism in the EU* (Oxford, Oxford University Press, 2014).
Keown, J, *Abortion, Doctors and the Law* (Cambridge, Cambridge University Press, 1988).
Komesar, N, *Imperfect Alternatives – Choosing Institutions in Law, Economics and Public Policy* (Chicago, IL, Chicago University Press, 1994).
Kingston, J, Whelan, A and Bacik, I, *Abortion and the Law* (Dublin, Round Hall Sweet & Maxwell, 1997).
Krisch, N, *Beyond Constitutionalism: The Pluralist Structure of Postnational Law* (Oxford, Oxford University Press, 2010).
MacCormick, N, *Legal Reasoning and Legal Theory* (Oxford, Clarendon Press, 1978).
—— *Questioning Sovereignty: Law, State and Nation in the European Commonwealth* (Oxford, Oxford University Press, 1999).
Mullally, U (ed), *Repeal the 8th* (London, Unbound, 2018).
O'Connell, D, Cummiskey, S, Meeneghan, E and O'Connell, P, *ECHR Act 2003: A Preliminary Assessment of Impact* (Dublin, Law Society of Ireland, 2006).
Phelan, DR, *Revolt or Revolution: The Constitutional Boundaries of the European Community* (Dublin, Round Hall Sweet & Maxwell, 1997).

Quilty, A, Kennedy, S and Conlon, C (eds), *The Abortion Papers Ireland: Volume 2* (Cork, Cork University Press, 2015).

Schweppe, J (ed), *The Unborn Child, Article 40.3.3° and Abortion in Ireland: Twenty-five Years of Protection?* (Dublin, Liffey Press, 2008).

Sieckmann, J-R, *Regelmodelle und Prinzipienmodelle des Rechtssystems* (Baden-Baden, Nomos, 1990).

Smyth, A (ed), *The Abortion Papers: Ireland* (Cork, Attic Press, 1992).

Sweetman, R, *On Our Backs: Sexual Attitudes in a Changing Ireland* (London, Pan, 1979).

Tully, J, *Strange Multiplicity: Constitutionalism in an Age of Diversity* (Cambridge, Cambridge University Press, 1995).

Weiler, JHH, *The Constitution of Europe* (Cambridge, Cambridge University Press, 1999).

Chapters in Edited Volumes

Alexander, L, 'Introduction' in L Alexander (ed), *Constitutionalism: Philosophical Foundations* (Cambridge, Cambridge University Press, 1998).

Arnull, A, 'The Americanization of EU Law Scholarship' in A Arnull, P Eeckhout and T Tridimas (eds), *Continuity and Change in EU Law: Essays in Honour of Sir Francis Jacobs* (Oxford, Oxford University Press, 2008).

Avbelj, M, 'Can European Integration be Constitutional and Pluralist – Both at the Same Time?' in M Avbelj and J Komárek (eds), *Constitutional Pluralism in the European Union and Beyond* (Oxford, Hart Publishing, 2012).

Avbelj, M and Komárek, J, 'Introduction' in M Avbelj and J Komárek (eds), *Constitutional Pluralism in the European Union and Beyond* (Oxford, Hart Publishing, 2012).

Bacik, I, 'A Human Rights Culture for Ireland?' in I Bacik and S Livingstone, *Towards a Culture of Human Rights in Ireland* (Cork, Cork University Press, 2001).

Barents, R, 'The Fallacy of European Multilevel Constitutionalism' in M Avbelj and J Komárek (eds), *Constitutional Pluralism in the European Union and Beyond* (Oxford, Hart Publishing, 2012).

Besson, S, 'The Reception Process in Ireland and the United Kingdom' in A Stone Sweet and H Keller (eds), *A Europe of Rights: The Impact of the ECHR on National Legal Systems* (Oxford, Oxford University Press, 2008).

Cahill, M, 'A Critical Assessment of Irish Scholarship on the Constitutional Reception of European Law' in T Mohr and J Schweppe (eds), *Thirty Years of Legal Scholarship* (Dublin, Roundhall, 2011).

Davies, G, 'Constitutional Disagreement in Europe and the Search for Pluralism' in M Avbelj and J Komárek (eds), *Constitutional Pluralism in the European Union and Beyond* (Oxford, Hart Publishing, 2012).

de Witte, B, 'The Closest Thing to a Constitutional Conversation in Europe: The Semi-Permanent Treaty Revision Process' in P Beaumont, C Lyons and N Walker (eds), *Convergence and Divergence in European Public Law* (Oxford, Hart Publishing, 2002).

—— 'The Use of the ECHR and Convention Case Law by the European Court of Justice' in P Popelier, C Van de Heyning and P Van Nuffel (eds), *Human Rights Protection in the European Legal Order: The Interaction Between the European and National Courts* (Cambridge, Intersentia, 2011).

Fassbender, B, '"We the Peoples of the United Nations": Constituent Power and Constitutional Form in International Law' in M Loughlin and N Walker (eds), *The Paradox of Constitutionalism: Constituent Power and Constitutional Form* (Oxford, Oxford University Press, 2007).

Gerstenberg, O and Sabel, C, 'Directly-Deliberative Polyarchy: An Institutional Ideal for Europe?' in C Joerges and R Dehousse (eds), *Good Governance in Europe's Integrated Market* (Oxford, Oxford University Press, 2002).

Gragl, P, 'The Reasonableness of Jealousy: Opinion 2/13 and EU Accession to the ECHR' in W Benedek, F Benoît-Rohmer, MC Ketteman, B Kneihs and M Nowak (eds), *European Yearbook on Human Rights 2015* (Vienna, Neuer Wissenschaftlicher Verlag, 2015).

234   Bibliography

Groussot, X and Bogojević, S, 'Subsidiarity as a Procedural Safeguard of Federalism' in L Azoulai (ed), *The Question of Competence in the European Union* (Oxford, Oxford University Press, 2014).

Halberstam, D, 'Local, Global, and Plural Constitutionalism: Europe Meets the World' in G de Búrca and JHH Weiler (eds), *The Worlds of European Constitutionalism* (Cambridge, Cambridge University Press, 2012).

Hogan, G, 'Incorporation of the ECHR: Some Issues of Methodology and Process' in U Kilkelly (ed), *ECHR and Irish Law*, 1st edn (Bristol, Jordan, 2004).

Kaupa, C, 'Maybe Not Activist Enough? On the Court's Alleged Neoliberal Bias in its Recent Labor Cases' in M Dawson, B de Witte and E Muir, *Judicial Activism at the European Court of Justice* (Cheltenham, Edward Elgar, 2013).

Keleman, RD, 'The Dangers of Constitutional Pluralism' in G Davies and M Avbelj (eds), *Research Handbook on Legal Pluralism in EU Law* (Cheltenham, Edward Elgar, 2018).

Komárek, J, 'Institutional Dimension of Constitutional Pluralism' in M Avbelj and J Komárek (eds), *Constitutional Pluralism in the European Union and Beyond* (Oxford, Hart Publishing, 2012).

Krisch, N, 'The Case for Pluralism in Postnational Law' in G de Búrca and JHH Weiler (eds), *The Worlds of European Constitutionalism* (Cambridge, Cambridge University Press, 2012).

Kumm, M, 'Rethinking Constitutional Authority: On the Structure and Limits of Constitutional Pluralism' in M Avbelj and J Komárek (eds), *Constitutional Pluralism in the European Union and Beyond* (Oxford, Hart Publishing, 2012).

Ludlow, A, 'The Right to Strike: A Jurisprudential Gulf Between the CJEU and ECtHR' in K Dzehtsiarou, T Konstadinides, T Lock and N O'Meara (eds), *Human Rights Law in Europe: The Influence, Overlaps and Contradictions of the EU and the ECHR* (London, Routledge, 2014).

MacCormick, N, 'Comment [on G Postema's "The Normativity of Law"]' in R Gavison (ed), *Issues in Contemporary Legal Philosophy* (Oxford, Clarendon Press, 1987).

Maduro, MP, 'Contrapunctual Law: Europe's Constitutional Pluralism in Action' in N Walker (ed), *Sovereignty in Transition* (Oxford, Hart Publishing, 2003).

Mason, L, 'Labour Law, the Industrial Constitution and the EU's Accession to the ECHR: The Constitutional Nature of the Market and the Limits of Rights-Based Approaches to Labour Law' in K Dzehtsiarou, T Konstadinides, T Lock and N O'Meara (eds), *Human Rights Law in Europe: The Influence, Overlaps and Contradictions of the EU and the ECHR* (London, Routledge, 2014).

Mayer, FC and Wendel, M, 'Multilevel Constitutionalism and Constitutional Pluralism' in M Avbelj and J Komárek (eds), *Constitutional Pluralism in the European Union and Beyond* (Oxford, Hart Publishing, 2012).

Moens, GA and Trone, J, 'Subsidiarity as Judicial and Legislative Review Principles in the European Union' in M Evans and A Zimmermann (eds), *Global Perspectives on Subsidiarity* (Dordrecht, Springer, 2014).

O'Connell, D, 'Watched Kettles Boil (Slowly): The Impact of the ECHR Act 2003' in U Kilkelly (ed), *ECHR in Irish Law*, 2nd edn (Bristol, Jordan, 2009).

Rosas, A, 'The European Union and Fundamental Rights/Human Rights' in C Krause and M Scheinin (eds), *International Protection of Human Rights: A Textbook* (Turku, Åbo Akademi University Institute for Human Rights, 2009).

Sarmiento, D, 'The Silent Lamb and the Deaf Wolves: Constitutional Pluralism, Preliminary References and the Role of Silent Judgments in EU Law' in M Avbelj and J Komárek (eds), *Constitutional Pluralism in the European Union and Beyond* (Oxford, Hart Publishing, 2012).

Schienen, M, 'Economic and Social Rights as Legal Rights' in A Eide, C Krause and A Rosas (eds), *Economic, Social and Cultural Rights*, 2nd edn (Leiden, Martinus Nijhoff, 2001).

Somek, A, 'Monism: A Tale of the Undead' in M Avbelj and J Komárek (eds), *Constitutional Pluralism in the European Union and Beyond* (Oxford, Hart Publishing, 2012).

Twining, W, 'Institutions of Law from a Global Perspective: Standpoint, Pluralism and Non-State Law' in M del Mar and Z Bańkowski (eds), *Law as Institutional Normative Order* (Farnham, Ashgate, 2009).

Walker, N, 'Flexibility Within a Metaconstitutional Frame: Reflections on the Future of Legal Authority in Europe' in G de Búrca and J Scott (eds), *Constitutional Change in the EU: From Uniformity to Flexibility* (Oxford, Hart Publishing, 2000).
—— 'Late Sovereignty in the European Union' in N Walker (ed), *Sovereignty in Transition* (Oxford, Hart Publishing, 2003).
Walzer, M, 'Nations and Universe' in D Miller (ed), *Thinking Politically: Essays in Political Theory* (New Haven, CT, Yale University Press, 2007).
Weiler, JHH, 'Fin-de-Siècle Europe' in R Dehousse (ed), *Europe After Maastricht: An Ever Closer Union?* (Munich, Beck, 1994).
—— 'In Defence of the Status Quo: Europe's Constitutional *Sonderweg*' in JHH Weiler and M Wind (eds), *European Constitutionalism Beyond the State* (Cambridge, Cambridge University Press, 2003).
—— 'Prologue: Global and Pluralist Constitutionalism – Some Doubts' in G de Búrca and JHH Weiler (eds), *The Worlds of European Constitutionalism* (Cambridge, Cambridge University Press, 2012).

Journal Articles

Alonso García, R, 'The General Provisions of the Charter of Fundamental Rights of the European Union' (2002) 8 *European Law Journal* 492.
Apps, K, 'Damages Claims Against Trade Unions after *Viking* and *Laval*' (2009) 34 *European Law Review* 141.
Avbelj, M, 'Questioning EU Constitutionalisms' (2008) 9 *German Law Journal* 1.
Avbelj, M and Komárek, J, 'Four Visions of Constitutional Pluralism' (2004) 4 *European Constitutional Law Review* 524.
Baquero Cruz, J, 'The Legacy of the Maastricht-Urteil and the Pluralist Movement' (2008) 14 *European Law Journal* 389.
—— 'Another Look at Constitutional Pluralism in the European Union' (2016) 22 *European Law Journal* 356.
Bateup, C, 'The Dialogic Promise: Assessing the Normative Potential of Theories of Constitutional Dialogue' (2005–06) 71 *Brooklyn Law Review* 1109.
Besselink, L, Claes, M and Reestman, J-H, 'Editorial: A Constitutional Moment: Acceding to the ECHR (or Not)' (2015) 11 *European Constitutional Law Review* 2.
Besson, S, 'The Truth About Legal Pluralism' (2012) 8 *European Constitutional Law Review* 354.
Bobek, M, '*Landtová, Holubec*, and the Problem of an Uncooperative Court: Implications for the Preliminary Rulings Procedure' (2014) 10 *European Constitutional Law Review* 54.
Bobić, A, 'Constitutional Pluralism is not Dead: An Analysis of Interactions Between Constitutional Courts of Member States and the European Court of Justice (2017) 18 *German Law Journal* 1395.
Bulterman, MK and Kranenborg, HR, 'Case Comment: What if Rules on Free Movement and Human Rights Collide? About Laser Games and Human Dignity: The Omega Case' (2006) 31 *European Law Review* 93.
Burrows, N, 'Question of Community Accession to the European Convention Determined' (1997) 22 *European Law Review* 58.
Cahill, M, 'Constitutional Exclusion Clauses, Article 29.4.6°, and the Constitutional Reception of European Law' (2011) 18 *Dublin University Law Journal* 74.
Claes, M and Reestman, J-H, 'The Protection of National Constitutional Identity and the Limits of European Integration at the Occasion of the *Gauweiler* Case' (2015) 16 *German Law Journal* 917.
Cohen, J and Sabel, C, 'Directly-Deliberative Polyarchy' (1997) 3 *European Law Journal* 313.
Connelly, A, 'Implications of the ECHR Act 2003' (2004) 98 *Law Society Gazette* 7.
Coppel, J and O'Neill, A, 'The European Court of Justice: Taking Rights Seriously?' (1992) 12 *Legal Studies* 227.

236 Bibliography

Craig, P, 'Constitutions, Constitutionalism and the European Union' (2001) 7 *European Law Journal* 125.

Crumley, C, 'Heterarchy and the Analysis of Complex Societies' (1995) 6 *Archaeological Papers of the American Anthropological Association* 1.

Davies, ACL, 'One Step Forward, Two Steps Back? The *Viking* and *Laval* Cases in the ECJ' (2008) 37 *Industrial Law Journal* 126.

Davies, G, 'Subsidiarity: The Wrong Idea, in the Wrong Place, at the Wrong Time' (2006) 43 *Common Market Law Review* 63.

de Londras, F, 'Declarations of Incompatibility Under the ECHR Act 2003: A Workable Transplant?' (2014) 35 *Statute Law Review* 50.

den Heijer, M, 'Procedural Aspects of Shared Responsibility in the European Court of Human Rights' (2013) 4 *Journal of International Dispute Settlement* 361.

—— 'Shared Responsibility Before the European Court of Human Rights' (2013) 60 *Netherlands International Law Review* 411.

Douglas-Scott, S, 'A Tale of Two Courts: Luxembourg, Strasbourg and the Growing European Human Rights *Acquis*' (2006) 43 *Common Market Law Review* 629.

Doyle, O and Ryan, D, 'Judicial Interpretation of the European Convention on Human Rights Act 2003: Reflections and Analysis' (2011) 33 *Dublin University Law Journal* 369.

Dunoff, JL, 'Constitutional Conceits: The WTO's "Constitution" and the Discipline of International Law' (2006) 17 *European Journal of International Law* 647.

Dworkin, R, 'Hart's Postscript and the Character of Political Philosophy' (2004) 24 *Oxford Journal of Legal Studies* 1.

Eckes, C, 'EU Accession to the ECHR: Between Autonomy and Adaptation' (2013) 72 *Modern Law Review* 254.

Eijsbouts, WT, Besselink, L, Reestman, J-H and Sap, JW, 'Preface' (2005) 1 *European Constitutional Law Review* 1.

Eklund, R, 'A Swedish Perspective on *Laval*' (2007–08) 29 *Comparative Labor Law & Policy Journal* 551.

Eleftheriadis, P, 'Pluralism and Integrity' (2010) 23 *Ratio Juris* 365.

Euzéby, A, 'Economic Crisis and Social Protection in the European Union: Moving Beyond Immediate Responses' (2010) 63 *International Social Security Review* 71.

Ewing, KD and Hendy, J, 'The Dramatic Implications of *Demir and Baykara*' (2010) 39 *Industrial Law Journal* 2.

Fassbender, B, 'The United Nations Charter as Constitution of the International Community' (1998) 36 *Columbia Journal of Transnational Law* 529.

Fennelly, N, 'Pillar Talk: Fundamental Rights Protection in the European Union' (2008) 1 *Judicial Studies Institute Journal* 95.

Fontanelli, F, 'The European Union's Charter of Fundamental Rights: Two Years Later' (2011) 3 *Perspectives on Federalism* 22.

—— '*Hic Sunt Nationes*: The Elusive Limits of the EU Charter and the German Constitutional Watchdog' (2013) 9 *European Constitutional Law Review* 315.

Franklin, C, 'The Legal Status of the EU Charter of Fundamental Rights After the Treaty of Lisbon' (2010–11) 15 *Tilburg Law Review* 137.

Gaja, G, 'Case-note on Opinion 2/94' (1996) 33 *Common Market Law Review* 973.

—— 'The "Co-Respondent Mechanisms" According to the Draft Agreement for the Accession of the EU to the ECHR' (2013) 2 *European Society of International Law Reflections* 1.

Halberstam, D, '"It's the Autonomy, Stupid!" A Modest Defense of Opinion 2/13 on EU Accession to the European Convention on Human Rights' (2015) 16 *German Law Journal* 105.

Hofmann, HCH and Mihaescu, BC, 'The Relation Between the Charter's Fundamental Rights and the Unwritten General Principles of EU Law: Good Administration as the Test Case' (2013) 9 *European Constitutional Law Review* 73.

Hogan, G, 'The Value of Declarations of Incompatibility and the Rule of Avoidance' (2006) 28 *Dublin University Law Journal* 408.

Jaklič, K, 'Liberal Legitimacy and Intact Respect' (2014) 27 *Ratio Juris* 409.

Joerges, C and Rödl, F, 'Informal Politics, Formalised Law and the "Social Deficit" of European Integration: Reflections after the Judgments of the ECJ in *Viking* and *Laval*' (2009) 15 *European Law Journal* 1.

Judge, I, '"No Taxation without Representation": A British Perspective on Constitutional Arrangements' (2010) 88 *Denver University Law Review* 325.

Keane, R, 'Judges as Lawmakers: The Irish Experience' (2004) 4 *Judicial Studies Institute Journal* 1.

Keleman, RD, 'On the Unsustainability of Constitutional Pluralism: European Supremacy and the Survival of the Eurozone' (2016) 23 *Maastricht Journal of European and Comparative Law* 136.

Kochenov, D and Pech, L, 'Monitoring and Enforcement of the Rule of Law in the European Union: Rhetoric and Reality' (2015) 11 *European Constitutional Law Review* 512.

—— 'Better Late Than Never?' (2016) 24 *Journal of Common Market Studies* 1062.

Komárek, J, 'Playing with Matches: The Czech Constitutional Court Declares a Judgment of the Court of Justice of the EU *Ultra Vires*' (2012) 8 *European Constitutional Law Review* 323.

Krisch, N, 'Europe's Constitutional Monstrosity' (2005) 25 *Oxford Journal of Legal Studies* 321.

—— 'The Open Architecture of European Human Rights Law' (2008) 71 *Modern Law Review* 183.

Kuijer, M, 'The Accession of the European Union to the ECHR: A Gift for the ECHR's 60th Anniversary or an Unwelcome Intruder at the Party?' (2011) 3 *Amsterdam Law Forum* 17.

Kumm, M, 'Who is the Final Arbiter of Constitutionality in Europe?: Three Conceptions of the Relationship Between the German Federal Constitutional Court and the European Court of Justice' (1999) 36 *Common Market Law Review* 351.

—— 'The Jurisprudence of Constitutional Conflict: Constitutional Supremacy in Europe Before and After the Constitutional Treaty' (2005) 11 *European Law Journal* 262.

—— 'Constitutionalising Subsidiarity in Integrated Markets: The Case of Tobacco Regulation in the European Union' (2006) 12 *European Law Review* 503.

—— 'Rebel Without a Good Cause: Karlsruhe's Misguided Attempt to Draw the CJEU into a Game of "Chicken" and What the CJEU Might Do About It' (2014) 15 *German Law Journal* 203.

Landau, D, 'Abusive Constitutionalism' (2013) 47 *University of California Davis Law Review* 189.

Lawrence, J, 'Contesting Constitutionalism: Constitutional Discourse at the WTO' (2013) 2 *Global Constitutionalism* 63.

Lenaerts, K, 'Exploring the Limits of the EU Charter of Fundamental Rights' (2012) 8 *European Constitutional Law Review* 375.

Lesch Bodnick, K, 'Bringing Ireland Up to Par: Incorporating the European Convention for the Protection of Human Rights and Fundamental Freedoms' (2002) 26 *Fordham International Law Journal* 396.

Liisberg, JB, 'Does the EU Charter of Fundamental Rights Threaten the Supremacy of Community Law?' (2001) 38 *Common Market Law Review* 1171.

Lock, T, 'Beyond *Bosphorus*: The European Court of Human Rights' Case Law on the Responsibility of Member States of International Organisations under the European Convention on Human Rights' (2010) 10 *Human Rights Law Review* 529.

—— 'EU Accession to the ECHR: Implications for Judicial Review in Strasbourg' (2010) 35 *European Law Review* 777.

—— 'Walking on a Tightrope: The Draft ECHR Accession Agreement and the Autonomy of the EU Legal Order' (2011) 48 *Common Market Law Review* 1025.

—— 'The Future of the European Union's Accession to the European Convention on Human Rights after Opinion 2/13: Is it Still Possible and is it Still Desirable?' (2015) 11 *European Constitutional Law Review* 239.

MacCormick, N, 'Beyond the Sovereign State' (1993) 56 *Modern Law Review* 1.

—— 'The Maastricht-Urteil: Sovereignty Now' (1995) 1 *European Law Journal* 259.

—— 'Risking Constitutional Collision in Europe?' (1998) 18 *Oxford Journal of Legal Studies* 517.

Maduro, MP, 'The Heteronyms of European Law' (1999) 5 *European Law Journal* 160.

—— 'The Importance of Being Called a Constitution: Constitutional Authority and the Authority of Constitutionalism' (2005) 3 *International Journal of Constitutional Law* 332.

238 Bibliography

Mantouvalou, V, 'Labour Rights in the European Convention on Human Rights: An Intellectual Justification for an Integrated Approach to Interpretation' (2013) 13 *Human Rights Law Review* 529.

McDermott, PA and Murphy, MW, 'No Revolution: The Impact of the ECHR Act 2003 on Irish Criminal Law' (2008) 30 *Dublin University Law Journal* 1.

Morijn, J, 'Balancing Fundamental Rights and Common Market Freedoms in Union Law: *Schmidberger* and *Omega* in the Light of the European Constitution' (2006) 12 *European Law Journal* 15.

Murkens, JEK, '*Bundesverfassungsgericht* (2 BvE 2/08): "We Want Our Identity Back" – The Revival of National Sovereignty in the German Federal Constitutional Court's Decision on the Lisbon Treaty' [2010] *Public Law* 530.

Nic Shuibhne, N, 'Margins of Appreciation: National Values, Fundamental Rights and EC Free Movement Law' (2009) 32 *European Law Review* 230.

Niedobitek, M, 'The *Lisbon Case* of 30 June 2009 – A Comment from the European Law Perspective' (2009) 10 *German Law Journal* 1267.

O'Donnell, TE, 'The Constitution, the European Convention on Human Rights Act 2003 and the District Court – A Personal View from a Judicial Perspective' (2007) 7 *Judicial Studies Institute Journal* 137.

O'Leary, S, 'Freedom of Establishment and Freedom to Provide Services: The Court of Justice as a Reluctant Constitutional Adjudicator: An Examination of the Abortion Information Case' (1992) 17 *European Law Review* 138.

Pech, L, '"A Union Founded on the Rule of Law": Meaning and Reality of the Rule of Law as a Constitutional Principle of EU Law' (2010) 6 *European Constitutional Law Review* 359.

Peers, S, '*Bosphorus* – European Court of Human Rights' (2006) 2 *European Constitutional Law Review* 443.

—— 'The EU's Accession to the ECHR: The Dream Becomes a Nightmare' (2015) 16 *German Law Journal* 213.

Pernice, I, 'Multilevel Constitutionalism in the European Union' (2002) 27 *European Law Review* 511.

Petersen, N, 'Karlsruhe Not Only Barks, But Finally Bites – Some Remarks on the *OMT* Decision of the German Constitutional Court' (2014) 15 *German Law Journal* 321.

Petersmann, E-U, 'The WTO Constitution and Human Rights' (2000) 3 *Journal of International Economic Law* 19.

Pliakos, A and Anagnostaras, G, 'Saving Face? The German Federal Constitutional Court Decides *Gauweiler*' (2017) 18 *German Law Journal* 213.

Rawls, J, 'The Idea of an Overlapping Consensus' (1987) 7 *Oxford Journal of Legal Studies* 1.

Reestman, J-H and Besselink, LFM, 'Editorial: After *Åkerberg Fransson* and *Melloni*' (2013) *European Constitutional Law Review* 169.

Reich, N, 'Free Movement v Social Rights in an Enlarged Union – The *Laval* and *Viking* Cases before the ECJ' (2008) 9 *German Law Journal* 125.

Ritter, C, 'A New Look at the Role and Impact of Advocates-General – Collectively and Individually' (2005–06) 12 *Columbia Journal of European Law* 751.

Robinson, M, 'The Irish European Communities Act 1972' (1973) 10 *Common Market Law Review* 352.

Sabel, CF and Gerstenberg, O, 'Constitutionalising an Overlapping Consensus: The ECJ and the Emergence of a Coordinate Constitutional Order' (2010) 16 *European Law Journal* 511.

Šaltinytė, L, 'Jurisdiction of the European Court of Justice Over Issues Relating to the Common Foreign and Security Policy Under the Lisbon Treaty' [2010] *Jurisprudencija/Jurisprudence* 261.

Sarmiento, D, 'Who's Afraid of the Charter? The Court of Justice, National Courts and the New Framework of Fundamental Rights Protection in Europe' (2013) 50 *Common Market Law Review* 1267.

Bibliography 239

—— 'Making Sense of Constitutional Pluralism: A Review of Klemen Jaklič's *Constitutional Pluralism in the EU*' (2015) 40 *European Law Review* 110.

Schütze, R, 'Subsidiarity after Lisbon: Reinforcing the Safeguards of Federalism?' (2009) 46 *Cambridge Law Journal* 525.

Shaffer, G, 'A Transnational Take on Krisch's Pluralist Postnational Law' (2012) 23 *European Journal of International Law* 565.

Smismans, S, 'The European Union's Fundamental Rights Myth' (2010) 48 *Journal of Common Market Studies* 45.

Stone Sweet, A, 'The Structure of Constitutional Pluralism' (2013) 11 *International Journal of Constitutional Law* 491.

Sutherland, PD, 'The Influence of United States Constitutional Law on the Interpretation of the Irish Constitution' (1984) 28 *St Louis University Law Journal* 41.

Temple Lang, J, 'Legal and Constitutional Problems for Ireland of Adhesion to the EEC Treaty' (1972) 9 *Common Market Law Review* 16.

Timmermans, C, 'The Magic World of Constitutional Pluralism' (2014) 10 *European Constitutional Law Review* 349.

Tulkens, F, 'La Convention Européenne des Droits de l'Homme et la Crise Economique: La Question de la Pauvreté' [2013] *Journal Européen des Droits de l'Homme* 8.

Twining, W, 'Normative and Legal Pluralism: A Global Perspective' (2010) 20 *Duke Journal of Comparative and International Law* 473.

Van de Heyning, C, '*PO Kokkelvisserij v the Netherlands*' (2009) 46 *Common Market Law Review* 2117.

van Peijpe, T, 'Collective Labour Law after *Viking, Laval, Rüffert* and *Commission v Luxembourg*' (2009) 25 *International Journal of Comparative Labour Law and Industrial Relations* 81.

Veldman, A, 'The Protection of the Fundamental Right to Strike within the Context of the European Internal Market: Implications of the Forthcoming Accession of the EU to the ECHR' (2013) 9 *Utrecht Law Review* 104.

Vėlyvytė, V, 'The Right to Strike in the European Union after Accession to the European Convention on Human Rights: Identifying Conflict and Achieving Coherence' (2015) 15 *Human Rights Law Review* 73.

Walker, N, 'European Constitutionalism and European Integration' [1996] *Public Law* 266.

—— 'The Idea of Constitutional Pluralism' (2002) 65 *Modern Law Review* 317.

—— 'Big "C" or Small "c"?' (2006) 12 *European Law Journal* 12.

—— 'Beyond Boundary Disputes and Basic Grids: Mapping the Global Disorder of Normative Orders' (2008) 6 *International Journal of Constitutional Law* 373.

—— 'Reconciling MacCormick: Constitutional Pluralism and the Unity of Practical Reason' (2011) 24 *Ratio Juris* 369.

—— 'Constitutional Pluralism Revisited' (2016) 22 *European Law Journal* 333.

Weiler, JHH, 'The European Union Belongs to its Citizens: Three Immodest Proposals' (1997) 22 *European Law Review* 150.

—— 'The Reformation of European Constitutionalism' (1997) 35 *Journal of Common Market Studies* 97.

—— 'Europe: The Case Against Statehood' (1998) 4 *European Law Journal* 43.

—— 'A Constitution for Europe? Some Hard Choices' (2002) 40 *Journal of Common Market Studies* 563.

—— 'On the Power of the Word: Europe's Constitutional Iconography' (2005) 3 *International Journal of Constitutional Law* 173.

—— 'The "Lisbon *Urteil*" and the Fast Food Culture' (2009) 20 *European Journal of International Law* 505.

Wendel, M, 'Exceeding Judicial Competence in the Name of Democracy: The German Federal Constitutional Court's *OMT* Reference' (2014) 10 *European Constitutional Law Review* 263.

240   Bibliography

Woolfson, C, Thörnqvist, C and Sommers, J, 'The Swedish Model and the Future of Labour Standards after *Laval*' (2010) 41 *Industrial Relations Journal* 333.
Ziller, J, 'The German Constitutional Court's Friendliness towards European Law: On the Judgment of the *Bundesverfassungsgericht* over the Ratification of the Treaty of Lisbon' (2010) 16 *European Public Law* 53.

Miscellaneous

Working Papers

Avbelj, M and Komárek, J (eds), 'Four Visions of Constitutional Pluralism (symposium transcript)' EUI Working Papers LAW 2008/21.
de Londras, F, 'Using the ECHR in Irish Courts: More Whisper than Bang?' (Public Interest Law Association Seminar, Dublin, 13 May 2011): www.pila.ie/download/pdf/pilaechrseminar130511fdelondras.pdf.
Halberstam, D, 'Systems Pluralism and Institutional Pluralism in Constitutional Law: National, Supranational, and Global Governance' (2001) University of Michigan Law School Public Law and Legal Theory Working Paper Series, Working Paper No 229.
—— 'Constitutional Heterarchy: The Centrality of Conflict in the European Union and the United States' (2008) University of Michigan Law School Public Law and Legal Theory Working Paper Series, Working Paper No 111.
Halmai, G, 'National(ist) Constitutional Identity? Hungary's Road to Abuse Constitutional Pluralism' EUI Working Papers LAW 2017/08.
Kochenov, D, 'Busting the Myths Nuclear: A Commentary on Article 7 TEU' EUI Working Papers LAW 2017/10.

Conference Papers

Costa, J-P, 'La Déclaration Universelle des Droits de l'Homme (1948–2008): Les Droits Economiques, Sociaux et Culturels en Question' (Strasbourg, 16 October 2008): www.echr.coe.int/Documents/Speech_20081016_OV_Costa_FRA.pdf.
McDowell, M, 'The European Convention on Human Rights Act 2003: What the Act Will Mean' (Law Society of Ireland/Irish Human Rights Commission Conference on New Human Rights Legislation, 18 October 2003).

Blog Posts

Enright, M, 'Ireland, Symphysiotomy and the UNHRC' (*Inherently Human*, 21 July 2014): inherentlyhuman.wordpress.com/2014/07/21/ireland-symphysiotomy-and-the-unhrc.
Scheinin, M, 'CJEU Opinion 2/13 – Three Mitigating Circumstances' (*Verfassungsblog*, 26 December 2014): www.verfassungsblog.de/cjeu-opinion-213-three-mitigating-circumstances/.
Weiler, JHH, 'Christmas Reading? Christmas Gifts? Some Suggestions from the Editor-in-Chief' (*EJIL: Talk!*, 29 December 2014): www.ejiltalk.org/christmas-reading-christmas-gifts-some-suggestions-from-the-editor-in-chief/.

Official Publications

Agreement Reached in the Multi-party Negotiations (10 April 1998): peacemaker.un.org/sites/peacemaker.un.org/files/IE%20GB_980410_Northern%20Ireland%20Agreement.pdf.
Constitution Review Group, *Report* (Dublin, Stationery Office, 1996).
Council of Europe, 'Fifth Negotiation Meeting between the CDDH ad hoc Negotiation Group and the European Commission on the Accession of the European Union to the European Convention on Human Rights: Final Report to the CDDH' (47+1(2013)008rev2): www.echr.coe.int/Documents/UE_Report_CDDH_ENG.pdf.

Department of Health, 'General Scheme of a Bill to Regulate Termination of Pregnancy' (27 March 2018): health.gov.ie/wp-content/uploads/2018/03/General-Scheme-for-Publication.pdf.

European Court of Human Rights, *Annual Report 2014* (Strasbourg, Registry of the ECtHR, 2015): www.echr.coe.int/Documents/Annual_Report_2014_ENG.pdf.

European Parliament, 'Completion of Accession to the ECHR': www.europarl.europa.eu/legislative-train/theme-area-of-justice-and-fundamental-rights/file-completion-of-eu-accession-to-the-echr.

Health Service Executive, *Investigation of Incident 50278 from Time of Patient's Self-Referral to Hospital on the 21st of October 2012 to the Patient's Death on the 28th of October 2012* (2013): cdn.thejournal.ie/media/2013/06/savita-halappanavar-hse-report.pdf.

Health Information and Quality Authority, *Investigation into the Safety, Quality and Standards of Services Provided by the Health Service Executive to Patients, Including Pregnant Women, at Risk of Clinical Deterioration, Including those Provided in University Hospital Galway, and as Reflected in the Care and Treatment Provided to Savita Halappanavar* (2013): www.hiqa.ie/sites/default/files/2017-01/Patient-Safety-Investigation-UHG.pdf.

Independent Review of Issues Relating to Symphysiotomy (13 March 2014): health.gov.ie/blog/publications/independent-review-of-issues-relating-to-symphysiotomy-by-judge-yvonne-murphy.

Justin Keating TD, Dáil Debate, 2 December 1971: www.oireachtas.ie/en/debates/debate/dail/1971-12-02/3/.

Rodríguez Iglesias, GC, 'Memorandum: Visite de Mme le Présidente d'Irlande, le 16 mai 1995' (No 212/95).

Referendum Results 1937–2015 (Dublin, Department of Housing, Planning, Community and Local Government, 2016): www.housing.gov.ie/sites/default/files/migrated-files/en/Publications/LocalGovernment/Voting/referendum_results_1937-2015.pdf.

Referendum Returning Officer, 'Referendum on the Thirty-sixth Amendment of the Constitution Bill 2018: Detailed Results': www.referendum.ie/detailed-results.

Report of the Inquiry into Child Sexual Abuse in the Diocese of Ferns (October 2005): www.lenus.ie/bitstream/handle/10147/560434/thefernsreportoctober2005.pdf.

Report of Dr Kevin McCoy on the Western Health Board Inquiry into Brothers of Charity Services in Galway (November 2007): www.hse.ie/eng/services/publications/disability/mcoy-boc.pdf.

Report of the Commission to Inquire into Child Abuse (20 May 2009): www.childabusecommission.ie/rpt/pdfs.

Report of the Commission of Investigation into the Catholic Archdiocese of Dublin (29 November 2009): www.justice.ie/en/JELR/Pages/PB09000504.

Report of the Expert Group on the Judgment in A, B and C v Ireland (Dublin, Department of Health, 2012): health.gov.ie/wp-content/uploads/2014/03/Judgment_ABC.pdf.

Report of the Inter-Departmental Committee to Establish the Facts of State Involvement with the Magdalen Laundries (5 February 2013): www.justice.ie/en/JELR/Pages/MagdalenRpt2013.

Supreme Court of Ireland, 'National Report', 26th Congress of the Conference of European Constitutional Courts (2014): www.confeuconstco.org/reports/rep-xvi/LB-Irlande-EN.pdf.

News Media Articles

Corazza Bildt, AM, 'This Time, Viktor Orbán Has Gone Too Far' *Politico.eu* (3 August 2018): www.politico.eu/article/viktor-orban-parliament-epp-hungary-has-gone-too-far/.

Kelly, F, 'President Signs Bill Repealing Eighth Amendment Into Law' *Irish Times* (18 September 2018): www.irishtimes.com/news/politics/president-signs-bill-repealing-eighth-amendment-into-law-1.3633601.

Smyth, J, 'Expert group on abortion to be set up by November' *Irish Times* (17 June 2011): www.irishtimes.com/news/expert-group-on-abortion-to-be-set-up-by-november-1.598305.

Index

A, B, and C v Ireland, 203
 conditional recognition principle, 188–91,
  195, 201–2
 discretion in moral matters, 201
 legal reasoning, 191–96
 margin of appreciation, 191–94, 201, 218
 remedies, 214
 reverse conditional recognition, 188–91
 right to private and family life, 186–88
 violation of Article 8 ECHR, 191–94
abortion law:
 case study, xix
  see also right to life of the unborn
   (case study)
 Irish situation, 151–55
  Attorney General v X, 85–86, 178–86
  Grogan case, 77–78, 163–66
  pre-1983, 155–58
  Open Door case, 78–79, 158–63
 United States, 157
  Ireland compared, 157
 see also right to life of the unborn
accession of the EU to ECHR, 51–52, 59
 see also Draft Accession Agreement;
  Opinion 2/13
accession of Ireland to European Community,
  62–64
 European Communities (Amendment)
  Act 1986, 66–69
 European Communities Act 1972, 62–64
 exclusion clause, *see* exclusion clause
 licence to join, *see* licence to join
 Third Amendment to the Constitution,
  62–63
 Title III Single European Act 1986,
  69–71
Advocates General, 145
 compatibility of role with right to a fair
  trial, 118–22, 134, 145, 211, 221
*AG (SPUC) v Open Door Counselling and
  Dublin Well Woman*, 202–3
 avoidance principle:
  High Court judgment, 160–61
  Supreme Court appeal, 162

defences, 158–59
ECtHR:
 freedom to impart information, 172–75
 legitimate aim of injunction, 175
 proportionality test, 175–76
EU exclusion clause, 160
EU law, 160–63
 failure of EU arguments, 162–63
 Grogan case compared, 163–64
 High Court, 159–61
 metaconstitutional interface norms, 166
 right to receive and impart information:
  freedom of expression, 171–76
  freedom to provide services, 167–71
 Supreme Court appeal, 161–63
  preliminary reference to CJEU, 161–62
Attorney General v X:
 right to travel, 178–79
  arguments, 179–82
  inconsistency of interface norms, 182
  Supreme Court appeal, 182–84
 removal of limit to freedom to travel,
  184–85
autonomy:
 autonomy of EU fundamental rights
  law, 124
 autonomy of EU law, 118–19, 129, 133,
  146, 218
  mutual trust, 127–28
 Crotty case, 74
 mutual recognition, 51
 pluralism principle and, 35–36
 specificity and autonomy, 115, 122
  Draft Accession Agreement, 124–29
avoidance principle, 159–61, 162, 184,
  198–99, 202
 Grogan case, 200–1
 Open Door case, 163–64

best-fit universal constitutionalism, 24
Bosphorus v Ireland, 114–15
 Bosphorus doctrine, 116–17
 conditional recognition principle, 117,
  121–22, 150, 213, 218

244 *Index*

manifestly deficient exception, 117–18, 121–22

margin of appreciation v presumption of compatibility, 116

presumption of equivalent protection, 117–21, 123, 129, 145–46, 149, 207, 211, 213
  conditional recognition, 150, 218–19
  national specificity, 215
  rebuttal of, 122, 131
  reconciliation of CJEU jurisprudence by ECtHR, 115–16

Brexit, xiii, 47

Bundesverfassungsgericht (BVerfG) (German Federal Constitutional Court):
  CJEU, relationship with, 37
  democratic statism, 37
  Maastricht judgment, 5–6
  metaconstitutional pluralism, 51–52
  relationship with CJEU, 37, 43
  Solange case, 3–4, 64, 115
  see also conditional recognition principle; *Solange* case

certainty, *see* legal certainty

Charter of Fundamental Rights of the EU (CFREU), 103, 110–11
  aide to incorporation of ECHR, as an, 207, 209–10
  Article 53, 146
    Art. 53 ECHR, relationship with, 125–26, 133–34
    mutual trust principle, 127
  ECtHR references to, 112
  legality principle, 211
  right to take collective action, 136, 143, 147–48
  role of Advocates General, 211
  status, 108–9

co-respondent mechanism:
  Opinion 2/13, 129–30, 213

collective action, right to:
  alternative forms of redress, 140–41
  balancing economic freedoms with, 136–37
  CJEU recognition of, 135–36
  conceptualising collective action, 137–38
  disruption, element of, 139
  freedom of establishment, 137–38
  freedom to provide services in the EU, 137–38
  justification for collective action, 138–41
  Omega case, 137

proportionality, 140
  Schmidberger case, 137
  Viking and *Laval* cases, 137
  see also freedom of assembly and association

Common Foreign and Security Policy (CFSP):
  jurisdiction, 128–29

competences:
  EU, 5, 55, 105, 124–25, 150
  national competences, 40–41

conditional recognition principle, xvi, 216–19
  A, B, & C v Ireland, 188–91, 195, 201–2
  Bosphorus presumption, 117, 121–22, 150, 213, 218
  Crotty case, 66–67, 87
    heterarchy/hierarchy arguments, 68–69
    plaintiff's arguments, 67
    response of the courts, 67–68
    scope and objectives test, 123–24
  European Communities (Amendment) Act, 66–69, 72
  Grogan case, 87, 182
  Omega case, 200
  reverse conditional recognition, 188–91, 195, 201–2
  scope and objectives test, 71–75, 123–24, 217–18
  Single European Act, 72–73
  Solange case, 42–43, 51, 58, 112, 158, 164–66, 208
  universal applicability, 217–19

Connolly gap, 116–18, 122, 149, 207

constitutional pluralism defined, xiv–xv, 205–6, 230–31
  abuse in Hungary, 224–27
  constitutionalism element, 14–19
  movement, as a, 11–12
  pluralist constitutionalism distinguished, 1–2, 21–23
  pluralist element, 19–21

constitutional tolerance, *see* Weiler

constitutionalisation, xiv–xv, 2–3

constitutionalism beyond the state, 37, 163–64

contrapunctual law, 34–35, 146, 160–61
  aims, 34–35
  contrapunctual law principles, 35
    consistency and coherence, 36
    institutional choice principle, 37
    pluralism principle, 35–36
    universalizability, 36
  cosmopolitan constitutionalism compared, 42–43, 54

Index 245

horizontal coherence principle, 36, 42–43, 97, 132, 182
interface norms, 35–37
national constitutional challenges, 64
  ex ante review of EU norms, 64, 65–75
  ex post review of EU norms, 64, 75–86
vertical and horizontal coherence, 36, 42–43, 182
coordinate constitutionalism, *see* **polyarchic coordinate constitutionalism**
cosmopolitan constitutionalism, 37–40
conditional recognition principle, 216–19
dual purpose, 40, 208
interface norms, 40–43, 208
  democracy principle, 40, 41, 212–16
  legality principle, 40, 41–43, 208–12
  protection of basic rights or reasonableness, 40, 42–43
  subsidiarity principle, 40–41
sui generist approach, 38–39
universal applicability, 43, 216
crises in the EU, xiii
abuses of constitutional pluralism, 226–27
Crotty **case,** 86–87
autonomy, 74
challenging Single European Act, 66–69
conditional recognition principle, 66–67, 87, 217
  heterarchy/hierarchy arguments, 68–69
  plaintiff's arguments, 67
  response of the courts, 67–68
  scope and objectives test, 123–24
democracy principle, 215
ex ante constitutional review, 65–69, 123–24
  penultimate judicial supremacy, 70–71
  scope and objectives test, 73–75
legislative interface norms, 100–1
scope and objectives test, 73–75, 81, 86, 123–24, 217

declarations of incompatibility:
duty to amend domestic law, 98–100, 187
interpretation of ECHR, 96, 98
priority, 98–100
democracy principle, 41
abortion question:
  Bosphorus presumption, 215–16
  Crotty case, 215
  Grogan case, 215
  overlap of democracy principle and national specificity, 214–15

cosmopolitan constitutionalism, 40–42
EU and ECHR, relationship between, 212–13
Irish law and ECHR, relationship between, 213–14
Irish law and EU law, relationship between, 214
overlap of democracy principle and national specificity, 214–15
universal applicability, 43, 216
democratic legitimacy, *see* **democracy principle**
democratic statism:
BVerfG, 37–38
consequences, 38–39
cosmopolitan constitutionalism, 39, 184
definition, 38
supremacy of national courts, 38
direct effect principle, 18
constitutionalisation of EU, 2, 49
ECtHR, 56
EU law, 47, 76
Draft Accession Agreement:
co-respondent mechanism, 129–30
failure to preserve specific features of EU law:
  CFSP, 128–29
  human rights standards, 125–26
  interpretation conflicts, 126–27
  mutual trust principle, 127–28
Opinion 2/13, 123–24
  co-respondent mechanism, 129–30
  CFSP, 128–29
  interpretation conflicts, 126–27
  mutual trust principle, 127–28
  no lowering of human rights standards, 125–26
  prior involvement of CJEU, 130–31
  circumvention of TFEU preliminary reference procedure, 131–32

ECHR and Irish law, relationship between:
constitutional polyarchy, 95–96
  effect of ECHR Act, 96–98
  priority and declarations of incompatibility, 98–100
declarations of incompatibility, 94–95
European Convention on Human Rights Act 2003:
  compensation, 95
  constitutional polyarchy, 95–100
  core interpretive obligation, 94
  declarations of incompatibility, 94–95

246 *Index*

interpretive approach, 94
just satisfaction, 95
method of incorporation, 93–94
obligation to act in accordance with
ECHR, 94
obligation to take due account of ECtHR
jurisprudence, 94
origins, 92–93
legislative interface norms, 100–1
pre-ECHR incorporation, 88–92
empowerment, 17–18
triangular constitutionalism, 56–57
epistemic meta-constitutionalism, 23
EU law and ECHR, relationship between,
103–4, 149–50, 202
CJEU attitude to ECHR, 104–5
CFREU, 108–9
direct applicability of ECHR rights,
108–9
normative status of ECHR, 106–8
reference to ECtHR case law, 109–11
Draft Accession Agreement, *see* Draft
Accession Agreement
ECtHR's perspective:
challenges to primary EU law, 112–13
challenges to secondary EU law, 113–16
EU's perspective, 104–6
ECtHR caselaw before CJEU, 109–11
normative status of ECHR, 106–9
interface norms, 132–34
metaconstitutional interface norms,
122–23
judicial conflicts, 145–49
labour rights, 134–35
CJEU, 135–41
ECtHR, 141–45
judicial conflict, 145–49
see also labour rights in Europe
EU and Irish law, relationship between:
accession to the EC, 62–64
closed legal order, 61–62
conditional recognition, 66–69, 71–75
democratic legitimacy, 82–86
ex ante review of norms, 65–75
ex post review of norms, 75–86
exclusion clause, 75–86
Grogan case, 77–82
incorporating Community/EU law, 61–64
legislative interface norms, 100–1
licence to join, 65–75
national specificity, 84–86
origins of Irish constitutional law, 61–62

penultimate judicial supremacy, 69–71
proportionality, 84–85
scope and objectives test, 73–75
see also Crotty case; *Grogan* case
European Communities Act (ECA) 1972,
63–64, 96–97, 159
legality principle, 209
European Communities (Amendment)
Act 1986, 66
compatibility with Irish constitution, 71–72
conditional recognition principle, 66–69, 72
Crotty case, 124
European constitutional supremacy, 26, 37,
45–47, 146–47, 163–64, 184
European Convention on Human Rights
(ECHR):
Draft Accession Agreement, *see* Draft
Accession Agreement; Opinion 2/13
dualist approach of Irish legal order, 95
EU, relationship with, *see* EU and ECHR,
relationship between
member states, relationship with, *see* ECHR
and Irish law, relationship between
European Convention on Human Rights
Act 2003:
method of incorporation, 93–94
origins, 92–93
European Court of Human Rights (ECtHR):
apportioning responsibility, 115
Bosphorus case, *see Bosphorus* case
caselaw before the CJEU, 109–12
challenges to actions of institutions,
116–18
challenges to primary EU law, 112–13
challenges to secondary EU law, 113–16
judicial conflict with CJEU, 145–49
jurisdiction, 207
labour rights, 141–43
freedom of assembly and association,
143–45
European Court of Justice (CJEU):
BVerfG, relationship with, 37
CFREU, 108–9
CJEU attitude to ECHR, 104–5
direct applicability of ECHR rights,
108–9
judicial conflict with ECtHR, 145–49
normative status of ECHR, 106–8
reference to ECtHR case law, 109–11
role of Advocates General
right to a fair trial, 118–22, 134, 145,
211, 221

Index 247

European Union (EU):
  legal order, 207
    ECHR as part of, 207
  member states, relationship with, *see*
      EU and Irish law, relationship
      between
  ECHR, relationship with, *see* EU and
      ECHR, relationship between
ex ante constitutional review, *see Crotty* case
ex post constitutional review, *see Grogan* case
exclusion clause (Art. 29.4.6° of Irish
      Constitution), 62, 63–64, 86–87,
      159–60, 206, 210, 212, 228–29
  ex post constitutional review, 75–86
  Grogan case, 77–79, 165
    democratic legitimacy, 82–84
    national specificity, 84–86
    Supreme Court appeal, 77–82
  Irish law and ECHR, relationship
      between, 88, 101
  primacy of Community/EU law, 75–77

final say in constitutional conflict, 2, 7,
      44, 48–49, 177–78, 197, 204–5,
      220–21
  conditional recognition principle, 72
  Jaklič, 13, 23, 24–25
  Kumm, 38–39
  MacCormick, 35
  penultimate judicial supremacy, 70–71
  Walker, 13, 23, 33
  Weiler, 26, 35
free movement, 84–85
  abortion law, 198–200, 215
  national specificity, 171
  public policy derogation, 181
  right to take collective action, 136, 137–38,
      140, 145
  see also right to travel
freedom of assembly and association (ECHR),
      135–36, 141–42
  CJEU's interpretation, 147–49, 150
  integrated approach to interpretation,
      143–44
freedom of establishment (TFEU), 136
freedom of expression (ECHR), 20–21,
      47–48
  Open Door case, 158–59
    injunction interfering with freedom to
        impart information, 173
    injunction's legitimate aim,
        173–74, 175

  interference necessary in democratic
      society, 174
  proportionality test, 175–76
  right to receive and impart information,
      171–76
freedom to provide services:
  Open Door case:
    no cross-border activity, 168, 169
    no economic activity, 168–69
    providing information and providing
        assistance distinguished, 167
    right to receive and impart information,
        167–71

Gerstenberg, *see* Sabel and Gerstenberg
good administration principles, 18
Grogan **case,** 77–79, 86–87
  conditional recognition principle, 87, 182
  democratic legitimacy, 82–83
    narrowness of application, 83–84
  national specificity, 84, 85–86
  proportionality, 84–85
  Supreme Court appeal, 77–82

harmonious discursive constitutionalism, 24
heterarchy/constitutional heterarchy, *see*
      pluralism
horizontal relationships, *see* EU and ECHR,
      relationship between
human dignity, xv–xvi, 21, 31, 83–84
  right to take collective action, 136–38

institutions of the EU:
  challenges to their actions, 116–18
  role of CJEU Advocates General
    right to a fair trial, 118–22
integrity, 44, 47–48, 49–50, 55, 57, 182,
      191–92, 222–23
  threats to, 2, 10, 86, 185, 199
interface norms:
  context dependent nature, 53
  contrapunctual law, 35–37
  cosmopolitan constitutionalism, 40–43
    democracy principle, 40
    legality principle, 40
    protection of basic rights or
        reasonableness, 40
    subsidiarity principle, 40
  evolution over time, 57–59
  metaconstitutional norms, xvi
  polyarchic coordinate constitutionalism,
      33–34

248   Index

rules, principles, demands and values,
29–30
substantive norms, xv–xvi
Ireland:
accession to the ECHR:
constitutional exclusion clause, 62–63
constitutional licence to join, 62–63
European Communities Act 1972, 63–64
legislation giving effect to EC law, 62,
63–64
constitutional order, 206–7
ECHR, relationship with, *see* ECHR and
Irish law, relationship between
EU, relationship with, *see* EU and Irish law,
relationship between
member of the EU, as a, 206
signatory to the ECHR, as a, 206

Jaklič, 11–12
analysis of metaconstitutional theories,
24–28
final say in constitutional conflict, 13, 23,
24–25
heterarchy minimised, 13
self-standing legal orders, 14–19
utopian pluralism, 28
judicial supremacy:
judicial conflict between ECtHR and CJEU,
145–49
penultimate judicial supremacy, 69–75
just satisfaction, 94–95

Kadi case, 31, 108, 202–3, 209
Keleman, 223–24
Hungarian situation, 45–46, 49, 224–27
Kompetenz-Kompetenz, 5–6, 20, 47
Krisch, 8
conception of constitutionalism, 13–17
ECHR, 188
interface norms, 28–30
margin of appreciation, 175
rejection of metaconstitutional
pluralism, 29
Kumm:
best-fit universal constitutionalism, 24
cosmopolitan constitutionalism, 37–40
interface norms, 40–43, 207
sui generist approach, 38–39
democratic statism, 37–38
final say in constitutional conflict, 38–39
legal monism, 37–38
see also cosmopolitan constitutionalism

labour rights in Europe, 134–35
balancing human/fundamental rights and
economic freedoms, 136–37
CJEU recognition of right to take collective
action, 135–36
balancing free movement rights, 136–37
collective action, right to, *see* collective
action, right to
conceptualising collective action, 137–38
freedom of assembly and association, *see*
freedom of assembly and association
horizontal direct effect, 137–38
justification for collective action, 138–41
market freedoms and labour rights, 135–37
proportionality, 140
right to collective action, 135
conceptualising collective action, 137–38
disruption requirement, 139
human dignity, 138
justification for collective action, 138–41
right to collective bargaining, 135
vertical direct effect, 137
Laval case, *see Viking* and *Laval* cases
legal certainty, xiii, 10, 29, 44, 222–23, 227
legal integrity, 2, 10, 44–50, 222
legal monism:
supremacy of EU law, 37–38
legal orders, relationship between, *see*
interface norms
legality principle, 40, 41, 122–23
application of legality principle in
metaconstitutional sense, 210–11
CFREU, 211
cosmopolitan constitutionalism, 40–42, 133,
166, 208
EU/ECHR relationship, 212–13
Irish/ECHR relationship, 209, 213
Irish/EU relationship, 209
protection of fundamental rights, 42–43
rebuttable presumption, as a, 210, 216
universal applicability, 211–12
'**licence to join**', 62, 64
attitude of the courts, 71–73
compatibility of EU norms, 65–66
conditional recognition, 66–69
scope and objectives test, 73–75, 86–87

MacCormick, xvi, 52–53, 96
final say in constitutional conflict, 35
pluralism under international law, 7, 14, 22,
26–27
radical pluralism, 5–7

Index 249

Maduro:
contrapunctual law, 34–35
interface norms, 35–37, 207–8
harmonious discursive constitutionalism, 24
see also contrapunctual law
margin of appreciation, 116, 138, 174–75, 181, 188–89, 191–95, 201, 218
member states and ECHR, relationship between, *see* ECHR and Irish law, relationship between
member states and EU, relationship between, *see* EU and Irish law, relationship between
metaconstitutional theories, xv, 1, 23–24
contrapunctual law, 34–35
interface norms under, 35–37
see also contrapunctual law
cosmopolitan constitutionalism, 37–40
interface norms under, 40–43
see also cosmopolitan constitutionalism
polyarchic coordinate constitutionalism, 30–33
interface norms under, 33–34
see also polyarchic coordinate constitutionalism
rule of law, threat to, 44–50
universality of interface norms, 51–53
monism and monist theories, 7, 15–16, 205
democratic statism compared, 37
European monism, 10–11, 26–27, 35, 37
legalist monism, 37–38, 39
pluralism compared, 12–14, 15–16
multi-level classical constitutionalism, 24, 25
mutual trust principle, 127–28, 133–34

national constitutional supremacy, 37, 163–64, 184
national specificity, 152–54, 227–28
EU and Irish law, relationship between, 84–86
exclusion clause (Art. 29.4.6 of Irish Constitution), 84–86
free movement, 171
Grogan case, 84, 85–86
proportionality, 84–85
overlap of democracy principle and national specificity, 214–15
presumption of equivalent protection, 215
proportionality, 84–85
see also democracy principle; right of the unborn (case study)

Omega case:
conditional recognition principle, 200
Opinion 2/13, 123–24
objections to Draft Accession Agreement:
CFSP, 128–29
circumvention of TFEU preliminary reference procedure, 131–32
co-respondent mechanism, 129–30
interpretation conflicts, 126–27
mutual trust principle, 127–28
no lowering of human rights standards, 125–26
prior involvement of CJEU, 130–31
overlapping consensus principle, 32, 33–34, 43, 51, 54, 58, 72, 87, 147, 175, 201–2
overlapping legal landscape, 1–2, 8–9, 39, 206–8
oversight by national courts, 47, 73–74

penultimate judicial supremacy, 70–71, 81, 95
final say in constitutional conflict, 70–71
Pernice:
multi-level classical constitutionalism, 24, 25
pluralism defined:
heterarchical pluralism, 12
heterarchy minimised, 13
legal pluralism, 13
pluralism and constitutionalism as binary opposites, 13–14
weaknesses regarding rule of law, 45–50
pluralism under international law, 7, 14, 22, 26–27
pluralist constitutionalism:
constitutional pluralism distinguished, 1–2, 21–23
polyarchic coordinate constitutionalism, xvii, 30–33, 86–87
conditional recognition principle, 216–17
interface norms, 33–34, 208
overlapping consensus principle, 33–34
polyarchic constitutionalism, 53–56, 204–5
conditional recognition, 216–17
interface norms, 33–34, 208
legality principle, 208–12
national specificity, 212–16
preliminary reference procedure, xviii, 79, 114–15, 119, 230

250   Index

circumvention, 131–32
right to travel, 161
presumption of compatibility, 116
presumption of equivalent protection, 121–22,
        123, 129, 145–46, 211, 213, 218
    see also Bosphorus case
primacy principle, 2, 5–6, 16, 18, 34, 40,
        47, 49, 56, 68–69, 76–77, 88, 124,
        125–26, 164, 182, 205, 226–27,
        228–30
protection of basic rights or reasonableness,
        40, 42
    legality principle, 42–43
Protection of Life During Pregnancy Act 2013,
        154–55, 190

radical pluralism, 5–7, 14, 22
reductionist constitutionalism, 24
referendums, 63, 69–71, 78, 86, 124, 152–53,
        157, 173–74, 177, 184–86, 191, 201,
        206, 214, 217
relationship between legal orders, see interface
        norms
restraint, 17–18
    self-restraint, 223–25
    triangular constitutionalism, 56–57
reverse conditional recognition, 188–91, 195,
        201–2
review of EU norms by national courts,
        46–47
    national courts informing debate, 47
right to a fair trial (ECHR):
    Advocates General and, 118–22
    right of reply in CJEU, 118–22
right to life of the unborn (case study):
    equal right to life of the born, 156–57
    Irish constitution, 151
        1937 Constitution, 156
        Eighth Amendment, 152
        Thirteenth Amendment, 152, 184–85, 197
        Fourteenth Amendment, 152, 177–78
        Thirty-sixth Amendment, 152
        referendum of 2018, 152, 197–98
    Open Door case, see AG (SPUC) v Open
        Door Counselling and Dublin Well
        Woman
    origins, 155–56
    saving the life (not the health) of a pregnant
        woman, 152, 185–88
right to private and family life:
    A, B, & C v Ireland, 186–88
    reverse conditional recognition, 188–91

right to travel, 178–79
    Attorney General v X, 178–79
        arguments, 179–82
        inconsistency of interface norms, 182
        Supreme Court appeal, 182–84
    removal of limit to freedom to travel,
        184–85
rule of law, 2, 222–23
    certainty, 223
    constitutional pluralism, threat from,
        44–45
    indeterminacy argument, 47–48, 50
    institutional independence, 223
    integrity, 223
    interdependence of constitutional orders,
        223
    legal heterarchy, threat from, 45–50
    self-restraint, 223
    sincere cooperation, 223
    stability, 223

Sabel and Gerstenberg:
    polyarchic coordinate constitutionalism,
        30–33
        interface norms, 33–34
    reductionist constitutionalism, 24
    see also polyarchic coordinate
        constitutionalism
scope and objectives test, 86–87
    conditional recognition principle, 71–75,
        123–24, 217–18
separation of powers doctrine, 61, 71–72
Single European Act 1986, 65–66
    conditional recognition, 66–69, 72–73
    ratification, 69–71
socio-teleological constitutionalism, 23
Solange case, 3–4, 64, 115
    conditional recognition principle, 42–43, 51,
        58, 112, 158, 164–66, 208
special significance of ECHR, 105–6, 108–9,
        114, 119, 171, 210–11, 212–13
stability, 22, 46, 49, 95–96, 208, 222–23
state and non-state legal orders, see ECHR
        and Irish law, relationship between;
        EU and Irish law, relationship
        between
subsidiarity principle, 40–42, 123, 132, 133,
        166, 198, 207, 208, 221
suicide, risk of, 179–80
    saving the life (not the health) of a mother,
        154, 185–86, 190–91, 196–97
supremacy, see primacy principle

triangular constitutionalism generally:
  defined, 53–55, 56–59
  ECHR as reference order, 55
  equality of interfaces, 220–22
  EU as reference order, 55
  Irish constitutional order as reference
    order, 55
  see also polyarchic constitutionalism

United States:
  abortion law, 154
universality of interface norms, xv, 2, 51
  conditional recognition principle, 217–19
  contrapunctual law principles, 36
  cosmopolitan constitutionalism, 43, 216
  democratic legitimacy, 52
  horizontal relationships, 51–52, 202
  legality principle, 211–12
  metaconstitutional theories, 51–53, 219–30
  reiterative universalism, 53
  right of the unborn, 198–99–202
  universalizability principle, 52
  vertical relationship, 52, 202
utopian pluralism, 27–28

vertical relationships, 202
  Irish law and ECHR, *see* ECHR and Irish
    law, relationship between
  Irish law and EU law, *see* EU law and Irish
    law, relationship between
***Viking* and *Laval* cases,** 145–49, 195
  disruptive intent, 139
  freedom of establishment, 136
  prevention of further action, 137–38
  proportionality, 139–40
  right to collective action, 136

Walker, 7–8
  constitutional pluralism:
    epistemic claim, 10–11
    explanatory claim, 8–9
    normative claim, 9–10
  epistemic meta- constitutionalism, 23
  final say in constitutional conflict, 13, 23, 33
Weiler, 26–28
  constitutional tolerance, 25–26
  final say in constitutional conflict, 26, 35
  socio-teleological constitutionalism, 23
  substantive pluralism, 24